TEACHING/WRITING
IN THE LATE AGE OF PRINT

RESEARCH AND TEACHING IN RHETORIC AND COMPOSITION
Michael M. Williamson and David L. Jolliffe, series editors

Basic Writing as a Political Act: Public Conversations About Writing and
Literacies
Linda Adler-Kassner and Susanmarie Harrington

New Worlds, New Words: Exploring Pathways for Writing About and In Electronic
Environments
John F. Barber and Dene Grigar (eds.)

The Rhetoric and Ideology of Genre: Strategies for Stability and Change
Richard Coe, Lorelei Lingard, and Tatiana Teslenko (eds.)

Teaching/Writing in the Late Age of Print
Jeffrey Galin, Carol Peterson Haviland, and J Paul Johnson (eds.)

Identities Across Text
George H. Jensen

Against the Grain: Essays in Honor of Maxine Hairston
David Jolliffe, Michael Keene, Mary Trachel, and Ralph Voss (eds.)

Directed Self-Placement: Principles and Practices
Dan Royer and Roger Gilles (eds.)

forthcoming

Black Letters: An Ethnography of a Beginning Legal Writing Course
Randolph Cauthen

Marbles, Cotton Balls, and Quantum Wells:
Style as Invention in the Pursuit of Knowledge
Heather Graves

Multiple Literacies for the 21st Century
Brian Huot, Beth Stroble, and Charles Bazerman (eds.)

Classroom Spaces and Writing Instruction
Ed Nagelhout and Carol Rutz

Remapping Narrative: Technology's Impact on the Way We Write
Gian S. Pagnucci and Nick Mauriello (eds.)

Tech Culture: Internet Constructions of Literacy and Identity
Gian S. Pagnucci and Nick Mauriello (eds.)

Unexpected Voices
John Rouse and Ed Katz

Who Can Afford Critical Consciousness
David Seitz

Principles and Practices: New Discourses for Advanced Writers
Margaret M. Strain and James M. Boehnlein (eds.)

TEACHING/WRITING
IN THE LATE AGE OF PRINT

edited by

Jeffrey Galin
Florida Atlantic University

Carol Peterson Haviland
California State University—San Bernardino

J Paul Johnson
Winona State University

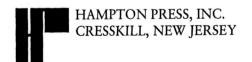
HAMPTON PRESS, INC.
CRESSKILL, NEW JERSEY

Library of Congress Cataloging-in-Publication Data

Teaching/writing in the late age of print / edited by Jeffrey Galin, Carol Peterson
    Haviland, J. Paul Johnson.
        p. cm. -- (Research and teaching in rhetoric and composition)
    Includes bibliographical references and index.
    ISBN 1-57273-457-4 (cloth) -- ISBN 1-57273-458-2 (pbk.)
        1. English language--Rhetoric--Study and teaching. 2. Report writing--
Study and teaching (Higher) I. Galin, Jeffrey R., 1961- II. Haviland, Carol
Peterson. III. Johnson, J. Paul. IV. Series.

PE1404.T27 2003
808'.042'0711--dc21

                                                                    2003042330

Cover design by Adrien Spano, Graphics Dept., Florida Atlantic University.

Hampton Press, Inc.
23 Broadway
Cresskill, NJ 07626

CONTENTS

*   *   *

The following tables may point readers to chapters of particular
interest; however, the categories should not be seen as mutually exclusive but rather as descriptive of the issues they raise or the assumptions
that undergird them. Both the introduction and the afterword elaborate
these complex intersections.

	1	2	3	4	5	6	7	8	9	10	11	12	13	14	15	16	17	18	19	20	21	22	23	24	25	26	27	28	29
2 year college	x																												
liberal arts																									x				
regional state univ. (15-20k)								x					x		x	x			x							x	x		
research 1 (15-20k)				x					x		x	x					x												
regional campus of research 1										x																			
research 1 state (20-30k)												x		x															
research 1(<30k)			x		x	x	x											x		x		x						x	x
Literacy							x		x	x	x	x									x						x	x	x
Motivation	x						x		x	x	x	x			x	x			x		x		x			x	x		
Portfolio				x																			x	x					
Postmodernism			x								x		x					x	x					x		x			
Project-based Learning																										x		x	
Reading	x						x		x	x	x													x	x		x		x
critical reading																								x	x		x		
Reflection	x		x		x	x								x					x		x								
Research			x		x				x				x		x	x	x		x			x	x		x	x			
Resistance/Alternative Pedagogies and Writing/Risk		x											x		x	x		x	x		x				x				x
Revision				x					x	x			x	x						x			x						
Sequencing Assignments		x							x	x							x	x			x						x		x
Service Learning																		x			x								
Social Construction			x				x			x		x			x		x	x			x			x					
Social Epistemicism												x					x		x		x								
Visual Rhetoric/Literacy									x								x	x									x	x	
Voice	x										x					x		x					x		x				

FOREWORD

Susan Miller
University of Utah

I was honored to be asked to contribute this foreword to *Teaching/Writing in the Late Age of Print*, to provide a ceremonial dedication that may mediate between the intentions of this collection and the varied itineraries for reading it will suggest. But as a contributor to William Coles and James Vopat's 1985 *What Makes Good Writing Good*, my appreciation goes beyond the normal pride involved in any such invitation. That is, as a contributor to that model for this volume, I am invited to rethink that earlier purpose for writing and its contents in light of these fresh new texts.

I was a relatively minor figure among those who undertook the earlier collaboration. As I review its list of contributors, I group them in three generations. I recall how much and how often I learned from the secure scholars of literature, linguistics, or English Education who had assembled around composition and pedagogy in the period after the Soviet Union's launch of Sputnik, which created the National Defense seminar and fellowship programs that were then wisely allocated even to humanists. That group included editor Bill Coles, James Britton, James Sledd, Walker Gibson, Wayne Booth, Bill Irmsher, Frank D'Angelo, Leo Rockas, Nell Ann Pickett, John Mellon, Richard Young, Janice Lauer, Steve Tchudi, Don Stewart, and Ross Winterowd. Many of these generous mentors no longer help our field in person. But they and those who stood with them in the 1970s were themselves the gravitas and energy that permitted me and others in that volume's second generation to name ourselves as having a distinct field, a composition studies that formed around their articulations of a significant history and a pedagogy that is capable of theorization. Their insight, tenacity and curiosity about noncanonical texts added up to what I now see as a relative toughness of spirit. It empowered the continuing work of Don Daiker, Toby Fulwiler, John Gage, Sandra Schor, Erika Lindemann, Ira Shor, John Warnock, Linda Flower, Carolyn Miller, Paul Eschholz, David Bleich, Joe Williams, Elaine Maimon, co-editor Jim Vopat, and more. Yet credit for even more professional daring goes to a third group of untenured contributors, among which I am happy to recall some of my students and then-colleagues, such as Janet Kotler. To see their work and that of their own later students cited here in the new essays that author *Teaching/Writing in the Late Age of Print* is to see maturing interests in an increasingly complex professional tradition.

At the time, however, Coles and Vopat were sharply reproached for selecting "star" contributors, as they were for reinforcing the ideology that their collection's selections were taken to embody, in ways I will take up later. Nonetheless, as Jeff Galin's, Carol Haviland's, and J Paul Johnson's call for contributions to *TWLAP* suggests, both collections are historical place markers, "document[s] for future researchers in our field who want to assess what claims, assumptions, and practices prevailed" in these two times. So as the lucky contributor to both volumes, I may be able to help chart the distance between these books by setting out categories of difference that current and still later readers may note.

That said, it is important to state that I do not mean to map those differences on the easily recognized maxim that attributes "growth" and "influence" to supposedly "evolving" traditions in art and intellectual inquiry. *Plus ça change. . .* is rarely more than fatalistic and relatively shallow thinking about time. That conservatory, actually corrective perspective on obvious variety forgets the array of material circumstances that inevitably sever already fragile threads across time, circumstances that make continuity not a routine narrative pattern but one hard won from overdetermined causes and their often ruptured results. The primary example here is that "process-centered" teaching did not suddenly appear, nor did it suddenly eliminate the gate-keeping that had been applied to first-year students. Nor was it a newly conceived grammar of interventions codified overnight to create teacher-proof curricula. Instead, it has been interruptions in the material and institutional circumstances that formed composition studies that have linked the modernist pedagogy of *WMWG* to references to its form and goals in the making of this postmodern volume. These disruptions include the men and women who fought in Viet Nam and those who resisted that fighting and its subtexts, the therefore "new" students of open admissions who appeared in a 1975 *ADE Bulletin,* and the ambivalently motivated new capitalists who now populate a computer industry that paraphrases its profitable results as "electronic communication" and a "service economy." From this materialist perspective, the more things change, the more they change. There are some absolute differences between then and now in the teaching of writing, as the ability even to think this title phrase, "the late age of print," and the allusions around it tell us.

Of course, "differences" is the key word here. Neither "repetition" nor "opposition" can account for activity in temporal spaces that are not "eras," where practices and their subtexts recirculate and trace many apparently wrecked trains of thought. Thus, *TWLAP* revisits what is in my view a stellar, never remembered, and much too rarely sought agenda from *WMWG:* to praise students and their texts, specifically in the situations that evoke them. There is consequently much repetition in the stated desires of the two projects. Coles and Vopat asked contributors only for three brief texts:

1. An example of a piece of college student writing . . . that for that teacher in some way demonstrates excellence, however flawed or unfinished the paper may be . . . writing that would start conversations rather than stop them.
2. The writing assignment.
3. A commentary . . . in which the teacher [explains] to a student audience why he or she finds the paper praiseworthy. (viii)

The articulation of authors' responsibilities for *TWLAP* is very similar:

1. A reflective analysis of a piece of student writing and the pedagogy that prompted, enabled, or supported it [to] explain how the teacher defines the work of composition, what goals are set for students, what contexts shape the work, and how the work reflects these goals and contexts.
2. A representative piece of student writing . . . however excellent, flawed, or unfinished, and
3. The assignment on which the paper was based.

Coles and Vopat's requirements are more simply stated. They want a piece of writing that "demonstrates excellence" and an estimate of why it does so. Galin, Haviland, and Johnson ask that the student text be "representative" rather than "excellent" and that the teacher include in analysis the pedagogy around it, the teacher's definition of composition's work, goals for students, contexts affecting the student text, and relations between these reflections and the student text. Each editorial position arguably invites almost infinite inventiveness among contributors. But among its other premises, *TWLAP* is clearly theorized outside earlier assumptions that writers might directly and independently control their language absolutely. It is clear from the call for contributions that *WMWG*'s contributors need not have evoked narrative examples ("a piece of college student writing . . . that for that teacher in some way demonstrates excellence"), but the many contributors whose assignments had evoked them were later charged with privileging student "voice" as the essence of excellence. The collection was seen to have equated personal expressivism with authenticity, "truth," "integrity," and "honesty" in the inappropriate self-revelations that comprised its content.

The conviction hereby impugned to the book is that excellence in academic writing depends on exposing one's character, not in a generic "personal essay" with a history traced back to Montaigne, but instead in an effusion of unmediated expression, very much the "breathing out" that ex-press defines and that lessons in rhetorical elocution actually teach. Of course Coles' prior reputation has a great deal to do with inferring this bias, as does the statistic that 30 of the 48 selections in *WMWG* are personal narratives. But other politics were also in play. For instance, I selected Vince Dawson's "Put it on A Matter Of" to share my unabashed awe at his writing to and for his classmates about the amputation of his leg, but not because it exposed a hidden experience that could be more direct and authentic than decorum dictates in public spaces. Strictly imitating a required "Matter Of" incident report, this forcibly retired Milwaukee cop's story conveys the power of "generic convention" more acutely than the paradox of expression could. With dry precision, his report format represents this one moment of encounter with a speeding reckless driver: "The driver of the car was apprehended. The blood began to cover everything."

I argue, as others did more and less directly, that it is familiarity with generic conventions that makes overwhelming devastation precisely "graphic." I am still persuaded that it is restraint made visible, a difference between always disappearing lived experience and clichéd renditions of it in circulating formulas, that defines "good writing." This often tacit knowledge of how this juxtaposition works results neither in correctness nor expressive liberation from it, neither in well-schooled imitation nor an illusory originality. As Candace Speigleman demonstrates in "Teaching Expressive Writing as a Narrative Fiction," a passionate rendition full of illuminating detail describing a personal joy or tragedy may turn out to be—in all "honesty"—a student's "own ways of handling the 'honest' and 'personal' aspects of an assignment, not truth" (par. 36). It is the space between these paired alternatives—the always escaping experience and the formula expectation for making it textual—where Vince (who sometimes spelled his name "Vinc") becomes an indigenous Capote-Mailer-Hemingway master of assembled detail. At the least, Vince's work warrants Jim Sledd's comment on the following selection in *WMWG*, that "our cruelty blocks the main function of language, communication, if we deny respect to other people because their different histories have not given them the kinds of English that we value" (35). My point is that Coles and Vopat called for no more nor less than this, representations of the ways in which student writing calls attention to acts of writing themselves, whether with Vince's imitative skill or with a "voice" portrayed well enough to sound like a "voice."

I am not here setting aside the many histories that include Coles in the 1966 Dartmouth Conference agendas. Like British educators who attended and Richard Ohmann, Wallace Douglas, James Sledd, and many other leftists in American composition, Coles lamented the shallow content of student writing and hoped to find ways to increase its texture. He emphasized self-expressive uses of language, interaction among teachers and students, collaborative activities, and the goals of a "process" pedagogy that opposed the then emphasized "transmission" theory of teaching by, for instance, giving quizzes on the logical fallacies named in most textbooks at the time. Yet what I and many others took to be the "trick" of *WMWG* was to publish student texts not as examples of the underlying cogency of error, but to bring to bear on many sorts of student writing the positive interpretative habits of literary English Studies. The "expressivism" of the Dartmouth conference, that is, pushed against a tradition of disciplined recitation. But it did so to place students and their writing in appropriate schooled interchanges, to find respect on their own terms precisely as situated students, not as psychologized recipients of either institutional sympathy or familial responses to their difficult moments.

Thus it is possible, and I think important, to see these agendas in composition's history vividly restated in the moment of *TWLAP*. It again opposes an earlier lecture model of teaching, but it now also takes on the later belief that there is a cognitive "key" to the brain and that we will find and apply it to what writers think and do. The current collection instead takes for granted that the norms of well-theorized writing instruction are collaboration, workshops, "network theory," student publication, multiple drafts, reading that gleans both rhetorical information and a source of literate content, and close interactions between teacher and student. But the difference is that now, it does not need to oppose these common practices to a hegemonic belief that "control" makes good teaching good.

It is here, in fact, that *Teaching/Writing in the Late Age of Print* represents a primary difference from *What Makes Writing Good*, a difference that cannot be attached to an elaborated composition theory, but one that is embedded in a much broader cultural shift over the last fifteen years. This collection obviously offers excellent and needed emphases on technologies as partners in pedagogy, both as tools of composing and commentary and as means toward writing new and varied genres such as web pages and e-mail conversations about texts. But its primary difference from earlier models for teaching writing is not in this new content. Its distinction is in its repeated praise of classes and of student writing that "extend the boundaries of the classroom" (Hult 240). This book prescribes a different sort of investment in an education that takes place outside proprietary ownership of "my" students and "what I do."

That is, these essays realize a new cultural stake in the academy, one that values its institutional cooperation with the resources that form and sustain it, specifically with the intellectual, financial, political, and social interactions with people who may join its interests—not, as has historically been imagined, who must either give to or take from it. *Teaching/Writing in the Late Age of Print* celebrates the many peer reviews, publication projects, electronic "meeting places" and conversations, service learning initiatives, community actions such as providing web pages for specific service groups, and other "public" interactions that do not repeat methods we applied as process teachers in the 1980s. Nor are these novel elements of our conversation reactions to what J Paul Johnson calls the earlier, "essentially modernist" view of purposeful composing as an individualistic pursuit (318). Instead, this emerging identity for universities and the students and teachers in them places our work in the totality of communicative practices that comprise cultures. The academy, that is, is no longer valued as a "free" space, a place where ideas must be (or can be) born and articulated in protected laboratory conditions. Certainly the material and emotional circumstances of the veterans returning from a brutal World War, the repressed conflicts of the cold war, and the carnage of Vietnam projected powerful images on American society that made universities refuges in more than figurative ways. But no matter how cautiously, their faculty members and students now cheerfully re-explore once obvious premises, especially that the space an academy occupies is within its immediately supportive context, which often includes the dread State Legislatures to whom some students are learning to write.

It is possible to see this new context for scholarly studies as a threat to more than closely held preferences for academic isolation. But the positive value of this shifted relationship to their contexts informs the practices and theories that make *TWLAP* a new temporal place-marker. This collection's diverse descriptions of pedagogic success convey a fresh spirit. They now describe always valued student publication as "participation in two discourses at once." They emphasize and facilitate not the judgments of "peer review" so much as ongoing conversations among students about how they are writing, what they are saying, and how they want their work to be evaluated. As George Otte notes, such conversations do not inhabit the same artificial and controlled site of scrutiny as typical "workshops," but are student-driven (95). In these and other ways, *TWLAP* emphasizes that successful pedagogy establishes participation in an assembly of learners who are peers in a fragmented but interdependent world, not the one-to-one teacher/student interactions billed as "what you need to learn here to go into a world outside this one."

Thus, it is important to name the categories of analysis that *Teaching/Writing in the Late Age of Print* suggests. My view of history precludes the idea of "late ages," as I have made clear. Any temporal present is a space of accumulated usages that are redeployed when new tools and new circumstances recall them; nothing is ever entirely "over." And as I have said, it is not the composition of web links, e-mail conversations, web page design, the ability to archive and return to drafts and exchanges, or on-line editing tools that are at stake in the subtexts of this collection. The required multivocality of electronic composing here is a theoretical assertion about the human making of textuality, not a window on recent technology. This assertion traces an earlier agenda in praise of student writing to open a different window onto identities for both students and their teachers. Students are credited, for instance, with what they already know and bring to the academy, especially with an emotional stake in composing that results in texts that are both highly textured and carefully crafted. As Libby Miles says of herself, these teachers often place student expertise and experience at the center of a curriculum (227). But as Miles and others do, they step outside the inherited Gnosticism around academic certification by revealing their own existing interests, desires, and emerging technological expertise. Their self-representations thus work against the gate-keeping that contributors to *WMWG* also rejected, but here with more awareness of a writing instruction that cannot be contained in privatized classrooms nor encompassed by relative evaluations of its result.

In sum, this collection begins to rewrite many interactions within the academy. Both teachers and students become people capable of helping themselves and others. Both have as great a stake in conversing in groups as they do in competing as individuals. Both can assess their own relatively successful performances and changes in a particular learning situation, and both move ahead with a meta-understanding of what writing entails. In sum, students and teachers here are joined, in a new chronicle of dedication and rededication to noticing that, and how, writing is the most important subject.

WORKS CITED

Coles, William, and James Vopat. *What Makes Writing Good: A Multiperspective.* Washington, DC: Heath, 1985.

Miller, Susan. "The New Student." *ADE Bulletin* (September, 1975): 11–16.

Speigleman, Candace. "Teaching Expressive Writing as a Narrative Fiction." *Journal of Advanced Composition* 16.1 (1996): 119–140. 7 July 2001. <http://www.cas.usf.edu/JAC/161/spigelman.html>.

INTRODUCTION

As both a print anthology of pedagogical essays and an extended website of teaching materials, *Teaching/Writing in the Late Age of Print* aims to chart the considerable growth, breadth, dispersal, and momentum that has marked the last two decades of postsecondary writing instruction in the United States. One of a number of influences on this project has been William Coles and James Vopat's 1985 *What Makes Writing Good: A Multiperspective*, a collection of what excellent writing teachers then valued as "good" in student writing. That representative corpus of assignments and responses has long provided composition studies an illuminating anthology of student work. Both lauded and critiqued, *WMWG* captured the teaching practices of its era and today serves an important archival function. *Teaching/Writing in the Late Age of Print* aims to provide for composition studies today what Coles and Vopat had for an earlier paradigm: a richly contextualized range of theories and pedagogies for teaching writing enacted in real classrooms, with real students, under real constraints.

Those familiar with the history of writing instruction know well the struggle of composition studies to define itself as a discipline. Yet what has long marked the enterprise is (aside from its roots in rhetoric and the humanities) its connectedness to the practice of teaching, a genuine understanding that writers, students, humans are central to its mission. In calling for the chapters and course materials that have come to comprise this volume and its companion website, we have aimed to elicit contributions that would demonstrate how writing is taught at the turn of the 21st century. These essays and their supporting documentation suggest that the teaching of writing occurs in a remarkable diversity of sites, by a remarkable array of teachers (who are themselves remarkable in their self-reflective practice), and with a remarkable body of students who accomplish far more than critics of contemporary higher education might ever surmise they could. Epideictic, then, in a sense, *TWLAP* celebrates the work of our era's accomplished writing teachers and their students.

In the mid-1980s, when *WMWG* appeared, David Bartholomae and Anthony Petrosky published *Ways of Reading*, Linda Flower and John Hayes received their first Braddock Award for cognitive research in the teaching of writing, and MegaByte University, the first listserv for teaching composition using computers, was formed. James Berlin published *Rhetoric and Reality*—in one sense concluding a history of writing instruction, at least as it was read by many a graduate student in the field, effectively with the year 1985. At the same time, poststructuralist and postmodern theories of identity formation and social dynamics began posing the first real challenge to process theory as the dominant paradigm for research and teaching within composition studies. Theories of social construction influenced the diffusion of writing instruction upward and outward across the curriculum, leading to the wide-scale emergence of writing in the disciplines, writing centers, and, more recently, service learning. Debates over literacy, the canon, and multicultural education informed our discourse and practices with the emergence of literacy ethnographies, culturally diverse readerships, and problem-posing pedagogies. The proliferation of networked computers accelerated the reconsideration of the dominant genres and practices of the composition classroom, and the more recent ubiquitousness of the World Wide Web dramatically increased the number of compositionists and their students navigating, researching, and building multilinear and multimedia texts. All the while, feminist critiques of language and gender interrogated the previously unchallenged histories of rhetoric and composition as well as the pedagogies that shaped teaching in writing classrooms. And PhD programs in rhetoric and composition appeared across the country, marking the coming of age of the discipline. All of this rapid change has taken place in an era of increased demands for accountability that have complicated the work of program administrators, students, and teachers alike.

In essence, since 1985, the field of composition has undergone rapid change on many fronts: epistemological, technological, pedagogical, political, and institutional. As we three co-editors—Jeff Galin, Carol Haviland, and J Paul Johnson—witnessed and experienced these paradigmatic shifts in our teaching, scholarly, and administrative roles, we felt compelled to chart them, to study them in some meaningful way. In essence, we felt, the changes since the 1980s warranted, for us, a project that would provide a second, a closer look at what our students write—and how their writing is read.

NINETEEN HUNDRED AND EIGHTY-FIVE: WHAT MADE WRITING GOOD

The publication of *What Makes Writing Good* in 1985 is germane to this current project in a number of ways. Its editors designed it as a textbook for composition courses. They invited composition teachers and program directors to contribute a single sample of student writing that "in some way demonstrates excellence" (viii), and they published those pieces, framed by the assignments that prompted them and critiques that assessed them, as a means of engaging and instructing the student writers who were imagined as the book's primary audience. Its roster of contributors read something like a Who's Who of Composition Studies in the 1980s: Susan Miller, Andrea Lunsford, Linda Flower, Edward Corbett, Donald Murray, James Williams, Erika Lindemann, and others, many of whom had migrated to composition after being trained in period literature. The collection, with its assignment apparatus, did not survive as a textbook for composition courses. It has, however, been cited as an "extremely valuable" source of assignments, student writing, and instructor commentary (Faigley 120).

Although *What Makes Writing Good* remains valued as a source of data, its contents have been critiqued. Certainly, the book suggests a homogeneity of practice that was quite different from the diversity generated by the increasingly complex demographics and pedagogies of the subsequent fifteen years. Few of its student papers seemed to arise out of any particular context or problem-posing in the Freirean sense; no papers focused on linguistics, literacy, or discipline-specific discourse; and there are no collaborative pieces, no portfolios, no research, nor service projects. In *Fragments of Rationality*, Lester Faigley discusses an emphasis on personal and autobiographical writing that characterized one-half to three-quarters of *WMWG*'s chapters, and concludes that this preponderance suggests a similar (and inappropriate) emphasis in the field (120). Indeed, the feature that most consistently seemed to "make writing good" in *WMWG* is that the writing convinced a community of readers of its goodness—and, apparently, the personal essay was, at the time, that most likely to carry suasive effect. It was, in fact, the prioritizing of such personal narratives in *WMWG* that led Patricia Bizzell and Bruce Herzberg to characterize the book's values as having served "a profoundly conservative political agenda" (247). In sum, its critics were wary of its predominance of personal essays and its lack of student work that might more fully have represented the diversity that, in theory and in practice, existed then in writing classrooms.

However, it is worth asking whether such critiques of *WMWG* represent it fairly. In his discussions of *WMWG* in *Fragments,* Faigley deleted the subordinated part of the title, that which attested to its "multiperspective": it is nowhere to be found in *Fragments* (neither in his appraisal of *WMWG* in pages 120-29 nor in his Works Cited list) even though he provides full titles for a number of other authors (among them Pierre Bourdieu, Michel Foucault, Jürgen Habermas, and Patricia Harkin and John Schilb). The fact that *WMWG* can be read from multiple perspectives—and can be seen to represent multiple perspectives—is in itself a perspective its critics seem to wish to dismiss. Despite Faigley's claims to the contrary, the student writing presented there did indeed represent at least something of a multiplicity of genres, including technical pieces, timed writings, informal work, and even short fiction. As Coles and Vopat pointed out in their preface, the writing included examples "as different in form and purpose as the résumé, the short story, the field report, the meditation, the fifty-minute diagnostic essay, the journal" (viii). The authors claimed that the 48 collected pieces are "a way of dramatizing how no judgments about writing can be taken as final or absolute" (viii). Although Faigley is correct to point out an emphasis on personal and autobiographical writing, and although the text did not represent the kinds of diversity of genres one might expect, *WMWG* was hardly as monologic in its presentation of student writers as its critics would intimate.

Thus, despite the scholarly dissensus regarding its value, the three of us still find *What Makes Writing Good* a meaningful collection—meaningful enough to motivate us to solicit and compile the essays that comprise this anthology, which we see as something of a companion piece, if not a sequel, to that earlier volume, and we hope that *Teaching/Writing in the Late Age of Print* represents the teaching practices of our era as interestingly as did *What Makes Writing Good* those of 1985.

TWO THOUSAND ONE: AN ODYSSEY

Ours are transitional times, as we noted earlier, on many fronts. Our tools, our contexts, and our practices for teaching and writing have changed dramatically, and thus the sites of change that affect this collection most profoundly are technologies, demographics, and pedagogies. In his 1991 book *Writing Space: The Computer, Hypertext, and the History of Writing*, Jay David Bolter called ours the "late age of print" (3), a phrase that has echoed with us for some time now, and especially as we sought a title that would suggest the extent to which writing technologies have shaped education generally and composition studies specifically.

Bolter coined his phrase to characterize an era in which the conventions of print still inform the thinking and practices of literate behavior, even as computer technologies foreground, question, and remake those traditions. In a 2001 keynote speech at the 17th Annual Computers and Writing Conference, Bolter amplified his phrase, noting that this late age of print is marked by what he calls "re-mediation," a process in which 'real media' forms such as print, cinema, and photography interact with digital media forms, each departing from long-practiced forms and, thus, "remediating from each other." He suggests that the WWW is the "quintessential remediator," illustrating with examples of the ways CNN Online remediates from news casting and TV news remediates from the Web by borrowing windows and frames. He reaffirms, however, that the late age of print does not mean the end of print any more than the late age of capitalism means the end of capitalism.

By the year 2001, of course, networked computers had become ubiquitous in American higher education, often transforming the practices of teaching writing. As Bolter suggests with his reference to late capitalism, our title does not celebrate an impending "death" of print culture; rather, it signals new directions, implications, and possibilities that may emerge from "remediations." Although computer technologies are hardly the only feature that have helped reshape the last two decades, they have marked an important shift in the means of production, distribution, representation, and consumption of texts, both in academic institutions and in American culture at large.

Only fifteen years ago, the teaching of composition in the majority of postsecondary institutions across the United States was governed by the same writing materials and strategies that instructors used across the twentieth century: pencils, paper, books, handouts, writing samples (student and professional), chalk and dry-erase pens, and black and white boards. Increasingly frequently, though, writing instructors began to use higher-end technology that is simultaneously more costly, more complex, yet just as frequently more time-intensive: computers, software, courseware, networks, printers, cd-roms, the Internet, LCD projectors, and Smart Boards. This change has prompted teachers, students, and researchers of writing to work with established pedagogies in new ways (communication, composition, revision, networked drafting workshops), in remediated or altogether new genres and fields (mixed-media research projects, digital slideshow presentations, hypertext, and document design), and using new tools (graphics and web development software, touch-screen projector systems, courseware interfaces). In *TWLAP,* the presence of technology looms large in many chapters, to be sure. Technology also played an important role in our editorial work, as the three of us kept our modems and networks busy with flurries of e-mails and attachments between San Bernardino, Boca Raton, and Winona—not to mention countless others between us and our contributors scattered across dozens of states. But perhaps more importantly, it allowed us to conceive of and develop the web component of the project, where we archive course materials for each chapter and thus initiate a much more detailed contextualization of our contributors' work than would have been otherwise possible.

This website includes a searchable database of all the chapter abstracts, the full texts of assignments, syllabi, excerpts from all contributions, extended course materials, and an online forum for teachers and researchers to meet and discuss their research interests. It also includes links to those technology-based submissions that are better presented online than in print. In the years to come, we will solicit and post additional contributions that do not appear in the print text. We ask that our readers consider this website an active, integral part of the project: as they use and contribute to it, teachers, scholars, and researchers can learn considerably more about each of the approaches to teaching writing that our individual chapters characterize. In essence, the new technologies have enabled us and our students to retool/remediate and thus re-envision the teaching of writing in this late age of print.

In addition to technological change, a second continuing area of change in American higher education has been, for lack of a better word, *demographic*. The contexts in which we work have changed. By most accounts, student social activism has decreased in comparison to previous generations. Indeed the student population has become like the general populace—increasingly culturally diverse yet increasingly politically centrist. Particularly, college students are today marked by greater, if by no means "optimal," diversity in representation of gender, class, race, culture, language, ability, and age. Today, nearly half of all high school graduates attend the thousands of postsecondary institutions across the United States, most of which require composition instruction in some form. Increasing numbers of part-time students (one recent estimate suggests that 40 percent of postsecondary students are enrolled part-time), first-generation college students, and nontraditional learners are noteworthy for their shifts away from humanities and social sciences to management, engineering, and paraprofessional degrees. These changes contribute equally to a general skepticism towards the traditional liberal arts and to an increasing focus on the technical aspects of education—a binary that composition, with its roots in one garden and its tendrils in another, has long sought to deconstruct.

Despite heated discussions of what composition is and who should teach it, composition requirements remain in place at most postsecondary institutions. Thus, the teaching of writing today takes place in a variety of types of institutions and at a number of levels. Influenced at least in part by the wealth of professional scholarship in the 1970s and 1980s, terms such as "process," "collaboration," and "publication" have become keywords for postsecondary and secondary student writers as well as those at the elementary and middle-school levels (Paul's daughter has a "Writing Center" in her elementary classroom, the mission of which is not wholly unlike the one he directs at his university). Advanced placement and college-level courses in composition now challenge high school students with college-level writing tasks. Alongside a continuously difficult job market for PhDs in English literature, specialists in Rhetoric and Composition have enjoyed burgeoning opportunities over the previous fifteen years. Yet, at postsecondary institutions, the required first-year course often is held primarily responsible for writing instruction, and part-time, adjunct, nontenured faculty, along with graduate students, still carry the bulk of the teaching load.

The growth of writing-across-the-curriculum, writing-in-the-disciplines, and writing center programs, however, has contributed to a general diffusion of writing instruction both upward and outward across the curriculum. Even as writing instruction is characterized more by the diversity of programs, requirements, and faculty across the United States, some recent efforts, such as the "Outcomes Statement" of the Writing Program Administrators, suggest the prospects of at least some degree of consensus about what first-year composition ought to accomplish, as well as what it can not.

Given the widespread changes in our technological and institutional landscapes, it should not seem too surprising that our practices have changed as well. And *TWLAP* is ultimately a book about pedagogical change, only some of which has been shaped by technology. There exists a wide variety of classroom practices, with composition classes that are subject-, project/problem-, genre-, or mode-based—and that address a variety of topics, from classical ideas to cultural studies, from personal expression to contemporary problems, from modal exercises to writing in the disciplines, from service learning to technical communications. And, of course, the writing that students do in these classes elicits a variety of responses, from formative appraisals to summative corrections—and just about everything in between. This variety of sites, participants, contexts, materials, and practices, then, gives rise to the variety of different pedagogies: writing can be taught as a mode of inquiry and self-examination; as a means of participation in civic, community matters; as an economic and social necessity; as humanistic, even belletristic adventure; as an introduction to (and immersion in) an academic community; as a means of understanding effects of race, class, gender; and as a means of challenging typically unquestioned assumptions that pass as the normal state of affairs.

Of course, no system can grow and expand infinitely on the principle of inclusivity, and composition teaching today is no exception. Many of these more current practices and theories have replaced or subsumed those that came before them. Gone today from the teaching of writing are some of the practices and goals of nineteenth-century (and earlier) instruction: memorization, rigid schemata, declamation, oral eloquence; and, of course, reduced are some of the various movements that have characterized the ebb and flow of composition teaching across the 20th century, among them exercises in transliteration, explication, paraphrase, imitation, and transcription. Current-traditionalism, characterized by Berlin as unduly emphasizing surface correctness and generic form, may still work its effects in certain classrooms, yet it is hardly a vital force in either published scholarship or classroom practice. And the once-close relationships with speech communications and literature have eroded from view, as separate departments of communications offer speech courses and forensics programs, and as writing about literature is now more widely seen as the province of a writing-in-the-disciplines approach.

What we see today, then, is that the practices of composition are so varied—and so demonstrably, so suddenly, so visibly different from 1985—as to warrant this anthology. In what follows, we hope to chart how composition teachers and their students today practice their craft, and how they do so in a multiplicity of ways, sites, and contexts. Whereas *WMWG* indeed provided a generation of composition professionals with a survey of the kinds of assignments and writing valued then, we hope that *TWLAP* likewise provides its audience with an understanding of the range of teaching and learning that characterize this late age of print.

REPRESENTING TEACHING—AND WRITING—IN THE LATE AGE OF PRINT

We invited contributors to select student texts that allow them to reflect critically on their teaching practices, values, and institutional contexts, modeling our call for contributions loosely on Coles and Vopat's. However, we use *WMWG* as a marker rather than as a model because in many ways we are representing a very different moment in composition studies. For example, Coles and Vopat made personal invitations to professors and program directors already known for their scholarship; we made multiple public calls as well as some private solicitations for contributions. Coles and Vopat asked for transcriptions of writing assignments and student texts; we asked that contributors contextualize and reflect on their teaching, and so in some cases our contributors necessarily truncated the language of their assignments or excerpted the work of their students. Whereas Coles and Vopat asked that the student texts (to be of no more than 1,000 words) demonstrate "excellence, however flawed or unfinished" (viii), we instead asked that the student writing be *representative* of classroom teaching, in the process acknowledging that some of the most interesting teaching moments occur before, after, or even in disjuncture with the submission of the final, polished product. We also encouraged our contributors to structure and frame their own discussions as they wished, guided only by the directive that they provide context, student work, and analysis, preferably in that general sequence.

The result has been that the pieces may seem less similar to each other than did those in *WMWG*, with its lockstep assignment-response-analysis structure. However, that latitude has allowed our contributors to reflect upon the interrelationships of their institutional contexts, teaching practices, and students' writing; furthermore, in many instances, the chapters are able to present the dialogism, recursivity, and self-reflexivity of the writing process as it is carried out between participants. *What Makes Writing Good* provided 48 short chapters; in this book, we offer about a third fewer, but we do so, we hope, with a considerably greater depth of detail about the practice of composition, one made even more fully realized by the supporting teaching materials available on the companion website. Our contributors also did not limit their reflections to first-year writing classes, as did those who contributed to the Coles and Vopat text. In addition to contributions on first-year writing, we include chapters from high school, honors, upper-division composition, and critical reading, professional writing, and graduate classes. Furthermore, we hope to include, both online and in a subsequent volume, even more contributions.

The call for papers for *Teaching/Writing in the Late Age of Print*, then, prompted our contributors to think about the connections between their teaching and their students' writing—and thus to consider more fully the contexts within which students write. Although at one point early in the process we invited each of the contributors to *WMWG* to author an article for our volume, only one accepted the offer. Our lone volunteer, Susan Miller, author of *Textual Carnivals* and *Rescuing the Subject,* contributed the foreword, which reflects upon the historical moments of both *WMWG* and *TWLAP.*

Several recent anthologies have collected articles on issues confronting composition studies, but *Teaching/Writing in the Late Age of Print* is unique in demanding that contributors ground their claims in their students' writing. In other words, we look to the pudding for the proof. Other than *Twelve Readers Reading* and the two anthologies that followed, *The Practice of Response* and *Sourcebook for Responding to*

Student Writing, no other volume we know of asks compositionists to use student writing to reflect on their teaching practices; no other, insofar as we know, aims to provide the rich breadth of response to student writing that reflects the current state of composition. We offer *Teaching/Writing in the Late Age of Print* to researchers who are interested in what composition has become as a discipline, including teachers of writing in high schools and universities, writing program administrators, graduate students entering the field, and students in composition classes who hope to study the kinds of work that is being valued in academia. We hope, then, that the book will be read in academic libraries, graduate degree-granting institutions, faculty development centers, teacher-training programs, and in composition and rhetoric scholarship.

TEACHING AND WRITING, INEXTRICABLY BOUND

In aiming to characterize a diversity of contexts and practices, *Teaching Writing in the Late Age of Print* raises a full range of issues and challenges. Some of our contributors sent us the kinds of work we might have expected, with emphases on collaborations, computers, critical pedagogies, and so on, but other contributions raised a host of issues for us as we planned and organized the anthology. In particular, we found that the influences of feminism, poststructuralism, multiculturalism, and social constructionism, and, more broadly, of postmodernism proved both interesting and revealing as we looked at the ways in which they were represented, although usually implicitly. For example, contemporary composition studies is heavily influenced by feminism, yet, like many other observers, we noticed that its presence in this volume is largely unspoken. We see it in our own call for contributors that invites what Joy Ritchie and Kathleen Boardman call "a dialogical relationship between theory and experience" (602), and we see it in the many chapters that feature "pushing for admission [of the other], working intuitively alongside, and interruption of the conversation" (600). The collaboration between Wini Wood and Nida Sophasarun that begins our volume may be our most compelling example. Even though the most explicit acknowledgment of feminism may be found here in this introduction, we also see it represented in the expanded notions of authorship and intellectual property, the visible risk taking and collaborative learning, and some of the divergence of textual forms this volume presents.

The issues of authorship have been addressed most directly by Andrea Lunsford and Lisa Ede, whose *Singular Texts/Plural Authors* both represented and advocated a new view of collaboration. Interrogating the academic traditions, particularly in the humanities, of solitary writing and strict delineation of authorial contributions, they argued for a more complex view of authorship, one that more closely reflects writing as a social act. In contrast to *WMWG*, where all chapters were singly authored and faculty and student texts marked as clearly distinct from each other, a number of the chapters in *TWLAP* are jointly authored, and some of those are authored jointly by faculty and students. However, we remain surprised, given the extensive discussion of collaboration in both journals and conferences, that these chapters remain in the minority. In fact, several contributors asked specifically if it would be "all right" if they wrote jointly with their students, suggesting that this kind of authorship is increasingly common but still recognized as possibly inappropriate—or insufficiently valued. What we did see more commonly is a greater interplay between student and faculty texts. Rather than uniformly following the *WMWG* pattern of student text followed by separate teacher commentary, Wini Wood and Carol Haviland wove their texts together with their students', evoking a dialogic approach to texts and teaching rather than presenting a named expert responding to unnamed novice. In fact, it is that very kind of recursive interplay that accounts for the way we present our title as "Teaching/Writing": it is intended to connote that relationships between teaching and writing, between teachers and writers, between assignment and response, are neither unidirectional nor always clearly demarcated. Teaching is itself a kind of authorship, a construction of knowledge, just as writing serves, in a way, as pedagogy.

So we note with anticipation these richly complicated notions of authorship even as we are dismayed that the opportunity to contest such notions remains located in privilege. Although our call for contributors to this book circulated widely, at conference proceedings, in journals, and on listservs devoted to writing teachers at all kinds of institutions, our proposals came chiefly from colleges and universities. Despite our seeking them out, few came from secondary schools or community colleges, we believe for two reasons, both reflecting privilege. First, is time. Very simply, although faculty who teach three or four classes per term may feel burdened with their teaching loads and scholarly demands, they still have more time to write than do their peers on high school and community college campuses—who commonly teach more and larger classes and are rewarded less for scholarly activities. A second, less visible difference involves the opportunity to reflect critically on one's work. In many high school and community college settings, faculty are pressed to "just teach" and to leave the critical conversations to department chairs and curriculum supervisors. This press to "just teach" also reduces or even eliminates the rewards for scholarly writing; university faculty are rewarded for publication, but secondary and community college faculty are offered little incentive to invest their time in research. Thus, even though we have been impressed by the critical reflection displayed by many such faculty, they were uneasy about how their writing might look alongside university faculty scholarship. This is a gap we hope future compositionists address, for universities are still noted more for berating—rather than their supporting—the very institutions that provide their students.

A second feature is the willingness of contributors to take risks, both in their teaching and in these chapters about teaching. For example, several chapters describe faculty teaching courses in which they are only beginning to develop expertise. Again, this might be expected, given the mushrooming field with which scholars struggle to keep pace, but struggles to keep up often are struggles kept secret. However, in such chapters we see an opening of these sites of learning. In some cases, they are open to new and differently situated participants as faculty draw on students' expertise, together investigating technological, linguistic, and cultural complexities. Such sites make the faculty role of co-investigator more visible as students participate as recognized knowledge-makers, not simply as washers of lab glassware or writers of imperfect texts.

Of course, this risk-taking invites a different view of students, and it must acknowledge the risks faculty ask students to take alongside them. When both faculty and students see difference, dissensus, and conflict as useful, they plunge into the potential quagmire of postmodernism. For example, when faculty view students as collaborators, the dynamics of writing assignments shift. Rather than asking students simply to write about themselves or to acquire the conventions of academic others, they ask students to write and speak to others about the intersections of self, issues, and others. This kind of risk-taking demands that faculty anticipate and insulate students from unacceptable risks, and it can make faculty members vulnerable if student evaluations of teaching rest chiefly on whether faculty are "masters of their subjects." But if chapters such as these salute such risk-taking as enriching rather than compromising learning, they may help rewrite criteria for good teaching.

The diversity of textual forms that *TWLAP* chapters took also differ from the more uniform chapters of *WMWG*, reflecting in part the choices of editors for both books and in part disciplinary expectations of each era. Early on, we editors struggled with our own visions of coherence as manuscripts began arriving. Some fit almost exactly with what we thought that the call for chapters invited, but others departed widely. Indeed, our own conversations continued right up to publication, the three of us struggling to achieve a careful balance between the needs of individual authors and the coherence of the whole volume. As it stands, the collection offers a compromise: many chapters follow parallel tracks as they situate their interrogations of teaching writing in complete student texts; others, meanwhile, address the core issues of context and pedagogy but seem less visibly similar to each other. Our contribution by Dickie Selfe, Karla Kitalong, and Michael Moore—which features an extended discussion of a cross-class collaboration—as well as the selections by Katherine Fischer, Daniel Anderson, and James Inman represent something of this textual diversity. We struggled, too, with determining how to present student writing within each chapter. Traditional conventions of indention and italics seemed to disrupt collaborative texts, and nearly full pages of set-off text looked, simply, typographically strange to us. Twenty years ago, when the lines between teacher and writer, teaching and writing were more clearly drawn, and when fewer forms of writing were common, such concerns were less worrisome, if at all present. But for us, writing about teaching in the late age of print challenges the typographic conventions that were more workable for *WMWG*.

These conventions, though, may be more than merely typographic. A generation ago, there may have been fewer questions about what made writing good, perhaps because writing itself had yet to be interrogated by technology and postmodernity. Certainly, one could assume that what got "composed" in a first-year composition class was a paper. And a good one, we could safely assume, was comprised of the synthesis, integration, and articulation of ideas into a linear flow of syntactic units intended to create a coherent whole. For Tuman, these are the very tasks that define the print literacy of high modernism and book culture, for writers of compositions are, in essence, creating "miniature books" (4). Some of our chapters, such as those by Rick Straub, J Paul Johnson, Helen Ewald, and Kathleen Welsch, feature—and sometimes interrogate—such work. But what counts today as a composition, when the word is used to describe what students write, is neither necessarily fixed nor finite. In other words, in *TWLAP*, the composition is not always a composition, and it is frequently not a "paper," as the student writing in this volume ranges from synchronous chats (in the chapters by George Otte and Joan Latchaw) to hypertext webs (Becky Rickly, Carrie Leverenz, Betty Eidenier), from portfolio self-assessments (Susanmarie Harrington) to service-learning projects or other semester-long projects (Jane Carducci and Gary Eddy, Libby Miles, Jeremy Ball and Judy Hawkins, Christine Hult), from email exchanges (Jeff Galin, Becky Howard) to teacher-student collaborations that extend long beyond the academic semester (Wini Wood, Carol Haviland).

Such are the effects of postmodernity on the subject of composition, then: no longer can we be certain what a student text is, just as we can no longer take for granted what a student text might mean. As co-editors, we have tried to encourage a range of submissions that would both foreground the diversity of student writing and reflect carefully on the intersections of institutional demands, student demographics, and theoretical assumptions that inform the teaching practices. Many of our authors—including Maureen Mathison, Steve Parks and Lori Shorr, Barbara Heifferon, Mariolina Salvatori, and Betty Eidenier—speak pointedly to those constraints and opportunities. In sum, we feel our contributors have responded well to that challenge: their contributions offer no grand narratives that promise to guide all writers towards a single predetermined outcome, but instead they reflect carefully on the goals and practices that make their work meaningful in their particular institutional contexts.

TEACHING/WRITING: A READING

All readings—or so goes a central tenet of the postmodernist—are partial ones. So, too, is our table of contents. Although we might have tried to arrange the chapters collected here by taxonomizing genres of student writing, types of institutions, or kinds of pedagogies, we have instead chosen to provide our readers with sections that would provoke thought and discussion by placing diverse perspectives in contact with each other. We realize that no single reading—no single organization—can fully represent the rich, diverse discipline of composition. We are, of course, keenly aware that we might have grouped them in any number of ways, by any number of topics. The four sections we describe below, however, are ones we hope provide readers with a purposeful framework for comparison and examination.

In the first section, "Teaching/Writing about the Self, the Subject, the Community," we have grouped chapters that focus on the development and articulation of the "writing subject" as students study, construct, and revise their positions. The chapters in this section range from students and teachers reflecting on nonacademic discourse for first-year writing (Rick Straub) to the relationships between personal and institutional writing: Richard Miller reflects on his student's exploration of the ways religious beliefs govern reading practices, and Wini Wood examines student subjectivity in a piece that uses a painting as an opportunity for self- and cultural-reflection. Were we to have received more of the kinds of personal essays and autobiographical narratives that predominated in WMWG, we might have placed them alongside these chapters, but few of our contributors, it seems, assign today the kinds of texts so valued a generation ago.

In section two, "Teaching/Writing with Computers, Classmates, and other Colleagues," the chapters share emphases on collaborative writing and computer technologies. Although fully two-thirds of our contributors use computer technologies in their classes in some manner, as their pieces demonstrate, this set of chapters focuses primarily on synchronous communications, web-based projects, and/or using computers to facilitate collaborative writing and peer review work: Joan Latchaw and George Otte explore the goals and successes of synchronous exchanges, and Carrie Leverenz, Becky Rickly, and Katherine Fischer discuss the possibilities of hypertextual class projects. Karla Kitalong, Michael Moore, and Dickie Selfe discuss their use of extended technology autobiographies in technical communications classes. Additionally, Daniel Anderson assesses web-based platforms for peer review. These are not the only chapters to address computers and collaboration, of course, and readers will find discussions of cooperative learning and technology issues threaded across a number of our other contributions.

The third section, "Teaching/Writing for Academics, Agencies, and other Audiences," includes chapters in which students have been asked to respond successfully to the variables of real-life rhetorical situations—some of them engaging in what Sandra Stotsky calls "participatory writing," which is "indispensable for protecting political rights in a democracy and for promoting the public good" (234). These efforts include service-learning courses taught by Christine Hult, Jane Carducci and Gary Eddy, and Libby Miles; Steve Parks and Lori Shorr's community-university partnerships; and Carol Haviland's, Lisa Toner's, and Susan Lang's explorations of their students' writing for external, multiple audiences. Aside from the widespread integrations of collaborative learning and computer technologies, the focus on writing for audiences beyond the classroom may be the most dramatic change between the students who wrote for *WMWG* and those writing is discussed in *TWLAP*.

The final section, "Teaching/Writing as Rhetoric, Reading, and Revising," is a diverse collection of chapters that emphasize critical reading, writing, revising, and rhetorical strategies. Mariolina Salvatori and J Paul Johnson explore the acts and effects of student reading practices. Jeffrey Galin and Helen Ewald provide explicit pedagogies for postprocess classes. And Becky Howard and Judy Hawkins and Jeremy Ball explore argumentation: the former describes the rhetorical strategies of a student who took part in a listserv dedicated to campaign issues on welfare within the Electronic Democracy Project, and the latter collaborators discuss the revision process of mock trial arguments in their project-based, cross-disciplinary honors class. Critical reading and rhetorical argumentation prove central to the teaching of writing in these chapters, as students read, discuss, argue, revise, and rework their positions amongst a variety of discussants and audiences.

From these short descriptions of the book's four sections, it should become clear that the categories are anything but mutually exclusive. Project-based, computer-mediated, liberatory, and collaborative pedagogies permeate all four sections. Over half of the chapters are situated in first-year writing classes, whereas others range from high school English courses to technical communications and advanced writing courses to graduate seminars. Critical reading, self-reflection, portfolio evaluation, social construction, and web design all inform numerous chapters. To help our readers navigate this multiplicity of paths, we provide a table of chapters following the Table of Contents that explore a certain topic, issue, or pedagogy, and our website provides a series of search terms for the chapters and the corresponding course materials.

We noted earlier that many of our contributors discuss the condition of postmodernity with some degree of specificity, pointing explicitly to its effect on the teaching of writing. And in the sense that *TWLAP* interrogates the status quo; revisits assumptions about authorship; resists grand narratives of progress; deconstructs the teacher/student binary; values play, interplay, heteroglossia, and indeterminacy; and acknowledges the complexities of context and ideology, we think it a purposefully postmodern project. We offer this description as an invitation. *Teaching/Writing in the Late Age of Print* is, in a sense, partial and incomplete, yet simultaneously ongoing and reconstructed. We invite our readers to participate in future revisions of this work by writing their own chapters, charting their own collaborations, exploring their own pedagogies as our contributors have done here. And we look forward to the many exciting ways in which those participations will revise and reconstruct the next age of print.

WORKS CITED

Bizzell, Patricia, and Bruce Herzberg. Review of *What Makes Writing Good*. William Coles and James Vopat, Eds. *College Composition and Communication* 37 (1986): 244-47.

Bolter, Jay David. *Writing Space: The Computer, Hypertext, and the History of Writing*. Hillsdale, NJ: Erlbaum, 1991.

———. "Hypertext, New Media, and the Future of Writing." Computers & Writing 2001 Conference: A Cyber Odyssey. Ball State University. Muncie, IN, 17 May 2001.

Coles, William, and James Vopat. *What Makes Writing Good: A Multiperspective*. Washington, DC: Heath, 1985.

Ede, Lisa, and Andrea Lunsford. *Singular Texts/Plural Authors: Perspectives on Collaborative Writing*. Carbondale: Southern Illinois UP, 1990.

Faigley, Lester. *Fragments of Rationality: Postmodernity and the Subject of Composition*. Pittsburgh: University of Pittsburgh P, 1992.

Ritchie, Joy, and Kathleen Boardman. "Feminism in Composition: Inclusion, Metonymy, and Disruption." *College Composition and Communication 50* (1999): 585-606.

Stotsky, Sandra. "Participatory Writing." *Nonacademic Writing: Social Theory and Technology*. Ann Hill Duin and Craig J. Hansen, Eds. Hillsdale, NJ: Erlbaum, 1996. 227-56.

Straub, Rick. *The Practice of Response: Strategies for Commenting on Student Writing*. Cresskill, NJ: Hampton Press, 2000.

———. *Sourcebook for Responding to Student Writing*. Cresskill, NJ: Hampton Press, 1999.

——— and Ronald Lunsford. *Twelve Readers Reading: Responding to College Student Writing*. Cresskill, NJ: Hampton Press, 1995.

Tuman, Myron. *Word Perfect: Literacy in the Computer Age*. Pittsburgh, PA: Pittsburgh UP, 1992.

ACKNOWLEDGMENTS

As we completed this manuscript for, we were stunned and saddened to learn of the death of Rick Straub, whose contribution to this project is thought-provoking and articulate, and whose contributions to the profession are numerous and purposeful. Our colleagues at Hampton Press, where Rick published three of his books, are especially grateful for his important contributions to the field, and, of course, particularly saddened by his passing.

Our sense of accomplishment is tempered by Rick's passing, yet we also appreciate the wonderful work that so many have contributed to this project. Our inspiration came from William Coles' and James Vopat's *What Makes Writing Good: A Multiperspective*. Lester Faigley's insightful critique of *WMWG* motivated us to conceive *Teaching/Writing in the Late Age of Print* as a study of the field since 1985. Our other colleagues contributed to the project in more direct and tangible ways. We would like to express our sincere appreciation to Barbara Bernstein and Joni Choi of Hampton Press for their collegiality and support; to series editors David Jolliffe and Michael Williamson for their insights and guidance; to all of the contributing authors for their collective intellect, patience, and good cheer; to William Covino, Joan Latchaw, Susan Miller, and Jacqueline Rhodes, for lending their generous and critical readings to drafts and portions of the manuscript; and finally, and most importantly, to all of our students, especially those whose work we feature here, who write so often and so diligently at our behest, for it is their work, ultimately, that gives this project its purpose, its shape, and its meaning.

I

TEACHING/WRITING...

...about the SELF, the SUBJECT, the COMMUNITY

1

"SEE THE SUBJECT FIRST"

Negotiating Subjectivity in a Disciplinary Context

Winifred J. Wood
Wellesley College
with
Nida Sophasarun
Wellesley College, Class of 1999

It is no longer possible to speak of composition as a unified subject. The multiple subjects of composition include the student as subject, the subject of writing, the subjects about which we write, and the disciplines (subjects) that create the context(s) in which we write. The student essay discussed herein, written by Nida Sophasarun in 1996 for a content-based first-year writing course, reveals a delicate balance amongst all these subjects. Nida's essay is striking both formally (it constitutes an artfully hybrid formal analysis/personal essay) and for the student subjectivity it develops, one caught between the passions and desires of popular culture and the critical awareness of the academic community. Nida, now a college graduate, comments on what it felt like to write this essay and to struggle with the constraints of academic writing. Both teacher and student argue that a defining moment in a student's writing life occurs when she learns to negotiate a stance for herself with respect to the subject(s) she writes within and about; teachers need to create spaces and instruction that foster such negotiations and relocations. This demands a reconsideration of the role personal writing plays in a program that emphasizes academic writing.

Originally from Atlanta, Nida graduated from Wellesley College in 1999 with a double major in English and Art History; she earned honors in English by writing a creative thesis in poetry. In addition to taking her first-year composition course with Wini (when she wrote the essay discussed herein), Nida worked with Wini during her senior year as a TA, designing and teaching a tutorial writing course of her own. Of that experience, she wrote this: "I wonder why I thought I would see a linear progression of improvements and lessons imaged in my tutee's writing, when I don't even see it in my own pieces. Progress is not always linear, but, I guess, more like upward, downward, forward, backward, expanding, and contracting circles."

Nida then earned an MFA in creative writing at Johns Hopkins, worked as a research associate at National Geographic magazine, and now lives in Shanghai, where she continues to work on her poetry. She has agreed to collaborate with Wini on this piece, reading and responding to Wini's interpretations of her work. Nida's comments appear throughout the piece in italics.

> If there is any method in the way I take pictures, I believe it lies in this. See the subject first. Do not try to force it to be a picture of this, or that or the other thing. Stand apart from it. Then something will happen. The subject will reveal itself.
>
> —*Bill Brandt, photographer, 1904-1983*

Bill Brandt was perhaps disingenuous in saying that a photographer need only stand back and let the subject reveal itself; his photography was anything but artless. Sometimes he presented us only a slice of his subject—a giant eye, or the side of a head with only the ear visible, poised against a barren landscape. But however the subject presented itself to Brandt, it was clear that something didn't "just happen" between photographer and subject. Rather, the photographer was busy making meaning himself; a transaction was clearly taking place between two actively engaged participants.

Of course, Brandt didn't say "Just see the subject." He said "See the subject first. . . ." These days, though, seeing the subject first—or even deciding which subject to see first—has become a complicated undertaking. In the paper we have chosen to discuss for this volume (it will not surprise you that it is a paper about one of Bill Brandt's photographs), the student (Nida) sees the subject first. (And then something else happens.) And in my (Wini's) description of her paper, I attempt, as well, to see the subject first. But there lies the rub. What is the subject? Is it Nida, who wrote the paper? Is it Bill Brandt's photograph, the subject about which she wrote? Is it art history, the discipline whose methods she evokes and then abandons in order to produce this prize-winning paper? Is it the subject of composition? How can we, teaching in the year 2002 and beyond, understand the relationship between writer, object, and methodology that frames that object? How can we create writing programs in which all writers, the most talented and the least experienced, can find productive and satisfying relationships for themselves within this tangled web? And how can we develop any single pedagogy when the very subjects we teach—the students, the disciplines, and the words that are used by both students and disciplines, not to mention the words that are used in the world outside our cherished disciplines—are changing faster than we are?

Nida's essay prompts me to raise far more questions than I can answer. And so, in my discussion of her essay, I have chosen to focus more on the subjects of our teaching than the methods of our teaching. I see these subjects, for the time being, as the products of our postmodern, postcolonial time: they are global, multiple, in constant transition. They are destabilized, but longing for a stable core; fragmented but with interestingly overlapping identities; highly visual but at the same time defined by discourse and text; unconventional, but constantly developing and redefining conventions to suit their needs and tastes. I cannot and will not argue for a particular pedagogy to meet their many needs, but my description provides glimpses of a pedagogy that may be useful to other teachers. It is a pedagogy that exploits the tension between individual subjects and disciplinary subjects, that asks these subjects to interrogate each other, that leaves open cracks and ruptures into which curious students can drive a wedge of resistance and that students who want a safer form of learning can ignore. It is a messy, but capacious, pedagogy, one that places a semblance of modernist order over its surface but allows spaces in which teachers and students with a postmodern bent can move.

The paper under discussion here—Nida's "*Home is Where. . .*"— was written for a first-year writing course at Wellesley College, one of the many content-based writing courses offered within our program. Each course in the program offers students instruction in the methods of analysis and styles of discourse specific to particular disciplines and asks students to reflect, as well, on how method and style vary across disciplines and within disciplines. The idea behind such a program is that students write better, and learn to write better, when they have some expertise within a particular genre of writing. In addition, students receive instruction in writing process (drafting, revision, and peer editing) and in the techniques of research writing.

I remember writing that essay. I was cramped into the right corner of my dorm room, wedged in between my closet and my dresser, so that I had to physically brace myself against the corners of my desk and shelf to lift and slide myself—Dukes of Hazzard style—into the college-issue wooden chair, which couldn't be moved or else it would bang against the wall or into the ill-fitting desk. There were five desk lamps burning full blast—to mask the true time of night—over the space where I sat with my knees pressed against my chest. My roommate was redecorating her side of the room—a ritual whenever she had a serious deadline. Under these auspices, and on a full stomach of ramen, I wrote that paper.

My section was called "Strong Women in Film." Most of my assignments asked students to write fairly conventional film analyses (analyze a scene; discuss how a character is presented visually; compare what happens to two characters within two different film narratives). To address a recurrent (and obvious) objection to genre-based instruction—when students learn to write within a narrowly defined genre, what transferable skills do they acquire?—I provided students with alternative options to these generic assignments.

In this case, the alternative was to visit and write about an exhibit of photographs at our campus's new Davis Museum and Cultural Center. The exhibit, called "Home is Where . . ." offered a wide array of interpretations of domestic spaces.[1] As I explained to my class (in an effort to link the exhibit to the subject of our course), the notion of domestic space is critical to the representation of women, in film and elsewhere. Although there might not be any direct connection to the films we were studying, I said, the exhibit might open up some new ideas they would like to explore in writing, and I would accept any and all explorations for this assignment. Three students, Nida among them, chose this alternative.

Here, I focus exclusively on Nida's essay, but it is impossible for me not to recall the array of student writing in which Nida's work lay embedded. One student (who later became a theater director) used the

---

[1]For this course, I worked with two of the Davis Museum's curators, Lucy Flint-Gohlke and Corinne Fryhle, to develop ways to integrate the museum's offerings with the curricular offerings of the Writing Program. These curators shared, with me, a deep interest in the relationship between image and text. The *Home is Where . . .* exhibit included essays as well as photographs; the essays, written specifically for the exhibit by members of our campus community, offered varied reflections on the meaning of home. Other exhibits have used text in other, less conventional ways. I take this opportunity to express thanks to Corinne and Lucy, not only for their imagination and support, but also for their vision of a museum that takes risks in bringing art to a wider public and that imagines a wider art to bring to its public.

exhibit's photographs to help her understand the concept of domestic space; she then returned to one of the films we were studying, *Mildred Pierce*, to write an analysis of the set designs for this movie, of the sequence of domestic spaces that defined Mildred's life over the course of the film. Another student—a returning student who makes a living photographing other people's children—chose not write about the photographs at all, but rather to write a highly personal account of her wedding day fifteen years earlier, a piece of writing that led her to question her traditional values. Her avowed goal was to use writing to help her understand herself better, which in turn would help her develop her own photographic style. Surrounding these three individual interpretations lay a dozen other papers doing conventional film analyses.

There must be another way to verbally communicate spaces— academic, domestic, personal, etc.—where the lines aren't so distinct and punishable. There is hardly any space in academia for students to write the here-and-now version of themselves onto paper. In most cases validation is earned through following the academic formula, and distrusting the other types of commentary. Wini's writing assignment created a necessary in-between space: it was an enabling exercise where the energy sprung from weaving formal and personal elements together in an overall visual-verbal statement. As long as teachers give students some sort of choice, there is space for creative interest and genuine investment in the subject. At some point we realize that expressing oneself in an articulate and eloquent manner is a valuable asset—one that prepares us for the real world, and one that defines who we are at the present.

Reading my paper now, I get the surreal feeling of watching my eighteen-year-old self think out loud. I also remember feeling that I was taking a risk by having so much fun with a writing assignment that allowed a vulnerable and earnest voice to seep in. Admittedly, there is some sort of line I walked in that paper, where I traded tit-for-tat critical analysis with my own observations about life. It's that tension which gives the paper some sort of energy, I think. If ever I was stumped about where the flow of the paper was headed, I would return to the photo, and from there I just bounced off the inspiration.

Perhaps it is best to provide you with Nida's paper in its entirety. I hope you enjoy it as much as I did when I first read it (and still do):

Home is Where. . . .
By Nida Sophasarun

One of the parlormaids wears a crisp, pressed uniform along with pursed lips and a sour countenance. Her starched white apron makes a big V against the chest of her black dress to emphasize the effect: prim and orderly. She stands tall and straight as a pin in clear focus in the center of the black and white photograph. Her face conjures up images of strict high school librarians and prudish aunts. Proper, aristocratic names like Georgianna and Anastasia come to mind. I almost walk to the next photograph when something catches my eye.

To the right, a little shorter, a little fuzzier, a little crowded, a little behind, and a little less severe, stands another parlor maid. She looks as if she is eager to please—eager to do things right. Her eyes are unfocused and glazed over; perhaps she is not thinking of the task at hand, and she wishes she were somewhere else. Her cheekbones are not hollow like the first parlor maid's, which look like something sucked the flesh out of them. This maid still has some shininess, some ruddiness about her; maybe it is the small, button nose or her unsure stature, but I know that I like her, and I look further.

Actually, the shine of the silverware is what caught my attention at first. The glorious spread of dinner utensils and flower arrangements garnish that mahogany table like a bright smile on a plain girl. Slowly I notice the crystal goblets, colored wine glasses, polished cutlery, bursting flowers, origami-esque folded napkins, hand-painted porcelain dishes, floral table cloth, and finally a gilded wine tumbler bedecked with jewels and intricate gold designs: this treasure of organized artistry spreads out for [what seems like] miles in front of these parlormaids, who do not admire their handiwork, but rather, let their eyes veer towards something right in front of them. The table takes up the bottom half of the picture, but we only see a portion of the dining-table—like half a racetrack. And then the attention turns toward the maids, who are photographed at a seemingly normal time (dinnertime), but with peculiar expressions.

Perhaps I have glanced too often and stared too hard at my *Town and Country*, because this picture of manor maids has attracted me. And even though I worship the bodies in *Vogue* and the Hollywood stars in *Vanity Fair*, I would much rather look at these two women than glossy page after glossy page of bottled and formulized humanity in a size 2 Mizrahi skirt. The parlormaids, though completely still, look as if they belong in the frame of a Merchant and Ivory film: full of repression and strict social standards. Like good actresses, they can emanate a sense of inner turmoil, duty, aristocratic tradition, and entrapment all in a single snapshot.

It is not the lifestyle to which I relate in this picture. Parlormaids do not wait on me in freshly ironed aprons. In fact, I am the one who is supposed to follow the motto: *non ministrari, sed ministrare.*[2] I cannot

---

[2]*Non ministrari, sed ministrare* is the motto of Wellesley College: not to be ministered unto, but to minister. Needless to say, this is a complicated ideal

help but admire the setting, however, and I readily admit that there is glamour in such a charmed lifestyle. I obsessively read magazines, not *Time* and *The Economist*, but prettier, more flowery materials like *Tattler* and *Bazaar*. My room at home is filled with stacks and piles of cut-up magazines. My room at college is almost the same except that the cramped space allows fewer corners and nooks for stacks of magazines; thankfully there is a recycling bin in the hall outside.

My roommate eyes me suspiciously when I come back from the Ville with more shiny magazines to rip up and stick on our claustrophobic walls; she finds it strange that I like to surround myself with waifish, doe-eyed gamines, except she does not call them that specifically. She says they look like corpses. But at $4, these supermodels are like the polished silver on the tables of the upper crust. They look over us like the eternal billboard advertisement in Fitzgerald's *Great Gatsby*, which pictures a huge pair of eyes wearing optical lenses, towering and overseeing the actions of the small humans below. They hold all of this promise and status that we like to watch like voyeurs; the hundreds of web sites and home pages, which contain pictures and trivial factoids of the famous and filthy rich, can attest to our odd preoccupation with things we find photogenic and appealing. We know that these girls are human like us, but somehow, they are meant to look so unreal and untouchable. They are beautiful, but they are menacing.

Despite the glare of the silver and the alluringly dark gardenias on the table, the parlormaids are still the center of attention. Maybe this is because their poofy white caps make them look more human and less like carbon copies of each other. Even though the taller, grave-looking maid appears unyielding and unmovable as a mountain, a sense of responsibility and duty can be seen in her stance. But it is the nervousness of the smaller maid which leads me to believe that she is like me. In her expression, one can see her insecurities and her genuine effort to emulate the taller parlormaid's actions. The natural, human emotions come through the medium of expression, making the setting a home.

So I overlook the glaring fact that our modest house and sloppy landscaping will never be in *Home and Garden* like my friends'. Our wild, weedy garden and funny mailbox is enough to make me break out into a huge smile as we drive down our street on our way back from the airport. My scruffy dog and his evil odor which my mom tries to cover up with baby powder, the small kitchen where everything seems to go on at once, my closet which is stuffed with everything possible, our photo albums which my dad told me to save first in case of an emergency fire (forget the stacks of *Seventeen*), and my bathroom with the

---

for an elite women's college, a complexity that is not lost on Nida, the child of Thai immigrants.

picture of Clark Gable clutching Vivian Leigh in *Gone with the Wind*: home is the natural, the recognizable, the comfortable.

The photograph is called "Parlormaid and Under-parlormaid: Ready to Serve Dinner." It is neither the sophistication of the owners nor the brand of crystal that matter. Neither the mahogany polish nor the gilded tumbler constitutes the image of home. Whether the paintings in the background were auctioned from Sotheby's or from Gatsby's does not make a difference. Rather, it is the parlormaid's face and her awkward expression. In the movies we have seen, it is Gilda's humming, the way Ilsa rummages through clothes in the market to avoid Rick's stare, Cynthia's pensive expression when she has been stood up by Christopher Strong, and Mildred's painful realization of her daughter's venomous nature: we relate. Everyone can see the emotions on the faces of Rita, Ingrid, Katherine, and Joan, and we know that they have the same feelings we do in real life. They get sad and feel joy. Even famous people eat dinner. We all eat dinner.

Forget images of supermodels and posh aristocracies. Trash "Lifestyles of the Rich and Famous" and "Entertainment Tonight." I would rather look at this photo, which would look as sophisticated as it is meant to look, except for the under-parlormaid's quirky expression, and know that I feel the same way sometimes—know that I am home.

Nida's essay is, in every possible way, about the nonprint world, and yet its beauty lies in its classic form, a form not of the "late age of print," but rather of print's elusive golden age. It surprises me that I have selected this particular essay to share with you, because it is not at all typical of the writing that emerges from my classes (I teach students to write in the so-called "academic form"; when they are not doing that, they are experimenting with electronic forms for me). From its opening zeugma, through its skilled use of parallelism, repetition, antithesis, and detail, Nida shows a startling comprehension of the tropes and figures of belletristic rhetoric (without ever, so far as I know, having been formally taught this style—certainly not by me).

But she also knows quite a bit about the tropes and rhythms of the multiple contemporary discourses that figure her life. When I first picked this essay to share with you, back in 1996, I was thinking less of its stylistic features than of its content. For one thing, in her opening paragraphs Nida displays great skill in visual analysis, her account of the photograph so accurate and so complete that it would be easy for anyone to pick this particular photograph out from among the many similar photographs in a collection of Bill Brandt's work. And indeed, my impression of her skill was later corroborated by others. At the end of the semester, I suggested to Nida that she submit the essay for our museum's Davis Art Prize. Both she and I were hesitant about the submission; as a fledgling first-year student, she would be competing against older students well into their art history majors. But she won the prize, and the judges—from the art history department, the women's studies department, and the Davis Museum—expressed unanimous and enthusiastic praise of her writing. They particularly liked the way Nida used her very fine formal analysis in the service of a larger, more interesting point. In the years since then, these colleagues and I have returned, over and over again, to the same question in our conversations with each other: What is the difference between the competent, workmanlike writing that we dutifully teach toward in our courses, and the bright, engaged writing like Nida's, to which we award prizes? Why can't we produce more of the writing that we yearn for, but rarely see, in our stacks of prize submissions?

What made Nida's paper so interesting to us was, in fact, not the formal analysis with which it began, but rather, what followed: her bemused postmodern-esque (to borrow from Nida's ways of talking) reflections on identity, popular culture, and the impact of the media. She provides hints of what is to come even in her formal analysis—her own double-take when she realizes that what appeared to be a conventional *haute-culture* image was disrupted by the imperfections of the underparlormaid. And it is the underparlormaid—the underbelly of her own fascination with the inaccessible—that she turns out to be interested in. Subsequent paragraphs take us from her reflections on the aristocratic ideal portrayed (and dismantled) in this photograph, back to Nida's own home, where the only elite ideals available to her lie in the photographs that fill the magazines she reads so avidly, and the movies she adores.

> *I stuck with the visual aspects of the photo because there was no way I could fail by describing the subject—it's functional, undeniable and pretty. The essay is also riddled with words snatched right up from my immediate surroundings: the magazines, advertisements, and movies I had been obsessively studying. The language construction is a mass media mix of brand names, listed material wealth, and celebrities. Though I had read a considerable amount, I had, in the past, watched more movies and television than anything else, and this undoubtedly affected the way in which I learned the English language and measured my value system. The essay is very much a construction of my world at the time it was written. I'm not as comfortable analyzing it as I am talking about how I felt when I wrote it, since much of the meaning feels like my own struggle to find meaning—not always pretty.*

Like so many women awash in our image-saturated world today, Nida is caught between pleasure and pain, between desire and critique. She consumes these images of women and is entirely conscious that, as a woman and as an intellectual, she should be disdaining both image and consumption of image. I still vividly recall a comment that popped up during one of our class computer conferences; I had asked students to scour the Web for sites relating to the films we were viewing, and keep a record of their findings by posting URLs and critical descriptions of the sites into our online class conference; Nida wrote: "Here's a great Rita Hayworth site! Lots of legs!" I despaired of being able to teach Nida, and many of her classmates, the kind of cultural critique that was so important to me. This paper illustrates her own approach to the dilemma, a pastiche of pragmatism and play.

Nida uses the essay to display (partly consciously and partly unconsciously, I think) the wide range of subjectivities that reverberate in her 18-year-old being: the self that consumes magazines and the self that critiques that consumption; the self that is discovering art and the self that parodies that self; the intruding voice of the roommate ("they look like corpses"!), and finally, the self that yearns for the old-fashioned kind of whole, centered, and nonfragmented self ("Home is the natural, the recognizable, the comfortable. . . . I would rather look at this photo . . . and know that . . . I am home.") Like many of the films we viewed in class, this essay works with a kind of Lacanian mirroring: Nida sees herself, with a start of distorted recognition, in the underparlormaid, and the light then bounces around among other versions of herself.

Nida's final paragraphs represent a turn away from the fragmenting and frightening landscape of the world of image and mirror, and toward the desire for the enveloping spaces of home. At the same time, she makes a nod to the films we have viewed in our class—all out of a hope, I think, of achieving some sort of closure, some sort of coherence, in an essay that has rapidly begun to scatter into shards. On the face of it, it appears she has found "home." But where is home for her? Home turns out to be not the "modest house" with the "wild, weedy garden and funny mailbox" (though we believe for a minute that that kind of home is just possible), but rather something elusive that lies just barely visible beneath the expressions of all the women in all these images she has viewed: a fragmented glimpse of the possibility of real person, after all.

This paper works, for both reader and writer, because it reveals something about the condition of our students' lives right now: of how they hang suspended among images, memory, the media, desire, and the written self they are trying to create for us in the academy.

As I said before, it was a fun assignment. While composing it, I must've been breathing some ether which allowed me to address the topic of domestic space, give a nod to my teacher, mention movie stars and parents in the same breath, and say something about my particular state of eighteen-year-old angst. This is clearly not an academic paper, but it was enjoyable to the people who read it; so, it must have its own office in the writing hierarchy. It's a paper that gave me confidence, sparked discussion, and was refreshing in the parade of academic papers I had to write. It allowed me to take a break and look at myself reflected by the things around me—something that helped me gain some control, perspective, and agency over the amount of material I was learning and the person I was becoming. And I suddenly remembered the reason why I liked school.

When Nida wrote this essay for me, back in 1996, I was fresh from a reading of Lester Faigley's "Judging Writing, Judging Selves." I was fully persuaded by Faigley's argument that, in most cases, the personal essays written by students revealed more about the clichés of autobiographical writing than they did about the students. Among the problems Faigley exposes, in his review of the many personal essays selected for Coles and Vopat's *What Makes Writing Good,* are these: "the illusion of a unified and knowing self that overviews the world around it" (408), a denial of "the role of language in constructing selves" (410), and the perpetuation of certain stereotypes through "the very ease of [their] recognitions" (409). The decade of the 1990s was marked, for compositionists, by a tension between expressivism and constructivism, perhaps most clearly defined by the strongly felt polarity of the Bartholomae/Elbow debate, a polarity that led me, and many like me, to rule out personal writing in favor of a course that emphasized academic writing. Nida's essay convinced me to allow the personal back into my classroom, not as the basis of a first-year composition course, but as one mode of writing that may well help students negotiate a presence for themselves as writers in the new and multiple public spaces they are entering.

In a recent article about the teaching and reading of essays by black feminist writers, Juanita Rogers Comfort makes a point quite similar to the point I want to make here, and I draw on her words to help me: Acknowledging that we still need to help students become good academic writers, she goes on to argue that:

> In a society that is so culturally diverse, technologically sophisticated, and hierarchically complex, finding a vantage point, a place to stand, and a locus of authority, respect, influence and power cannot be ignored as a teachable subject in rhetoric and composition courses. What many student writers seem to long for, even without knowing exactly how to articulate it, is meaningful

instruction in using writing to assess, define, and assert who they
are becoming as knowing human beings. (558)

This is a privilege that we often deny our students; the subject of their
writing is too often a subject we assign to them, not a subject that allows
them to explore their own subjectivities, or to develop a subjectivity in
relationship to the discipline they are studying. Ironically, established
scholars in the fields I most often teach—film and electronic discourse—
seem to assume this privilege for themselves; it is almost a commonplace
for books of film theory, for example, to begin with an introduction in
which the writer names himself or herself as a spectator of film, often
exploring the personal experience of viewing film. If even established
thinkers need to orient themselves to a subject—and understand the
extent to which they are constructed by the subject—why should we
expect that students do not need and desire a similar orientation?

*Wini gave us the option of choosing that assignment; she creat-
ed the first space. With maturity and experience, a student learns to
trust and ground herself in the ideas and opinions that outfit each phase
of her life—an ever-changing second space. Then there is a third space
in between one's instinctive personal reaction to a piece of art and the
conscious, intellectual unpacking of its formal qualities. The meaning
is somewhere in between the two and that is what I was trying—I am
still trying to find.*

WORKS CITED

Arts Council of Great Britain. "Parlourmaid and Under-Parlourmaid
    Ready to Serve Dinner, 1933." Photograph. *Bill Brandt:
    Photographs.* Exhibition Catalog. London: Hayward Gallery, 30
    April-31 May 1970.
Brandt, Bill. *The Photography of Bill Brandt.* Forward by David
    Hockney. New York: Abrams, 1999. (Produced as a catalog to
    accompany a travelling exhibition, "Bill Brandt: A
    Retrospective.")
Comfort, Juanita Rodgers. "Becoming a Writerly Self: College Writers
    Engaging Black Feminist Essays." *College Composition and
    Communication* 51.4 (June 2000): 540-559.
Faigley, Lester. "Judging Writing, Judging Selves." *College Composition
    and Communication* 40.4 (December 1989): 395-412. (rpt., with
    some revision, in *Fragments of Rationality.* Pittsburgh: U of
    Pittsburgh P, 1992).

2

TEACHING WRITING AS WRITING
Teaching Students as Student Writers

Richard Straub
Florida State University

This chapter outlines a first-year writing course designed to help students gain a practical understanding of writing as a way of thinking, a means of discovery, an act of saying something to someone else, in some context, for some purpose. The writing- and response-intensive course is built on two sequences of writing assignments and focuses mainly on one genre: a version of the personal essay that emphasizes exploration and reflection. No textbooks or reading anthologies are used. Instruction grows inductively out of the discussion of student texts and is sequenced to allow students to focus on certain areas of writing at certain times. Learning to read texts rhetorically and critically is viewed as instrumental to students' improvement as writers. Instead of individual texts in isolation, the course privileges the students' ongoing texts across the semester and their overall performance as "learning" writers.

For William Coles, Jr., a teacher I have never had who has taught me so much about teaching and learning.

I grew up in the field in the early 1980s, in the heyday of the process movement, so when I look to define the work of composition, I think of teaching writing. I think of helping students gain a practical understanding of writing as a way of thinking, a means of discovery, an act of saying something—really saying something—to someone else and adding to the community's storehouse of knowledge. I think of helping students become better readers and writers. This is what I think teachers such as James Moffett, Wayne Booth, Ken Macrorie, and Janet Emig had in mind when they began to formally investigate writing and looked to legitimate composition as a field of study, and it's what I have in mind when I think of the work of composition and teach any first-year writing course.

To realize this idea of composition, I have students do a lot of writing—ten-twelve essays across the semester, most of them personal essays, especially a version of the personal essay that emphasizes exploration and reflection. Students write mainly from their own experiences and perspectives, what Michael Polanyi would call their personal knowledge. I build our work around sequences of assignments on a common general subject, in the manner of William Coles and David Bartholomae (and, before them, for 30 years at Amherst College, Theodore Baird). The writing in the first half of the course is, for the most part, submitted only as final drafts; our work with drafting and revising is held for the second half, after we've developed a sense of direction and a vocabulary for our talk about writing. I look to sequence my instruction—and, in turn, my ways of reading, evaluating, and responding to student writing—around these sequences of assignments, highlighting certain things at certain times so that we can keep our work focused and manageable: getting something worth saying; naming experience and thoughts more sharply and concretely; constructing a simple, direct voice and negotiating various perspectives; giving substance to key statements; considering matters of focus, proportion, and arrangement; improving sentence structure. Typically, students hand in their papers, I read and respond to them, and then we discuss sample papers in class. All of the writing is done out of class, and most of our class time is given to reading, commenting on, and talking about the writing. Throughout the course I look, above all, to help students develop the content of their writing and nurture their sense of how form shapes thought in text. I am less concerned with individual writings or even better writing than with the students' individual development in the course, over time.

This is the pedagogy I used in the course from which the following piece of student writing came, a number of years ago now, at Lehigh

University, a private institution in eastern Pennsylvania that enrolls some 5,000 undergraduates, enjoys a strong reputation in engineering and business, and attracts exceptional students. It's also the pedagogy I've used in my first-year writing courses at Florida State University, a much larger institution with a broader base of students, and the pedagogy I would use in almost any instructional environment, with almost any type of students. The course looks to work in the space between process and product pedagogies and between expressivist and social constructionist approaches to teaching writing. But I want to resist such easy labels, such reductions, and let my talk about the class in the pages to come, through my discussion of one student's work, speak for what the course is really all about. It is in the writing we have students practice and the values of writing we hope to instill—the ways we read, evaluate, respond to, and talk about the work of our students—that we most clearly define ourselves as teachers and characterize our courses in composition.

Below are two informal essays written for a sequence of six assignments on the subject of accomplishment, the first (Writing 2) coming in at the start of the second week of class, the second (Writing 4) coming in at the end of the third week. I present the first as a touchstone for talking about my real interest here: Writing 4 and the work it represents for this student writer.

Assignment 2 (short version):

In an essay, describe an experience in your recent past where you accomplished something you set out to accomplish or something you were expected to accomplish. Try to recover for yourself and your readers a sense of the circumstances surrounding this experience and your attitudes toward what happened. How did you look at the goal and the effort it took in order to achieve it? How did you look at the goal or effort once you reached it? Using this experience as a case in point, what can you tell us about your outlook on striving after goals?

Lee's Essay:
Target: Lehigh

To me, achievement is Lehigh. I read about Lehigh in U.S. News and saw it listed among the top schools. I took my first step and set my goal. Many goals have obstacles and this one was no different. Two major obstacles were the high selectivity and the cost. I was in all of the advanced classes except English but never considered myself a "brain." I was average among my classmates. Nonetheless, I buckled down and worked. It was hard because my freshman and sophomore years earned me no bragging rights. The cost was astronomical. For a third of the cost I could have easily gained acceptance to a lesser but closer university. But what glory is there in achieving the easy or obvious? Not only did I set a goal, but I took a risk. Lehigh was the only school I applied to and I applied early decision. Even if I would have failed, I would still have a sense of accomplishing something because I tried. Trying is the most important part of achievement. Many of my more intelligent friends applied to lesser schools. What's the challenge? Achievement doesn't always involve accomplishment. The harder you push, the farther you go.

Lee was a quiet student, one whose voice you wouldn't recognize if you weren't looking at him. He handed his papers in on time, followed the guidelines of the assignments, and did his classwork well enough, but he did nothing extraordinary in his writing and didn't have much to say in class. I knew little about him other than what I learned from his first few papers. (He was not an exceptional student, but he expected to do well in school. He was delighted to be at Lehigh and maybe a little intimidated by the setting. He liked to play basketball, although he did not play on his high school team.) His first three writings in the sequence were nothing to write home about. Like "Target: Lehigh," they seemed like answers to an exam, assignments only. They have their moments, statements that go beyond the obvious and cut against—or cut into—the grain: "Achievement doesn't always involve accomplishment"; "Henry Wadsworth Longfellow suggests that you aim higher than your goal so that when you fail, you are still on target. This is morbid advice. It takes away that confidence you need to risk." But for the most part, the essays trade in broad generalizations and commonplaces and offer little to readers:

> Every achievement is a success.
> Many goals have obstacles and this one was no different.
> Trying is the most important part of achievement.
> The harder you push, the farther you go.
> Numerous steps must be taken in reaching a goal.

Lee rarely gets beyond these easy generalizations and does little to explore the promising assertions he does make in order to find something more to say and make his writing more meaningful for readers. "I buckled down and worked," he tells us in Writing 2, but he never tells us just what "buckled down" means, how we are to take it. Buckled down how? What did he do exactly? How was it different from what he did before? "I took a risk," he claims. A risk how? What did he put at risk? What was there to lose? Notably, all three papers are short—a half or a third of the length of most students'—and starkly undeveloped. Lee, it seemed to me after his third paper, was not giving enough to his writing, was not pushing to develop what he had to say. His third paper showed some signs of life, a noteworthy attempt to try out a different voice from the detached, all-knowing voice that he (and most students) fell into in the first couple of papers, one that was more animated and engaging, but still the paper languished, coming in under 250 words. Writing 4, I knew, would be an index of what students were getting from and putting into the course, now that we had taken up several assignments, had a chance to discuss, at length, seven or eight sample student papers, and had begun to establish (through what would become a class-long conversation about writing) the value in getting something to say and finding a way to share it with readers.

Assignment 4 (short version):

Look back on one of the experiences you wrote about on Writing 2 or 3 or on another experience where you put a significant amount of effort into trying to accomplish something (whether you actually attained the goal or not) and examine the role that somebody else played in this experience. What influence or impact did this person (these people) have on what you did and how you did it—on your way of seeing the goal, your way of going about trying to achieve it, or your feelings toward the work you put into it or toward the goal itself? On the basis of this experience, what can you learn—and share with us—about how others influence our achievements or our way of striving after goals?

Lee's Essay:
Just Like Mike

A major goal in my life was to learn how to play basketball and to be good. I learned how to play in eighth grade when I became involved with the YMCA basketball league. My team didn't do too well, in fact we came in second to last. I also didn't learn too much that year for two reasons. First, my father was our coach and he knows next to nothing about basketball. Actually, this was his first taste of basketball. He really didn't understand the finer rules and couldn't really develop any plays. Secondly, we were one of the lesser teams and I was one of the lesser players. I had an average shot but couldn't jump or get rebounds. Losing numerous games, we sort of lost our drive and gave less than 110%. We didn't practice our shooting and dribbling and didn't practice like a team. At least I got a shirt out of it.

My second and more meaningful basketball experience started after that. I started playing for my church. My church had a basketball league with other churches and all the games were at my church. It started the same until the day I met Michael Leake.

Mike was the star of the varsity team at my church. He could dribble and pass like Magic and shoot like Bird. He could play guard or forward. Mike held the record for most scored points in a game with fifty-seven. Being the nice guy that he was, he took me aside and schooled me in the art of basketball. He taught me to dribble and how to crash the boards. I did much better in the JV games and even played a few minutes in some of the varsity games. After leading the varsity team to two consecutive league titles, Mike left to play at Penn State McKeesport. While he was gone, I kept practicing, hoping to be a force next year.

The next season rolled around and Mike was going to be our coach. I got to play a lot. I sat out maybe five minutes per game. That year I scored twelve points in a game which was a career high. It was also the most scored by any player in that game. All the while, Mike kept tutoring me. Teaching me power moves and how to dominate inside and to utilize my height and strength. He gave up on ball handling because I had hands of stone. My tutoring continued until I had to leave for college, with my skills ever improving. Mike played a very important role in my trying to learn how to play basketball. I can almost beat Mike one-on-one but not yet. My new goal is to be just like Mike.

Three weeks into the course, beyond pushing students to get more to say and look at their writing in terms of what they might offer readers and add to our classroom discussion about accomplishment, I am looking to encourage students to craft a casual voice, name their ideas sharply and evocatively—in Emerson's words, to attach their words to things—and give substance to their key statements. Later, we'll do more with the overall shape and form of their writing, in time, more with arrangement and sentence structure, and, by the end of the course, more and more with correctness. We'll look increasingly, in other words, to do more to shape their writing into formal, full-fledged essays. But for now I want to focus on content, voice, and development—these primary concerns.

Lee's Writing 4, "Just Like Mike," is not an exceptional piece of writing. It probably did not even rank among the top half of papers turned in for this assignment. But it is an exceptional piece of work for him in the course—and a good example of what I look for from students, especially at this point, in a first-year writing course. I like the easy, direct voice he constructs in the writing, the way he creates the sense of someone talking with someone else. I like the way he uses the language of basketball to create context and establish a sense of authority:

> Mike was the star of the varsity team at my church. He could dribble and pass like Magic and shoot like Bird.
>
> All the while, Mike kept tutoring me. Teaching me power moves and how to dominate inside and to utilize my height and strength.

The strength of the paper, however, lies in the substance he gives to his key statements. Lee makes seven assertions in the essay. With almost every one of them, he does something he hasn't done much of in his previous papers: he goes back over the ground of the statement and gives substance (see the sentences in italics) to what he has to say:

1. He says he didn't learn much in his first year of playing basketball and then goes on to suggest what he means: *First, my father was our coach and he knows next to nothing about basketball. . . . Secondly, we were one of the lesser teams and I was one of the lesser players.*
2. He says his father knew next to nothing about basketball and then gets even more to the point: *Actually, this was his first taste of basketball.*
3. He indicates that he wasn't particularly good and the team wasn't particularly talented or dedicated, and then he grounds the claims in something more specific and makes it mean: *I had an average shot but couldn't jump or get rebounds. Losing numerous games, we sort of lost our drive and gave less than 110%. We didn't practice our shooting and dribbling and didn't practice like a team.*
4. He makes what is his sharpest and most substantive assertion in his writing thus far in the semester when he says that Mike was the star of the team and then adds: *He could dribble and pass like Magic and shoot like Bird. He could play guard or forward. Mike held the record for most scored points in a game with fifty-seven.*
5. He says Mike "schooled him" in the art of basketball and, by going on to indicate what he taught him, begins to establish what he means: *He taught me to dribble and how to crash the boards.*
6. He says he played a lot the next season and suggests he did well, statements he goes on to substantiate: *I sat out maybe five minutes per game. That year I scored twelve points in a*

game which was a career high. It was also the most scored by any player in that game.

7. Mike kept "tutoring" him the next year. Tutoring at what? He explains: *Teaching me power moves and how to dominate inside and to utilize my height and strength.*

Such going back over his key statements—showing what's wrapped up in his assertions and making them mean—is a key strategy in the course, and I'm delighted to see Lee finally working at it in his writing. There may be something a little too mechanical about the writing. There may be additional things he might do to give it greater substance. He might tell us more, for instance, about what he did to develop his dribbling, shooting, and rebounding. He might explain what he means by learning the art of basketball: does it have to do with moving more precisely? thinking more strategically? developing better concentration? Nevertheless, one thing is clear: he is getting the idea of using detail and adding other statements to show what is underneath, or involved in, his key terms and statements and helping readers understand what he has to say.

I also like the way, in several places, Lee plays one idea off another, one perspective off another, in this writing. "My team didn't do too well," he tells us early in the opening paragraph, "in fact we came in second to last"; then, after admitting that the team didn't give 110 percent, he adds with a shrug: "At least I got a shirt out of it." He explains how Mike kept working at making him better; then he marks the limits of Mike's instruction, making another playful shift in voice, something he hasn't been willing to try very much up to this point in the course: "All the while, Mike kept tutoring me. Teaching me power moves and how to dominate inside and to utilize my height and strength. He gave up on ball handling because I had hands of stone." More broadly, I am taken by Lee's developing sense of how texts work. He seems, for instance, more alert about providing background information for readers. He seems to be intuiting better when to go into detail. He seems to be more aware of the power of a single statement to carry the weight of a key idea, capturing as he does the futility of his first season with the glib understatement, "At least I got a shirt out of it," and indicating how far he has come as a basketball player—and how far he still has to go—with the single statement, "I can almost beat Mike one-on-one but not yet." Lee is learning to read writing more closely, more analytically. He is playing with the languages in and around him and experimenting with conventions, seeing how he can use the text to act on the world and achieve certain effects. I'm encouraged with what I see.

There is still a lot that could be done with this writing—and learned from it. It's far from doing the kind of thinking, searching, and reaching I'd like to see at this point in the course, and at the same time it opens up a lot of possibilities for Lee's work as a writer. Lee doesn't push his thinking in the essay, doesn't really tell us anything about accomplishment that we don't already know or that might get us thinking along different lines. He never gets beyond the simple premise that a friend helped him become a better basketball player. He never explores his claims or looks at these experiences more discerningly for what they might tell him—and what he, in turn, might tell us—about *how* Mike tutored him in dribbling and shooting or how he "schooled" him in the art of basketball. What exactly was the nature of his impact? Was there anything that Mike did that another player or coach could not do? Was it purely a matter of expertise—inside knowledge? Or was it something more? Did the successful instruction have something to do with Mike's stature in Lee's mind—with the impression Mike may have had on him as a local player who makes good? By turning these experiences around in his hands, seeing what's wrapped up in them, Lee might get beyond simply illustrating a commonplace and discover something more—more distinctive, more original, more interesting—to say: perhaps about the ways in which his own drive to excel might actually have been accelerated, not mitigated, by the lackadaisical attitude of his church team; perhaps about how he gave (how we all tend to give?) more weight to any sort of teacher or mentor who has achieved some public status or whom we esteem. Still, I don't want to push Lee on this point. I don't want to ask for more. Right now I want to celebrate this paper and the work it represents. I want to recognize what he's accomplished and build on it in the writing to come. It is a critical time in Lee's work in the course. I want to be sure we both take advantage of the opportunity.

I expect great things from students in a writing course. I assume that every student is capable of getting something more to say and develop as a writer. At the same time, I realize that learning to write better takes a lot of work and plenty of time. Writing is intricate, learning how to write, demanding. Trying, even more, to develop the content of writing and really say something to readers is exacting. I realize that different students are in different places and need to work at their own pace, according to their own schedules and scales. So I want to take the long view and see my course as only a short interval in their unfolding history as learning writers. I want to look at their texts not so much as individual papers but as part of their ongoing "text" across the course. I want to look at the students themselves not so much as writers but as *student* writers, as students learning to write. I want to use the writing before me as the best material for helping them develop their concept of writing and learn to write better—not necessarily write well, but write and read and come to understand how texts work *better*—than they did last week, on their last paper, or when they first walked in the door. Lee, as it turned out, would come to distinguish himself in the course. By the end of the semester, he was not among the best writers in the class, but he was one of the best students of writing, one of the students who learned the most about rhetoric, discovery, and making meaning through texts and put it into practice in his writing. His work in the course is representative of the kind of work I look for from students in a composition class. It is the kind of dedicated performance that I hope for and revel in as a teacher of writing, the story of success that keeps the fire burning.

*   *   *

The method of the course follows from my conviction that a writing course should devote itself first and last to the teaching of writing as writing: teaching writing, namely, as at once an act of discovery and an act of communication, a way of using writing to come to terms with experience and sharing one's thoughts and views with others, writing that is as much concerned with *what* is said as *how* it is said: writing as rhetoric *and* dialectic. The design follows just as much from my belief that a writing course does best when it focuses not on competency or fluency or better written products—but on the content of writing, on how words and texts come to mean, and on the students' gradual and long-term development as writers, as students learning to write.

I use the *reflective* essay—and its more informal counterpart, the exploratory essay—because I want students, above all, to work on developing the content of their writing. This primary form of the essay, which emphasizes writing as an attempt to come to terms with one's thinking, seems well-suited to writing that looks for writers to forge something distinctive to say out of their own thoughts, experiences, and perspectives. I use the *personal* reflective essay because there is no better subject matter for writing that looks to engage the writer in original thinking and help her gain some sense of authority over her texts than the writer's own views and her own first- and second-hand experience. I focus so much of our work across the course on a *single* genre, rather than skipping from one type of writing to another because, more than rhetorical versatility or the study of various conventions, I want students, again, to focus on developing the content of their writing and developing their practical understanding of texts. I think both of these goals are best pursued through practice in a single genre, over time. By having to give less attention to the differences between one type of writing and another, students can become more and more familiar with the conventions of one genre and focus more fully on what they have to say. I have students work with the *same subject* in sequences of assignments, because I think that only by involving themselves in a subject over time can they pierce the surface of commonplace thinking and begin to see for themselves how writing might be a way of thinking, a mode of discovery, an act of really saying something to someone else. Finally, I sequence and coordinate my assignments, instruction, and response, focusing on various strategies of writing in a certain order, incrementally, across the course—getting something more to say, constructing a simple, direct voice, naming experience and thoughts more sharply and concretely, giving substance to key statements, all along nurturing a sense of how form shapes thought in text—because I am convinced that such emphasis, repetition, and clustering, such deliberate, cumulative practice, is essential to learning an activity as complex as writing, especially writing as authoring.

The course has a crosshatching of touchstones and precedents. It draws abundantly, as I've already suggested, on the work of William Coles, with its use of sequenced assignments, its emphasis on writing as a way of thinking, and its attempt to make the writing classroom into a community, but without his emphasis on writing as art or writing as a mode of self-creation. It draws on David Bartholomae's practice of teaching writing as inquiry, but without his emphasis on the conventions of academic discourse. It draws heavily on James Moffett's concept of writing as authoring, a writer's carving the content of her writing out of her experience and views, through her own act of composing, without his emphasis on playing across the universe of discourse. It attempts to put into practice the conviction, extolled by the likes of Wayne Booth, Ken Macrorie, and Donald Murray, and by figures no less than Plato and Kenneth Burke, that writing is as much a matter of dialectic as it is rhetoric—that writing must involve a writer in discovering something that is hers, something that is worth saying, something that she sees as true, and finding a way to share it with others. The course is also informed by Peter Elbow's emphasis on giving students practice in the processes of writing and focusing on the development of writers over time; John Dewey's learning by practice, in a social setting, in manageable steps; and, more recently, Bakhtinian theorists who view discourse as a struggle and negotiation of competing voices and literary theorists such as Stanley Fish and Stephen Mailloux, who view discourse in terms of social conventions.

The agenda of the course is not really expressivist. It is not merely rhetorical. And it is not social constructionist. It is an attempt to distill the essence from each of these ways of looking at composition and create an alchemy that will involve students in practicing writing as a way of saying something to someone else through the mediating form of the text, in some social context. It is an attempt to help students develop as writers and readers. Ultimately, the course is devoted to the pursuit of a liberal education, liberally construed. I am not interested very much in technical training or in a pedagogy of preparation, that is, in getting students ready for tasks or situations they will supposedly be confronted with in the near or distant future: writing in the disciplines, writing in the manner of published authors, writing they may eventually be expected to do on the job. I want the introductory writing course to have its own goals, its own reason for being, its own integrity. I want it, first and last, to be a course in writing, a course in learning to read and write better, because better reading and writing by themselves can make a real difference for the student—and for the student as more than just a student or a job candidate or a worker—now and across her life.

3

BRIAN'S "ACHIEVED UTOPIA"
Disabling the Disability Label

Barbara Heifferon
Clemson University

Our earlier euphoric assumptions about networked classrooms may be revised from a new perspective, that of the differently abled student. Faigley's ironic term, the "achieved utopia," can be turned back on itself to reveal that early euphoria about using computers in the writing classroom can sometimes still be validated within the culture of the differently abled. A classroom experience as a "representative anecdote" points to two implications of using technology in our writing classroom: first, there was an important and unexpected shift in perspective and in roles, one that we as postmodern, computer-literate teachers trying to achieve a student-centered classroom need to keep in mind; and second, the "disability" label first attached by other students to Brian in the first part of the semester was at least to some extent itself disabled. Brian's role as differently abled student changed as a direct result of his own computer expertise. He was differently abled not so much because he was in a wheelchair, but because he was able to become a co-teacher as our resident computer expert.

When I asked Lester Faigley what he meant by "achieved utopia" in *Fragments of Rationality* in the chapter called "The Networked Classroom," he wryly answered, "I mean what happens to the dog when he finally catches the bus." Not only was he referring to his own terms as ironic, but he also perfectly depicted our dilemma as teachers who are trying to figure out what to do with networked classrooms once we have them. As we strive to find new assignments and invent new ways of using technology in our writing classrooms in the late age of print, we also collect data and attempt to analyze some of the implications of our actions on the new frontier we are settling. Although we cannot generalize from anecdotal evidence, as we collect our stories, some of these narratives point us toward important directions for future analysis. I present the following as a "representative anecdote" that points to one implication of the networked classroom often overlooked in the pedagogical spaces we inhabit (Burke 510).

Although we would like to buy into Trent Batson's vision of "entirely new pedagogical dynamics" as a result of networked classrooms in which teachers are decentered, often in the multivocal transcripts of chatrooms, only chaos or meaninglessness seem centered (32). Cynthia Selfe and Paul Meyer also saw traditional classrooms evolving into more "egalitarian classrooms," but others such as Susan Romano critiqued this notion (Cooper 141, Romano 21, Selfe and Meyer 165). Faigley "bracket[s]" his own "conclusions," suggesting that "subsequent experiences have problematized the concept of a student-centered classroom" and admits that "postmodernity [has] some bearing on our present circumstances for teaching writing" (*Fragments* 167). Thus our initial euphoria of "the networked classroom" as utopian has changed and become much more sophisticated in the years since *Fragments of Rationality*, as we all carefully examined and studied the implications of our electronic forms of discourse within the context of teaching/writing in the late age of print.

However, with this representative anecdote, I would like to further complicate the picture by reversing the term *achieved utopia* yet again and have us look at one site that such early euphoria can still be validated within a culture still not widely acknowledged: the culture of the differently abled. Working with a student, Brian McCracken, in our two-semester composition curriculum, I experienced the potential of computer-assisted instruction (CAI) without a fully networked classroom.[1] Brian was placed by chance in my 101 classroom, but then

[1]In Disability Studies, an often-heard motto is "Nothing about us without us!" Brian not only wanted me to use his words and experience in the classroom, but also insisted that I write his experience for a wider audience. Brian wants

asked me to insure that he would also be in my section of English 102. Although my role as teacher was not fully decentered by any means, there was an important and unexpected shift in perspective and in roles, one that we as postmodern, computer-literate teachers need to keep in mind. And as a further result of the shift of power, the "disability" label first attached by other students to Brian in the first part of the semester was at least to some extent *disabled*. Brian's role as differently abled student changed as a direct result of his own computer expertise. He was differently abled not so much because he was in a wheelchair, but because he was able to become a co-teacher as our resident computer expert. I saw Brian empowered to take his rightful place as a full member of my classroom, and, often, as a mentor to the rest of us for enabling our own sometimes less-than-able computer skills. When Brian became the computer expert in our classroom, my role was decentered, at least in that area. In some sense, then, we had achieved some "new pedagogical dynamics" (Faigley 167).

On the very first day Brian and I met, I was greeting students as they filed into my English 101 classroom. I had already arranged the brightly colored desks in a circle, barely finding enough room for the 25 students I would have in that class. The class filled up quickly; students hurried to claim the last few seats. Then in the door came an athletic-looking young man in a motorized wheelchair with a huge boombox strapped to the chair behind his head. I looked around the room and realized that there was only a very small place not taken up by a student in one of the desks in the circle. Brian very deftly whizzed into the center of the room and backed his chair perfectly into the only tiny space left in the room. I looked at him in amazement and said, "You do a better job of parking than I do!"

Somehow that set a tone for the rest of the year together. In fact Brian did many things better than I did, many things better than the rest of my students did. We often engaged in a joking repartee in front of the class before class began. Brian and I also played with the words *disabled* and *enabled*. I talked often about our class being computer disabled, lamenting both the fact that there was limited access to a computer classroom for English classes as well as my own lack of expertise in that area. Sometimes I exaggerated my personal lack to make my point, but often I was dismally behind Brian, especially in designing web pages and working in hypertext. Brian and his typist had a nickname for me, too, one that we discussed in class: "The Comma Queen." I know he often

---

the word out to raise the awareness of the needs of differently abled people everywhere. At that point in time, the University of Arizona had no Humanities computer classrooms, but Brian always brought his laptop with him to class.

requested that I disable that comma-making pen that seemed to go crazy on his and other students' drafts. I realized that I was unconsciously promoting such an exchange to put all of us at ease, especially the students. Although I had often worked with differently abled individuals, the students in the classroom obviously had not. Their anxious faces reflected their discomfort that first day.

The main way we subverted the disability label was not only through humorous repartee within the class, but through Brian's enviable computer expertise. It wasn't long in each of the two classes that Brian's skills became evident. He was generous in offering to help students design homepages and to teach them other computer skills. We found that students had varying degrees of computer skills, but none as accomplished as Brian's. Students would gather around Brian, his chair, and his boombox after class, requesting help on various computer programs and problems. When this process was in full swing, student faces reflected very different expressions from those on the initial day of class and first few class meetings. Instead their faces were accepting and eager, friendly and relaxed. Some offered their help to Brian in exchange for his help with their computer requests. As the semester wore on, the disability label became more and more disabled.

One of the first assignments I give in class is for students to reflect on their writing before coming to the university. The only way Brian has been able to read or write is by means of a computer. A trauma at birth resulted in cerebral palsy and confined him to a wheelchair with limited use of his hands and limited sight. Even though in the piece below Brian talks about using typists, one of whom was also a student who was in both my English 101 and English 102 classes, he used a laptop for writing in class and was frequently online, sending me drafts of his writing and asking questions. I would respond by writing in between lines of his drafts. His writing skills, poor at first, grew, and my computer skills grew as a result of his teaching. Brian was also my staunchest supporter of e-mail correspondence between instructor and students. (That resistance has broken down since the year Brian and I were in class together).

As I mentioned earlier, part of our process included such drafts arriving from Brian over e-mail. I would then type comments and corrections within the draft in all capital letters so Brian could enlarge the text and read the comments. As is clear from the introduction, this process was the most effective form of feedback for Brian's revisions, although we also met one-on-one and talked about the possible changes and questions I had about various aspects of this and other papers. Brian's typist was also an active member of his group workshop. They worked together all year long, giving each other feedback and forming part of a strong and good writing group. This group in the first semester class was the only one that met outside of class on a regular basis for extra workshop sessions. Meeting outside of class was not a requirement.

Brian also had a tutor from the Writing Skills Improvement Center on our campus. She was a Ph.D. who specialized in working with minority students and students on financial aid. We had also worked together in a summer bridge program for the same population for two summers. During the year the four of us: Brian, his typist, his tutor, and I became a very close-knit writing team. His disability thus enabled an especially effective collaboration, still another instance of that label being subverted by the writing experience. As within the other settings, Brian was the one with the most expertise in computers among us four.

When I asked Brian to reflect on the role of writing in his life, he replied in the following e-mail:

> Due to my physical disability I am unable to use a pen or pencil for extended amounts of time. Computers enable me to compose academic papers by dictating my thoughts to a typist, since my disability hinders me from using two hands to type. Since I have a severe vision impairment, I am also unable to read most handwritten material. Having the material typed on a computer allows me to enlarge the font to my liking so I can read it. (E-mail 17 March 1996)

In the classroom Brian often talked about computers and writing. Although it was not always easy to understand him when he talked, as the first few weeks of the semester passed, he seemed also to relax, speak somewhat more clearly, and our skills as listeners increased. I also was able to learn about the equipment available on campus so that I could be more aware of access issues with other differently abled students.

On another question for that response piece, that asked students to talk about when they first "met" computers, Brian said,

> I was introduced to computers at a very early age, somewhere between third and fourth grades. Since then I have used them to write my papers, both academic and non-academic. About six years ago I was introduced to a voice-activated computer. This voice input device would allow me to type my thoughts instead of

dictating them. Unfortunately, the technology was not advanced enough to understand persons with speech impediments like my own.[2] (E-mail 17 March 1996)

Brian felt particularly helped by computers in his lack of mobility because of his wheelchair. I have to chuckle, though, even as I write the sentence, because Brian had a motorized wheelchair that sped quickly over University of Arizona's extensive campus. We had ongoing jokes about who could get back and forth to my office the fastest several blocks away. Sometimes as we walked/rolled together, if I critiqued his writing vigorously (which I sometimes needed to do), he'd take off in a huff, then pause ahead and wait for me to catch up. We'd laugh, but I'd realize that it might be a good time to back off. Because further distances were difficult for him, even with a fully outfitted van, Brian was particularly grateful for his chance to communicate with people in other cultures in places he might not ever reach physically. In Brian's words, "As a result of computers I also am able to communicate with people around the world without leaving my home by using my computer" (E-mail 17 March 1996).

When Brian asked me to request that he be placed in my section of 102, I was especially happy. Not only did the other students and I learn much from him, but also I liked the way he and I worked together to include computers in our writing and discussions, even though I was frustrated by not yet having a computer classroom to teach in.

In the first paper of our second course together, all of the students wrote about Barbara McClintock, the Nobel-winning scientist. We had read *A Feeling for the Organism* as a class, and students were given the option of writing either a rhetorical analysis or an interpretive analysis. Many of the students were resistant to Keller's feminism; one of the most vocal at first was Brian. But in his paper he chose to concentrate on the discrimination McClintock faced as a woman in a man's world in the 1920s and 1930s in this draft:

Barbara McClintock was one of these women eager to experience life beyond the home. At the age of 23, McClintock graduated with a Ph.D., and later became an excellent scientist. All through her life she encountered numerous occasions where she was discriminated against based on her sex because she was in a so-called man's profession. She did not let this stand in the way of her dreams. In Keller's biography, McClintock is represented as a woman who struggled for acceptance in the science field.

---

[2]As we are aware, this capability continues to improve. Because Brian's speech patterns differ as a result of the c.p., his voice recognition is even more difficult for the computer.

Keller uses McClintock's life experiences to inspire other women who want to contribute to the world in a way other than that of a housewife.

Keller demonstrates how much McClintock is dedicated to science by explaining to us that she had to overcome certain obstacles on her road to becoming a scientist. McClintock first became aware of her desire to become a scientist when, "At Eramus Hall High School, she discovered science" (Keller 26). From that point on McClintock would have to constantly prove to her mother that she would be happier as a scientist than as a housewife. One method she used to prove her dedication to receiving a higher level of education was by studying science alone at the library in the evenings after working all day. As Keller points out, McClintock said, "I had a schedule—things I'd read—and I was going to educate myself one way or the other" (30). Keller devotes several pages to this difficult decision to go in the direction of science, quoting McClintock as saying, "Whatever the consequences, I had to go in that direction" (28).

Through the years McClintock encountered many struggles as a woman scientist. One of her struggles is that she had trouble finding a suitable job. Keller makes us aware of the fact that McClintock was not the only one that was unable to find a job as a scientist. During the Great Depression, "Times were hard for everyone, and university job opportunities were almost nonexistent, even for her male colleagues" (Keller 73). Keller also points out, however, that men with less impressive qualifications were finding job opportunities. The Great Depression was not the only factor of her not being able to find a suitable job. Her being a woman also added to her problem. Two of her colleagues tried to get her an appointment at Iowa State, but "the Director of the Station will not appoint a woman" (Keller 74).

Even though McClintock found a job at the University of Missouri in 1936, she later learned that she was not working out there. Even though one of her colleagues said, "Everything she did would turn into something big," Keller speculates that perhaps her other colleagues found her 'difficult' (80). However, Barbara explains that if she were a man they would not have been concerned with her being "difficult." Since Keller presented both sides of the story, as a reader it is up to the reader's view as to why McClintock was not rehired. I feel she was not rehired because she was a woman. Her colleagues did not want to say the real reason that they did not want her back, which was because she was a woman, so they labeled her as difficult. . . . (E-mail 2 February 1996)

Those worried faces early in the semester, a repeat of the first days of the 101 class, made me wonder if Brian, even with his limited vision, could pick up on the tension in the room. I felt he answered my question when he elected to write about discrimination against Barbara McClintock in his first paper for English 102. I realized he identified with her being discriminated against, although she was often discriminated against because of her gender. Or as Brian put it, "she was discriminated against based on her sex because she was in a so-called man's profession." Brian undoubtedly experienced similar discrimination because of his disability. In the third paragraph of Brian's second writing sample, he rhetorically analyzes that the author, Keller, is giving the reader "both sides of the story." He acknowledges that the interpretation is dependent on the "reader's view." Brian's view is clearly that she was discriminated against. Brian, even as a very young student at the University, was already head of the Student Council's Advocacy Team for Disabled Students. He talked frankly in class and out of class about discrimination faced by disabled students. Thus both his choice of a focus for his essay and his "reader's view" was one with which he could easily identify: discrimination. And without my having to be overt and engender more resistance, Brian's changes and subsequent identification in class with another marginalized group were persuasive to other students as well. In short, they got it.

In his paper Brian also focuses on the term, *difficult*, within the book and within McClintock's life. People called her *difficult* both because she was a woman and because she was different. People did not give the real reason for not renewing this accomplished scientist's contract. I would imagine Brian is often not given the real reason for rejection in his world. He is very aware of the antidiscrimination laws regarding disability. So are many other people. They know it is illegal to discriminate, but by finding other excuses, they often continue discriminatory behavior. I also imagine in many ways Brian's life has been *difficult*. And how many times are arrangements that need to be made to accommodate his chair *difficult*? That term seems to hide many layers of meaning, both for McClintock and for Brian. But as *difficult* as it must have been for Brian to take two writing classes in a row, in our classes the disability label was at least partly challenged.

In the second paragraph, one that I suggested he move to another part of the paper, Brian focuses on McClintock's determination. This determination was another point of identification for Brian. He also had "certain obstacles to overcome" and "was going to educate myself one way or the other." For Brian this meant moving to another part of the country and being on his own for the first time, a hard enough task for people not in wheelchairs. Every day Brian was faced with obstacles to overcome, and every day he must have had to renew his commitment to getting an education.

In each of the courses the second and most demanding essay is the documented one. Students are expected to do extended research.

Most were intimidated by our large and well-stocked library on a campus of 37,000 students. Brian was at home in the library, even though he could not read the books without the help of the enlargers centered in the disabled student area. He was even more at home among the rows of computers loaded with various databases. He often volunteered to help students who came to me with research problems before, during, or after class. I would patiently explain to them about various key searches they could initiate using our online system and how to find various databases. But Brian was the one who would volunteer to meet them there and show them how to start their online research. I should mention, too, that at this particular time we had very little or inadequate curricular support for online research. That weakness in our program was being addressed and remedied.

Because of the intimidation students felt when entering the large library, I scheduled a class session in the library on the several computers loaded with the databases useful for English 102, the literature-based writing course. I had talked to Brian in advance about operating one of the computers with the appropriate databases, while I operated the other. That way we could have students crowd around in groups of ten-twelve, rather than one unmanageable clump of over 20. Brian was a patient teacher and didn't get frustrated when the online library system didn't function as smoothly as we hoped. Several times I had to consult him about glitches in the system. He could find ways around most problems. Then we had students work individually or in small groups on various computers to start their research while Brian and I cruised the room to give individual help.

Brian's role in the classroom, partly made possible by his computer expertise, began to decenter some of my authority in a very useful and powerful way. I noticed other students would come forward with suggestions and input, more relaxed about sharing the expertise on various subjects they knew about. Perhaps it was a coincidence, but the class discussions were among the best I've experienced within my classes. They were at times heated, but students were not afraid to voice their own opinions. Students also felt free to critique the textual choices I had made and other aspects of the course. It is possible the decentering brought about by Brian's role also empowered other students within the class.

The biggest obstacle to decentering the teacher is always grades. We are the ultimate arbiters and judges; we cannot gloss over that source of power. With Brian this area was especially difficult for us both. He worked very, very hard at writing, completing multiple drafts, correcting, changing, revising, and editing. In the first semester class he began with what I would honestly evaluate as low C or D level writing. By the end of the semester he was writing at a B level according to our Composition Program's standards. We had, however, constructed our own classroom criteria, with Brian contributing very vocally to the language (often humorously but effectively) of the grading chart we drew up. Even on that chart, Brian had clearly earned a B. I knew he wanted an A, as all students do. I was faced with a dilemma. With the obstacles he had to overcome, I could take those into account and give him an A. Or I could look at the writing as I would look at the writing of any student and give him a B. I agonized over the decision. Finally, I decided that I would be discriminating against him if I gave him a grade based on anything other than his writing ability. I gave him a B. I have always wondered if that was the right decision.

Even though our classroom was not networked, Brian's and my relationship was a networked one. Although it was no "achieved utopia" in most senses, the fact that without computers Brian could not write and would not have been in my classes made a sort of "achieved utopia" for him, for me, and for the class. Also the decentering brought me closer to the ideal classroom I envision in which I am facilitator rather than dictator and ultimate authority. Brian and I were in a somewhat different position from the one Faigley spoke about. We figured out what to do when we caught that bus. Or perhaps I figured out that I just needed to follow Brian up the ramp. We hopped on that bus and took it to where we needed to go.

WORKS CITED

Batson, Trent. "The ENFI Project: A Networked Classroom Approach to Writing Instruction." *Academic Computing* (February 1988): 32-33, 55-56.

Burke, Kenneth. *Grammar of Motives*. Berkeley: U of California P, 1945.

Cooper, Marilyn. "Postmodern Pedagogy in Electronic Conversations." *Passions, Pedagogies, and 21st Century Technologies*. Gail E. Hawisher and Cynthia Selfe, Eds. Logan: Utah State UP, 1999.

Faigley, Lester. "Beyond Imagination: The Internet and Global Digital Literacy." *Passions, Pedagogies, and 21st Century Technologies*. Gail E. Hawisher and Cynthia Selfe, Eds. Logan: Utah State UP, 1999.

—. *Fragments of Rationality: Postmodernity and the Subject of Composition*. Pittsburgh: U of Pittsburgh P, 1992.

Keller, Evelyn Fox. *A Feeling for the Organism*. New York: Freeman, 1983.

McCracken, Brian. E-mails. Paper. University of Arizona. Tucson, Arizona. Fall 1995 and Spring 1996.

Romano, Susan. "The Egalitarianism Narrative: Whose Story? Which Yardstick?" *Computers and Composition* 10: 5-28.

Selfe, Cynthia and Paul Meyer. "Testing Claims for Online Conferences." *Written Communication* 8: 163-92.

4

ON PROJECT SIX

The Role of Reflection in First-Year Writing Course Outcomes

Susanmarie Harrington
Indiana University Purdue University Indianapolis

The increased use of portfolios has brought with it many changes in pedagogical practice. Portfolios affect how we teach revision, and they have had profound effects on grading strategies. But perhaps the most important, and understudied, impact of portfolios in the writing class-room involves the genre portfolios have popularized: reflective statements. Analyzing the reflective statement produced by Katherine Ellison at the close of a first-semester honors writing class, I argue that self-assessment is an integral part of writing instruction. Active reflection helps students learn to see patterns in their learning, their past achievements, and their future plans. Reflective writing can help us understand how students experience our courses. First and foremost, we should be in the business of teaching writers, not writing. Making reflection the central activity in our classrooms keeps the focus on writers moving towards personal and institutional goals.

Portfolios have been one of the greatest change agents in composition classrooms in recent years. Now widespread, portfolios have allowed teachers and students to suspend grading, at least for a time, to focus on revision, and to focus on conversations about an accumulated body of work. As the NCTE Position Statement on Writing Assessment eloquently states:

> any individual's writing "ability" is a sum of a variety of skills employed in a diversity of contexts, and individual ability fluctuates unevenly among these varieties. Consequently one piece of writing—even if it is generated under the most desirable conditions—can never serve as an indicator of overall literacy, particularly for high stakes decisions. Ideally, such literacy must be assessed by more than one piece of writing, in more than one genre, written on different occasions, for different audiences, and evaluated by multiple readers.

Portfolios are an assessment vehicle ideally suited to teaching writing, for they allow students to collect multiple pieces, written for multiple purposes, over time, and submit them for evaluation. Kathleen Yancey and Irwin Weiser note that portfolios had ambitious aims: "nothing short of changing the face of American education" (1). And portfolios have indeed changed many educational practices, as the varied essays in Yancey and Weiser's *Situating Portfolios* or Donald Graves and Bonnie Sunstein's *Portfolio Portraits*, to name just two starting places, demonstrate. Portfolios allow both teachers and students to pause, reflect, and explain to others, and this has profound implications for grading, reading, and organizing student work. Portfolios encourage us to make assessments more valid and useful.

Useful as portfolios are for best representing realistic pictures of writers' abilities, their most transformative impact in the classroom is connected to the new genre they introduced: the reflective statement. Although there are as many ways to use portfolios as there are teachers, a common feature of portfolio use is some kind of reflective statement about choices made in compiling the portfolio. Reflective statements have made self-assessment an important part of classroom work. This is an area of teaching and learning that has not received as much attention in our published scholarship, and partly for that reason, I have chosen to discuss it here, in my contribution to an anthology about changing notions of teaching and writing. Understanding reflective self-assessment is key to understanding teachers, readers, and students of writing. Reflecting on reflection will challenge us—a point I'll make through the consideration of an essay written by Katherine Ellison at the close of an honors first-year composition course.

Katherine's work as presented below is excerpted from the cover essay for a final portfolio. It was the last in a series of formal assignments, and the last of a series of reflections. Students had written short assessments of each formal assignment during the semester, working through activities focused in part on argumentation, in part on research. The syllabus promised students:

> At the end of the semester, if you have completed all the work for the class, you should be able to demonstrate the ability to:
>
> 1. *analyze arguments, examining structure, evidence, and claims (we'll use Toulmin's rhetorical framework here).*
> 2. *evaluate your own work, engaging in a recursive process where you evaluate and set goals over an extended period of time.*
> 3. *research issues of some complexity and integrate outside sources into your writing.*
> 4. *use argumentative techniques appropriate to varying rhetorical situations.*
> 5. *make deliberate and effective choices about style and diction appropriate to the rhetorical situation.*
> 6. *use writing skills in the service of real needs in the community.*
> 7. *work with others at varying stages of writing projects, including consulting experts who can help you plan or research projects, and consulting with peers in class as both giver and receiver of diligent and careful peer reviews, written and oral.*
> 8. *complete at least one long essay (about 7 pgs). Although I will not mandate essay lengths for each project, you must consider this issue as you plan each project. We will consult during the term about each project. This course goal merely sets a minimum requirement.*
>
> *Here's some space for you to note what you would like to demonstrate at the end of the semester:*

I devised these goals (including space for students' personal goals) to serve the needs of fairly new students on our commuter campus. I've always been ambivalent about honors curricula. Honors programs put many resources at the disposal of students who already have access to a great deal. Students who have flourished in high school arrive on our campus and get access to research opportunities and small seminars—the very opportunities that their high school success prepared them for, to be sure, but also the very opportunities that could really make a difference for at-risk students. Why can't we teach all students like honors students, I wonder? But my experiences teaching honors at a commuter campus, one that caters to large numbers of first-generation college students, has given me a new view of honors. An honors writing curriculum can help ground students who are at-risk in some overlooked ways, and it can invite them to construct their own goals for their first-year work. Katherine's reflection will illustrate the ways in which her own goals for education—many of which were only tangentially related on the surface to writing goals—were always in play during the semester.

A bit more local background: my department attracts students to our honors writing class via a placement test (not through the official honors program mechanisms, based on high school GPA—not all the students in honors writing are officially affiliated with the honors program). So the students we get are an eclectic bunch. Often, their academic records don't reflect extraordinary academic success, but their writing samples reflect an engagement with some hobby or interest: honors students have passions. Those passions are not usually for writing. Not all students in our honors course say they like to write and read, but they all have an ability to put a sentence together with some flair. On a commuting campus, where many first-year courses are large, an honors class provides a way for these students with passions to find each other. And that serves a valuable social need. I've come to believe that honors students benefit from a homogenous grouping where their interests, and their advanced curiosity, can play out.

As I look at the course goals listed above, I see several ways in which I would revise them now: they need to provide more guidance for the service learning component in particular, and they probably need to structure the formal assignments a bit more. On the whole, though, the goals continue to reflect my teaching and language philosophies. The course creates a community of writers who understand language as a set of overlapping and sometimes contesting systems, systems that both reflect and shape the world in which we live. Toward that end, the course goals emphasize the importance of response in writing, and the importance of writing in varied rhetorical situations. Focus in these areas helps students learn that communities of writers, readers, and thinkers share certain knowledge, biases, and passions, and that writers new to those communities need to learn these dimensions of community life. The emphasis on argumentation in a Toulmin model helps students see the debates and running conversations that help keep communities going (and that sometimes divide communities). Arguing is one of the most human of all activities, and our study of argumentation paves the way for analysis of academic issues, as well as the analysis of civic issues necessary to a democratic society.

The essay below, from Katherine's final portfolio, offers some insight into how she experienced these goals. The final assignment for the course, *Project Six: Finishing the Semester,* was:

> Essentially, this final project provides a cover argument for your portfolio. It should be a definition argument in that it examines your work in light of the grading guidelines and makes an argument about the category into which your portfolio best fits. . . . It should also reflect on the semester to discuss and analyze what you did, what you learned, and where you're headed next as a writer. In addition to reviewing the course goals and your personal goals, you may find some of the following questions helpful. I learned (and then adapted) these questions from Louie Crew, a wonderful writing teacher at Rutgers University in New Jersey:

- *A big problem I had this semester was. . . .*
- *My major global revision was. . . .*
- *My favorite local revision was. . . .*
- *A risk I took. . . .*
- *I made project [1,2,3 etc.] my own when I. . . .*
- *I thought about audience at this moment and then. . . .*
- *My personality affected my writing when. . . .*
- *A place where I'm especially proud of my style is. . . .*
- *Why a good student in another writing class could/could not write like this. . . .*
- *The response I'd like from you is. . . .*
- *I responded to the structure of the assignments by. . . .*
- *You influenced me by. . . .*
- *My classmates influenced me by. . . .*
- *What I learned about audience was. . . .*
- *What I learned about my community was. . . .*
- *I responded to earlier readings of my work by. . . .*
- *I broke a rule (and enjoyed it!) when. . . .*
- *I broke a rule (and worried!) when. . . .*
- *I got more efficient. . . .*
- *The biggest style/usage/grammar problem I faced. . . .*
- *If I had another week I'd. . . .*
- *if I had another month I'd. . . .*
- *If I could do it all over I'd. . . .*
- *I was intimidated by ( ) but I responded and. . . .*
- *I hope you won't notice. . . .*
- *I made a connection between this course and another course when. . . .*
- *I made a connection between this course and my friends/family when. . . .*

- *I made a connection between this course and my job when. . . .*
- *I tried [name a strategy] but rejected it when. . . .*
- *I felt a little childish when. . . .*
- *I was most creative when. . . .*
- *I worked and worked and worked until . . . success! . . . when. . . .*
- *I worked and worked and worked but it's still not right. . . .*
- *I got help/hindrance in writing from. . . . .*
- *I wanted . . . but you wanted . . . I resolved this by. . . .*
- *Please, please, please notice. . . .*

Project Six: My Argument
Katherine Ellison

I have noticed something very odd this past week. I have noticed that usually, the most dramatic changes to my work have been visible to everyone except me. I spend my months working frantically, staying up until television stations go off the air, and I never realize that I am making definite advances, that my work is building on each previous piece and I have compiled a considerable foundation for future endeavors. I write separate essays and in my mind they stay just that—separate. It isn't until I am in the final stages of reflection, until I am shuffling through past papers in search of that one I shouldn't have thrown away, that I see it, I see the patterns and the foundation I have created. This semester has sparked some of the largest improvements in my writing. Each course which I have taken has added a new side to my outlook and my style. Each subject, whether it be history, logic, drawing, anatomy, creative writing, or argumentative writing, has added a much needed stone to this building I am creating. What will this structure look like when I am finished? Will it be the one I will live in, or will I go on to build new ones, improved ones, stronger ones? I have no idea, but I am very excited at the possibilities.

The anticipation I have of my future has caused me to take my education rather seriously. I am an impatient student. I don't like to repeat myself and I don't like to waste time. In order to get everything out of my classes, I try to dedicate myself fully, without hesitation and without boundaries. If I read a novel and the author refers to another novel, I will read that one next. It is all a part of this foundation. A weak stone, a stone with a crumbled corner, will throw everything off balance and someday, when I am probably most comfortable, my structure will slide off into the soil and I will be sitting on the ground rubbing my sore behind in confusion. What does this all mean? It means that I try to meet all of the goals, both standard, and personal, for every class, and this class has been no exception. In fact, I feel that I have worked harder in this writing class than I had even anticipated I would, and I feel that my collection meets the standards of an "A" portfolio. My use of the Toulmin's scheme has grown to such proportion that I now use it for all argumentative writing I do for other classes. I have "grappled" with complex subject matter and I now have a greater understanding of not only writing techniques but also of our government, our laws, our history, and the ways in which I can convey my findings to diverse audiences. This audience awareness, in turn, has forced me to demonstrate the use of my different styles. I have written you many writers' letters which I feel have shown my analysis of my own work and the extent to which I have thought about each revision and the reflection involved in these revisions. The definite difference between the first drafts of my papers and the final drafts illustrates that I have listened intently to the suggestions of others and I have responded to those suggestions. I have been constantly aware of the goals of the course and my own personal goals and I have geared my work accordingly. The combination of my works also creates a definite timeline of improvement and the pieces are each related in this way. I think that, for the most part, my portfolio is free of glaring mechanical errors. Finally, I have met a very important goal I have set for myself. I have learned how to connect the different fields which interest me. I have linked them not only to each other, but to other fields which don't necessarily interest me yet are mandatory to the advancement of my writing skills. I am speaking primarily of anatomy, drawing, creative writing, and (my not-so-favorite) formal writing.

The most effective tool I have learned during this semester is the Toulmin Scheme. At first I approached this device with great apprehension—a formula for writing, how preposterous! I never used outlines before this semester. I was a die-hard stream-of-consciousness advocator. Soon I realized, however, the importance of approaching a paper with a notion as to how the content is going to be organized. I worked out a rough enthymeme and outline before beginning my research paper. . . . At this point I only got as far as saying "Literature should not be censored because . . . ." I then developed a quick outline according to the reasons...This represented my first efforts with the scheme. Suddenly, after seeing the scheme you used in my response, I wanted to know more about it. . . . The final draft of my research paper grew right along side the growth of the Toulmin's scheme, and I think this proves the extent to which I have worked in this area. . . . I learned how to step back from my paper and ask these questions of myself. I also used the Toulmin's scheme in my responses to the work of my peers. I was ecstatic when I constructed one for Susan's anthology submission and found that there were a few conditions of rebuttal which she left wide open. I would have never suggested that the dictionary might not be an adequate source for an argument about freedom and liberty if I had not used the scheme, and after I thought about it I realized that I, personally, would not believe such an argument which used only that source. . . . I also constructed one in response to the later stages of

Doug's research paper . . . each of these pieces of writing, whether they be writer's statements, peer reviews, or the research paper itself, prove that I have worked with and made definite progress in the construction of Toulmin schemes. I now understand them fully and have used them in other classes. Dr. Turner [our department chair who was teaching another English course she took that term] has even witnessed this, but he admits, he's "not as good as I should be in this regard." (Now I don't feel so bad about not understanding in the beginning.)

I have learned how to integrate the different fields I am interested in, and I think this is illustrated best by the drawings I have included in the portfolio. I have not yet reached the point where I think they (the drawings and writing) are balanced, but I have drawn upon the concept of a "circle" and the other emotional connotations different shapes have for me. I have slowly transformed into a sort of cubist I think! I am not sure why this is, but perhaps it stems from my fresh experiences with organization and logical thinking. Maybe the faces I draw out of shattered glass-looking triangles and rectangles are actually my way of giving the portrait an analytical personality. I'm not sure. I must point out that the included portrait is of no one I have ever seen. I drew it while working on "Myself as a Writer." I had the paper next to the keyboard and when I reached a slow-point I would switch back and forth. The other two drawings related to the subject matter. One depicts a girl trying to read but a serpent is bothering her and breathing fire onto her book (how annoying!). The book is also on fire, which related to the introductory passage of my research paper. The other drawing of a woman crouching above a pile of books. This is how I see myself, this is my ideal work. Just me and a pile of books. She is nude (not naked—nude, like that poem "Naked or Nude?" Who is that by I forget?) Anyway, the reason she is "nude" is because that is most natural, and when I write that is how I feel, mentally nude. Actually I feel mentally naked (I must find that poem again). I feel slightly different when I read. . . .

I feel this portfolio is a wonderful representation of my efforts and my growth as a writer. . . . Everything is starting to come into focus, and I am very excited. Perhaps I will someday look back on my writing career and point a bony finger at this thread in my web and say "There, that is where it all started to change."

I chose to excerpt Katherine's essay here for several reasons, the most important of which is the way in which this reflective essay represents Katherine the writer, someone who is working, reflecting, choosing. Goals—my goals, her own goals—are a key element of this essay. Katherine's personal goals (to integrate her diverse interests, to move with dispatch through her education) became an explicit element of the course. Her reflective writing gave us an avenue to pause together, assess progress, see what all her work added up to. Goal setting is something my students and I do frequently; we talk about weekly goals, unit goals, course goals, personal goals, and academic goals on a regular basis. But in many ways, traditional course goals are almost irrelevant to what we should accomplish in first-year composition. Traditional course goals convey a teacher agenda—reflective writing allows students' agendas to come into the classroom in a powerful fashion. And more than anything else, students should emerge from their semester(s) of composition as writers who understand and manage their own agendas. This ability will allow them to function effectively in a variety of settings: other writing classes, disciplinary classes, workplaces, homes, churches, and so on. And although I could have chosen Katherine's long-researched argument on censorship and its effect on writers to illustrate how well she learned formal argumentative structures, or I could have chosen her public service announcements written for an agency that sponsors high school exchange programs to illustrate how well she learned to analyze audience, or I could have chosen her peer responses to illustrate how well she developed as a peer responder, none of those pieces would have shown you Katherine as a self-conscious writer.

Her reflective essay, on the other hand, shows her increasing awareness of form and stylistic concerns, and it demonstrates the ways in which she immersed herself in the demands of the semester, set personal goals in addition to those I listed in the syllabus, and thoughtfully reflected on her progress. In short, it demonstrates that she is a writer making choices, sharing text, reading, writing, and revising. Kathleen Blake Yancey's study of reflection argues that students become "agents of their own learning" when we ask them to reflect (5), and Katherine ably illustrates Yancey's points in her own discussion of her impatience about learning. Reflection makes it possible for Katherine to bring her goals to the surface, to talk with her teacher and her peers about her desire to bring together an impressive array of interests. Reflection allows Katherine to set the composition course in the context of her life. Arthur Applebee's notion of curriculum as conversation highlights the connections between "broader cultural traditions and schooled knowledge" (37). Reflection provides another domain for conversation: it asks writers to use writing as a bridge between formal assignments and prior experience, between in- and out-of-school activities. In our classroom, reflection functions on several levels. On one level, it helps students: here Katherine engages in a dialectical review of what she has accomplished, how she accomplished it, and what her accomplishments mean. She moves back and forth between her "schooled" knowledge, her personal goals, and her private passions. On another level, it helps me: as

Yancey suggests, juxtaposing reflective texts with other course texts promotes understanding of "how students experience the curriculum I think I'm delivering" (140).

To find out how students experience that curriculum, reflection can be integrated in several ways. The most obvious is the formal sort of reflection I encourage here. But smaller reflective moments—class discussion or informal course assessments (the "minute papers" advocated by Thomas Angelo and Patricia Cross, where students take a minute at the end of class to write down a question or comment, for example)—are essential for the development of effective self-assessment. Hilgers et al. summarize the literature on self-assessment and note that these conditions lead to positive effects: self-assessment must be systematic, embedded in a context that considers motivation and reward; self-assessment must be taught; it should break complex tasks into smaller portions; and it should interrupt behavior at points where it can "make a difference" (6). In my honors composition course, self-assessment was linked both to course and individual goals; we practiced it weekly on an informal basis, and at the end of each unit with a formal reflection. We used reflection as a vehicle to negotiate individual work toward course goals—which assignment would a student choose to revise into the long essay required? How much of the course would be devoted to the service learning component?

Katherine's essay demonstrates how she, in the end, responded to these kinds of questions—and then some. She integrated a range of writing over the semester; she treats both peer responses and formal essays seriously, which indicates the degree to which she integrated course goals. Often students treat the process-oriented course goals as less important than the product-oriented ones, preferring to put effort into writing their own essays and missing the connections between reading and writing. Katherine clearly views reading and writing as all of a piece, and she forges connections between all elements of the class as she assembles the portfolio. According to John Dewey:

> the method of intelligence manifested in the experimental method demands keeping track of ideas, activities, and observed consequences. Keeping track is a matter of reflective review and summarizing, in which there is both discrimination and record of the significant features of a developing experience. To reflect is to look back over what has been done so as to extract the net meanings which are the capital stock for intelligent dealing with further experiences. It is the heart of intellectual organization and of the disciplined mind.

Katherine illustrates a disciplined—yet impatient, as she names it—approach to keeping track as she looks back over her work from the semester, choosing which pieces to include in the portfolio and which pieces to discuss. Without much explicit prompting from me on this score, she pulls in work from other classes, mentions previous reading and writing experiences, and cites conversations with other teachers. She refers to her interests in art, and she sees her portfolio as a resting place, not simply a culmination of the semester. Hephzibah Roskelly and Kate Ronald, drawing on John Dewey and Ann Berthoff, argue that a romantic/pragmatic rhetoric is our best hope for making real change in education. Katherine's nimble mind reflects the kind of rhetoric they call for, one that is "active, restless, imperfect, hopeful, and brave" (139). Katherine's reflection is a vehicle for considering the consequences of her current work—what pragmatic difference will it all make? She closes her reflection by wondering what the end of this semester will signify in the future—what kind of beginning it presages, a beginning she cannot then even dream of. Dewey also notes that reflection demands that we see "every present experience as a moving force in influencing what future experiences will be." Reflective writing assignments allow students to capture snapshots of those moving forces, just as Katherine did. (One tangential point that keeps coming to mind here: Katherine uses web as a metaphor for the patterns she sees as she closes her reflection. She wrote this essay before the World Wide Web was in common use—and now she has developed a beautiful web site of her own that integrates text and art to show the intellectual foundations she continues to construct in her graduate work.)

Elizabeth Chiseri-Strater has described her experiences using an open approach to portfolios, in which students construct a portfolio using only general guidelines from her (a system much like the class that produced Katherine's portfolio, where students were free to construct portfolios that reflected progress with course goals in any way they saw fit). Chiseri-Strater saw three patterns in her students' responses to these guidelines: students who "emphasized writing as craft or skill," students who "focused on learning," and students who "constructed their portfolios as a kind of mirror of who they were and where they stood in their lives" (64-67). Katherine's reflective essay combines all three of these strands, although the reflective piece puts the most emphasis on her reflection of herself. Chiseri-Strater saw these three patterns as reflecting back different strands of her own curriculum, which enables her, like Yancey, to see portfolios as something that help her to refine her teaching and to assess her work.

What I have learned from Katherine and her classmates is that students make choices about writing that are sometimes indirectly related to the assigned curriculum. I have learned that my original views of reflection were too limited, geared only toward understanding why and how a student revised from draft 1 to draft 3 or 4. Katherine is a deft writer, and she certainly had much to teach me about how revision can work—her thorough consideration of the deep structure of each essay led her to become a better writer and a better peer responder. Her essay reflects a graceful style, a broad grasp of the issues involved in her writing, and a willingness to work very hard. Her essay reminds me, in fact, of how hard students work. My original dreams of various assignments for this semester were not bound up with images of a student working long after the television station has gone off the air! Katherine's portfolio humbled me—its glorious collection of art and words, drawn from academic and private moments, represented a staggering amount of work. Katherine was, to be sure, an exceptional student. But even her classmates who were less talented, or perhaps worked less hard, still devoted an enormous amount of time to their work. And so I have learned to value that time and to make assignments that are worthy of that kind of investment.

Katherine's hard work is not something she resents, nor is it something she objects to; she sees it as simply the work of a writer. What is most compelling here is her determination to succeed at academic goals that are driven, frankly, by external forces (represented in the course goals I devised, *and* her determination to succeed at personal goals, driven by her own desire to integrate her interests in art and literature). Her portfolio (which unfortunately cannot be reproduced here) contains not only essays, letters, peer responses, and drafts produced for our writing class, but also some work produced for another English class, and seven pieces of art. Katherine illustrated the cover of her portfolio with a collage, and she drew sketches to accompany each of the six major projects represented in the portfolio. Her reflective essay discusses the connections she created through the course of the semester in this regard.

Perhaps the most powerful lesson I learned from Katherine is that writers need support in learning how to think and reflect (a lesson I might have learned sooner from John Dewey, of course, who argues in *How We Think* that educators have a responsibility to help students learn to reflect in oral and written language; see Yancey 9). Overall, Katherine's essay reminds us that writers need time to write, time to reflect, and a community of supportive and challenging readers. As her essay notes at the start, it is through reflection that writers see the patterns that have emerged in discussion, and the threads that need to be followed, and the threads that are already in place. Elsewhere in her portfolio, Katherine noted that she was satisfied with some dimensions of an autobiographical essay, but that she "would like to keep adding to it, to keep reflecting. I just thought of an obvious metaphor—if you stop reflecting, you lose your shine. Hmm. A little jagged yet catchy. I will remember that. . . ." And on that "little jagged yet catchy" note I will end this reflection, by noting that reflection is the heart of a writing class, and that reflective writing is what will show us most clearly the writers that emerge from our classes. First and foremost, we should be in the business of teaching *writers*, not writing. Making reflection the central activity in our classrooms keeps the focus on writers moving towards personal and institutional goals.

WORKS CITED

Angelo, Thomas A. and Patricia Cross. *Classroom Assessment Techniques: A Handbook for College Teachers.* San Francisco: Jossey Bass, 1993.

Applebee, Arthur. *Curriculum as Conversation: Transforming Traditions of Teaching and Learning.* Chicago: University of Chicago Press, 1996.

Chiseri-Strater, Elizabeth. "College Sophomores Reopen the Closed Portfolio." In *Portfolio Portraits.* Ed. Donald H. Graves and Bonnie S. Sunstein. Portsmouth, NH: Heinemann, 1992. 61–72.

Dewey, John. *Experience and Education.* New York: Macmillan Press, 1938. <http://www.cas.usf.edu/~dlewis/publications/Experience andEducation/7.htm>.

Graves, Donald H. and Bonnie S. Sunstein. *Portfolio Portraits.* Portsmouth, NH: Heinemann, 1992.

Hilgers, Thomas, Edna Hussey, and Monika Stitt-Bergh. "The Case for Prompted Self-Assessment in the Writing Classroom." In *Self-Assessment and Development in Writing: A Collaborative Inquiry.* Eds. Jane Bowman Smith and Kathleen Blake Yancey. Cresskill NJ: Hampton Press, 2000. 1-24.

National Council of Teachers of English. *Writing Assessment: A Position Statement.* http://www.ncte.org/positions/assessment.html. March 1995.

Roskelly, Hephzibah and Kate Ronald. *Reason to Believe: Romanticism, Pragmatism, and the Teaching of Writing.* Albany: SUNY Press, 1998.

Yancey, Kathleen Blake. *Reflection in the Writing Classroom.* Logan: Utah State University Press, 1998.

Yancey, Kathleen Blake and Irwin Weiser. "Situating Portfolios: An Introduction." In *Situating Portfolios: Four Perspectives.* Eds. Kathleen Blake Yancey and Irwin Weiser. Logan: Utah State University Press, 1997. 1-17.

5

MAKING RHETORIC EXPLICIT

Demystifying Disciplinary Discourse for Transfer Students

Maureen Mathison
University of Utah

In recent years the population of students transferring from two-year colleges into traditional four-year universities has increased. Although these numbers are climbing, very little has been written about courses designed specifically to suit the needs of these students. This chapter describes such a course, "Ways of Knowing in a University Setting," designed to assist students in learning about academic practices, and more specifically, those associated with their unique discipline. In the course, one returning student was able to design a study in which she pursued her personal interest in voice and initial self-presentation by analyzing the introductions of articles. Her own text illustrates this gendered genre as she begins by disclosing parts of her own self as they are relevant to her topic in the form of a narrative. Finally, she approached her research as a social scientist would, designing a study that included a knowledge of method and procedure, and an analysis that allowed her to say something "novel" about rhetorical voice in anthropological writing. In this sense the personal and the academic were made compatible and more importantly, made relevant to others.

Composition isn't just for first-year students anymore. At least, that's what demographics are beginning to indicate in higher education. Increasingly, university populations are shifting, and it is now likely that the term "first-year student" refers to transfer students who are juniors or seniors, as much as it refers to students entering immediately from high school. Educational trends in student populations have changed over the past twenty years, with more students beginning their education at two-year institutions. According to W. Norton Grubb and Associates, almost half of all first-year students in higher education now enroll in community colleges (3). Many of these students choose to fulfill many, if not all, of their general education requirements at two-year institutions prior to transferring to four-year institutions where they pursue a bachelor's degree. Jerry Gaff has also demonstrated that the cultures of the two- and four-year institutions differ (8-9) and transfer students from the two-year institution sometimes have a more difficult time adjusting to the four-year institution, a phenomenon commonly known as "transfer shock." Generally, this is reflected in a lowered GPA (grade point average) for transfer students during their first or second semester at the new institution (Knoell and Medsker 48).

Whereas many students may overcome the challenges of this initial phase of adjustment, some do not. There is a relatively large attrition rate for the first transfer year. Many reasons have been provided that help explain this rate, but one that transfer students themselves have cited as causing some challenge at the four-year institution is the expectations for writing. In her study of transfer students' perceptions of four-year academic environments, Barbara Townsend found that students perceived writing to be one of the most critical means to success. Said one student, "I have found the key to doing well at the university is being able to write" (183).

Students coming from one institution into another often find themselves entering a new community with its own unique beliefs and values. According to James Paul Gee individuals belong to multiple communities that have their own *Discourses*, ways of thinking, being, and doing (74). *Discourses* are associated with the different values and beliefs of a community and are manifested in, for example, the speech and writing of its members. Students are not born with these *Discourses*, but as research conducted by Nancy Nelson Spivey and myself has shown, they are enculturated into them, learning them over time (134). For transfer students this transition can be especially difficult because they have come from the more familiar and, in their eyes, the more congenial atmosphere of the community college into the research university, which is large and overwhelming.

To help transfer students become more immersed in university culture and in their major fields of study, a program called Horizons of Possibilities (HOP) was initiated by the College of Undergraduate Studies at the University of Utah. The course I describe in this chapter, "Ways of Knowing in a University Setting," was part of that initiative. The course was designed to assist students in making the transition by making explicit some of the tacit demands of thinking and writing that students will be expected to learn and produce in their respective majors. I believe that in studying disciplinary practices, transfer students are better able to adapt to the scholarly atmosphere of a large research institution such as the University of Utah, where academic practices differ from many of the institutions from which they transferred. In the Fall 1999, approximately 41 percent of the incoming student population at the University of Utah were transfer students.

"Ways of Knowing in a University Setting" was a composition course that was designed to train students to be student-researchers in their classes, and in doing so, to help them develop an understanding of academic practices as they are lived in a research institution, where at the upper-division level of course work, students are expected to: (1) go beyond the immediate syllabus and synthesize relevant material to define problems and solve them; (2) apply information and construct novel perspectives; and (3) collaborate with peers on projects. They are also expected to write well, as if they were "professionals-in-training," to use Barbara Walvoord's and Lucille P. McCarthy's term (8). It is important to clarify that undergraduate students are not expected to perform as professionals, but to engage material, and to think and write about it in ways that are specific to their discipline. A pedagogy that emphasizes a rhetoric of the professional (i.e., thinking and writing like a biologist or an historian or a psychologist) allows students to make information their own and transform it for their purposes. "Ways of Knowing" attempted to create an environment that, by putting students through an intense scholarly process over the term, demystified academic practices so that they could better engage material and understand the relationship between thinking and writing in their majors. The course was divided into three segments: (1) rhetoric *about* students, (2) rhetoric *for* students, and (3) rhetoric *by* students. Students read research articles written by authors in rhetoric and composition that demonstrated how students tended to perform writing (and in some cases, reading) in four-year institutions, as well as articles that deconstructed disciplinary practices and rhetorical conventions. Students put into practice what they had been learning by contributing to the conversations about which they had been reading in the last segment of the course, rhetoric *by* students.

Four major writing assignments converged over the term to produce a line of inquiry. The final writing assignment, called a "contribution paper," was based upon a question that emerged out of their journal responses to the readings and/or class discussion. This assignment allowed them as student-researchers to contribute to the ongoing theoretical discussions regarding the types of thinking (about which they had been reading and experiencing) that occur in academic communities. Students in the course have written about a number of academic topics, from what makes a good study group, to how to predict what will be on a test, to conducting their own research about a question they have in their area of interest.

The following abridged paper was written by Liz, a junior, who was a 25-year-old returning student from a traditional family that seemed more concerned about her welfare as a wife than as a student. According to Liz, they equated her well-being with being married. They worried about her being single and having no one to "take care of her." At the same time, it is important to note that Liz was a fiercely independent woman who was attempting to create a space for herself, a sense of purpose in her life. By the time she enrolled in my classroom, she had attended three universities and a trade school (for court reporting). According to her, she had stopped and started her education many times because she felt no urgency to get her Bachelor of Arts— she assumed that sooner or later it would be awarded to her. Her experience attending the university this time, however, was different, she told me. For some reason she did not view being awarded a degree an insignificant event.

Liz's contribution paper was imperfect, yet professionally and personally compelling on a number of levels. Her topic dealt with issues of gender and voice in anthropology, a discipline she was considering as her major. Liz undertook the project because she wanted to examine how anthropologists inserted themselves into their own work, how they achieved a sense of voice, something relevant to her own personal/professional goals. Because of the length of her paper, I have included her introduction, a summary of the body of her paper to provide some detail (which is my interpretation), and her discussion/conclusion.

Searching for a Voice: An Analysis of How Authors Position Their Claims in Anthropological Texts
Elizabeth Hendricks

In How to Make an American Quilt, *Whitney Otto tells the story of Finn Dodd, a graduate student who has difficulty deciding who she is.*

At first I thought I would study art. Art History, to be exact. Then I thought, No, what about physical anthropology?

Literature was my next love. Until I became loosely acquainted with critical theory, which struck me as a kind of intellectualism for its own sake. It always seems that one has to choose literature or critical theory, that one cannot love both. All of this finally pushed me willingly (I later realized) into history.

I knew in a perfect world, I would not be forced to choose a single course of study, that I would have time for all these interests. I could gather up all my desires and count them out like valentines.

Further, confusing Finn's life is that Sam, her boyfriend, has just proposed to her when the story begins. "I have lost track of the sort of girl I am. I used to be a young scholar, I am now an engaged woman. Not that you cannot be both—even I understand that—yet I cannot fathom who I think I am at this time" (Otto, 1991).

Though my life does not mirror Finn's I am sympathetic of her struggle. I, too, have had difficulties choosing a field to study. Continually, I fight our society's demand to pigeon-hole my scholastic interests into one field of study. Further, I am frustrated by the continual societal pressure I feel to secure my life, to get married.

I hope one day soon to be the first female in my family to finish college. In spite of my feeling of fulfillment, I have found that I am facing some painful choices in creating a life for myself. Often, I am faced with making decisions that are beneficial to my educational goals, but misunderstood by my family and the traditional values in which they believe. In my rebellion against my family's traditional norms, I have found it difficult to voice why my education and career is important to me.

Often, when telling the stories of my achievement, I am interrupted with questions about the status of my social life at the university. This is not the same for my brother, who is also attending university. He is constantly asked about his future career plans. When my brother and I speak to our family of difficulties we are having in school, my brother is reminded how beneficial education is to his future, while I am asked if I have found any new marriage prospects.

Because so frequently I feel my own voice is muted by what others around me are thinking, I write. I write to sound my voice in black and white. When I write, I imagine my audience listening to me. There is a reality that exists for me as I write—that I am being heard. One of my goals in attending the university is to refine my written voice, not only as a student, but as a woman. In this paper I will examine the similarities and differences in male and female authorship in the social sciences, specifically, how authors position their claims within the text, and the ways that authors create a rhetorical voice.

Liz chose to write in the genre of a research report and her process as a researcher reflected that choice. She systematically collected her data. "There were three requirements for each article," she stated. "The article had to come from an anthropology journal, the gender of the author had to be obvious, and the articles had to begin with a personal story or personal account." She then randomly chose six articles (three female-authored articles and three male-authored articles) to analyze for the types of voice she found authors employing, and then further analyzed voice for gender effects. She denoted three voices: "1) the I voice, 2) the we voice, and 3) the field voice." Liz found that what she termed the "I voice," the one which "created greater intimacy" with a reader, was more prevalent in the female-authored articles than the male-authored ones. The "we voice" was almost equally distributed among male and female authors (with the exception of one female author). This voice, Liz concluded, created more of a distance between the author and reader by invoking the field as authority. Finally, Liz found that the "field voice" created a sense of objectivity and distanced the author from the text. This voice was indicated generally through the passive voice, where no agent could be identified. Liz found that male authors were much more likely to employ this voice in their writing than either of the other voices.

[Liz's] Discussion and Conclusion

From my experience in writing and research, I am convinced that how an author uses his or her voice is important. However, I am not clear whether or not one voice is "better" than another. From analyzing these articles, I cannot determine whether or not these authors modified their rhetorical voice in order to be published. In this paper I have determined that there are different rhetorical voices. These rhetorical voices are used in different circumstances by different authors.

It is not by coincidence that [Renato] Rosaldo has chosen to integrate all three voices in his article while the other men have not. In his article he states, "how rhetorical forms of discourse are read depends not only on their formal linguistic properties, but also on how narrators are positioned" (105). The detached objectivity of the dominant legitimate form in the anthropology discourse can work against the author who is trying to describe other cultures in ways that render them familiar enough to their readers that he or she can understand the culture. Instead of looking for one specific recipe for writing as a man, writing as a female, or writing as a student, I feel it is more important for a novice writer, whether female or male to study the range and forms of rhetorical voices that are being used by the community they are entering. By being accustomed to the different approaches authors take in relationship to their writing, we can advance as writers. Rather than blindly mimicking the discourse, we can achieve a new range of possibilities.

Perhaps this is an optimistic claim for me to make. It is possible that as I finish my education and begin my career, I will determine that I am not allowed to make the choices of how I wish to position myself to my text. I will not be able to determine my voice, but instead I will be urged to utilize the dictates of the community. It is too early to tell. However, one thing I have learned from my research is that there are three different possibilities available. As an author of this discourse, I hope to use wise choices to define myself—to make a home for myself.

My role in the course was to help students situate themselves in the university—to understand their reasons for choosing a particular major and to help them understand how someone in their discipline might think and write. In supporting these course goals, I hoped to develop in students a sense of inquiry and a means by which to act on it. I also wanted to develop in them a sense of confidence and worth in their academic performance. Throughout the course I monitored students for their ability to adapt to this new culture and its expectations in order to assist them in achieving a sense of belonging.

In monitoring Liz I realized that she was certain of herself, yet uncertain about her abilities (similar to other transfer students). In many ways, she was an exceptional student because she had reached a point in her own life where she wondered where she fit into a "larger world" (her words). Being awarded a Bachelor of Arts degree to her became more than getting just a degree; it meant that she would learn to situate herself in a larger context. At the same time, she did not want to lose her sense of self.

Her contribution paper exemplifies the multiple ways Liz's personal and scholarly life began to merge and emerge in terms of inserting and asserting the self. She was learning to find a stronger academic voice that was compatible with her private voice. This was important to me as an instructor because throughout the course I had emphasized the importance of students making their work relevant to the community into which they were speaking. I had reminded students that all academic contributions are personal—they come from *our* questions, *our* knowledge, *our* creativity, and *our* labor. The problem that I often see is students mistaking their opinions for claims by writing personally rather than rhetorically in their respective discipline (see Maureen Mathison, 1996, for a discussion of this challenge). In general, however, Liz was successful in taking a very personal issue and making it relevant to a broader, interested, academic audience—something that helps students develop knowledge, understanding, and confidence in their area.

Her project was impressive in its scope, depth, and articulation. Whereas the majority of students demonstrated a way of knowing and writing in their respective disciplines in their contribution papers, Liz demonstrated an awareness of knowing and writing and *being*. She applied James Paul Gee's notion of the identity kit and wrote as if she were a member of the anthropological community, utilizing as much as possible the values and beliefs of the field. She did this as if she were a *female* social scientific anthropologist undertaking research, which was the topic of her contribution paper. In short, Liz's contribution paper fused content and form to examine gendered identity in anthropological writing in a manner that resonated with her research findings on female anthropologist authors. She achieved this through several means.

First, she designed a study in which she pursued her personal interest in voice and initial self-presentation by analyzing the introductions of articles, another form of initial self-presentation on the part of academics. She specifically analyzed the texts for different types of professional voice, which she termed the "I Voice," the "We Voice," and the "Field Voice." Her basis for this approach was justified because as Liz herself explains, "Anthropologists must know how to tell stories of another culture so that they sound familiar but without losing sight of their own contributions—their own voice in the process." She also utilized her findings that female anthropologists are more likely to employ the "I Voice" and begin their articles with stories. Liz's own text illustrates this gendered genre as she begins by disclosing parts of her own self as they are relevant to her topic in the form of a narrative. Finally, Liz approached her research as a social scientist would, designing a study that included a knowledge of method and procedure, and an analysis that allowed her to say something "novel" (Kaufer and Geisler 287) about rhetorical voice in anthropological writing. Her conclusion is cautious, which also demonstrates an academic maturity; she does not make claims beyond the scope of her data, and although she argues there are gender differences, she admits that she does not know the implications for this. She only hopes that her research can alert students to the possibility of different rhetorical voices in their disciplines, and suggests they study them carefully before choosing to engage them in their own work. Essentially, Liz has produced a paper that would fall into the course category of "Rhetoric For Students: What Researchers are Saying About Different Disciplines." She has learned to write with a degree of authority as she pursued her own intellectual interests and placed them within the concerns of a larger community. In this sense the personal and the academic were made compatible and more importantly, made relevant to others.

Since the pilot course was taught, the University of Utah has mandated that students fulfill, in addition to the lower-division writing requirement, an upper-division requirement in their discipline. This requirement can either be fulfilled through courses offered by the University Writing Program or through students' home departments. "Horizons of Possibilities" (HOP) has undergone a transformation and is now entitled "Writing in a Research University." It is one of three courses in the University Writing Program that fulfills the State upper-division writing requirement. Although many of the assignments are similar to that of HOP, the curriculum has been modified and it is this curriculum that is found on the web site. The goals for the course remain the same, and it is important to note that the contribution paper Liz wrote for HOP would be an acceptable contribution paper for the current course and would be supported by the revised syllabus. Since this course has been made permanent, it is interesting to note that student evaluations rate it as one of the best writing courses they have ever taken and that it has helped them to think and write more like a member of their disciplinary community. Overwhelmingly, they claim that it has made them feel more at ease in achieving their academic goals.

WORKS CITED

Gaff, Jerry G. "Toward a Second Wave of Reform." *Directing General Education Outcomes.* Monograph Series for New Directions for Community Colleges. Ed. Neal A. Reisman. San Francisco: Jossey-Bass, 1993. 5-12.

Gee, James Paul. *Social Linguistics and Literacies.* Philadelphia: Falmer, 1990.

Grubb, W. Norton and Associates. *Honored but Invisible.* New York: Routledge, 1999.

Kaufer, David S. and Cheryl Geisler. "Novelty in Academic Writing." *Written Communication,* 3 (1989): 286-311.

Knoell, Dorothy and Leland L. Medsker. *From Junior to Senior College: A National Study of Transfer Students.* Washington DC: American Council on Education, 1965.

Mathison, Maureen A. "Writing the Critique, a Text About a Text." *Written Communication,* 13 (1996): 314-354.

Otto, Whitney. *How to Make an American Quilt.* Universal Pictures, 1996.

Rosaldo, Renato. "Where Objectivity Lies." *The Rhetoric of the Human Sciences: Language and Argument in Scholarship and Public Affairs*. Madison: U of Wisconsin P, 1987. 87-101.

Spivey, Nancy Nelson and Maureen A. Mathison. "Development of Authoring Identity." *The Constructivist Metaphor: Reading, Writing, and the Making of Meaning*. Ed. Nancy N. Spivey. New York: Academic P, 1997. 223-234.

Townsend, Barbara K. "Community College Transfer Students: A Case Study of Survival." *The Review of Higher Education*, 18 (1995): 179-93.

Walvoord, Barbara and Lucille P. McCarthy. *Thinking and Writing in College: A Naturalisitc Study of Students in Four Disciplines*. Urbana, IL: National Council of Teachers of English, 1990.

6

REFLEXIVITY AND COMPUTER-BASED PEDAGOGY FOR FIRST-YEAR COMPOSITION TEACHERS AND STUDENTS

Looking Back, Thinking Broadly

James Inman
University of South Florida

Inman emphasizes teacher and student reflexivity in this contribution by rereading an earlier draft of this chapter, composed more than three years earlier. That initial draft, written collaboratively with student Erica Williams,[1] presented a narrative assignment challenging composition students to prepare narratives of their early computer literacy experiences, and it argued in particular that students need to come to terms with both the opportunities and challenges of working with computers. This revised version, written by Inman alone, shows how teacher reflexivity is just as important—that both teacher and student, then, must engage their own experiences carefully and thoroughly in order to best understand the way computer literacy develops in the composition classroom. This chapter is, in many respects, a model of the sort of reflective practice Inman believes is critical.

---

[1]Erica is no longer a student at Valdosta State University, where we first wrote together, but she has given me permission to include her essay and all of our original draft.

This chapter emerges from one specific teaching moment that highlights the importance of reflexivity. However, even with its specificity, it is a moment that has shaped my pedagogy in a number of courses and classes beyond the first-year composition course in which Erica Williams completed this essay at Valdosta State University, an 8,000-student regional public university in South Georgia. Indeed, the chapter itself is a study in reflexivity, for it is not simply the final revision of the draft that Erica and I began almost three years prior to completing this chapter. Rather, I am annotating excerpts of that draft—reading it, if you will. I am, in essence, reflecting on Erica's and my reflections. My goal is to demonstrate simultaneously my own reflexivity in teaching with writing technologies, thus indicating how important I believe it is that teachers also think reflexively about them, and Erica's reflexivity in completing the assignment with and about writing technologies. In addition, I seek to demonstrate how much knowledge has advanced about computers and writing in the past several years, indicating then just how large a challenge many teachers face in the academy today in terms of keeping up with professional practice.

When I originally gave this assignment, I knew little about computers and writing—not even that there's an annual conference—and I didn't have any idea about discussions of "computer literacy" and other like terms. I was unconnected, trying to find my way on what seemed to be a hazy, rocky, and ever-changing path towards professional growth, and I know that this is a feeling many teachers still experience today as they think about their work with students in individual contexts, not knowing that the important larger professional connections exist.

Reflexivity is a complex concept emerging largely from the social sciences that may be understood as individuals' abilities to see themselves and their impacts on social spheres through informed, critical lenses, a perspective that makes visible the social, cultural, political, and historical implications of any experience. Given the rise of ethnography in writing studies research, readers may be most familiar with reflexivity in terms of its relation to anthropological field work.[2] Whereas early works in anthropology assumed that researchers could come to know native cultures by being participant-observers for an extended period of time, contemporary hermeneutics has shown us that such research can never be fully successful, that observers always change the culture in which they are immersed, resulting in a less-than-native view. As scholars such as Charles Briggs have shown us, reflexivi-

---

[2]Readers can learn more about ethnography in writing studies by looking at Wendy Bishop's *Ethnographic Writing Research: Writing It Down, Writing It Up, and Reading It* (Heinemann, 1999).

ty comes into play in terms of researchers' abilities to perceive their specific influences.[3] Reflexivity is not autobiography, as that genre does not require self-consciousness, and it is not self-referential, that genre more aligned with allegory or the metaphorization of life experiences.

In attempting to encourage reflexive computer use among first-year composition students, I make several pedagogical assumptions:

* That students rarely have thought reflexively about their own computer use patterns and those patterns' significance in terms of writing projects;
* That students will grow as critical thinkers and more generally as learners if they begin to think reflexively about their writing; and
* That students will be well prepared for future writing technologies if they can examine the influence of the computer on their writing reflexively in this era.

I have taught in a host of environments—a regional university, a community college, a military college, a specialized university for aeronautical studies, a Research I university, and a liberal arts college—and these assumptions have proven reasonable in each place. More important, the assumptions I make are not unlike those of other compositionists, as described in books such as *Scenarios for Teaching Writing: Contexts for Discussion and Reflective Practice.*

ONE ASSIGNMENT AND ITS IMPLICATIONS

This assignment calls on students to write reflexive narratives about their technology uses: Recognizing the role of computer literacy and the natural relationship it possesses with identity development, I ask students to compose narrative essays that pinpoint and describe what they believe to be their first significant experiences with technology. Although experiences are not limited to classrooms, I explain that I am referring to computer technology only, and I establish an e-mail dialogue with to help students as they develop and revise their ideas and to be certain that no one mistakes my instructions and writes about a toaster or a video arcade.

---

[3]Readers interested in learning more about Briggs' work should see his *Learning How to Ask: A Sociolinguistic Appraisal of the Role of the Interview in Social Science Research* (Cambridge UP, 1986).

Narrative, as a genre, provides a sound way for students to think about their experiences with technology, and if critical commentary or analysis is encouraged, it also enables students to think reflexively about the experiences being related. Without such critical analysis, narrative cannot associate as well with reflection, but with it, the connection is clear, whether one grounds it in hermeneutics, phenomenology, or another foundation of social science knowledge.

In Erica's essay, reflexivity is visible as she thinks critically at about the way e-mail impacts her life and the sorts of computer requirements she and her peers should see in successful curricula. That is, she doesn't simply write autobiographically or without awareness of her social position; instead she looks at her subject critically, with a conception of consciousness and a clear sense of her visibility in any cultures she enters. When this critical perspective is merged with her enthusiasm for and wonder about e-mail, responses typical of any new user of a writing technology, the result is a well-voiced discussion of multiple perspectives about the technology.

Erica begins by introducing e-mail as a genre for communication, a common tack. Her approach, however, which is to connect e-mail to telecommunications technology broadly, proves unique as it reflects the sort of informed perspective Erica brings at times in her essay:

> As we enter the information age, technology surrounds and enthralls us. . . . Telecommunication, but one example, has been greatly enhanced by technology, from the invention of the telegraph, to the telephone, facsimile, and computer. A recent technological advance I have found particularly exciting is electronic mail, better known as e-mail. In the 1990s, with the large increase in the number of desktop computers, it has become possible for many people to exchange messages by e-mail.

Here Erica notes the social dimension associated with the advance of any writing technology, a savvy perspective for a novice user. Erica sees e-mail's popularity as directly related to the "increase in the number of desktop computers," not only in terms of e-mail itself.

From this introduction, Erica moves to identify the specific technology experience that she will describe throughout the essay: her work in my English 101 class. Certainly this choice could be read skeptically: I was the teacher who would be grading her essay and thus might look generously at an essay extolling the virtues of my class, and the course text she mentions specifically was one authored by me to help composition students use writing technologies. Knowing Erica, however, and interacting with her in the class, I understood this move to be less about teacher-friendly strategies and more about excitement to learn e-mail and other writing technologies. She orients her discussion around one of the textbooks for the class:

> The book we use is called *Electronic Communication and Research: An Introduction* . . . The first chapter introduced brief descriptions of the basics needed to operate a computer, and I read the second chapter and was able to type my first essay successfully. In the third chapter, I learned basic electronic mail. E-mail transmits messages from computer to computer over ordinary telephone lines under the direction of an intermediate service, which provides a host computer to receive messages, hold them, and send them to the proper destination. . . . A user of electronic mail simply needs a computer, a modem, a telephone line, and some sort of electronic mail service.

In this last sentence, Erica identifies hardware and software components associated with e-mail, a technical understanding uncommon in most students. It is my experience that most students who use the World Wide Web regularly are unable to describe the technical requirements and composition of the technology that enables it. They can use the Web, that is, but they do not understand its operational components. For Erica to think about a modem and a "telephone line" only several weeks into using e-mail shows significant thought, and, perhaps more importantly for this chapter, it shows an interest in the medium itself. Erica doesn't want simply to use e-mail; she wants to know its components and their various implications.

In the next paragraphs of her essay, Erica appears to put on rose-colored classes as she describes the large-scale positive impact e-mail has had on her academic and social experiences. Often such excited and overtly positive rhetoric is critiqued as problematic, and I begin to hint at that by referencing "rose-colored glasses," but I also believe that excitement is natural and should not be immediately imagined as uncritical. As her teacher, I was glad that Erica was excited about e-mail, just as I am pleased when my students are excited about learning new writing technologies in my classes today. However, the excitement must partner with informed reflection. Excerpts of Erica's paragraphs read:

E-mail has greatly enhanced my life in the short time I have used it. I have always enjoyed receiving mail, and e-mail gives me another way to communicate with friends and family. . . . There is no comparison when it comes to e-mail and handwriting a letter: the convenience of e-mail is amazing.

Communicating to whomever I choose at any time has allowed me to see the great value of e-mail. . . . Whenever communicating is made easier, it seems there is always some technological device at the heart of the change. There are not many communication devices that I can use at any time and also free of charge, but e-mail possesses such features for me. The free of charge feature is a benefit of having an account on-campus at VSU, but even if I had to pay for the service, like many people do, I'd still want to continue using it: it's become that important for me in only a very short time . . . I feel that e-mail is more a form of talking than writing; if I write a letter, it takes a long time to think just exactly would I would like to write about, and I feel more comfortable e-mailing my messages because I am not forced to be so formal and can get straight to the point.

Erica's enthusiasm parallels the enthusiam I have seen in other students. Realizing that e-mail arrives more quickly than postal mail is exciting, as is it reduces costs and enables friends to communicate in ways that add to their relationships.

Erica's next paragraph, however, best represents the way she developed reflexivity about e-mail as a writing technology through completing the assignment. Whereas many composition students would base their perspectives solely on enthusiasm, Erica thinks reflexively about her social position and the way it determines her ability to use e-mail. She writes about her appreciation for both her physical access to e-mail and her access to guided experiences in using the technology, a savvy approach that helped her classmates and me to understand more about social dimensions of e-mail:

Many people every day are fortunate to experience the . . . convenience of e-mail, but there are also those who are not so fortunate. This is a challenge facing e-mail and other technological devices. Everyone is not so fortunate as to have access to a computer. Not only am I allowed a place to work on a computer, but I am also able to operate a computer successfully. To me, having the opportunity to use a computer is only half of what is needed; I think experience with and general education about computers are equally important.

As Erica rightly implies, access to even basic networked technologies such as e-mail and knowledge about them cannot be assumed in the contemporary academy. Teachers and students alike bear the burden of trying to bridge this digital divide, and clearly the first step is to gain an informed critical perspective, as Erica demonstrates reflecting on her use of e-mail as a writing technology.

Erica concludes her essay with a brief, but broad explanation of the degree to which computers and the writing technologies they offer will be connected with her future:

> Computers and computer skills are essential for my future. My knowledge of computer skills began in the public school classroom, but I did not learn how to operate computers successfully until I was a freshman in college. I wish I could have learned more about computers when I was in high school or even junior high, and I now believe very strongly that education about computers must begin earlier in the classroom for everyone.

Erica's essay offers much of value for educators, I believe, as it models a reflective perspective on e-mail and thus an informed reflexivity about that writing technology's influence on her work in the class and beyond.

The final section of Erica's and my original draft for this volume was an analysis of the assignment and its contribution to knowledge about contemporary writing instruction. Although the volume's overall focus called for a reading of the assignment as is being done in this revision, Erica and I took the opportunity to discuss the out-of-class conferencing the assignment involved for us both, as well as features of the assignment and essay we thought especially important for readers to consider. Our purpose in this analysis was to describe all phases of the assignment to give readers a sense of the considerable work computer-based writing requires of teachers and students alike.

Two paragraphs of analysis demonstrate my lack of professionalism at that time, as I voice claims about Erica's work that do not resonate with the current scholarship. Again I indicate the immaturity of my view not to berate myself publicly, but to recognize the position many teachers may be in, as they think about their work carefully but without knowledge of professional activity in the area. Clearly I would have been a more savvy thinker about Erica's work had I known this scholarship and participated in the professional conversations. First, in Erica's and my draft, I attempted to describe Erica's attention to the communicative dimensions of e-mail as unique:

> One of the elements which first attracted me to Erica's essay was her non-traditional treatment of the topic. . . . Erica, it seems, had a reasonable amount of experience with computers before entering my class, but had never done much more than use word processing software; computers were quite simply a tool, just as a plow would be to a farmer . . . and they were quite uninspiring, though the ability to save files and edit documents quickly was nice. As Erica details in her essay, using e-mail to communicate with others through computers is where the excitement began for her and where she marks the beginning of her appreciation for the potential of computing, both in and out of the classroom. I was very pleased to see this unique perspective and even more so to see how well Erica dealt with explaining her views.

I know now that this approach was typical of many students' perspectives. Next I voice appreciation for Erica's sense that computer literacy is more than pushing buttons on a keyboard or knowing how to insert a disk into a CPU, not thinking about how literacy itself had been defined as a social concept for years:

> One of the first characteristics of Erica's essay which proves to be outstanding is in her examination of computer literacy, specifically in how she defines this term in quite a non-traditional manner. For Erica, computer literacy is more than a basic understanding of proper terminology and computer components and their functions: it is utilizing technology to communicate, to define and participate in a relationship not between two real-life people, but between two virtual identities, two computer users more or less. Though she is not yet familiar with contemporary critical constructions of computer-mediated communication, she raised many key questions in e-mail dialogues and offers observations consistent with the complexity of the issue.

Somewhat embarrassingly, I do not know to which "contemporary critical discussions of computer-mediated communication" I was referring then. I imagine myself as a much better teacher now that I am more professionally aware and involved because I can reference important experiences others have had in the classroom and because I have opportunities to interact with such colleagues at length in various professional forums.

One component of effective computer-based writing pedagogy that Erica and I did have right in the early draft of this chapter is our understanding of the way writing technologies enable conversations between teachers and students outside of the classroom and of how effective these conversations can be. Erica and I discussed audience, formality, and computer literacy through e-mail, and, as we describe, our conversations were rich and sustained: In one of our first e-mail dialogues I had with Erica about her project, she raised the question of audience, describing how she felt more connected with the people she communicated with electronically than with those to whom she wrote letters or sent postcards. I introduced a few critical perspectives, such as Lisa Ede and Andrea Lunsford's *Audience Addressed/Audience* Invoked, into the dialogue, but I stopped short of suggesting that these perspectives were more or less valuable than her own, as the purpose of the class was not for students to find and utilize other opinions to inform their own, but rather to delineate and rationalize their own, unique stances.

In similar e-mail discussions, Erica further questioned the issue of formality, explaining that she felt she could make comments via e-mail that she would not make in person. As I noted, this reflection represented almost the opposite of the closeness and connection she also described because the distance the electronic forum provided allowed her to feel comfortable commenting more freely. To this observation, Erica was quick to respond that she feels a great deal of distance in her face-to-face communications as well. She observed that this may be due to her natural shyness, but she also noted that it was more likely common element to any communication: "I don't connect with people all the time, and I know my friends feel like that too sometimes. It's weird."

Another issue Erica addressed by e-mail as she began generating ideas and drafting her essay was her own definition of computer literacy, especially the reasons she believed communication, as opposed to just basic computer skills and knowledge, was both fundamental and essential. I encouraged her to use her essay to examine how her concept of computer literacy differs from her concept of literacy itself.

Although audience, formality, and computer literacy were ultimately elements of her final essay, many other ideas she explored in our e-mail conversations were not, and I think it is important here to emphasize that such an outcome is positive: E-mail conversations should not need to be efficient or productive in terms of a single assignment; the emphasis should be on encouraging students to think critically and grow intellectually.

Erica and I last delineated the individual character of "computer literacy," as we were describing it at the time, along with noting the role community plays in the development of any such literacy. We began by emphasizing Erica's attention to individualism and computer literacy in an e-mail. She explained how pleased she was that I had assigned a narrative essay form because she believed that computer literacy is individual and cannot be defined or taught by blueprint standards. Each individual is different, but within the narrative form, each class member could express his or her unique experiences. For Erica, working with e-mail represented an awakening, an epiphany, of the potential computer technologies have to impact our lives. The narrative form allowed Erica and others in the class to think not only about the way computers change lives, but also both how their particular lives were changing and how they came to recognize and undergo those changes.

Building on the notion that individualism is important, we next imagined how community could play a strong role. At Erica and her classmates' request, we held an in-class, two-day workshop for each student to outline the experience described in his or her essay. In addition to its informative value, this workshop helped establish community among students. In this late age of print, computers are becoming more and more central in pedagogy, and the more we as teachers and researchers can share what we have done and what our students have done, the more we will be able to take full advantage of the opportunities that arise. It is, after all, those scholars who cautiously embrace the potential of technology and dare to question how and why such technology is used in the classroom who will be tomorrow's leaders. Thus Erica and I encourage all teachers and students to share their experiences as they learn to use technology.

Reflecting on these remarks now, I believe this call for conversation and that Erica and I experienced is vital for teachers and students alike, whether we imagine communities in terms of particular institutions or across our profession. Perhaps now the idea of communities is all the more valuable, as computer-based writing technologies have moved further into the mainstream academy since we began our chapter. Yet even with multiple influences, individuals encounter technologies themselves, so reflection must always occur alongside community.

As I have attempted to show in this chapter, it is critical for both teachers and students to become reflexive users of writing technologies, such as computers. Too often teachers do not take on these challenges themselves, despite the obvious links to personal growth and intellectual development, and that lack of participation must change if writing technologies are to be more than add-ons to already packed curricula. Erica's essay offers one example of how an assignment can foster such reflexivity in students, but many more options exist, and readers of this volume can imagine the possibilities in their own individual contexts, sharing their attempts and results through publications and presentations. With teachers and students from across the academy working together as reflexive users of computers and other writing technologies, we can move carefully and responsibly into the future.

WORKS CITED

Anson, Chris M., et al. *Scenarios for Teaching Writing: Contexts for Discussion and Reflective Practice.* Urbana, IL: NCTE, 1993.

Bishop, Wendy. *Ethnographic Writing Research: Writing It Down, Writing It Up, and Reading It.* Portsmouth, NH: Heinemann, 1999.

Briggs, Charles. *Learning How to Ask: A Sociolinguistic Appraisal of the Role of the Interview in Social Science Research.* London: Cambridge UP, 1986. 2

Ede, Lisa, and Andrea Lundford. Audience Addressed/Audience Invoked: The Role of Audience in Composition Theory and Pedagogy. *College Composition and Communication* 35 (1984): 155-171.

7

EVERYDAY LITERACY

Secular Institutions, Religious Students, and the
Commute between Incommensurate Worlds

Richard E. Miller
Rutgers University

*What shapes the way students read in school? This chapter looks at the
role that religious training plays in determining what powers students
accord the books they've been assigned in their courses. Literacy
instruction in the 21st century is bound to be as profoundly shaped by
this unacknowledged influence as it was in the 20th century. By having
students consider how the reading practices they use outside of class
differ from the reading practices celebrated in the academy, however,
we can begin the process of bridging the gap between spiritually-driven
practices that rule in the domestic sphere and the intellectually
engaged, self-reflective practices that define literacy in the academy.*

Over 48,000 students are enrolled at Rutgers University, where I teach;
of these, some 33,000 are undergraduates and, of these, some 1,000 are
English majors. This is not a place, in other words, where students get
to know their professors very well. Rather, as is the case at most institutions this size, progress towards degree here is, for most students, just a
matter of stacking up credits until the magic number is hit and the pris-
oners are set free.

The English department has done its best to combat the incoherence that comes of having to serve so many students with such diverse interests. The department has revised its curriculum and now requires all majors to have a broad knowledge of the history of literatures written in English to complement their elective course work in more specialized areas. The department decided, as well, that, given the role critical theory has come to play in all phases of the discipline, all majors should take a theory course of some kind. It was this new departmental requirement that ended up bringing Rachael Biberfeld, the student I wish to discuss here, and her peers to my 200-level course, Reading Theory. Although there are many ways for English majors to fulfill the new theory requirement (i.e., they can take large lecture courses or advanced seminars), the 200 level course offers beginning students an introduction to theory that is writing-intensive and student-centered. In my section of this course, I wanted them not just to learn *about* theory, I wanted them to *do* theory. From the first week in the course to the last, then, the students in this course were asked to try to see the world from the vantage point of the assigned materials in the hopes that they would come to understand the theories under consideration from the inside out.

I have spent most of my teaching life in required courses, working with novices of one sort or another, and whether I'm teaching first-year writing or the graduate seminar for first-time teachers or an intro to theory course, I tell my students the same thing: I am only interested in writing that engages with the assigned materials. "If you could have written your paper without having done the readings, without sitting in on the conversations, without coming to class, that's a problem," I say. "You already know your own thoughts: the work here is to put your thoughts into conversation with what others have to say on the subject at hand. And the goal is to see what happens after that moment of connection." "Engagement," "conversation," "connection": these are the words I rely on in my teaching; they are the metaphors that point to the kind of writing I value most—speculative, deliberative, meditative writing. I don't want the students to produce writing that starts at some given place ("my thesis is X") and stays at that place ("and these are the examples that prove my thesis"). I want the students to produce writing that moves from here to there, writing that teaches as it goes. My job, as I define it, is to show the students how to produce such writing.

Why read? Why read when the world is saturated with more interactive, more responsive, more stimulating modes of communication? Does reading have a future in "the late age of print"? These were the questions that were at the core of this course. I wanted these students—seniors, those new to the major, and those on the fence—to think seriously about what the value of reading might be said to be. I wanted them, when asked to explain why they had committed their college years to the study of literature, to be able to say more than, "I like to read."

We started with excerpts from David Denby's *Great Books* as a way into the canon wars: here's a guy in his mid-forties, a successful film critic, who voluntarily decides to go back to college and become a novice once again. What are we to make of someone who takes books so seriously, someone who thinks reading and going to school are so important? Why should we care what he thinks? We studied Columbia's list of great books; we read some of Denby's scathing film reviews; I sent the students home to construct a list of texts that they would consider "great." Their lists were overrun with the literature of the high school English curriculum; they were also littered with religious and inspirational texts.

We then turned to the first book of Genesis, which appeared both on their lists and on Columbia's list, and spent some time discussing how the Bible might best be read in school. (Rachael refers in her paper to how disruptive this moment proved to be.) What does it mean to read a sacred text in a secular setting? What happens to the text when it's moved from here to there? What happens to readers in these different locations? For some students, it was heresy to suggest that there were two versions of creation in Genesis; for others the discrepancy was obvious. Suddenly, the question of how one reads and why one reads that way seemed to matter. The relatively impersonal work of reading books for class moved closer to home as the links between one's reading habits, one's upbringing, and one's cosmology started to line up.

Next we read Carlo Ginzburg's *The Cheese and the Worms*, which is explicitly concerned with exploring the connections between the way one reads and the way one views the world. Ginzburg focuses on the curious case of a fifteenth-century Italian miller, known as Menocchio, who was tried and eventually executed for heresy. What interests Ginzburg most is Menocchio's reading practice and the culture that supported his fanciful, oppositional readings. (Menocchio believed that, in the beginning, the cosmos was a primordial ooze like fermenting cheese and that God and the angels emerged out of this ooze just the way worms spontaneously appear in cheese. Eventually, he was executed for maintaining these beliefs.) What, I asked my students, would Ginzburg make of your reading practice? What kind of evidence would he rely on in making his case? Would he find traces of your cosmology in those materials? This, then, is the set of circumstances and the assignment that gave rise to Rachael's paper.

Preservation, Not Creation:
A Personal Rendition of the Methodology of Ginzburg's
The Cheese and the Worms
by Rachael Biberfeld

My name is Rachael Biberfeld, and Rachael is what I have always been called. I was born in 1974 in New York, a large city in the United States on the East Coast. Three years later, I moved to Miami Beach, where I lived until I married and moved to Lakewood, a small suburban town in New Jersey fifty miles south of New York. I have four children, and I earn my living as a teacher, and other things. But mostly I work as an Orthodox Jewish housewife; I also wear the traditional Jewish housewife's costume, a long skirt, a long-sleeved top, and a wig. Thus I present myself at my Reading Theory course in 1999.

With just such a superficial description, Carlo Ginzburg begins his study of Menocchio and the way he reads the printed and oral words around him. But a summary like this one only begins to nibble at the edges of what eventually becomes The Cheese and the Worms. These brief biographical facts hint at who I am and how I might think about my world, but it would take research with the depth of Ginzburg's to discover that those facts are not as revealing as they seem. If Ginzburg were to study the world I read and the ways I read it, he would see that in many ways, I read like Menocchio does, "isolating words and phrases, sometimes distorting them, juxtaposing different passages, firing off rapid analogies" (51). But my manipulations of my reading are different in one important point. Ginzburg posits that Menocchio's oral tradition served as a filter that "acted on Menocchio's memory and distorted the very words of the text" (33), presumably also causing his omissions, juxtapositions, and other unorthodox ways of reading, almost as if his way of reading was "wholly involuntary" (47). But my own methods of reading, while very similar to Menocchio's, are not an involuntary product of the filter of my own traditions as much as they are a conscious effort to screen my secular readings through my religious beliefs.

For the purposes of this analysis, my readings will be defined as secular items; I consider those written works that are part of my religious tradition as part of a culture and lifestyle that precedes and goes beyond secular readings. I read religious books, newspapers, magazines, etc. differently than I read secular works. That reading practice could perhaps be the subject of another paper, but for now it serves as part of what shapes my way of reading rather than the reading material itself. This is much like the way Ginzburg treats Menocchio's oral culture as formative for his ways of reading and interpreting written words. The Orthodox Jewish tradition that's formative for me is not an oral one, but a written tradition that is extraordinarily deeply rooted and much venerated in my community and family. Everything else that I read is seen through the screen of those beliefs. I consider them absolute truths through and against which I can measure good and bad, just and unjust, right and wrong in everything.

Ginzburg begins his investigation into Menocchio's life by examining the village he lived in and his relative position there. It is clear that he ascribes a vital importance to the society that shaped Menocchio's world in terms of its religion, economic status, and isolation from new, radical thinking trends (13-20). A similar inquiry into my own community would explain a lot about the religious commitment that so greatly affects the way I read. Lakewood is about as close as one can currently get to a European, ghetto-like, shtetl village. Nearly all the local people I deal with on a daily basis are Orthodox Jews; my husband is one of several thousand men who devote their hours to religious studies; my children attend Orthodox schools; I shop in mostly Orthodox Jewish stores—it is an extremely socially homogenous and sheltered environment. While my personal experiences do extend beyond this enclave to Rutgers and my teaching job in another community, a home base like this one serves as a bedrock for fervent religious ideals that permeate everything else I do.

A more focused search would evolve into an examination of my own home. I have three kinds of books in my house: many bookcases of Hebrew, Aramaic and English religious volumes; several shelves of secular works, nearly all "classics" and academic texts, as well as stacks of secular magazines (mostly Gourmet); and many children's books, both religious and secular. There is no TV, no VCR, and no functional radio in the house. Faced with this mass of evidence, what would Ginzburg deduce? Before even looking at the books themselves, the ways they are stored provide clues as to how I see them. The religious books are displayed in open, floor-to-ceiling bookshelves in the living room, while the secular ones are crammed in double rows on two shelves in a closed cabinet. Am I hiding them because they are somehow taboo? Or does the placement demonstrate a difference in their importance to me? The way one would answer such questions is the way he or she would be reading me.

Along with the secular literature, I have various textbooks for teaching literature. I am a twelfth grade English teacher in an Orthodox girls' school that strives to teach a standard academic curriculum within a framework of religious values and beliefs. My notebooks and lesson plans would be invaluable to Ginzburg in determining my understanding of literature, in the same way that he scrutinizes Menocchio's under-

standing of the texts he read, like the Rosario (34). In this example Ginzburg shows how Menocchio emphasized some details over others to produce a reading that is quite different from the intended one. As a reader and teacher, I sometimes do the same thing. When I teach Romeo and Juliet, I try to emphasize to my teenaged students that Romeo is not someone they would want to marry, because his rash, passionate, emotional reactions cause him to make mistakes; his love at first sight for Juliet is not an ideal of love in marriage. This reading is clearly not Shakespeare's intention, but read through the filter of my personal value system, this is the one that emerges.

Another source for Ginzburg to examine is my collection of my own papers on various works of secular literature. Assuming he would sift through all the Hebrew documents on my computer (my husband's religious notes and papers), he would find a wide range of texts that I read and commented on, since Rutgers University tries to expose its students to many different kinds of literary texts. The books in my possession do not necessarily reflect a personal choice as much as they reflect what I allow myself to be exposed to. A sampling of these papers would display more of the kinds of readings and manipulations that Menocchio worked with, but again, done in my own ways and for my own purposes. In my reading of Andrew Marvell's Seventeenth Century poem, "The Nymph Complaining for the Death of Her Fawn," I chose to downplay some overtly Christian images like a bed of lilies and read them as symbols of temporal purity rather than Christian purity. This was an effort to avoid discussion of Christian symbolism and ideology which might prove heretical to my Jewish beliefs. In a paper on Nathaniel Hawthorne's The Marble Faun, my criticism of Hawthorne's attitude toward spirituality as being "sad, overbearing, and gray" would be noteworthy to Ginzburg; I read this negative outlook as a sign of confusion and a lack of fulfillment in Hawthorne's work. To me, from my personal mental framework, a negative attitude toward the triumph of spirituality over physical joys is evidence of just such a lack of fulfillment. This is a value judgment based on my own values, and another reader would see this differently.

My readings of even the final category of books in my house, the children's books, are filtered through my religious beliefs. Aside from the religiously themed books, I verbally edit some of the secular ones to better reflect the values I am trying to communicate to my children. Sharp language is toned down, references to Christian holidays are omitted, and moral lessons are played up and repeated. Again, I "assimilate, transpose, and remold words and phrases" (47) like Menocchio does. But while he does this "in a wholly involuntary manner" (47), I do in consciously and proudly, in order to fit these texts in with my own set of truths.

There are some texts that I can not interpret or reinterpret in a way that fits my beliefs, and these texts I am forced to reject. Most modern novels fall into this category, as they are too explicit in their language and imagery for me to even read, let alone interpret. These texts are absent from my library. Also included here are texts such as the English version of Genesis that we received in this course earlier in the semester. The footnotes were clearly antithetical to Orthodox Jewish beliefs in the divine authorship of the Bible, and I could not read them. The New Testament and much of the writings of the ancient philosophers are in this group as well. Ginzburg could learn from what I do not read along with learning from what I do read.

These secular works that I would define as "Great Books" are the ones that best express those truths that I am committed to. An Anglo-Saxon poem called "The Seafarer" can be far greater than a classic like Paradise Lost if in it, I can see an outlook on materialism, life, and death that speaks to what I believe in. In a work like Jane Eyre, good triumphs over evil, and repentance leads the way to happiness. In The Grapes of Wrath, loving-kindness and virtue create heroes out of very ordinary, unheroic people. These are examples of books that are "Great" to me.

While Menocchio is proud of the "explosive mixture" that results from his "encounter between the printed page and oral culture" (51), as evidenced by his attempts to convince the Inquisitors of the truth of his views, I try desperately to avoid "explosion" by reconciling my secular readings with my religious traditions where I can and rejecting my readings where I can not reconcile. Like Menocchio, I search "for confirmation of ideas and convictions that [are] already firmly entrenched" (36), but these entrenched ideas are the screen though which I do my reading, not a wholly new creation based on a combination of that screen and the written word. Do I read like Menocchio? Yes. Does that practice result in a new, personal, unique reading of my world? I hope that it will not. It is preservation and enhancement that I seek, not enlightenment.

There is much that I find remarkable about the work that Rachael has done: she has adopted Ginzburg's theoretical approach, reading her world through his critical frame. Taking on this project has led Rachael to focus her attention on the kind of evidence that most interests Ginzburg in his study of Mennochio: Rachael looks at the books she owns, the community she lives in, the talk she participates in. Following in Ginzburg's footsteps, Rachael thus sets out to reconstruct the social and spiritual worlds within which her reading takes place. Doing this does not, however, lead her to the same set of conclusions that Ginzburg reaches in his study. Rachael makes it clear that she is unlike Menocchio in one very important way: she is fully aware of the filters that are at play while she reads. Her manipulations and distortions of the text are conscious. When she reads it is for "preservation and enhancement" of her belief system, "not enlightenment." For those who expect the reading and writing that is done in school to be transformative and for those committed to the notion of false consciousness, this conclusion is bound to be disappointing. From my vantage point, though, Rachael has done everything that can reasonably be expected of a student: she has reconsidered her experience in light of the assigned material; she has demonstrated her command of the assigned approach; she has noted the limits of that approach's explanatory power; and she has done all of this in prose that is simultaneously lucid and thoughtful.

Obviously, Rachael has done something else, as well: she has told a story about reading and its limited significance in a secular institution, a story about faith and religious community, a story about the incommensurate worlds she shuttles between. Her story is not, as I came to understand that semester in Reading Theory, all that unique: all the students were, to one degree or another, trying to figure out how to bridge the gap between the literate practices of their homes and the literate exercises they were expected to perform at the university; they were, as well, trying to make sense of the role that reading and writing might have to play in the development of a powerfully resonant inner life. It is important, I think, to keep such students and such concerns in mind as we consider what shape writing instruction might assume in the future. Why do we read the way we do? This is the question, ultimately, that rests at the center of any course I teach. Answering this question, as Rachael's paper shows, requires embarking on a journey that is simultaneously personal and impersonal, introspective and analytic, metaphysical and academic. It is in the movement between these worlds that learning occurs.[1]

---

[1]Readers interested in learning more about how to sequence assignments along the lines discussed here are encouraged to read David Bartholomae and Anthony Petrosky's Facts, Artifacts, and Counterfacts (Boynton/Cook: 1986).

II

TEACHING/WRITING...

...with COMPUTERS,
CLASSMATES,
and other COLLEAGUES

8

THE IMPROVING POWER OF E-CONVERSATION

George Otte
The City University of New York

When chronic failures stonewalled by a standardized assessment get passing scores, the question is less whether their experience of computer-mediated communication made a difference than why. The difference seems to be an "in your face" experience of audience, of the thoughts of others rendered visible. And this is more than the felt presence of interlocutors: the experience, dynamic and social, helps the students sense the social dynamic of what it means to make a point, to share an opinion, to confront disagreement. In this instance—basic writing students facing second and third attempts at a standard exit exam, the City University of New York Writing Assessment Test—the writing sample is collectively authored, because that was fundamental to the students' reconception of what it means to write. All the online writing was perceptibly what all writing arguably is: response to the writing of others.

Frequently, almost unavoidably, examples of student performance such as those contained in Coles and Vopat's *What Makes Writing Good* (or, for that matter, those collected for this project) elide the social and temporal dimensions of writing instruction. Too often, they focus instead (for reasons of space and simplicity) on a snapshot-like product. That's a tendency to be resisted here because the argument is that it's precisely the experience of multiple perspectives at an earlier point in the process that makes the key difference in the final product. What this amounts to is really just a chance to talk things through beforehand with the crucial qualification that this is talk made visible, a written exchange of ideas made more immediate by computer mediation, and this makes all the difference.[1]

The proof of the pudding is a radical hard case, even as hard cases go: a special section of chronic failures, "multiple repeaters" who could not pass a standard exit exam and thus emerge successfully from basic writing. All these students had repeatedly failed the CUNY Writing Assessment Test—for two decades the most widely used of the sort of test commonly called the 50-minute impromptu. Procedures at the time (they have since changed) ensured that each student's test was not scored by the instructor but cross-read by scorers who knew none of the students. When seventeen out of eighteen of these students who had repeatedly failed this exam passed it (the standard pass rate, even for first-timers, is consistently about 50%), the results amounted to compelling evidence of something people are profoundly curious and skeptical about: whether the experience of computer-mediated communication translates at all into effects on "ordinary" writing.

---

[1]The emphasis on conversation here ought to call to mind a major informant behind the method outlined here, Kenneth A. Bruffee. The final articulation has, in fact, been very much influenced by two very recent works—so recent they are not yet published. One is "What College Is For," which argues that "we can increase craft of interdependence through networked computers" but cautions that "existing educational software is almost exclusively designed for the vocational education of individuals working alone" (24). The other, "What Goes on in Teaching Writing with Computer Supported Collaborative Learning," holds that "teaching writing collaboratively at a distance, given currently available software, seems unlikely to succeed without concurrent, ongoing classroom consensual conversation" (14). Bruffee's concerns about computer-mediated instruction (particularly distance learning) helped to crystallize my thinking about what made this particular use of computers work. As I note later, I think the success has less to do with the use of computers in a computer classroom than with the use of computers (wherever they are located) to allow students to engage in sustained exchange, particularly what Bruffee calls (in "What College Is For") "substantive conversation." I am grateful for Bruffee's work and input, grateful, too, for the permission he has given to cite the two unpublished pieces mentioned here.

Just what CMC means is context-bound, of course, and we are speaking of a course offered over half a decade ago—a distance of time making it easier to see the principles and dynamics underlying the procedures. In this case, the test could not be taken on the computer, and none of the students were computer adepts. (Most, in fact, were not even native speakers of English.) They used computers primarily in untimed, unpressured exchanges in real time, via the Daedalus subprogram InterChange. The class read Jonathan Kozol's *Savage Inequalities* together, and discussions of it on InterChange were tough problem-solving activities, challenges to wrestle with questions even Kozol couldn't answer. Students were asked to air their thoughts and work with the thoughts of others—to see what's out there as grounds for discussion in terms of attitudes, premises, different value-based and experiential takes. The example that follows is atypical only in being so short. (Usually InterChange session transcripts ran twice as long, but this was a quick one, weighing in at only about 1,000 words.) As was often the case, students were given a choice of conferences, and over half the class participated in this one, which occurred halfway through the term.[2]

****
Start of conference CHANGE
****

Msg #1 George Otte:

In Chapter 6, Kozol tells the story of someone who sued the state of Texas over unequal funding—and won. But that's not the whole story. "In San Antonio, where Demetrio Rodriguez brought his suit against the state in 1968, the children of the poor still go to separate and unequal schools." If the court system takes so long (the verdict in the '68 suit was handed down in '89) and doesn't have much effect even then (Kozol notes "a series of delays and challenges and, doubtless, further litigation"), what are we to conclude? Is there no real hope for change? Must change come about by other means? If we shouldn't accept "savage inequalities" in education, what should we do?

Msg #2 Paula Ruiz:

Changes take time specially those changes that will favor the poor and black people. I believe there is hope in many people that changes to these situations can occur. The problem is that there are also people (those people who have the money and the power) who have hopes that these changes will not favor the poor and black people.

---

[2]Students' actual texts (and real names) are used—with their permission.

Msg #3 Rhadames Delacruz:

To achieve change in the educational system we must unite as a society and take a stand. We control the polititions, we control there political future. They work for us. Most of Americans don't vote. We are letting a small persent of people make all the decisions for us. If we want to stop the inequalities we must let the polititions know and then use the vote. If they don't want to work for us we kick them out and put some one who will.

Msg #4 Paula Ruiz:

I don't really see what other means we can use to change the situations that poor and black kids have at their school. I think that the situations that Kozol wrote about in his book are very strong to let these people (government people and rich people) know and understand that we need changes fast. They don't care and I believe they will never care no matter what.

Msg #5 Yanjun Zhou:

Changes will occur sooner or later, but it will take a lot of people's williness to do something about it. People must fight the battles to win the war on equality. Every case like the Demetrio Rodriguez, people win something; moreover, other case can come out and look to the case as a battle won. We can look at the case with hope; eventhough, it took so longer we can at least said more and more people will fight for their educational equality.

Msg #6 Ana Estrella:

Paula this is absolutly true. I agree with your first message.

Msg #7 Abdul Yusifu:

When we want something changed let us say a law something tragic must happen in order for a change to take place. I conclude that if we want change in the education system something tragic must also take place. The problem is that the people in charge of the states do not want changes because they are scared of it. Until these people realize that we will all be affected by savage inequalities there will be no changes.

Msg #8 Hanh Van:

Believe it or not, this country have change a lot. It have change from black and poor not getting an education at all to given the chance to an education. This change took along time to accomplish, but we did change it and that is the main idea. Everything take time, if we stick it out and keep on demanding changes we will get it, but we must be patience.

Msg #9 Ana Estrella:

The poor people will never get the same rights that rich get because of the position of the poor. The rich are always the first one in everything held for the public and what is left is what the poor get.

Msg #10 Taisha Knowles:

There is hope for a change in this unequal opportunity for school. The people who have the authority to give better schooling is holding it back from the people of color and other minority groups. The only thing we can do is come together an fight for what we know belongs to our people.

Msg #11 Ana Estrella:

All this people living on those conditions hope for change but they know that it will take too long to occur. The only solution that I can think of is to discriminate the rich if they discriminate the poor. Give the same kind of education to everyone.

Msg #12 George Otte:

A lot of the discussion I see so far is really, at bottom, about who controls this country—and so Rhadames talks about the importance of voting, Yanjun talks about the importance of little victories, and Hanh speaks of gradual progress. Can you say more about WHY you believe change for the better will or will not occur?

Msg #13 Rosa Chabla:

Paula: I agree government and rich people will never care no matter what. If they did care they would have done something a long time ago.

Msg #14 Oy Ng:

There is a saying "Good things comes to those who wait", I think changes are possible, but it will take time. As Hanh said it took a long time before blacks and the poor were allowed to attend schools. As for now we must accept it, but this doesn't mean we have to like it.

Msg #15 Indira Mercedes:

It is going to be difficult to hope for changes, especially for the minority since they have little to hope for. However, hope can occur at any time. I believe it will.

Msg #16 Flor Barrientos:

Is true this is going to stay the same. We just have to deal with our lives and do our best. For some people this is a problem, but not for everyone. There are a lot of minorities with their careers and that have achieve what they wanted, so now they have to wait for their children to follow their steps.

Msg #17 Indira Mercedes:

I think that change will be made with time. However, the "haves" and the "have nots" will always be there. Since the rich will never give the poor the opportunity to become as rich as them.

Msg #18 George Otte:

I see a fair amount of hope and a fair amount of despair, but it's all pretty general. I want each one of you to take a specific instance—not from Kozol's book but from your life—and explain how it supports your belief that things will or won't change. Don't do this here in InterChange but switch the computers off for a while and avail yourself of good old fashioned pen and paper.

****
End of conference CHANGE
****

The single most striking thing about this extended example is how it confirms something we could get from theory but don't need to—because as teachers it's the very air we breathe: students do not so much *get* ideas as *give voice* to them. The student's role is less to have the idea (as one has a vision or a flash of inspiration) than to articulate it for herself, to fashion it for her own purposes. This, in fact, is at the heart of what the "compose" in "composition" means. Just about all the students have to work with, in the way of ideas, is already out there, circulating in the general currency of thought. The key thing is to put these ideas into play. We may wince a bit at the declaration that "Good things comes to those who wait," but we're likely to encounter no less of a cliché (if better grammar) with, say, the McLaughlin Group. What the basic writers lack, fundamentally, is sophistication in knowing what spin or elaboration to give the idea, in showing sensitivity to what context they are to use it in—the sort of savvy we've come to call a sense of an audience.[3]

And why shouldn't they lack this? Institutionalized education obscures both the shaping (spinning, elaborating) role and the social nature of what's being shaped. In the student's experience, school is too often about *what* to think (and maybe just what to remember), not how to think. And though this *how*, this process of shaping ideas to fit contexts and purposes, is eminently social (not least of all as the manipulation of received wisdom), school can cut the students off from seeing that. Knowledge (I use the word loosely) is channeled to them through authorities, while their work, done in isolation, participates in a disconnection, a dis-integration, a de-composition of what it means to articulate ideas. (We acknowledge as much whenever we—or the textbooks we use—invite the students to *imagine* an audience, especially one socially constituted, genuinely interested. They need to conjure what they don't really have.[4])

A reintegration into collectively effected discourse, a chance to rejoin and respond is precisely what synchronous composition makes possible by making the audience vocal—and what is vocalized visible.

---

[3]Just how complex this issue of context and audience can be is no doubt best disclosed by Mikhail Bakhtin. It is, in fact, the "problem" in the "The Problem of the Text": "The transcription of thinking in the human sciences is always the transcription of a special kind of dialogue: the complex interrelations between the text (the object of study and reflection) and the created, framing context (questioning, refuting, and so forth) in which the scholar's cognizing and evaluating thought takes place" (106-07). The special problem for the inexperienced writer is that these "complex interrelations" are not registered experientially. The writing is discrete, radically cut off from a sense of participation in a larger "conversation." Reading and writing are compartmentalized, disconnected activities, forms of intake and output that have almost nothing to do with each other. For Mina Shaughnessy, for instance, no problem afflicting the basic writer was more critical than the problem that "when a student writes his papers, it does not occur to him that he is a writer producing reading; he remains a writer producing writing. This alienation of the student writer from the text robs him of important insights and sensitivities, for it is only when he can observe himself as a reader and imagine that a writer is behind the print of the page that he imagines his own situation as a writer" (223).

[4]Richard Ohmann famously railed against this sort of thing in *English in America*, encountering injunctions like "When we come to write we must decide who and what our audience is." "Decide?" Ohmann rejoined. "What kind of writing have 'we' undertaken to do, that we have not conceived an audience as integral to it?" (164).

The traditional writing classroom militates against genuine communication (instead, the exchange of papers becomes a kind of labor exchange in which grades are dispensed as pay or punishment for work done), but synchronous conversation is an in-your-face experience of verbal interaction. (By the way, I would argue that this is scarcely less true of the asynchronous discussions my students engage in these days on web-based discussion boards; there are trade-offs we make for the sake of any-time access: exposure to multiple viewpoints is less immediate and rapid-fire, even as reflection becomes more sustained—but these are differences of degree rather than kind.)

Let's look to the example to see what the exposure to multiple viewpoints means in concrete terms. The first one out of the gate is Paula Ruiz, who sounds a note of cautious optimism: "Changes take time. . . . I believe there is hope. . . ." But after only one intervening message—from Rhadames Delacruz about the need for determined political action—Paula seems to have changed her tone, her tune, her stance. Perhaps because Rhadames has reminded her that hope means faith not just in change but in agents of change, she says of "government people and rich people," "They don't care and I believe they will never care no matter what." She has, moreover, undercut the hope held out by gradual progress, the sort of "changes [that] take time," saying that "we need changes fast." By the time Ana Estrella (the fourth student contributing) says to Paula, "I agree with your first message," there is some question as to whether Paula herself agrees with it.

Who's in the better position to start writing at this point, Ana or Paula? Most of us would say that Paula is—although her initial statements, equivocatingly complex, also suggest she would be the one who would have more trouble beginning a formal essay on this subject. By contrast, there's real confidence, a ring of real conviction, about Ana's "Paula this is absolutly true." But there's also something a little too pat, too easy. For one thing, she seems to miss the two-edged quality of Paula's first message, which acknowledges both hope and obstacles to its realization: "The problem is that there are also people (those people who have the money and the power) who have hopes that these changes will not favor the poor and black people." So there is some question as to just what "this" is that Ana proclaims "absolutely true" about Paula's message. Subsequent posts from Ana suggest it is not the hope of change Paula spoke of but the resistance to change: "The poor people will never get the same rights that rich get. . . ." But Ana, too, has her ambivalence, and her last message has her searching for a solution, issuing a call to action: "Give the same kind of education to everyone." Ultimately, as the short discussion comes to its arbitrary end, Indira

Mercedes articulates a kind of synthesis of the positions Paula began with: "I think that change will be made with time. However, the 'haves' and the 'have nots' will always be there."

Indira's comment is not a culminating consensus by any means, but it is a microcosmic instance of how the dynamics of such a conversation work. We can see—what is more important, the students themselves can see—how their perspectives are at once shared and diverse, how they participate in one another. Rosa Chabla's "I agree government and rich people will never care no matter what" is one way to respond to Paula, but Taisha Knowles, like Rhadames, uses the same sense that "people who have the authority" aren't doing enough as reason to "fight for what we know belongs to our people," and Abdul Yusifu acknowledges the same resistance to change but sees hope that enlightened self-interest may overcome it, if only once "these people realize that we will all be affected by savage inequalities." Similar premises, in other words, lead to different conclusions, as do similar strategies. For instance, Rosa looks to the past as a support for pessimism—"If they did care they would have done something long ago"—whereas Hanh Van, in a point first made by Yanjun Zhou and later elaborated by Oy Ng, sees past victories, even little ones, as incremental causes for hope: "Believe it or not, this country have change a lot." Self-reliance advocates Indira Mercedes and Flor Barrientos even find the lack of clear grounds for hope a kind of reason not to despair, to "do our best" (Flor) and believe "hope can occur at any time" (Indira).

This whirlwind tour (by no means an exhaustive inventory) of the positions articulated in this short discussion makes several things clear. First, even from a small group, a number of positions can come, and it doesn't take special pleading to suggest they're all tenable, viable as points of argument—at least potentially (for they would need further elaboration and substantiation). Second, these positions are often interrelated, not least of all divergent and opposing ones; seeing them ahead of time invites students to know they're out there, use them as counters to or qualifications of their own points. Third, there's real ambivalence and uncertainty, which the online discussion helps to flesh out, complicate, sometimes perhaps even resolve. Though issues of daunting complexity can be expected to call up mixed feelings, generate perplexity or ambiguity, students tend to try to excise such things from their papers; these often productive lines of thought, which we've learned to label (and sanction) as "problematizing," are often seen as threats to coherence. Our valorization of the controlling idea and the consistent argument threatens to turn students into Johnny-One-Notes—but not in online discussion, a reduced-risk activity.

Of all these virtues, the last is, to my mind, the most important. Were I to ask the students, as I often have (and maybe did in this instance), who was right, their experience of one another's online discourse would give me my desired answer: "It depends. . . ." They've seen enough to know that as an experienced fact. And with some experiential inkling of what "it depends" on in their own cases and those of others, with some look, however glancing, at specific premises and strategies as well as the larger rhetorical issues of purpose, audience, context, they are primed to write, have in fact written themselves into a readiness to write. Having talked together, they have seen enough to say so much more than any one of them could say alone.

And so it went with the class. Students who had been taught (no, drilled) to organize papers in formulaic fashion began to see development not as a ticking off of reasons but a testing of perspectives. Messages appeared under their log-on names, investing them with an important sense of ownership but also a consciousness of other's positions, while competition to get one's thoughts out there increased fluency, and reading what others said included the instructive *experience* of error (as opposed to its dissective disclosure by the instructor). All these things gradually helped transform the students' writing, building in a special sense of audience, developed interactively, conversationally, in writing.

Important as this was for perennial "basic writers" verging on believing what they'd so often been told—that they "couldn't write"—this special sense of audience was made still more important by the looming exit exam. It was an extreme instance of what academic writing too often can become: a demand for writing that, apart from institutional strictures, lacks any clear purpose or context or audience. An invitation to comment pro or con on some major controversy—what causes violence in society, what shapes educational reform might take—it was evaluated so that what respondents said didn't matter; all that mattered was how they said it. And yet what they said *did* matter; it mattered enormously: without some sense of how to address a point (and, not so incidentally, an accompanying sense of how that response would be received), they would be hobbled from the start, perhaps even silenced. Knowing they had very little time to write, they would also know they had very little reason to. That had been the case for them all too often. One member of the class had failed this exam no less than nine times. But she passed—all but one of these nineteen "multiple repeaters" passed—and the difference this time was that online conversation, the collective composition. Students knew that equivocation could mean more development (not mere waffling), that uncertainty could be a hedge against seeming oversimplification, that conviction was more likely rooted in their premises than the "rightness" of their positions. Above all, they had some sense of how others took—and responded to—positions. Although no single concluding essay would blind a reader with its brilliance, they were all (save one) certified as competent. (All of the students in the example given were students who passed, and again, the instructor had no role in the scoring, which was done by two certified readers who cross-read the exams.)

Such an unprecedented pass rate for a group of chronic failures seemed to call for a "Stand and Deliver" moment, and there was one. Convinced that it was the computer-mediated group-thinking/writing that got them to that pass, I led a faculty development workshop on this use of InterChange, circulating transcripts including the one given here. A senior colleague, sure that the pass rate was too much of an anomaly, had the Chief Reader (the person supervising the scoring of the exams) "pull" these students' particular exams and deliver them to her office, where they were not so much reviewed as scrutinized. Shortly thereafter, this senior colleague pulled me aside to tell me that she had been properly amazed: the essays struck her as not only competent but unusually thoughtful—and long. (A standard tactic for students on this exit exam is to produce a carefully edited bare minimum as a means of playing it safe. But these students had filled their test booklets, in many cases cramping their writing or spilling onto the back cover to get it all in.)

Confident as I am that the use of computers made the decisive difference for these students, I'm not interested in making sweeping claims for computer use. Any claims worth heeding have to be clearly situated and delimited, anchored in specific practices. In this case, perhaps the best way of registering just what it is that computer use did is to draw on what my wife once told me long ago, back in the early 1980s, when I was first waxing enthusiastic about what could be done with computers. She said I shouldn't use (much less advocate using) computers to do what I could do just as well by other means (overhead projectors, photocopiers, paper exchanges, etc.); justifying the expense and expertise computers required, she said, should mean using computers to do what otherwise couldn't be done, at least not in the same way and to the same extent. Times have changed (perhaps even the experience of change has changed), but that still seems to me a good prescription, and not an easy bill to fill.

This class I've described is a case in point: the computer use may seem to approximate any number of things—class discussions, workshop groups, and the like. But there are crucial differences. Class discussions and even workshop groups usually have their holdouts: not everyone contributes (or is even mentally present). But in these computer-mediated discussions everyone was certifiably both witness and participant. What's more—in a way that once was rare but is much less so as those coming of age converse by "IM-ing"—the discussion was both written and immediate: if writing is thought on paper (or screen), this was such thought caught in flight. And that's important: this enactment of thinking, in written form, was prelude to more writing, so the process—and its utility—could be made visible to the students. Above all, this experience of writing was collective, interactive: students didn't write and then review or respond to each other's writing in separate stages. All the online writing was perceptibly what all writing is arguably: response to other writing. Authoring was answering. The author was also the audience and the audience was also the author. No other student constituency I can think of could have needed that more desperately, and no other medium I can think of could have provided it more effectively. In this instance, then, I think this highly touted, rather costly technology (Moore's Law notwithstanding[5]) did what we ought to call on it to do: something that needed doing and that needed to be done by just such means. Computer-mediated communication is a clumsy term but also a useful one: when we use it so the emphasis is on that last word, communication, we bring something to writing instruction that needs to be more in evidence, and we make it visible, palpable, consequential.

WORKS CITED

Bakhtin, M. M. "The Problem of the Text in Linguistics, Philology and the Human Sciences." In *Speech Genres and Other Late Essays*. Eds. Caryl Emerson and Michael Holquist. Trans. Vern W. McGee. Austin: U of Texas P, 1986. 103-31.

Brown, John Seely, and Paul Duguid. *The Social Life of Information*. Boston: Harvard Business School P, 2000.

Bruffee, Kenneth A. "What College Is For." Unpublished manuscript.

——. "What Goes on in Teaching Writing with Computer Supported Collaborative Learning." Unpublished manuscript. http://web.nwe.ufl.edu/cw2konline/bruffee/.

---

[5]Moore's Law (the prediction of Gordon Moore, Intel founder, that computer power will double whereas the cost will drop every year and a half) is not only defined, but the unreflective optimism it has spurred is taken to task in *The Social Life of Information* (14–15). That entire book, by the way, is very relevant to the argument here, particularly Chapter 5, which stresses how critical community support is for effective learning.

Coles, William and James Vopat. *What Makes Writing Good: A Multiperspective.* Washington, DC: Heath, 1985.

Kozol, Jonathan. *Savage Inequalities: Children in America's Schools.* New York: HarperCollins, 1991.

Ohmann, Richard. *English in America: A Radical View of the Profession.* New York: Oxford UP, 1976.

Shaughnessy, Mina P. *Errors and Expectations: A Guide for the Teacher of Basic Writing.* New York: Oxford UP, 1977.

9

MAKING RHETORIC VIABLE/ MAKING RHETORIC VISIBLE IN FIRST-YEAR COURSES

Rebecca Rickly
Texas Tech University

How can writing courses that utilize technology prepare students as responsible participants in a democratic society? What literacies will university and community citizens find necessary in this new century? How can we encourage/enable students to think critically and reflectively about their ideas and their representations? In answering these questions, this chapter describes an early course in which students wrote for publication on the Internet, "Writing the Information Superhighway," and analyzes one student's "webfolio" rhetorically for audience, purpose, context, delivery, navigation, style, and so on. The student's text is then analyzed visually, and a discussion of how "user-centered" a web text should be ensues. The student's subsequent revision of her entrance page is noted, and her growth in terms of how she presents herself visually and rhetorically is analyzed. The chapter concludes by suggesting that students who have successfully integrated computer technology and writing not only become critical, reflective consumers of information, but also become critical, reflective producers of information, technology, and rhetoric.

So, the Internet will, on the one hand, change everything and, on the other hand, change nothing.

—Tom Rocklin, "Do I Dare? Is It Prudent?"

Although I would probably locate myself firmly in the ubiquitous social construction camp, I have always believed in the power of *imitatio,* of learning through imitation. Not surprisingly, then, I see as the roots of my educational philosophy the integrated process of *imitatio,* production, reflection, and application found in the influential school of Isocrates.[1] While not nearly as popular today as his rival, Aristotle, Isocrates nonetheless shaped the look and feel of public education until the 1800s. His integrated, reflective approach had at its core a primary objective: to prepare citizens to participate responsibly in a democratic society. With the growth in various modes of the Internet as a means of information and communication, this society has expanded beyond the city-state that Isocrates had in mind, however. In this new era, the late age of print, what does it mean to be a responsible participant in a democratic society, and how can we foster such an attitude and aptitude in our writing classes? In this chapter, I outline how I addressed this philosophy in an early course involving both writing and the Internet, I analyze several selected pieces of writing, then in retrospect I illustrate how this course has, in a very real sense, helped to garner such a citizen. I conclude by surmising why this course worked and positing how the concepts might be re-applied in other contexts.

In the winter of 1996, Wayne Butler and I taught a first-year seminar entitled "Writing the Information Superhighway."[2] The course, which fulfilled a first-year writing requirement, was one of the first courses to require that students produce, study, and critique online writing. The class centered around a web-based syllabus (a "syllaweb"), and in this class we asked that students not only complete four writing assignments but also critique each other online. They were required to web their documents by using simple html coding. The final product

---

[1]Probably the two most important works of Isocrates for me have been *Antidosis* and *Against the Sophists.* To get an excellent take on Isocrates and his theoretical importance in today's screen-based cultures, see Kathleen Welch's *Electric Rhetoric.*

[2]I am grateful to have had the chance to work with Wayne Butler on this course, which he developed a year earlier and then he and I re-envisioned in terms of the then exploding Internet. Wayne and I co-taught two sections of this course, and although the original pages have been removed from the University of Michigan, they can still be found on my own site at http://english.ttu.edu/rickly/ecb/infohighway.html.

would be an online portfolio (a "webfolio") consisting of two "traditional" assignments that had been webbed (though the students had the option to insert links for the revised final product) as well as two hypertexts—a final project and a reflective self-evaluation in which they justified the grade they believed they deserved based on how well they'd met the criteria of the course. A course overview follows:

> The "information superhighway," an international conglomeration of computer networks, offers access to data through ftp, gopher and the World Wide Web and supports written communication through electronic mail and various forms of electronic conferencing. Those building, cruising, and studying the information superhighway predict it will have profound effects on society, education, and perhaps language itself by effectively altering our definitions of knowledge, reading, and writing. The purpose of this course is to explore and learn, through writing, the literacies of the various networks available to UM students for research and correspondence. Through a series of computer-mediated writing activities that encourage them to learn about and from the information superhighway, students will enter electronic discourse communities within the class, across the university, and across the nation. The activities will begin at the local level, using the university's local area networks, e-mail, and Mirlyn (UM's on-line library catalog), then move out to the Internet to correspond with other students and researchers on the superhighway, and then on to various gophers and Web sites to gather information.
>
> Since this course also fulfills the Introductory Composition requirement, we will be writing four major papers that will undergo a number of drafts, with each draft receiving critical feedback from peers, cybertutors, and the instructor.

By starting locally, we hoped to foster the literacies students would need to participate as citizens of the university; by expanding our assignments to include virtual communities, our intent was to help students reflect critically on the literacies necessary to participate responsibly as citizens in a larger global context.

Many First Year Composition (FYC) classes begin with the personal, move into information-based or analytic papers, and then finish with argumentation and research assignments. This progression from the personal to the objective, from the "known" to the "unknown" is both common and pedagogically defensible. In our course, we opted to make a similar progression, first by asking students to work collaboratively to learn about key terms, tools, and technologies in the local computing community, then to observe and analyze an online community, then to identify and research an issue concerning the Internet, and finally, to research a topic concerning their discipline. As a final exam, we asked that students engage in self-evaluation by reflecting on their participation in the classroom community, their evolution as students, and their evolution as technologists. They were to produce a hypertextual analysis of the above in which they included hypertextual support for why their participatory, writing, and technology skills warranted a particular grade in the course. The assignments build on each other in that each one requires more reflection, more technological expertise, more sophisticated analytical skills, and more research/support for their ideas. We supplemented these assignments with outside reading—Howard Rheingold's *The Virtual Community: Homesteading on the Electronic Frontier* and Theodore Roszak's *The Cult of Information: A Neo-Luddite Treatise on High-Tech, Artificial Intelligence, and the True Art of Thinking*—as well as frequent group work both in and outside of class, and online class discussions on email and InterChange, a local area networked chat-type program. Below are shortened versions of the actual assignments as they appeared on the syllaweb:

Project I: It's a Beautiful Day in the Neighborhood
The purpose of this first assignment is to work collaboratively to learn as much as we can about the key terms, tools, and parts of the U-M computing community.

During this project, you will be teamed up with a partner. Your team will receive from me a word, acronym, or phrase. Your team's task is to scour the campus, conduct a scavenger hunt, and otherwise do research on the word, acronym, or phrase you've received. Your goal is to learn all you can about it, collaboratively write a "brochure" that you will share with your classmates, and lead a demonstration for your classmates on how to do whatever it is you learned how to do.

Project II: Look Who's Talking Now
Write a 5-7 page analysis of an electronic conference of your choosing. You may choose an IRC channel, a listserv, a usenet group, a MOO, or a number of our InterChange sessions. Your analysis is an attempt to figure out the rules of the group (who talks, who "listens," particular netiquette), the group's function (what is discussed, what is learned), and the group's dynamics (how many different people participate over a given period of time, what is the relationship between males and females, what different kinds of roles are played by different types of people).

Project III: Writing About the Internet
The information superhighway excites many people about its per-
ceived positive impact on society, culture, politics, and education.
A number of critics of the information superhighway are concerned
with issues of economics, politics, class, gender, and so forth.
During this part of the course we will look at the Internet critically.

As we have already learned from reading *Virtual Communities* and
from the recent events here on campus, a number of controversial
issues arise as the information superhighway grows. For Project III,
we would like to you to identify one controversial issue, research it,
and write a 5-7 page argumentative essay about it.

**Project IV: Writing in the Disciplines on the Information
Superhighway**
So far this semester we learned various tools of the Internet, read
two books, wrote a discourse analysis of a virtual community,
learned how to conduct research on the World Wide Web, and
wrote an argumentative essay about some controversial issue concerning the information superhighway. For Project IV, we'd like
you to write a new kind of "research paper"—a bibliographic
hypertext—on some topic related to your major or the field in
which you intend to major.

Traditionally, the purpose of a research paper is to give students
an opportunity to explore some topic in depth. In most cases, a
research paper involves a broad and deep review of articles and
books about the topic. The writer then synthesizes those sources
into a clearly written, logically organized, and focused essay, one
that includes internal references or citations and a bibliography or
works cited page.

When we consider writing "research papers" in cyberspace, however, we are forced to question the traditional structures of the
research paper without eliminating the intellectual goals of providing opportunity to learn and practice research skills, reading critically, synthesizing source materials, and writing clearly.

Students entered the course with varying levels of writing and technological ability, and their responses to the assignments described above were
both fascinating and troubling. Whereas students today might enter college with at least some exposure to gaming, to "surfing" the web, and to
using e-mail and/or chat programs, many of our students were not only
technologically inexperienced, but some were initially almost hostile to
the idea of communicating online (as opposed to the security of the
more familiar face-to-face variety of communication). Too, students'

first attempts at web-based writing (writing beyond merely saving their word documents in html) were a bit disappointing; we had hoped that the primary mode of writing on the Internet—hypertext: would allow students to explore ways of "chunking" and presenting information so that it suited the medium, the purpose, and the various audiences inherent to publication on the web. However, students seemed to feel constrained by the traditional essay form. The breakthrough, for many, came when we asked students to brainstorm criteria by which they could analyze a web site, then to apply those criteria to four selected web sites. After a heated discussion about which ones were easier to navigate, more pleasing to the eye, had easy access to information, and so on, several students began applying similar criteria to their own emerging web presences. We took the calculated risk of using these students as examples for the two classes, and students began to recognize that representation of information on the Internet was, necessarily, much different than the more traditional academic representations they'd learned.

In the following sections, I'd like to take this idea—that of representation for different audiences, purposes, and media—a bit further by examining the complex self-evaluation of one of my students—Julie—and by looking at how she took what she learned and applied it to her own web pages (and work she'd done for others on the web) in subsequent years.

Again, because this course was one of the first to ask students to foray onto the Internet, the products may seem a bit less sophisticated than those generated by similar courses today. These students programmed their work "by hand" in "raw" html (using an editor such as BBEdit, rather than an application specifically for creating web pages such as DreamWeaver), and they were experimenting with what was, at the time, a relatively new medium. With that caveat in mind, I'd like to take us briefly through Julie's webfolio and linger a bit on her final hypertext—the self-evaluation.

Julie links to her webfolio from her home page. The link doesn't lead directly there, however; instead, an intermediary page opens, which gives the reader two options for viewing the webfolio: via the index, or via the self-evaluation.

From the start, then, Julie has acknowledged the rhetorical situation of the Internet: she is aware that her readers will have different needs, different desires, and different backgrounds, and these differences might make them want to navigate her pages differently. Some may be interested only in her final hypertext on women in engineering; others may wish to get a sense of Julie's personality by seeing how her self-evaluation guides readers through her work. She also includes a naviga-

WELCOME

You are about to enter my wonderful world of writing!!

But first, you have to make a decision. You can take a guided tour through my writings, by means of my self-evaluation, or you can go directly to my portfolio index.

Take your time and enjoy!!!

Return to Main Page

tional link back to her own main page at the bottom. Her obvious awareness of audience and the medium is not without problems, however. Although she does give her readers a choice, one I'm sure they appreciate, she commits the sin of overzealousness in both her web design and content, frequent among those who've just begun to put up their own words for public display on the Internet. In this seemingly small, innocuous page, she sets the tone for her readers in terms of what they can expect: her background is busy and unnecessary; she overuses formatting devices such as lines to separate titles, and so on; she plays around with font sizes; and she mixes very personal writing ("You are about to enter my wonderful world of writing!!"), complete with overuse of exclamation marks, with a more academic purpose (submitting her webfolio for a grade in the first-year seminar). Should this level of evaluation—that of design on an opening page, there primarily to aid in navigation—be part the overall assessment of Julie's webfolio? Because we did not teach page layout, design, and so on, we chose not to evaluate this aspect of the webfolios, yet I will argue that it should be. Consider, for a moment, the power of this seemingly small opening page: it is the first thing people see; it sets the tone, the expectation, for everything else that we will see, and we will have likely formulated some kind of expectation before we enter the webfolio or self-evaluation. The visual impact of this page is, in fact, extremely rhetorical. The fact that this page is not only public, but also its potential audience is limited to those with access to the Internet, makes this point stronger.

When we navigate Julie's webfolio via her self-evaluation, we bring up the following page:

This page, with its plain blue background, clearly delineated bulleted items, and traditional black text, while not fancy, conforms more closely to the rhetorical situation of the class: that of an academic requirement, which asks students to analyze their own work in a particular class according to course objectives. Although the background is a bit dark, for the most part it is clean, neat-looking, and easy to navigate, and it sets the scene rhetorically in terms of both content and design.

The information to which Julie links from this page follows the same basic design. She follows the same color scheme (with the addition of a rainbow divider), she experiments with intertextual links to work she produced for the class (including course project descriptions and objectives, her course projects, her e-mail exchanges, her participation in InterChange transcripts, peer critiques and how she used them, others' responses to her critiques, etc.), and she includes a complete set of navigational links at the bottom of each page. In these pages, she supports her argument well, for she describes her contributions and then links to specific incidents from the course that illustrate her assertions. In my final assessment of Julie's webfolio, I wrote that I wished she'd been a little less descriptive of what she did and a little more analytic, saying more about the significance of her work. For instance, the section "Assessment as a Critical Thinker," Julie ends with the following paragraph:

> I have also become a critical consumer of information. The research for my papers was conducted through the Internet.

> Unfortunately, not all of the information found on the Internet is reliable; therefore, I learned to critically read the information I came across and decide whether it was legitimate, or not. . . .

Although I may appreciate her acknowledgment that she has become a "critical consumer of information" as a result of this class, Julie never articulates specifically what her criteria were, how she came up with them, or how she applied them. What Julie learned, though, was important: the information online does not come with automatic legitimacy; she needed to determine the level of legitimacy by applying critical assessment criteria to it. But knowing what to do and knowing how to do it are two separate issues; although I was convinced that Julie had, in fact, learned what to do, I wasn't completely convinced she had learned how.

When I was first contemplating this chapter, I went back to Julie's home page so that I could re-examine her webfolio. I was surprised to find a new, much cleaner-looking home page than the one I remembered (the initial home page was much like her intermediary page to her webfolio: busy background, graphic overload); she had redone it, with much the same information, but with a much more traditional "home page" feel.

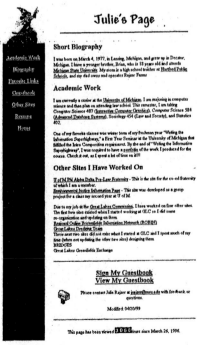

Although still incorporating graphics and language specific to Julie's own personality, the page was laid out in a traditional fashion: a navigational bar with links on the left, and on the right, sub-headings indicating personal information, academic information, and professional information. Below she places her guest book links, contact information, and a "hit" counter. The background is a textured white, the navigational bar blue, and the text traditional black with blue hotlinks. In addition to linking to her webfolio, she links to a fairly sophisticated online resume. A computer science major, Julie graduated from the University of Michigan in 1999 and is currently completing a law degree (specializing in intellectual property issues).

With her revised web page, Julie has physically acknowledged the rhetorical situation of visual representation for both specific audiences for her web pages—friends, teachers, potential employers—as well as for a more general public, who expect a more traditional, more professional look and feel. Information is still easily accessible, and her tone is, for the most part, consistent (except for when a bit of her initial overzealousness resurfaces as she encourages people to visit her online portfolio: "Check it out, as I spent a lot of time on it!!!"). She also lists and links to sites she has helped design, based on the experience she gained as a member of the first-year seminar course. Although it is similar to her first attempt at a home page, Julie has taken the time to examine the genre. She noted what worked, what she liked, and she imitated these conventions in her revisions. What this revised home page brought home to me when I viewed it for the first time was that Julie had matured rhetorically: she had not only learned what to do, but she had proven that she was, in fact, continuing to learn how to apply those ideas. She was moving beyond merely being a critical consumer of information to becoming a reflective, critical producer of information.

One of the questions Wayne and I struggled with in our courses was how much time we should spend teaching technology in a writing course. Because our course title was "Writing the Information Superhighway," we felt justified in teaching rudimentary skills associated with e-mail, chat, Internet research (both local and global), and basic web page creation (and asking that students research and become proficient in others on their own). We tried to locate these skills rhetorically, in terms of audience and purpose, but in retrospect, I believe that we overemphasized text and navigation; I don't think even we recognized the power of the visual in terms of legitimizing—or de-legitimizing—information on the web. Although not every first-year writing course will ask for students to construct hypertexts, for papers to be webbed, or for students to construct a home page or other web/public presence, we nonetheless need to be aware of the power of the visual in the overall rhetorical situation we focus on. Depending on the specific situation of our class, program, or institution, we need to teach technology accordingly. It should be located rhetorically, and we tried to do this in our courses, but it also needs to be presented—and critiqued—in a number of ways. Howard Gardner, the "father" of the idea of multiple intelligences, notes that "intelligences always work in concert" and that sophistication—and maturity—involve the melding of these multiple intelligences, or different ways to comprehend the world. Ann Marie Barry goes beyond merely agreeing that we need to comprehend and participate in visual literacy; she maintains that we must strive towards visual intelligence, "a holistic integration of skilled verbal and visual reasoning. . . the utilization of the visual in abstract thought" (6). It's likely that students will leave college and be required to participate in some form of technological production, and this kind of integration will be vital for their success. Robert Johnson argues that we need to put users—those who actually use/interact with technology—at the center, interacting with the design, development, implementation, and maintenance of technology, rather than serving as a mere end for a programmer's knowledge. This philosophy seems to be in concert with the pedagogical notion of the social construction of knowledge, but it places a huge responsibility on the shoulders of the user/participant in that to interact successfully at the center, the user/participant must *take responsibility* in terms of learning enough about the various components he or she is working with to have a successful, productive interaction. As the rhetorical situations our students are placed in—both in and outside of school—become increasingly complex, part of our job as writing teachers is to foster this kind of responsibility, these intelligences—visual, rhetorical, and otherwise—so that students leave with experience in a "rhetoricized space," becoming "active participant[s] who can negotiate technology in use and development" (Johnson, 33). Students must feel comfortable being "critical consumers" as well as producers: of information, of technology, and of rhetoric. We can do this through an integrated process of examination, imitation, reflection, and production in our classes, but we need to look beyond traditional forms of representation—and we need to spend more time examining the representations themselves.

WORKS CITED

Barry, Ann Marie Seward. *Visual Intelligence: Perception, Image, and Manipulation in Visual Communication.* New York: SUNY Press, 1997

Gardner, Howard. *Frames of Mind: The Theory of Multiple Intelligences.* Basic Books: New York, 1983

Johnson, Robert R. *User-Centered Technology: A Rhetorical Theory for Computers and Other Mundane Artifacts.* New York: SUNY Press, 1998.

Rheingold, Howard. *The Virtual Community: Homesteading on the Electronic Frontier.* New York: HarperPerennial, 1993. [The entire text is available online at htttp://www.well.com /user/ hlr/vcbook/index.html.]

Rocklin, Tom. "Do I Dare? Is It Prudent?" *The National Teaching and Learning Forum.* Vol. 10, No. 3, 2001. <http://c+l.stanford. edu/teach/NTLF/v10n3/techped.htm>.

Roszak, Theodore. *The Cult of Information.* New York: Pantheon Books. 1994.

Welch, Kathleen. *Electric Rhetoric: Classical Rhetoric, Oralism, and a New Literacy.* Boston: MIT Press, 1999.

10

CRITICAL THINKING IN THE DIGITAL AGE

Joan Latchaw
University of Nebraska-Omaha

This chapter describes the function of an online group discussion in a second semester first-year English course at North Dakota State University. The structure of the course required students, through cultural diversity and research projects, to think critically: construct a position by analyzing, challenging texts, theorizing, and drawing conclusions. The analysis of the Norton Connect discussion session tests how notions of critical thinking, social construction, and process pedagogy operate in practice. For instance, the best dialogue, resembling mini-arguments, included strong positions supported by evidence and reasoning. This analysis convinced me that online discussions are likely to be more successful if conceived as an intermediate phase of the writing/thinking process.

Critical thinking has always been central to my mission as a teacher. My interest originated in John McPeck's cognitive approach, which asserts that critical thinking includes methodology (research, statistics, ethnography) strategies (problem solving, decision making, theorizing), and techniques (spectrometry, argument): skills informed by their intellectual foundations. Each of these components is discipline-specific; nursing relies heavily on decision making, physics on problem solving, and art on summary, analysis, and evaluation. As a composition specialist, I define critical thinking as the ability to construct a position by speculating, forming alternative views, theorizing, drawing conclusions, and offering solutions or other visions. In the ideal situation, I want students to challenge texts, extend them, investigate their assumptions and the author's motivation—higher order skills, difficult to achieve in beginning writing courses.

At the same time, I value collaboration and negotiated meaning, values emerging from social construction theory and composition studies. Social constructionists argue that knowledge construction and learning occur in particular cultural, historical, or social communities. In philosophy, Richard Rorty argues for a new hermeneutics, that "understands the notion of culture as a conversation" (319). Knowledge construction, within a culture, is an open-ended conversation, whereby "human beings [are] generators of new descriptions rather than beings one hopes to describe" (378). In composition studies, Kenneth Bruffee's "Social Construction, Language, and the Authority of Knowledge" theorizes that "we generate knowledge by justifying those beliefs [about physical reality] socially" (777). And in "Collaborative Writing and the 'Conversation of Mankind,'" Bruffee demonstrates how writing tutors and tutees negotiate knowledge through dialogue. Each participant contributes a particular expertise that the other lacks. Proponents of these theories believe students learn best through a process approach, becoming the focus of their own activities. However, teachers must carefully construct and guide such activities. Because I believe writing is best learned through reading and responding to challenging texts, my students enter into ongoing "conversations" with those texts as well as the ones they and their peers write and revise. By thinking critically about both reading and writing, students can begin to position themselves—through argument, which might include personal experience.

As always, these principles laid the foundation for my English 111 course at North Dakota State University (NDSU). Although NDSU is a land grant institution committed to a general education core curriculum, it emphasizes engineering, agriculture, and the sciences. At the time of this study, the university had recently mandated English 111 as a required core course—with considerable and continuing resistance from other departments. Students, completing this second composition course in a two-semester sequence, would produce a substantial research paper and a shorter paper on cultural diversity—two projects that are not necessarily related.

My use of the Norton Connect program (a word processor, online grammar book, and discussion forum) was predicated on the notions that computer technology should be integral to the work of the course, and pedagogy should drive technology. The students had learned and used Connect collaboratively for examining arguments: fallacies, invalid reasoning, and insufficient evidence. In the sixth week of the semester course, having previously analyzed sections from E. D. Hirsch's *Cultural Literacy* and pieces by Stephen J. Gould and Elaine Morgan, students wrote summaries of M. Scott Momaday's "The Way to Rainy Mountain" and Marianna De Marco Torgovnick's "On Being White, Female, and Born in Bensonhurst." In preparation for a formal essay, students discussed one of the two readings in small Connect groups.

In analyzing these small group discussions, I wanted to test how my notions of critical thinking, social construction, and process pedagogy actually operate in practice. Being a pragmatist, I wanted my students to make productive and efficient use of technology, to consider the computer as a "machine for thinking." I guided students toward this philosophy by preparing them in advance of the discussion. Students would first write summaries of the readings, by which I meant "not just paraphrasing and quoting, but isolating the important issues and themes, and intentions/purpose of the writer." I provided a sample summary that I posted within the Connect program. By having students select significant issues and speculate on authorial intention, I meant to prime the critical thinking process. Students, I reasoned, would come to the lab believing the computer is a machine to think with.

Although online discussions in academic settings usually include elements of play, they often revert to idle chitchat. I have seen many long MOO logs, discussion threads, and e-mail exchanges that hardly seem worth the effort, in terms of intellectual engagement. I was eager to discover what computer technology prevents, obscures, or limits and what it reveals, aids, or enables. Keeping these questions open prevents teachers from making utopian assumptions or drawing despairing conclusions. To reinforce a serious dialogue, I asked students in each group to address one question for at least an hour. Each person would contribute ideas and receive a grade based on his or her participation. I promised to poke in on each group's conversation.

The five questions produced varying levels of critical discussion. However all groups, to my surprise, stayed on task for the entire period (1 hr. 15 min.), diligently asked each other critical questions, and tried to reach new insights. The three questions including Momaday (importance of scenic visions, shifting perspectives, and comparison with Torgovnick) were more successful than the two devoted only to Torgovnick (essay as a class or personal narrative and thematic identification).

My analysis focuses on Group 5's question: "In both the essays (Momaday and Torgovnick), there seems to be a kind of longing, obsession, concern, or desire to recapture the past. What do you think motivates that desire (or any other term you wish to label it)?"

The best dialogue, resembling mini-arguments, demonstrated positions supported by evidence and reasoning. In response to Group 5's question, Danita writes:

> Momaday appreciates his grandmother's people and their way of life as he remembers the summers when the "aged visitors" (82) would come. Even his grandmother and her people were concerned with the past. On page 82, paragraph 13, Momaday says, "They were an old council of warlords, come to remind and be reminded of who they were." I think they want to remember the past because as time goes on you learn a lot from your past. If you remember the past you can make sure you don't make the same mistakes you made in the past.
>
> The same holds true for Togovnick's essay. She looks at her past and sees how her neighborhood classified people as either insiders or outsiders. The outsiders were treated badly. This is proven by the fact that three black men were attacked by a group of whites because they were walking through the neighborhood. (179). By realizing this is what happens when a group of people feel they are superior, Togovnick learns that it isn't right to say some people belong and others don't. Even if someone doesn't belong she learned that she wouldn't treat them badly.

This post was remarkable in a number of ways. Although it was not my original intention to teach rhetorical tropes, the response resembles a comparison/contrast essay, which begins to explore two complex themes: identity (Momaday) and insider versus outsider (Torgovnick). Admittedly, the first section focuses more on learning from the past, a theme that offers fewer possibilities for extensive examination. However, buried in the middle of the first paragraph is an intriguing quotation, which suggests a unique, and perhaps surprising, relationship between respected elders, "warlords," and others in the community. That these venerated ancestors must themselves be reminded of their roles is rich material. The student might explore and begin voicing insights about Native American values and standards. (Note that the parenthetical citation in this paragraph marks quotations and paraphrases Danita uses as evidence for *observations* about Momaday's past—information typical of summary. At the end of that paragraph, she speculates on *reasons* for recalling the past—so as not to repeat it. Although this idea is a commonplace, it is moving toward argument.)

The second section is more thoroughly developed because the insider/outsider theme is more clearly articulated. It's clear that Danita is beginning to think about this response as an essay. This paragraph marks a comparison/contrast trope with three reasoning-type claims ("She . . . classified people," "By realizing," "Even if"). The only citation she uses supports the outsider theme. Here we see the heart of an argument that, I will argue later, was stimulated by intellectual exchanges similar to those on some academic listservs—where colleagues explore issues and extend another's analysis. These exchanges resemble writing more than speech. Thus, I saw Group 5's online discussion as both productive and efficient.

The Torgovnick mini-essay is an auspicious beginning for a full-length academic essay. The paragraph might be teased out into a two-part section: the first explaining the outsider's role and the second the insider's. Danita has only to examine her critical thinking markers ("This is proven by," "By realizing this," "Even if") as a way to develop the insider section. As her teacher, I could easily point out these cues to stimulate the revision process through which an internal two-part structure might be developed. And because focus and organization are primary considerations in a composition class, Danita has efficiently and productively profited from the online discussion.

When students began forming these mini-arguments, they were preparing for the next task—planning, organizing, and composing the paper. I understood successful writing in this upcoming assignment would mean the ability to create and defend a position about an ethnic, racial, or gender issue—using the assigned readings. The paper, reflecting the larger goals of the course, should represent a logical mind working out the complexities of the situation.

Group 5's collaboration signaled critical minds at work and interestingly generated the smallest number of pages and responses (22 total). The length of individual posts varied from 3/4 of a page to more than a page of double-spaced text (when printed). These findings were somewhat surprising because the question was more complex, requiring a comparison of the two essays and a number of issues: obsession, concern, desire. Sixteen of the 22 posts began with a claim in the first or second sentence, and most of them directly addressed the longing or desire to recapture the past. The claims were generally *informed* opinions based on careful examination of the two essays. And in many cases, students provided "good reasons" for their observations, perspectives, and positions. I speculated that this group's performance might be explained by a variety of factors: that the activity was graded and students took it seriously, that these were strong readers, writers, and thinkers, and that the discussion was useful in composing the formal paper.

One student, Jill, observed that "in both essays there is a sadness, because both Momaday and Torgovnick have lost a part of themselves from their childhood." What follows is another mini-essay: three well-developed paragraphs, exploring the origins of the sadness each writer experienced, the isolation from family and culture, and the loss of identity and memory. The "essay" concludes by discussing why Momaday had more difficulty releasing the past than Torgovnick.

What is significant about this post and others like it is its force as an argument, recognizable by the strong claims and evidence from Momaday's and Torgovnick's essays—the grounds upon which the student interprets, speculates and draws conclusions. My task was to identify which claims could be transformed into powerful theses. Trading the past for the future, experiencing internal and external conflict, or comparing the degree to which each writer became an outsider would make excellent topics for an extended essay.

The five posts preceding this one addressed identity, nostalgia and appreciation for the past, beliefs and values, and the outsider versus insider theme. For instance, the very first post begins, "I think that in both the essays the motivation to recapture the past is so that the narrators of each essay can figure out who they are. . . . Torgovnick is concerned with her past because it was a time where she wasn't free to be herself." The fourth short post reveals how returning to the past isn't possible: "I think that Torgovnick realizes something when she goes back to her old neighborhood. . . She is not accepted because when she left her neighborhood she became a different person through influences outside of place she knew before she left." A third student extends this idea in the fifth post, "While growing up in the community, she [Torgovnick] was treated like an insider and things were simple." The use of the word "insider" may have signaled a theme. Yet another student, Jill, responded to her classmates' ideas, which she likely integrated into her insider/outsider theme. In the seventh post, her mini-essay, she says about Torgovnick, "Even though [she] didn't necessarily agree with this attitude, she knew that once she left her old neighborhood, she would never be allowed back in. She would be treated as an outsider . . . ."

The second post signals another theme of social and cultural values. It states that Momaday "feels that the world his grandmother knew had a strong set of beliefs and values." Jill expands on beliefs and values (in her mini-essay) when she states that Momaday's grandmother "came to believe in christianity, but didn't totally give up her belief in the Sun Dance Doll. She gave up much of her way of life because of the white man's interference." It is likely that Jill was able to extend (build upon) these threads that her classmates had begun to tease out.

What impressed me was the students' willingness and ability to "think alongside" their peers. They extended ideas from earlier posts and offered alternative or additional reasons for their opinions. These moves represented the kind of critical thinking that is the bedrock of my teaching practices. Close to midterm, I was satisfied with isolating themes, analyzing, speculating, considering alternative views, and drawing conclusions.

Clearly, Group 5's interaction demonstrates negotiated meaning. This process occurred without intervention, as two other groups needed my help. Through careful, considerate responses to each other, students uncovered significant themes. In the following exchanges, an argument begins to develop. Danita gave three reasons why Momaday might want to recapture the past: to determine his identity, discover current patterns, and return to a simpler and happier time (because of his grandmother's influence). The next post picks up on the grandmother's influence: "N. Scott Momaday feels that the world his grandmother knew had a strong set of values and beliefs. I think he wants the present time to have such a strong set of beliefs and values." Jason built on Danita's comment on the grandmother, but took it in another direction. "They [Momaday and Torgovnick] are both motivated by the feeling that the past has something to offer that the present time does not." This idea is more complicated than just stating we learn from the past. Jason explains *why* this is the case and given more time and space could expand on the grandmother's values and beliefs.

Even the more silent students gained insights although, in some cases, it took nearly the whole hour to manifest. Tony "spoke" only a few times, primarily toward the end of the hour. He seems to have synthesized the conversations about Momaday's and Torgovnick's experiences but comes to a different conclusion than many of the others. "I think the past signifies something different for each writer." For Momaday it was the desire to preserve his native culture "in the modern world" and for Torgovnick it was a "feeling of entrapment." To Torgovnick "the past signifies what her life might of been like, If she hadn't left." It appears that Tony was thinking silently about these issues and perhaps needed more time to articulate a position. Taking a cue from the other participants, he may have realized that asking a simple question or making an idle comment, which did not reflect a reasoned response, was less desirable than waiting to form a real contribution. After all, I had emphasized that quality contributions would determine the grade.

I concluded that focusing on identifiable themes throughout the entire hour made the session fruitful. The discussion was productive because students were learning the strategies and skills they would need in composing their essays: focusing, analyzing, interpreting, and drawing conclusions.

Analyzing the group discussions revealed personal dynamics of social construction—specifically building a collaborative community, which developed within most of the groups. Participants queried each other for answers, asked for feedback when they put forward a theory, and built upon each others' ideas. The members of Group 5 seemed confident about their opinions, notable by the extended use of "I think" and the careful use of evidence and reasoning. They built on each others' *arguments*—without teacher prompting or intervention. This is the kind of student-centered learning teachers dream about. I suspect students understood, because of previous online discussions, that collaborative work was not for idle chat or even intellectual, playful chat. Rather it developed within a structured context and assigned topic, both of which I provided.

As opposed to Group 5, Group 1 illustrates a less confident but dogged willingness to reach group consensus in addressing their question: "Momaday spends a good part of his essay describing the landscape of Oklahoma, Canada, South Dakota, other plains states, etc. Of what importance are these scenic visions to the *meaning* of the essay?" Jodi addresses David,

> David,
> So now you think he didn't write the essay about his grandmother. Well, I agreed with you that it was about his grandmother and now I will agree with you again. Momaday probably feels left out because he didn't get to experience the true traditions of the Kiowas. He is expressing his feelings by describing the land to us so he can feel like he is more centered around the Kiowas.

This post represents a collaborative effort because Jodi supports David, by adding to his argument, with additional evidence and reasoning. She also relates to David on a more personal level than the students in Group 5. This stylistic difference might suggest that students develop community according to different levels of intimacy. Or their perception of the task may have been different: a discussion to improve their

---

[1]Readers interested in learning more about how to sequence assignments along the lines discussed here are encouraged to read David Bartholomae and Anthony Petrosky's *Facts, Artifacts, and Counterfacts* (Boynton/Cook: 1986).

understanding of the essay, rather than the beginning of a formal paper. Whereas Group 5's exchange was quite formal and literary, Group 1's dialogue was informal and more interactive. (The posts were generally quite short, 1-5 lines.) Students seemed more comfortable, not proclaiming their opinions, but testing them out. David says, "The landscape he [Momaday] describes reminds him [Momaday] of his grandmother and of how his people used to live. It is almost as if the land can tell the story of his people. What do you think?" In this case, the exchange resembles both speech and writing. It begins with a summary statement, explores the implications, and then asks for feedback. David is beginning to think critically, though hesitantly.

The next post is a short but meaty paragraph showing how "scenic visions" symbolize Native American beliefs and cultural values. David then asks whether Momaday ever explained the origin of the name Rainy Mountain. David is learning by testing out the waters very judiciously. This time he offers an opinion, but uses a question mark. "I think that the spirit of the people lives on through the land. It is as if his grandmother will always be with him. Maybe when he describes the land he is actually describing his grandmother?" Here is a student who may not have the confidence to speak out in a whole class discussion, but develops courage through small group interaction, marked by some strong opinions, some queries, some speculations, and general good will. Jodi praises David in a later post, "You have a good point David, that he may be describing his grandmother when he describes the land. He says some beautiful things about the land and they could actually be all about his grandmother." I would encourage these students to search Momaday's text for other illustrative excerpts and then analyze the effect of this dual discourse.

After this expression of praise (perhaps because of it), David offers a personal reaction, "I like the little story of Devil's Tower in Wyoming and the Big Dipper. I have heard this story before . . . . I get this feeling in the summer when I am working on the farm. What do you think, is this true?" Although he is tentative in his responses, David now reveals himself as a reader who knows something about literature, who feels more comfortable expressing personal taste, and who is ready to join an academic conversation.

Students were becoming invested in Momaday, interested in ways I hadn't seen in traditional classroom settings. One student who posted only twice in 25 minutes said, "His book would be interesting to read for the very descriptive writing and the tremendous feeling he puts into his writing." Although the student didn't post for another twelve minutes, his interest suggests he was a silent participant, that he had, in fact, been engaged in the dialogue. Three minutes later another student asked if anyone thought Momaday would ever return to Rainy Mountain. In my twelve years of teaching, I cannot recall a single instance of a student exclaiming anything like, "I'm interested in Momaday's idea of the land representing his grandmother and her beliefs," then turning to a classmate and asking, "What do you think?" Teachers typically must prompt their students to support their opinions, provide sufficient textual evidence, and justify their arguments with further reasoning. Often students resist, insisting on their rights to believe—just because. The issue, then, becomes a power struggle between the student and the teacher. However, in most of the online discussions, students either provided reasons on their own or after requests for clarification from their peers. Learning, then, was a friendly but rigorous exchange, whereby they depended on each other, another benefit of collaborative communities (although this is not always the case).

This analysis convinced me that online discussions are likely to be more successful if conceived as an intermediate phase of the writing/thinking process. Summaries, reader responses, or reflective journals should begin "priming the intellectual pump"—for the next stage. The online discussions might naturally lend themselves to full-length essays, by developing one of the mini-essays. Or each group discussion might be analyzed for features that produce fruitful collaborative dialogue, or in my terms, critical thinking. Similar analysis of a traditional classroom might seem invasive (tape recorder or video) and would be labor intensive to transcribe.

On a more affective level, these online conversations clearly have different functions for different students. Some interact more verbally, some silently. Some brainstorm ideas, apparently synthesizing information slowly. Others are able to synthesize more quickly, producing an argument on the fly. (Some students develop similar strategies when writing essay exams for various classes. In this case, successful essays typically provide succinct, direct answers, which provide claims and "good reasons.")

A few others, one group in particular, gained little benefit from the hour's work. I discovered, too late, that the students had little background knowledge of the Bensonhurst incident. Thus, their inability to understand the essay sufficiently killed the conversation. However, it wasn't until I studied the transcript that I understood the severity of the problem. Thus, teachers can learn about their own teaching strategies. They might learn how to form more effective groups, perhaps by assessing personality types, learning styles, and intellectual abilities. They might learn more about which environments are more effective for particular tasks.

From these observations and reflections, I would like to further interrogate my conclusions about teaching with technology. I have speculated that Group 5 was more successful because they interpreted the discussion as a more formal composing task; because they understood the reading better; because they valued high grades; and because they are stronger students. In terms of critical thinking, the students accomplished a great deal, in demonstrating some analytic and interpretive skills. However, they did not challenge ideas or texts or read against the grain. In future classes, I might use the technology later in the term to develop those strategies.

Though I have claimed the technology was integral to the work of the course, was it necessary? In a whole class discussion, rarely do all students contribute. In the online groups, participation was required. Shyness prevents speech, according to some of my best students; admittedly some reticent students do better in small classroom groups. Others in the online groups were reluctant to participate, but praise seemed to mitigate that difficulty. Furthermore, monitoring classroom discussions is difficult because the teacher can't be everywhere at once and students are often intimidated and silenced when the teacher lurks. Students may not know when the teacher is lurking in online discussions. Students can also ignore teacher comments without retribution. Discourse analysis comparing online and traditional classroom discussions would reveal which types of utterances occur in both environments, which are specific to each, and under which circumstances.

One could argue that students could compose mini-essays in a traditional classroom. But how? Certainly people create texts in a computer lab, but generally composition students write in drafts and collaborate in peer review sessions. Teachers commonly conceive of discussing and composing as two separate processes. I've found that giving students time to write in longhand during class is rarely productive, with the exception of essay exams. Either they can't concentrate and sit idle or they compose very slowly and unproductively. I have never seen a mini-essay like Group 5's produced in fifteen minutes or even an entire period. When students discuss in traditional classrooms, they rarely take notes; if they do, the notes are brief. I have seen little evidence that students in traditional classroom activities have learned to "think along with" their peers, synthesize the knowledge, and put it into a written form—productively and efficiently.

I am reminded of my own work, thinking alongside colleagues in a MOO as we prepare a joint class, brainstorm ideas for a conference presentation, or collaborate on an article. I reflect on our critical thinking practices: coming "to the table" already familiar with certain texts and ideas; thinking in advance about our opinions, attitudes, and beliefs; being open-minded to other positions; leaving the session with ideas (we archive) or with rough text; and finally assigning tasks for the next stage in the process.

Though my students are inexperienced, they have also demonstrated some facility to think and write alongside their peers. Admittedly, they have not achieved some of the critical thinking skills I most admire. They have not challenged the text or each others' ideas. They have not read against the grain. However, some did extend each others' ideas, express informed opinions, and begin composing on the fly. Those strategies might be developed later in the term or in a higher level course. I believe that with careful sequencing of assignments and activities, preparing and guiding students, and imagining the computer as a thinking machine, teachers can help students become stronger readers, writers, and thinkers.

WORKS CITED

Bruffee, Kenneth. A. "Collaborative Learning and 'The Conversation of Mankind.'" *College English* 46 (1984): 635-52.
——. "Social Construction, Language, and the Authority of Knowledge." *College English* 48 (1986): 773-90.
McPeck, John. *Teaching Critical Thinking: Dialogue and Dialectic.* New York: Routledge, 1990.
Rorty, Richard. *Philosophy and the Mirror of Nature.* Princeton: Princeton UP, 1979.

11

JEREMIAH'S GIFT
The Stained Glass Computer

Carrie Shively Leverenz
Texas Christian University

This chapter explores the challenge of evaluating and responding to web-based student writing when the student's expertise with computers is greater than the teacher's. In a graduate seminar titled "Cyberliteracy," one student chose to present his research on postmodernism and computers in the form of a help file that made extensive use of linking, images, and an informal authorial voice. In addition to challenging traditional academic forms, a logical outcome of the course focus on how computers affect literacy, this student's text challenged the teacher to rethink her criteria for evaluating graduate student writing as well as her role as guide.

The first time I taught a graduate seminar in cyberliteracy, I was an assistant professor at a large PhD–granting institution in the Southeast where most graduate students in the English department pursue a specialization in creative writing or literary studies, with only a few students in the rhetoric and composition track. Although I was originally hired to direct a writing center, I was soon asked to supervise two networked computer classrooms. The challenge of preparing TAs to teach in those classrooms led me to the computers and writing community, where I discovered a wealth of research, theory, and pedagogy that I had never been exposed to as a graduate student. By offering a seminar in cyberliteracy, I thought, I'd be introducing graduate students to issues and texts that I had come to believe were crucial to the future of English studies. The course also gave me the chance to assign all those books on my "must-read" list.

For this new course to "make" its enrollment, I knew I had to attract students with a variety of interests in literature, creative writing, and composition. I thus made it clear in the list of course requirements that students' final projects could take a number of possible forms:

> A final project, subject to the approval of the instructor, which may take the form of an extended critical paper, the design of a web-based writing or literature course (accompanied by critical commentary), hypertext fiction (also accompanied by a critical reflection), etc.

My emphasis on "critical commentary" and "critical reflection" reveals that I was concerned about the *academic* content as well as the *creative* content of students' projects. Although I granted students creative license with the form of their projects, I expected them to engage in the intellectual work of a traditional seminar paper—to articulate a significant question, to position that question within an ongoing conversation in the field, to formulate an argument, and to present authoritative evidence.

Given the subject matter of the course, it only made sense to include the writing of hypertext as a viable option. However, because I had never written hypertext myself (my syllaweb for this class was my first, and I had used a university-created template), I was not in a position to teach my students *how* to write hypertext. What, then, would be my teacherly role? Typically when I work with graduate students on their writing, I am concerned both with helping them accomplish their goals and with guiding their entrance into an established disciplinary discourse. Students who chose to write hypertext were thus in a challenging position: as our course readings had shown us, the rules of academic hypertext were still being written and as an inexperienced writer of this discourse, their teacher was of little help. I had not anticipated how graduate student–authored hypertext would challenge both my assumed authority regarding the teaching of academic writing as well as my assumptions about what good academic writing is and might be.

Certainly one might worry, as I did, that I foolishly had entered water far deeper than I knew, and indeed, I would list many advantages to having come to that class as a computers and composition expert. I also recognize that had my students not been as savvy as Jeremiah and his classmates were, I might not have chosen to write this chapter. However, I also believe that inviting students to do a kind of writing I was not an expert in had multiple benefits. Having to create a structure for their ideas required students to develop skills of invention and rhetorical analysis not typically required when using already established forms. In addition, as students struggled to invent appropriate forms to express their ideas about cyberliteracy, they were doing what they were writing about. Working with new forms also led students to question the assumed benefits of traditional genres, helping them to see how genres both enable and constrain meaning.

In particular, writing hypertext gave students the opportunity to question the relationship between form and effects in traditional academic argument. Rather than mapping out and developing a linear, hierarchically organized text, students experienced first-hand the challenges to authorial control that Jay Bolter, George Landow, and Michael Joyce all tout as benefits of hypertext writing. By constructing (breaking down?) arguments into nodes with multiple links, students were giving up control over how their arguments would be read. Multiple readings became possible; the reader—I, the teacher—became a contributing author of sorts in as much as I chose which links to follow and created connections, often associative rather than linear, between the various elements of their arguments.

Jeremiah's writing, especially his course project, "The Stained Glass Computer," exemplifies all of these benefits. Jeremiah was the only student of the twelve enrolled whom I didn't know from past classes or TA training. When queried, he admitted that he had started an MA in creative writing a few years earlier, and then he had taken a break to work for a while. He also confessed to having had some trouble fitting back in—no one knew him, and no one seemed willing to supervise his thesis (a novel). Although I didn't know what to expect from Jeremiah, he impressed me as one of those students who said little in class but seemed to be taking it all in. Jeremiah first made himself known as a writer when he presented a report on Dinty Moore's *The Emperor's Virtual Clothes*. Instead of e-mailing the report to me so that I could add it to the class bibliography, Jeremiah posted a notice to the class web board:

Tuesday's presentation
Now you can get the jump on basically everything I have to say
about Dinty Moore's hypeless classic "the Emperor's Virtual
Clothing." I wrote a webpage around it: http://tlh.fdt.net/
~jdm9717/cl_moore0.htm
enjoy,
-jeremiah

Even though the subject of the course was cyberliteracy and we
had already read several books on hypertext theory, it was still a surprise to click on Jeremiah's URL and be led to a web page with the title,
"The Average User Undressed," printed against a red feathery background. On the left was a column of yellow text against black, and on
the right, an image of a Renaissance-era male wearing only a crown and
a strategically placed black box. Jeremiah's review did everything the
other students' reviews had done—it summarized, it commented, it critiqued—but it did more: it wowed; it entertained.

Jeremiah's hypertext book review radically changed the dynamics of the class. As a result of his text, Jeremiah was transformed from a
quiet creative writing student whom nobody knew into a role model for
avant garde scholarly writing. By writing hypertext, he revised his ethos
as a writer. His classmates immediately began competing to see who
could create the most impressive hypertext response journals and book
reports, spending hours on assignments that would have taken much
less time if written conventionally. Several students chose to create their
first-ever hypertexts as their final projects for my class. In their eyes, it
became a limitation to produce only a well-written traditional scholarly
essay. They were persuaded by the course readings and by Jeremiah's
performance to want to do more—to write something they could
admonish readers to "enjoy."

Although I'm sure students learned important things about the
challenges of both conceptualizing and producing hypertext (all of them
complained about how long it took, even as they acknowledged they
chose to put in this extra time), I believe they were motivated as much
by the effect their use of links and images had on readers as they were
by the ways in which hypertext allowed them to construct more complex arguments and invite the reader into the meaning-making process.
Theorists may emphasize the degree to which hypertext calls into question the agency of the author, but ironically, in my students' experience,
hypertext invited them to feel their agency more dramatically than if
they were writing in more conventional forms.

As a reader of their work, I especially liked the element of surprise—opening students' web sites was like opening a gift. Like the stu-

dents in the class, I found myself highly engaged by the *look* of their texts—the color and the images—and I was intellectually stimulated by the associative nature of their writing, by the challenge of following students' representations of their thought processes in the form of links. But when called on to respond and evaluate such texts, I felt a conflict between my unabashed admiration for my students' web-writing ability and my obligation to critique their work. First there was the practical difficulty of responding to a text that did not allow me to insert myself into the margins and between the lines. But I also felt less authority to do so. Granted, there were things I didn't like about students' webbed texts; like most writing in early drafts, ideas were often fuzzy and not adequately developed, even if the visual presentation of them was clever and engaging. But hadn't the rules changed? Didn't "clear" and "well developed" mean something different in this medium? Didn't images and other elements of the visual presentation "count" as part of the argument, in contrast with traditional print texts where the delivery of the argument is not typically evaluated?

Jeremiah's course project was a case in point. After his virtuosic hypertext book review, I was surprised to find that the rough draft of his course project had many of the weaknesses typical of graduate student drafts: lack of a focused argument, lack of adequate support for claims, loose or missing connections between parts of the argument. I should point out that, although Jeremiah was planning to produce a hypertext, his draft was presented in more or less traditional form—on paper, with no visuals. Here's the opening:

The stained glass computer: a very rough draft:

An end to postmodernism?
Or just another permutation? {link: definition of POMO} As I have witnessed it, in the days before the Internet what the public read was largely determined by a semi-corporate conglomeration of editorial offices, advertising agencies, and book review writers. This old modernistic system was slowly being undermined (or possibly infiltrated, since it still exists) by the disunified ideals of a younger generation desiring more freedom of thought. However out of financial feasibility complete postmodernism still seemed like a Marxist pipe dream. Those texts that made it through the grist mill into print largely sold out of novelty as well as the world's readiness to assume that everything sandwiched in a dustjacket also contains some coherent system of thought and intention. Thomas Pynchon's career is a perfect example. There are many reasons why the world went gaga over Gravity's Rainbow. One of the primary ones seems to be an inability to believe that the highbrow end of the publishing industry could release what

might just be a 760-page densely written joke, a prank where the humor lies in the illusion of depth when in fact all is surface. (Of course Mr. Pynchon could not be reached for commentary, but I will keep trying :) {research gravity's rainbow}

And here are some of my comments:

> You're making some large generalizations that I'm not sure I'm willing to believe—unless you're willing to admit that they are your readings of the situation. Seems hard to believe that the motives of the publishing industry could be explained in a single sentence. Same with the explanation of why books sell.

> [After the reference to *Gravity's Rainbow*] Hmmm, I'm not sure what this statement supports. I know lots of good not-for-profit sites that are very good, particularly .edu sites. You might need to be more specific in your criticism. At the very least, you could provide links to sites you think illustrate what you describe.

My comments about Jeremiah's draft are representative of the way I typically respond. Even though some suggestions show my sensitivity to the medium he has chosen (I suggest that he link to examples of the bad sites he lambastes), for the most part my responses reflect my assumption that Jeremiah should limit and develop a single idea, that he should use hypertext to represent an otherwise conventional academic argument. And although I acknowledge that he can make the kinds of bold statements he wishes to make if he scales back his claims by identifying these statements as *his* reading of the postmodern condition, I might just as well have used the phrase "*merely* your reading." My other comments, asking for clarification, for more (authoritative) evidence, clearly urge compliance with the rules of traditional academic writing. Not until I saw Jeremiah's final hypertext did I come to question both what I thought Jeremiah was doing in that early draft and what I thought I was supposed to be doing when I responded to it. Jeremiah had given me what looked like a conventional draft, and I had responded by advising him how to write an even better conventional argument. His final project revealed, however, that although he may have made some use of my advice, as a writer he had clearly gone beyond anything I could have imagined or advised him to do. One example of this shift in authority is that when Jeremiah handed me his project on disk, he pointed out that to prevent readers from having to use scroll bars, he had used software for creating help files. Although he explained how to access the software needed to open the file ("If you have Windows, you have 'Winhelp,'" he said), I still had that sweaty-palm feeling I get when asked to do something new with technology. Suffice it to say, it was the first time I had that feeling when handed a final project in a graduate seminar.

From the moment I opened Jeremiah's file, questions about whether he had successfully articulated and developed an important idea related to cyberliteracy were pushed to the back of my mind as I enjoyed the Christmas morning experience of opening page after page. One measure of Jeremiah's success was that I spent two hours reading his course project and didn't mind. Although his argument was more fully worked out in this final version—the assertions were more clearly linked with more evidence supporting those assertions—other elements influenced my positive response: his explicit explanations of how to read his text, his logical ordering of associative relationships (made clear in the hierarchical structure of the help file's pull-down menus), and his use of images. These features of Jeremiah's text suggest how much he continued to resist those theories of hypertext that praised its unpredictability and the degree to which it made possible postmodern pastiche. Indeed, although Jeremiah was an expert web designer, he was also a creative writer who frequently objected to hypertext theory that argued for the benefits of setting aside authorial control. The fact that I responded positively to Jeremiah's technical efforts to "help" me read his text suggest that I also continued to value a writer's control over a logical argument, whatever its form.

On his opening page, Jeremiah introduced his idea of the computer as both a mediator of reality and itself a mediated object by drawing a computer using the image of a stained glass window in place of the computer screen (Figure 11.1). His use of the stained glass colors for the computer's outline was another creative flourish that made his opening page effective. Although we might use the word "original" to praise a scholarly paper, we rarely use the word "creative." Jeremiah's hypertext represented a hybrid between creative and scholarly writing that was appropriate, effective, and fun.

As I soon learned, Jeremiah's choice to construct his project as a "help" file meant that the reader was literally "helped" with the reading of the text (Figure 11.2). Because scholarly hypertext does not look like a traditional seminar paper or journal article, readers can feel disoriented. By making it possible to see the whole project (and to see how parts of the text are related to each other, just like an old-fashioned outline), Jeremiah minimized the potential for reader disorientation. Another advantage of providing a full list of contents was that at the end of my hours of reading, I was certain that I had read the whole text. The help file format, then, eased me over the gap from my experience reading linear texts to the experience of reading scholarly hypertext.

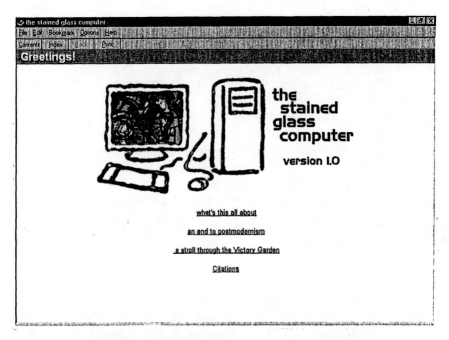

Fig. 11.1. The Stained Glass Computer

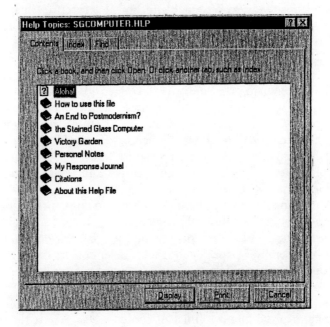

Fig. 11.2. Help File Format

In the first lexia, "what's this all about," Jeremiah explains why he wrote the text as a help file, how to use help files in general, and how he intended his particular file to be used, going so far as to set up the help file so that by clicking in the same spot on every frame, the text could be read straight through "like a book" (Figure 11.3). By moving through the text in this way, I was reading the argument as Jeremiah intended. In giving me this option, Jeremiah showed his awareness that readers need help making sense of new, unfamiliar forms. But he was also demonstrating a writerly insistence on maintaining control. Because much of his grade in my class rested on this project, he was not going to take the chance of being misunderstood. His text, both content and form, thus enacted much of what we'd been discussing all semester— both the possibilities and the limitations of digital texts. As with his

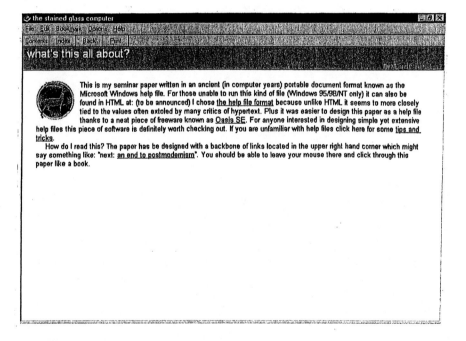

Fig. 11.3. What's This All About

show of technical prowess in his initial book review, providing this kind of "help" for the reader allowed Jeremiah to construct an authoritative ethos, an important move for all writers but especially important for graduate students who often bury their authority under dense paragraphs of references to outside sources.

In addition to taking risks with form, Jeremiah took risks with tone.

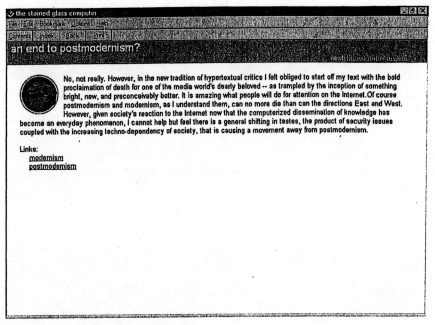

Fig. 11.4. An End to Postmodernism?

Jeremiah's web design skills gave him one kind of writerly authority, but his authority was also expressed in his construction of a textual voice that was jocular, ironic, self-conscious, not at all disembodied. The opening page for the section titled "an end to postmodernism?" is characteristic. First, the title "an end to postmodernism?" presented in the form of a question was answered "No, not really" in the first line. Here, Jeremiah is playing with readers' assumption that questions in the title of academic papers are merely rhetorical. In case we missed the point that he is playing with received forms, he comments: "in the new tradition of hypertextual critics, I felt obliged to start off my text with the bold proclamation of death for one of the media world's dearly beloved."

Jeremiah's handling of sources was also innovative. References to other authors were set up primarily as links listed at the bottom of each lexia/screen/page. For example, at the end of the lexia titled "the death of the author," Jeremiah offers links to quotes from Jay David Bolter, Julian Dibble, and George Landow. In contrast with the treatment of sources in traditional scholarly writing, Jeremiah does not introduce, appropriate, or apply this author's words. Visually, these quotes are tangential rather than integral to Jeremiah's argument; they extend rather than support his ideas, and Jeremiah himself called them "optional." The effect is to give Jeremiah's ideas center stage, again a provocative notion for graduate student writers just coming into a new field of knowledge. Such attention to the author's voice is additional evidence of Jeremiah's determination to invest his hypertext with the kind of agency he exhibits in his conventional creative writing.

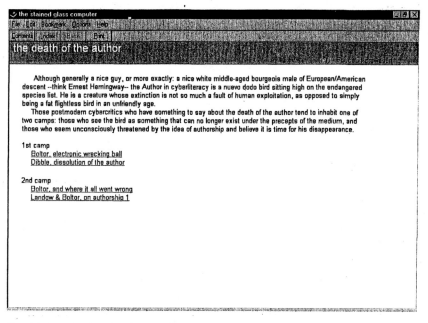

Fig. 11.5. The Death of the Author

Perhaps my favorite feature of Jeremiah's text was also the most perplexing: his use of abstract images to represent concepts related—in an associative way—to his argument. These images appear as a separate category at the end of the list of help file options, which serves to position them as auxiliary rather than integral to the text. As a reader, I experienced these images as icing on the cake. Had they appeared as part of a traditional linear text, I would have expected them to be connected explicitly to the main argument. And if they weren't, I would have seen their inclusion as problematic. Here, they seem to be Jeremiah's way of enacting postmodernist questions about meaning. The

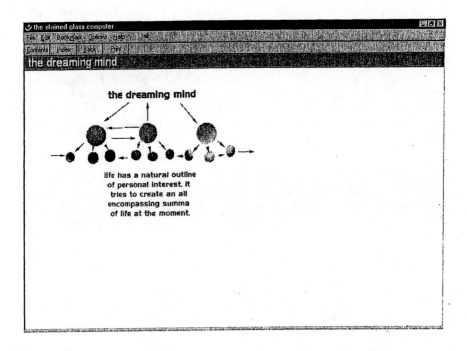

Fig. 11.6. The Dreaming Mind

images still don't make complete sense to me, but I like it that they make me wonder what they mean. Perhaps it is these images that bring Jeremiah's text closest to the utopian ideal of hypertext put forward by Bolter, Landow, and Joyce. The images, more than anything else in his text, required the reader to play author by determining a meaning that was not yet there. In "The Stained Glass Computer," Jeremiah demonstrated the promise of hypertext scholarly writing—the ability to work associatively rather than linearly, to be multivocal, to be rich with meaning made by multiple means. But the strong presence of its author's guiding hand (and the positive effect of that guidance) also demonstrates our continued attachment to what has made writing good in the past: a sense that we as readers are being led somewhere by an author's recognizable voice. The future of writing rides on texts like Jeremiah's that seek to bridge that gap.

WORKS CITED

Bolter, David J. *Writing Space: The Computer, Hypertext, and the History of Writing*. Hillsdale, NJ: Erlbaum, 1991.

Joyce, Michael. *Of Two Minds: Hypertext Pedagogy and Poetics*. Ann Arbor: U of Michigan P, 1995.

Landow, George. *Hypertext: The Convergence of Contemporary Theory and Technology*. Baltimore: Johns Hopkins UP, 1992.

12

TECHNOLOGY AUTOBIOGRA-PHIES AND STUDENT PARTICIPATION IN ENGLISH STUDIES LITERACY CLASSES

Karla Saari Kitalong
University of Central Florida
Dickie Selfe
Michigan Technological University
Michael Moore
Michigan Technological University

Emerging technologies influence our students' (and our own) literacy practices. In the context of the technology autobiographies we assign in various classes across several institutions, we discuss research on the connections between literacy and technology, the place of literacy narratives in composition and technical communication, and our attempts to engage and understand students' attitudes, assumptions, and self-reported literacies. We argue that Technology Autobiographies represent important data and reflective materials for teachers concerned with user-centered design, participatory literacies, and critical approaches to computer-mediated pedagogy.

Teachers of writing often find that asking students to consider the history of their literacy practices, early memories of reading and writing, and the writing and literacy expectations of their parents and teachers can help reveal the personal—and oftentimes unspoken—contexts that students bring to the classroom. Accordingly, literacy narratives and autobiographies are sometimes employed as a way for students to write about and reflect on those memories, as noted by Soliday as well as by

Eldred and Mortensen. Our primary interest in this chapter is with changing technologies and their influence on our students' (and our own) literacy practices. We see both the technologies and the literacy practices changing in the classes that we teach. But our approach has been influenced by scholars of literacy practices in general, scholars who explore the elements of our culture and our educational institutions that influence those practices. It seems reasonable, then, to lead off with techniques and methodologies that tie our efforts more generally to literacy education.

Literacy autobiographies are used by both instructors and students to help contextualize a particular pedagogy; for example, a class that emphasizes collaborative exercises and activities will benefit from an early discussion of students' experiences and expectations about the nature of individual versus shared tasks, or the implications of single or multi-authored documents.

One particularly thoughtful and systematic model for uncovering literacy practices and expectations is Deborah Brandt's approach in "Accumulating Literacy: Writing and learning to Write in the Twentieth Century." Brandt interviewed 65 participants with the goal of discovering the "institutions, materials, and people" that inform the acquisition of "practices that haunt the sites of literacy learning" (651; 661).

Brandt's goals for discovering these practices mirror and complement those that teachers of writing traditionally find to be useful in the classroom. Among the "guiding questions" in her study, Brandt asks students:

- to what they have been responding when they learn;
- how they describe the scenes of their learning; and
- what institutions, settings, sponsors, mediators, materials, and events they consider significant in their learning to write and read. (Brandt, 1995)

An "escalation in educational expectations" is among Brandt's findings, which highlight the effects of technological innovations on literacy practices both in the home and in the workplace (650). We see these heightened expectations articulated by a wide variety of educational stakeholders, including the media, state legislatures, industry, and any number of special-interest groups. Our approach highlights the contradictions and ambiguities among these institutional goals and the communicative acts and literacy practices of our students, articulated in their own words.

We find questions like the ones Brandt asks to be immediately applicable in our classes, especially if we think of such questions in light of our students' histories with technology. Like a literacy autobiography, a technology autobiography makes sense as a writing assignment in many types of English Studies classes because it makes explicit the students' experiences with technologies and clarifies how they understand the new technologies that are moving so quickly into the 21st-century classroom.

Similarly, Richard Miller describes "institutional autobiographies," which illuminate how students come to understand the larger contexts in which technologies operate. In his effort to map out territory between "two representations of schooling as either radically liberating and empowering or ceaselessly oppressive and instrumentalist," Miller suggests that in order for students to begin to imagine other ways of framing their experience of schooling, they must first be given an opportunity to formulate a more nuanced understanding of how power gets exercised in the social sphere (23).

The technology autobiographies on which we base this chapter provide students an opportunity to formulate such nuanced understandings, not only of how power gets exercised in technology-rich educational contexts, but also of how their life experiences with technology have influenced their attitudes, learning strategies, and approaches to living with technology. We would argue that these attitudes, strategies, and approaches should likewise influence how future technological power relations get exercised in the social/technological sphere of the classroom.

THE VALUE OF TECHNOLOGY AUTOBIOGRAPHIES AS WRITING ASSIGNMENTS

We, the authors of this chapter, are teachers of composition and technical communication. In this study, we used the following common questions as the basis for formal, informal, extended, or primarily diagnostic technology autobiography assignments.

- What were your earliest experiences with technological devices or artifacts? What devices do you remember using, and what do you remember about using them?
- What gadgets were popular in your house while you were growing up?

- Whom do you identify as being technologically "literate" in your life? What does it mean to be technologically literate? How do you measure up?
- What technologies are on your desk at home? What technological devices are you carrying now? What's on your technological "wish list"?
- How do you see technology as a force in the future, either in your career or personal life?

The students' responses to the initial questions prompted several follow-up questions and subsequent activities.

- What technological expertise can you share with the rest of the class during the term?
- Interview a family member (or a significant technological other), explore their technological literacy experiences, and report back to the class.
- What is your relationship with technology? Represent it visually through collage, drawing programs, or any other means at your disposal.

RATIONALE FOR ASSIGNING TECHNOLOGY AUTOBIOGRAPHIES

We are convinced of the value and usefulness of assigning technology autobiographies in a variety of literacy classes for several reasons. First, and perhaps most obviously, we already know—though it's seldom mentioned in the context of literacy education, and academics understand it only at surface levels—that some students enter our classrooms armed with sophisticated technological literacy skills and charged with excitement about technologies (Tapscott 1). As teachers, we need to know, and know more intimately, what's behind these literacy skills and attitudes, and how they will or should influence the complex social systems of postsecondary education. Perhaps selfishly, we also want to tap into this knowledge and this excitement.

Secondly, we have observed that teaching is an increasingly complex system of technologies within technologies. By that we mean that on one level, teachers are important stakeholders in the construction of systems of teaching and learning that are, in themselves, technologies (Johnson 9, 33, 89; cf Miller). English teachers' objectives for teaching and learning may vary considerably, but we all start out with the intention of creating learning systems or environments for students that will also function effectively within the social systems or institutions within which we work. In short, teachers attend to a variety of explicit and implicit influences on the technology of teaching and learning. Such influences include (but are certainly not limited to) the work of curriculum committees, institutional missions and values, building layouts, time schedules, book ordering conventions, the abilities of support personnel, administrators' needs, the work of state and national professional organizations, and our own intellectual interests and physical capabilities. Whether we acknowledge it or not, we are also influenced by what we think our students know. Our perceptions may or may not correlate with reality.

Increasingly, teachers attend as well to a range of electronic systems that influence and complicate course and curriculum planning. Such electronic systems make up another set of technologies within the technology of teaching and learning. As we construct classes (or, more accurately, construct learning and teaching environments), we often have the opportunity to decide whether—and how—to incorporate technologies such as e-mail, web pages, web development tools, electronic classrooms, chat systems, online class development tools, audio or video systems, and interactive TV networks. All of these possibilities now exist for many teachers on top of the now standard word processors, document design software, and network file systems. Teachers do not, therefore, merely design classes: they are the architects of increasingly electronic environments—or information ecologies—for teaching and learning (Nardi and O'Day). The complexity of designing technology-rich instruction has convinced us that we need to predict more accurately how students will react to our efforts. At some level, to use a card-playing metaphor, teachers are cognizant of the technological aces they hold in their own hands. Technology autobiographies, then, can provide us with a window into what literacy practices students can bring to the table. We get a peek at their cards as well.

A third reason for our interest in technology autobiographies as assignments in literacy classes is also related to the fact that teachers create or design courses and curriculum, in the same way that architects design buildings and engineers create cars, appliances, and other mundane artifacts. However, unlike architects and engineers, teachers usually work alone on the design of teaching and learning technologies, influenced, of course, by the institutional affordances and constraints alluded to above. In contrast, engineers usually work as productive partners in development teams. We don't dispute that teachers should adopt the label of creator and curriculum designer: this designation certainly makes clearer our responsibilities to those with whom we share the learning environments that we create, namely students. It is, however, not enough for teachers to imagine themselves as creators. They must also acknowledge the needs and values of the people for whom they create teaching and learning spaces and incorporate such needs and values into the curriculum design process.

As Robert Johnson suggests in his recent book on user-centered design, we believe that we are "obliged to learn how to value, how to see, the knowledge that users produce and then to learn how to make this knowledge an integral part of the technologies we use"(61). Quoting Aristotle, Johnson connects the discursive theories and practices of the rhetorical tradition with the mundane technological experiences of the end-users of technologies.

> [T]he user, or, in other words, the master, of the house will even be a better judge than the builder, just as the pilot will judge better of the rudder than the carpenter, and the guest will judge better of the feast than the cook. (*Politica*, qtd. in Johnson 3)

Johnson's fundamental claim is that our culture—in particular the culture of technical communication, but equally true of other literacy disciplines—falls easily into the "system-centered" philosophies that have dominated our understanding of technological experience for the last several centuries (Johnson 25-30). A similar, system-centered understanding of educational contexts leads teachers to downplay the importance of their own and their students' everyday technological experiences, despite the presence of "stories that beg to be told of people as they work with, against, and through the technologies that abound in [their] lives" (Johnson 4).

Our work is influenced as well by the work of anthropologist Margaret Mead, who compared the technological and social experiences of the turn-of-the-century immigrant generation with those of their American-born children and grandchildren.

> Today, everyone born and bred before World War II is an immigrant in time—as his forebears were in space—struggling to grapple with the unfamiliar conditions of life in a new era. Like all immigrants and pioneers, these immigrants in time are the bearers of older cultures. The difference today is that they represent all the cultures of the world. And all of them . . . have certain characteristics in common. (Mead 56)

Among these common characteristics, she noted that people born before World War II "grew up under skies across which no satellite ever flashed" (57). Another common characteristic is that the pace and quality of change in their worlds was so rapid and so profound that traditional "postfigurative" educational models, in which adults teach children, no longer functioned effectively.

In immigrant cultures, which were characterized by extreme social upheaval, and in today's Western technoculture, which is similarly disrupted by accelerated technological innovation, children acquire the necessary survival skills and social expertise much more readily than do their parents. Both of these situations necessitate an educational model in which children teach adults—a "prefigurative" model (Mead 51). "When the number of such young people is large," adds Mead, they are likely to "become models for one another" (32), thereby bypassing postfigurative education entirely in favor of a third educational model. Mead's name for this third model is "cofigurative culture," the cultural situation in which the "prevailing model for members of the society is the behavior of their contemporaries" (25). Acknowledging that "most commentators still see the future essentially as an extension of the past" (51), Mead suggested that because the desire for technological progress ensures that we are "committed to life in an unfamiliar setting," attempting to live in the past is like "building makeshift dwellings in old patterns," albeit "with new and better understood materials" (58).

As we considered our own experiences and discussed our own understanding of students' technological backgrounds in light of Mead's prescient insights, we acknowledged that we had each, at various times, taught and learned in all of the ways that Mead describes. Moreover, we each valued and routinely assigned group work in our classes, recognizing that in the "real world," collaboration is the norm, and that students have much to learn from each other. Nonetheless, we still took for granted that teachers alone are responsible for the construction of courses and other learning environments. Consequently, we had made very little effort to understand our students' approaches and attitudes toward the technologies that we were integrating into our classes. Student input had been circumscribed and limited. We regard this as an unfortunate lapse, given our recognition of students' status as cultural repositories of technological expertise.

Moreover, we came to recognize that by assuming full responsibility—and credit—for the construction of learning environments, we were denying students the opportunity to practice the type of technological activism that we find necessary for participatory citizenship. Robert Johnson states that "user-centered approaches should rethink the user as being an active participant in the social order that designs, develops, and implements technologies" (64). For us, of course, technologies are an increasingly important part of our teaching and learning environments. Johnson continues with an overview of the diverse roles users can play in the co-construction of technological environments, as well as the benefits of such roles.

> Users as producers have the knowledge to play an important role in the making of technologies; users as practitioners actually use the technologies and thus have a knowledge of the technologies in action; users as citizens carry user knowledge into an arena of socio-technological decision making the arena of the polis. (64)

We hope to understand students' knowledge, to put it bluntly, in order to better understand how their technological experiences can and should influence our literacy pedagogies, which prominently include our own uses of technology in the classroom. But in the process, we also hope to demonstrate to students how they can effect changes in technical systems and processes. We believe, in short, that better learning environments can be constructed. To do so, we must pay attention not only to other teachers, administrators, and technicians, who are typically credited with the design of educational systems. We must also heed the voices of the students.

Indeed, faith in the veracity of student/users' mundane technological knowledge prompted us to design the assignments discussed in this chapter and incorporate them into a variety of courses at several different institutions in order to invite students into our design of technology-rich courses. The bottom line, we believe, is that teachers don't just teach and students don't just learn. The authors of this chapter sense teacher/student collaborations in the making. In the remaining pages, we will try to make clear why we think that collaborating with students to redesign our literacy courses is important.

In sum, then, we employ the technology autobiography assignment in response to the following observations:

1. The literacy skills of students seems to be changing rapidly and diversifying;
2. The classroom experience is increasingly complex as we integrate communication technologies within the technologies of teaching and learning; and
3. Recent descriptions of technological design compel us to integrate users (students) into any design that is this important and complex.

TECHNOLOGY AUTOBIOGRAPHIES IN THREE
EDUCATIONAL CONTEXTS

Our students' technology autobiographies express both enthusiasm and ambivalence in personal examples of the social impacts of technological innovations, explicit references to communicative acts complicated or facilitated by technology in the home and classroom, and, above all, descriptions of the strategies they've developed to negotiate this complex and changing landscape. In the remaining pages of this chapter, we highlight students' responses to our technology autobiography assignments to suggest that these writings provide teachers, administrators, and technicians with unprecedented learning opportunities.

SELFE AT MICHIGAN TECHNOLOGICAL UNIVERSITY

One collection of technology autobiographies comes from a Publications Management course for third- and fourth-year technical communication majors at Michigan Technological University. As one course of six from which students might choose to fulfill the media requirement for the major in Scientific and Technical Communication, Publications Management assumes a basic knowledge of many publishing software and hardware systems, including document design, scanning and photo manipulation, output devices and formats, and web development. Knowledge of such advanced technologies is built on top of the expectation that students will understand and use basic communication devices and capabilities such as word processing, e-mail, and web searching, and will have in-depth knowledge of common hardware and operating systems. The "mundane artifacts" (Johnson 1) associated with this course have a substantial impact and illustrate the remarkable investment that Publications Management students have in the technological infrastructure around them: These students paid nearly $200 in general and course-specific computing fees when they enrolled in this course. They live at the technological crossroads of our culture, not only because of their technological backgrounds, but also because of the significant social and financial obligations they incur with respect to technology; consequently, they expect a great deal of themselves and the systems on which they depend.

The technology autobiography was not a substantial "graded" portion in this class of eighteen women and two men.[1] It was one of

[1]The gender balance was quite rare; at MTU men outnumber women at least 3 to 1.

approximately twenty ungraded daily assignments that account for the participation portion of their final grade. It was, however, described as an important component of their first large assignment, which asked each person to design a two- to five-page technology module that would bene- fit people much like themselves, working on communication projects in Michigan Tech's Center for Computer-Assisted Language Instruction (CCLI).[2] The technology autobiographies offered an inside look at a sam- ple of the technological experiences of people who would use and benefit from their technology modules. In other words, the students enrolled in Publications Management were to design technology modules for an audience very similar to themselves. Instead of describing typical users of these documents globally and vaguely, each technology module author would get to know the sample population with some intimacy.

For the technology autobiography assignment, then, Publication Management students were asked to read the questions, to respond only to those that seemed useful and interesting, to edit once, and then to hand in their responses electronically. It was an informal writing assign- ment with no chance for substantial revision. Still, it afforded Dickie Selfe a diagnostic preview of their future writing, as well as important insights into the technical literacy patterns of students who would use technology constantly over the course of the term. Even as his students were extracting useful generalizations about how typical document users might react to the documents they were designing, Selfe was extracting useful material from the technology autobiographies for the purpose of redesigning the way technologies might be used in literacy classes. Those insights are reflected in this chapter.

KITALONG AT UNIVERSITY OF CENTRAL FLORIDA

For students enrolled in Karla Kitalong's honors composition course at the University of Central Florida, the technology autobiography played a slightly different role. It was the students' first major writing assign- ment in their first college writing course, one of several "Gordon Rule" courses that they would take during their time at UCF.[3] Eleven men and

---

[2]Projects included modules on how to use important options in Adobe Photoshop, how to scan and use images in web pages, how to translate Microsoft PowerPoint presentation into web pages, how to create cascading style sheets for web sites, and many others.

[3]In Gordon Rule courses, by statewide mandate in Florida, students must write at least 6000 words during the course of the semester.

four women had self-selected the general education course based on its theme, "Technology, Community, Identity," and all were enrolled in technical majors such as engineering, forensic or premedical science, computer programming, math education, or accounting. After reading technology criticism from authors such as Kenneth Gergen, Langdon Winner, and Howard Rheingold as well as popular journalism accounts about growing up in the digital age, students constructed personal narratives of their own lives with technology. Although an immediate opportunity to revise was not afforded them after the paper was graded, students wrote several drafts of their papers and submitted them twice for peer review before they were graded.

Diagnostic information was gathered from this first paper and incorporated into future course lessons. In addition, at the end of the semester, students collaboratively produced on-line or printed zines focusing on some aspect of the course theme and aimed at an audience of their peers, instead of at an academic audience. For the zine assignment, each student revised and resubmitted one major paper, taking a new audience and rhetorical purpose into account.

MOORE AT MICHIGAN TECHNOLOGICAL UNIVERSITY

The technology autobiographies served a still slightly different purpose in Michael Moore's technical communication course for an interdisciplinary mix of juniors and seniors at Michigan Technological University. Students began the term by discussing various approaches to understanding and articulating their relationships with the forms of technology typically used in classrooms, in campus labs, and in homes. The technology autobiographies were introduced as student contributions to research into literacy practices and pedagogical assumptions and planning, as well as a way to develop a framework for the class, as mentioned below. More than in either of the other two classes, Moore's use of the technology autobiography was explicitly tied to course content and to a process in which students and the teacher could reflect together throughout the term on writing, designing, and collaborating in a networked communication classroom. The technology autobiographies also offered initial diagnostic clues into student writing features because the class members were asked to write in a narrative, reflective form— one that differed from the form that they had early on identified as "technical communication."

This perceived dissonance between the autobiographical narrative and the genres of technical communication that students more typically wrote allowed for class discussion on the choices writers make and the implications of such choices for research, audience, and effective communication. On at least two occasions during the term, students were asked formally to reflect on their attitudes toward technology and to articulate how their attitudes, experiences, and assumptions might be affecting design and collaboration decisions for their major projects.

The first occasion for reflection was provided when students wrote a 10- to 15-minute in-class, informal response just after reading Ellen Bravo's essay, "The Hazards of Leaving Out the Users." In the essay, Bravo argues from a clerical worker's point of view in favor of the active participation of users in the design of systems that will affect them. A second formal occasion for reflection came while groups were brainstorming their project reports. In these reports, students describe the workplace culture of the agency with which they conducted their service-learning projects, emphasizing in particular the uses of technology in that culture. Other less formal occasions for reflection on the technology autobiographies occurred while students were working collaboratively in the networked classroom (CCLI) and when the students' clients were actively involved in the document and editing process.

LEARNING FROM THE TECHNOLOGY AUTOBIOGRAPHIES: OBSERVATIONS

The technology autobiographies from all these classes, then, were useful on several levels:

1. Generalizations gleaned from technology autobiographies could, depending upon course goals, be consulted as a source of audience information for course projects, form the basis for future writing assignments, or be folded into follow-up discussions about how people learn to use technology.
2. Technology autobiographies revealed technological attitudes, approaches, and worldviews that demonstrated to us what we could learn from students and how they could become codesigners or redesigners (along with us) of the technology-rich instruction in a literacy class.
3. Technology autobiographies provided useful diagnostic writing samples.

In this chapter, we focus on the second level of usefulness by asking what these brief writing samples can tell us about students' approaches to technology. Further, we explore what that knowledge implies about how teachers might collaborate with students in the redesign of technology-rich English classes. Student responses in this area revealed for us the following kinds of expectations, strategies, and values:

- A certain technological facility is expected, and its value is, by and large, taken for granted. Attitudes toward generational differences in technological expertise are colored by these expectations.
- Students employ a variety of learning strategies, including gaming and games, what we call "surgical strike" or "just-in-time learning," and learning that takes place in spite of—not because of—teachers or other authority figures.
- The accumulative technological experiences of student groups often influence the direction of their projects, particularly when those projects are participatory, community-based, and involve real audiences. Because students are encouraged to make project decisions based on prior knowledge—in this case, technological experiences and literacies—their work can be grounded in increasingly complex, collaborative, knowledge-making activities.
- Despite their affinity for technology and their high expectations about technological facility, students express a variety of attitudes toward technology, including ambivalence, fear, and what we call "fear of fear."

In the next four sections of this chapter, we explore each of these insights in turn, highlighting revelatory passages from our students' technology autobiographies, summarizing what we learned, and proposing some implications for teachers. Patterns as well as anomalies are revealed in the anecdotes cited here. If we previously had been predisposed to regard technological literacy as a definable, quantifiable entity, we are no longer so inclined.

A CERTAIN TECHNOLOGICAL FACILITY IS TO BE EXPECTED

Students in the courses that we studied expect of themselves and others a relatively high level of technological facility. Moreover, they agree, for the most part, that such facility is both necessary and desirable. The

Central Florida first-year students were arguably the group for whom technologies were most immediate and naturalized. Most of these students recorded their first substantive interactions with technology in grammar school, making them early adopters by anyone's standards. Although these students' experiences are not overwhelmingly positive, all of them grew up with television, and all remember (although not necessarily with pleasure) their first experiences with video game systems. They all had worked with computers by junior high if not before, and they currently live in a high-tech region a mere 50 miles from Cape Canaveral, the site of now-routine, though nonetheless spectacular space shuttle launches.

Ashley Dunning's[4] expectations were established when she first worked with a computer before she could sit up. By the time she was fourteen, she carried a pager so she could easily communicate with her friends at any time. In high school, she did clerical work at a local business, but her title was "accountant," a position that normally requires at least a vocational school education. She credits this status to her ability to understand and explain the business's complex computer systems to her boss and coworkers.

Parents had a lot to do with students' expectations.[5] Sean Fortier's bedroom was wired with cable television when he was four years old. He had a computer of his own by the time he was fourteen. When a lightning storm destroyed their VCR, his father, after determining that it couldn't be repaired, took it apart to see how it worked. When he was satisfied that he understood the inner workings of the machine, Sean wrote, his father

> collected the parts and put them into a paper bag. That is when he issued the challenge. He said, "Hey, Sean, if you can put this whole thing back together, I'll give you a hundred dollars." To his astonishment, I did. Of course, it still didn't work, but it looked just like it did before. . . . I was only 12 years old.

---

[4]Unless otherwise noted, all of our student colleagues are identified by their real names. Truthfully, they should be accorded co-authorship of this chapter, because of the degree to which they have helped us arrive at the understandings we have.

[5]A number of parents were invited to participate in the Technology Autobiography Project beginning in the spring of 2000. Respondents were unanimously enthusiastic about participating in their children's coursework and assignments, and unfailingly generous in sharing their memories. The next phase of our research will incorporate this range of intergenerational data and stories.

Danny Deaton was also educated about technology by his father, a bio-medical instrumentation technician.

> As far back as I can remember I spent a lot of time either helping [my father] or . . . doing the work on my own. . . . [B]ecause of my age and lack of experience, I was not allowed to do the actual repairs. But I did take things apart, and prepare them to be repaired.

These students already depend on many different technologies, but they are always on the lookout for the next innovation that will help them while preserving their accustomed mobility. Crystal Spivey, who keeps up-to-date on new and useful technological developments and regularly shares her findings with her classmates, says this about her desire for new, useful, portable technologies. "I have come to like . . . the disc writer hardware systems that copy almost anything onto a CD. That will soon be a major attachment to my laptop." Other UCF students explored the relationships between their parents' technology experiences and attitudes and their own. Sometimes these remarks took on the tinge of impatience or amusement. John Roth, a UCF student, expressed his attitude toward the grand narrative of progress by coining a new term for those who resist technology: "Hopefully, some of the techno-obliviates will realize that technology is here to make life easier." In his technology autobiography, he wrote,

> My father and I bought my mother a CD player for mother's day this year. . . . [s]he asked me which button to push to play a CD. I told her, "the one with the sideways triangle on it"; she said, "Why don't they just write 'Play' on it?"

But, Michigan Tech student Renee Marion, a nontraditional student and mother who works full time as a coordinator of telecommunications services, speaks from a position that spans several technological generations. She grew up with parents who were selective about the technologies they adopted.

> My father, an iron ore miner, followed new technologies that enhanced his hobby with equipment such as state of the art fish locators and electric reels. My mother, the daughter of a Finnish immigrant, practiced old fashioned methods and shied away from new kitchen devices that sat untouched on our counters.

Students' technological facility and the literacy practices they exhibit—as well as their astute awareness of the cultural meaning of these issues of facility, literacy, and access—suggest a need to rethink the composing process in ways that include, even build on, the multiple technological fluencies of our students. Instead of lamenting that students don't read anymore, and using that lament as an excuse to discourage the presence of technologies ranging from web resources to cell phones and pagers in our classes, perhaps we ought to be asking, "Of what productive use is web literacy in our classes? Are cell phones simply classroom distractions, or can they be transformed into tools of the composing process?" After all, news reporters, teachers, engineers, forensic pathologists, and computer repair technicians all take full advantage of cell phones in their work; why shouldn't students who aspire to these careers be encouraged to employ and develop such fluency in our literacy classes? And why should English teachers be relegated to the role of "bearers of older cultures" (Mead 56), locked into reproducing single-mindedly postfigurative educational models?

It's fairly clear that English studies teachers will not find their classrooms populated with homogeneous groups of technology sophisticates, even in elective courses billed as technology-intensive. But it is also fairly clear that our students, like us, are accustomed to learning not only postfiguratively, but also co- and prefiguratively. We will have to be ready to accommodate a range of skills and attitudes not only in our teaching styles and class activities but also in our own expectations of students' work. At the same time, we can avail ourselves of a smorgasbord of learning opportunities if we allow for the possibility in our classes of a variety of educational models. We found clues for incorporating and accommodating these new opportunities in an analysis of learning strategies and preferences that students revealed in their technology autobiographies.

LEARNING STRATEGIES: GAMES, COLLABORATIONS, AND THE VALUE OF *KAIROS*

Among the preferred learning strategies students wrote about in their technology autobiographies, we identified gaming and games as highly significant. We also identified a goal-oriented pattern of learning that we call "surgical-strike learning," in which students acquire exactly the kind and amount of knowledge they need when they need it to accomplish a particular task. Finally, we identified a type of learning, often collaborative in nature, in which students acquired technological literacy, not because of teachers, parents, or other postfigurative authority figures, but in spite of them, behind their backs.

Nearly half of the Michigan Tech Publications Management students (9 out of 19) recalled games or gaming as an important, positive, and usually early influence on their attitudes towards technology. Some came to gaming on their own, reporting worn-out buttons on hand-held devices. Most, however, played with siblings, parents, or friends: "[A] day with Dad always meant video games." Several, like Laura Bentley (pseudonym), reported a bit of rivalry over the valued objects:

> I was jealous of my younger brother because he received a Speak and Spell for his birthday and he was way too young to even get any real use out of it. I was always convincing him he did not want to play with it. I would hide the batteries or put them in the wrong way and told him that it was not functioning properly.

For Chad Singleton and other students in the Central Florida class "technology has always found a way to incorporate itself into . . . daily routine[s]," beginning with early exposure to video games. Like Laura's brother, Chad recalls early exposure to the Speak 'N Spell.

> At the age of four, I didn't know that it was the first electronic duplication of the human vocal tract on a single chip of silicon. All I knew was that the guy inside the red box didn't mind teaching me how to pronounce D-O-G for hours upon end.

By purchasing games and playing with—and undoubtedly often losing to—their children, parents actively encouraged the development of this learning process. Some parents even use their own creativity to produce engaging electronic "toys" for their young children. Jeff Langley (pseudonym), one of the Central Florida students, writes about his first electronic toy, which appeared soon after his first birthday.

> My dad, who has a strong interest in electronics despite being a full-time musician, built me a small, blue box that had some buttons and switches on it that would cause lights to blink or glow and buzzers to buzz. According to them, I wouldn't let go of this new "toy" that I had. My mom rolls her eyes when she tells this story of the beginning of my "fascination with buttons." She attributes my interest in computers and my choice of Computer Science as a major to this blue box.

On the other hand, several students suggested that they had grown out of gaming and that those systems were for the young who had time to "waste." Their schedules, these students claimed, worked against this less direct, gaming approach to learning. Indeed, although the luxury of taking time to enjoy and puzzle out gaming situations seems to work against some of the other characteristics that the Technology Autobiographies suggest, Dickie Selfe, a lab director for over 15 years, observes that some students consistently make time for gaming, even as adults. Moreover, an increasingly large percentage of our student population recognizes and responds knowledgeably to gaming situations, whether they currently "play" or not.

Dickie Selfe felt compelled to ask more about the gaming trend he found in students' early technological experiences. Follow-up e-mail questions to students about the importance of gaming and how it trains or educates young people brought some interesting replies. He asked specifically, "What did gaming train you to do physically, mentally, attitudinally? Did that early gaming experience help you learn how to learn?"

Laura Bentley (pseudonym) credited participation in games and gaming with the often-noted "fearlessness" of young people towards new technologies. "Believe it or not, games can make children less frightened of technology. I thought of computers as a toy for years before it actually became a tool." Other students concurred, not only suggesting that gaming reduces computer anxiety, but also hinting at specific learning strategies that games encourage. As Glenda Axford (pseudonym) suggests in the following extended quote, in some situations students enjoy learning collaboratively, in what Mead called a cofigurative mode.

> What gaming taught me is that there are always little tricks to doing things. For example, when i played supermario bros. i learned how to "warp" to different worlds and that meant that i could skip 4 levels of playing without losing points. So i would always try to do new things regardless if there was a hint that i could do it or not. . . . The hidden shortcuts really got to be fascinating. . . . But what is also key is that i learned a lot of tricks from my friends. . . . So that is getting a reward from other's experience with the game.

A number of Central Florida students reported that they had quickly graduated from playing games to producing their own games and programs. These early adopters didn't just play with what the computer gave them; they became producers of new material. Luke Levesque characterizes this move from playing to programming as curiosity. When his family purchased their first computer, a second-hand Commodore 64, Luke began by playing the games that came with the computer. But he quickly mastered these rudimentary technologies. He writes

> [A]s always, I got curious about what things the computer could do besides games, which is when I opened up the manuals. The computer had BASIC built in, so I started by learning some simple programming. At this time, no one else really used the computer, so it was mine to play with upstairs in the spare room.

Luke learned to use a computer by playing with its capabilities and by studying the documentation. This two-part learning strategy extends to other areas of his life, as well, always prompted by curiosity. "After I bought my first car," he wrote, "I was curious about how it worked, so I bought a repair manual." Luke's overall view of technology changed as he became more familiar with the inner workings of cars. Working on cars, he said,

> taught me about mechanical technology, which is a bit different from the electronic kind that I am used to. It not only requires intelligence. It takes strength, coordination, and precision, as well. I find it very beneficial to work and learn about this sort of technology because not only can I save money, but it gives me a different perspective on things (both mechanical and electronic), and I find it fun to do.

For Richard Marens, programming knowledge was acquired during visits to his grandparents' home in Holland, while he was growing up in Germany.

> [M]y grandfather was a self taught computer programmer. . . . And so I began writing programs at one of his three computers. I started by copying code that people with no lives sent into these magazines that my grandpa had a stack of, and thus the saga begins. The first program I remember writing (or should I say "copying") was a little code that had a thing that looked like Snoopy walk around like a drunk and say, "Hallo, Richard!" in the end. Everyone praised me and I was proud that I could copy things into a computer console.

Collaborative learning was the norm for many of these students, beginning in early elementary school. Jeff Langley, for example, was the architect of a third-grade newsletter cobbled together with a classmate. After securing the teacher's approval, Jeff writes,

> I teamed up with a girl in my class who had a more advanced computer (an Apple) and she became co-editor with me. . . . She had a popular word-processing program that allowed us to use color graphics! Surprisingly, we were able to pull it together and print a one-page edition once a month using her computer for formatting and typing up the one paragraph articles on our classroom's ancient Acorn computers. The last time I communicated with my third grade teacher (about 5 years ago), her class was still publishing their paper, but with more advanced equipment.

We noticed that gaming and collaboration are often accompanied by a learning strategy we've termed "surgical-strike learning." Derived from the military practice of zeroing in on and attacking a specific target, the combative appellation seems to describe a learning practice, similar to the "just-in-time" learning that we hear so much about these days in relation to educational technologies, in which learners "swoop in" at the opportune moment, find and learn exactly—and only—what they need, and then move on. As Lisa DeMarco (pseudonym) puts it,

> In order to stay competitive I believe that it will be necessary to "roll with the punches" of technological change. It will never be possible to learn every new thing or always keep up but it will only be to my benefit to stay current with those things that pertain to my field or are positioned in it.

Diana Stendhall, another thoughtful student, writes,

> If I had more time, I'm sure my interest and drive would increase. I don't have the time to match my electronic/computer drive as it is though. I have a hard time throwing off other, maybe older, values for the sake of my computer literacy. I recognize that it takes a tremendous time commitment to stay fluent. I don't know what other part of my life I want to give up so that I can learn yet another piece of software. I will probably manage the learning of future skills by crisis, doing only what I have to do to remain literate enough.

We also found that many students described learning in spite of, rather than because of, their teachers or other adults. Students in the UCF honors composition class, fresh from their high school experiences and often still living at home with parents, were more likely than the older Michigan Tech students to employ this variation on surgical-strike learning. Travis Murray, for example, having already mastered the skills taught in his ninth-grade keyboarding class, found other collaborative opportunities for learning. In this class, he wrote, "I had my first experience in hacking."

> The kid I sat next to already knew how to type; the only reason he was taking the class is because, like I said, it was a pre-requisite for all other computer related classes. Just by watching him, I was able to pick up on the school system's loopholes, loopholes I couldn't resist trying myself. Both of us were only caught once, so we never got kicked out of the class.

Technology enthusiast Crystal Spivey concurs.

> A lot of the things I have learned about technology have been through trial and error. I have only taken one word processing class, and that was in the fifth grade. Basically with all the new technology, I have stayed enlightened by it through my own efforts.

Kristin Zangenberg, on the other hand, expressed one of the few reported instances in which a teacher actually fueled a student's interest in computers. Although the computers she used in her ninth-grade keyboarding class were "from way back when," her teacher left a vivid impression her and influenced how she approaches computers to this day.

> My computer teacher . . . wanted us to like computers as much as she did. . . . It seemed as if she was happy if you had a problem, because that way, she had something to help you with. I became proficient in Word, enjoyed doing our activities that involved spreadsheets, and often helped my fellow classmates when they needed assistance.

A tentative conclusion that we draw from the prevalence of game-style and just-in-time learning is that technology instruction may be more successful—and may be viewed by students as more relevant—if it is integrated throughout the curriculum, rather than conducted in stand-alone computer literacy courses. Required computer literacy courses such as the one Travis and his hacker seatmate endured may encourage students to find ways to circumvent the teacher's authority, especially when the students' knowledge surpasses that of the course content. The examples our students provided convince us of the value of channeling students' expertise into something more productive, such as helping less proficient students or conducting independent research.

TECHNOLOGICAL EXPERIENCES INFLUENCE THE DIRECTION OF PARTICIPATORY, COMMUNITY-BASED PROJECTS

As noted earlier, Michael Moore incorporated the student technology autobiography assignment in three service learning–oriented technical communication courses at Michigan Technological University to serve as a framework throughout the course, grounding progressively more complex, creative, and collaborative tasks in students' own experiences and attitudes. Students were asked to employ participatory design principles in projects with off-campus social and cultural agencies (Moore 1999), considering multiple audiences (parents, school administrators, students, district technology staff, perhaps even prospective community residents), as well as conventions of web design and usability. Students also collaborated with each other and with local agency participants on a series of writing assignments and HTML experimentation that culminated in websites that community participants were able to update and maintain after the course ended. Finally, project groups were asked to reflect critically on various aspects of their work throughout the quarter, beginning when they wrote their technology autobiographies, prior to project selection and group formation. Paying early attention to the students' own experiences and attitudes gave the class a framework for identifying and understanding the usability and access issues that arose during the development of their projects.

For example, Kelly Benson (pseudonym) acknowledged in her technology autobiography that her lifestyle will "depend on my technological capabilities," and expressed some amazement that "even minimum wage jobs" require some form of computer literacy. Kelly's perspective on access and skills was partially informed by her memory that her father "was extremely strict on buying only American-made products," and because "new technological items were assembled overseas," she was not exposed to computers until she reached school.

Kelly's team project involved designing a website with commonly requested forms and instructions. The client was a local family agency that provides food stamps, counseling, and other benefits for local families with children in need. When one of her group members pointed out that many of the agency's potential clients might not own computers or have Internet access, Kelly brainstormed—on the spot—a plan to distribute memos and flyers to local libraries and other service organizations to help educate the community about this new resource.

In another project group, three engineering majors, all male, worked with a local elementary school to develop the school's website. Their technology autobiographies were, upon first reading, quite dissimilar. David Claus was an older nontraditional student—a self-described "transitional" graduate student awaiting acceptance into a master's program in civil engineering—whose technology autobiography thoughtfully recollected his family life and how the introduction of technological devices, such as the family television, the first computer, and the microwave, affected life at home:

> Money was tight for my parents back then, and the TV proudly took its place in our living room with all the second-hand furniture. It was the first TV my parents had ever had with a remote control, and they were notably proud of it. They used to keep the remote controller in the kitchen on top of the refrigerator so my brother and I wouldn't play with it . . . By the time I was three I was already fascinated with technology.

Many students' technology autobiographies referred to their families' economic status when recalling what technologies found their place in the household, and David Claus notes his school's status in this regard, as well:

> By the time my family moved during my third grade year of elementary school, computers were starting to be used for educational purposes in the classroom. My school district was quite rich as far as school districts go, and each classroom had either an Apple IIe or a PET computer. I had a hard time making friends that year because I came halfway through the school year, so my teacher often let me stay in during recess and after school to play [on] the computer.

These recollections served as excellent critical and contextual reflections as the group began to consider the elementary school's day-to-day activities, and the students' potential participation in the project.

Mark Cicero, another of the project's team members, recalled that,

> We never got a new computer until I was in 10th grade. My Dad never really cared about the computers that we had at home because by the time he got home from work, he was sick of dealing with computers for the most part.

One thing we learned from these students' technology autobiographies was that their experiences inform the attitudes and motivations brought to bear on collaborative projects. In the short excerpts from Moore's class technology autobiographies, for example, issues of control (the TV remote hidden in the kitchen; access to computers dependent on the father's daily workplace environment) almost certainly affected project decisions at many stages of development. The elementary school website group's project proposal reflects students' attention to such issues:

> Our intention [is] to have the students and faculty of Houghton-Portage Township Elementary provide the guidance where content and appearance are concerned. In order for the web page to be useful to the children, they need to have a hand in its creation.

Obviously, the students' sensitivity to the needs of the end users comes, at least in part, from the participatory-design emphasis in the course. But the project group also actively articulated at each step their recognition that the elementary school students were already active users of technology. As the project progressed, the group encouraged increased participation between students and parents as well, and they attempted to make the design-decision process as collaborative among constituent groups as possible.

AMBIVALENCE: RESISTANCE, FEAR, AND THE "FEAR OF FEAR"

In discussions about how to apply our knowledge of such learning styles and interaction patterns to the projects that our students were developing (and, more importantly for this chapter, how these fascinating relationships with technology might inform the development of literacy courses), we noted a tension. On the one hand, the strategies that students employed—games, collaboration, surgical strike learning, idiosyncratic project development processes, and cofigurative learning—proved to be useful ways to introduce computers and other new systems. On the other hand, however, students across the board expressed varying degrees of ambivalence toward technologies and toward their own and others' relationships with technologies. We found these ambivalent feelings, embedded as they were within technology autobiographies that seemed largely enthusiastic about technology, to be particularly telling.

It is quite easy for teachers (including the authors of this chapter) to adopt a rather monolithic view of students' attitudes toward technology. We know, for example, that they are technologically sophisticated, they are quick to pick up new technologies and determined to use them, and they are convinced by a cultural "grand narrative of progress" that expects and values technological change. And of course a number of our student technology autobiographies fit this profile: Bill Dexter (pseudonym) writes, for example, "Technology has always played a large and deciding role in my life. I have always been called a tech-nut, a gadget man, or something like that." But, despite their adeptness, students carry with them a strong ambivalence toward technology, a fact that came as no surprise to us; we were aware of previous research that revealed similar ambivalence toward technology among English department computer users.

In 1996, Dickie Selfe surveyed students, teachers, technicians, and administrators working in 55 technology-rich English studies facilities around the United States. Of the 191 respondents who ranked themselves on a five-point scale designed to measure attitudes toward technology use, students self-reported the lowest enthusiasm levels of any of the groups. In this study, the average for general students was a rather enthusiastic 4.29; however, students who actually worked in technology-rich facilities reported themselves as somewhat less enthusiastic than the average, scoring 4.0 on the five- point scale. The levels of enthusiasm reported by teachers, administrators, and technicians, in contrast, ranged from 4.38 to 4.83 (R. Selfe, 1997). The technology autobiography assignments put a more human face on the student ambivalence revealed by Selfe's survey. In fact, the similarities between the numerical and the narrative responses may suggest a connection between students' relatively lower levels of enthusiasm and a diminished sense of control over the technological environments in which they work. If teachers ever preferred to believe that students were mindless technological drones, unaware of the impressive cultural hegemony that drives technological change in our culture, the technology autobiographies that we have reviewed appear to dispel that myth in clear and substantial ways. It was, for instance, common to find rather deterministically enthusiastic statements about technology like this one, from Kristen Bigari, one of the Michigan Tech Publication Management students. "[W]here would we be without these remarkable innovations? . . . there would be turmoil, for me at least. Technology is powerful source that influences the social elements in our society."

Interestingly, Kristen, in almost the same breath, indicated her ambivalence toward technology.

> Do not get me wrong, technology is amazing. As you can see I support technology and the many advancements that have been made for human kind. I just want to state that it should be taken seriously. We should not let technology enslave us, nor should we let it influence our social attitudes in our daily lives. Power is good, if it is used righteously.

Several technology autobiographies suggest an active resistance to technologies of all kinds (including the ones we most often use in our instructional planning). Brenda Polk of MTU made a suggestive comment after reporting on her early technological experiences: Even though her family had had computers in the house since 1984, she wrote, "[My] parents are still Internet-free." Later on, Brenda is more pointed in describing her reluctant approach to new technologies.

> So, today's "wish list" would contain an absence of technology. I wish I could get rid of my stereo, calculator, pocket dictionary, cell phone, and even my watch. I've weaned myself from TV/VCR and computer dependence, but haven't solidified my stance enough to get rid of everything yet. I can't convince myself that I need technology to survive, to learn, or to communicate. At the core of every person, there is no power button.

It is all too easy to assume that all students have had--or will soon have—substantial exposure to technologies, in spite of evidence to the contrary. A number of scholars have noted that exposure to technology, particularly early in a students' lives, is currently and will likely remain skewed along the axes of race and socioeconomic status (Moran and Selfe; C. Selfe). Yet, several students hinted in their technology autobiographies at some correlation between early positive technological experiences and successful learning of new technologies later in life. For instance, Dickie Selfe asked his Publication Management students, "Do you think there are social consequences or potential impacts on your lifestyle that depend on your technological capabilities?" Beth Tarkenton (pseudonym) answered in this way: "Yes I do, because in my house we have never had a computer. My mother finally broke down in the last couple of years and purchased a word processor."

This lack of early exposure may be connected to Beth's approach to new technologies; later in her response, she writes, "I think I will probably go about learning how to use new technology the same way I always have—very hesitantly. But once I adjust to it, I will probably just jump in and play around with it until I can understand it."

Ambivalence toward technology may also result in part from negative impacts that technology has had on friends, acquaintances, classmates, family, or self. MTU student Ann Culpeper (pseudonym) acknowledged that her "life revolves around computers." Nonetheless, she has guarded against some of the negative influences she sees in others: "While I've noticed that a lot more people are impersonal now that they can deal with you through the web, I haven't steered away from interpersonal relationships. I don't think I've fallen into the hole."

For Chad Singleton of UCF, "Although a majority of [the Internet's] effects were constructive, it also brought along with a variety of baggage. Feelings of isolation, extra temptations, and physical dependencies were all brought into my life from the computer and the Internet." Chad writes of having to "set down some personal rules" for himself to counteract the negative effects he believed the technology was having on his life. "To this day," he adds, "I still apply the rules strategy when I feel that I am spending too much time on the Internet." As a Christian, he also found himself struggling with "the temptations [the Internet] had to offer," including opportunities to view pornography and engage in piracy. "Why wouldn't I want to save $200 by downloading a program I didn't own, or see pictures of Pamela Anderson nude?" His "rules strategy" came into play again.

> To say that I never pursued these temptations would be a lie. Luckily, my conscience wouldn't allow me to continue either of them. I had to again set up ground rules for myself. These rules required more self-discipline than I thought I had.

Chad credits his early mastery over what he calls "temptation" as an important opportunity for recognizing his own weaknesses and intensifying his religious convictions. Today, his part-time job involves creating web pages for a UCF department, and he also reports with relish his money-making ventures on the Internet. He knows that the seamier side of the Internet exists, but he doesn't go there any longer. And he learned something about himself by testing and rejecting the aspects of the Internet that worked against his personal values.

Enslavement, painful values, reluctant learning, impersonal behavior, temptation, are all words and phrases that make it clear why the students in our classes might approach classroom use of communication technologies with a well-seasoned ambivalence. But the word "ambivalence" doesn't begin to describe the difficult position that many students perceive themselves to occupy. Although they may not always be able to articulate it, at some level most of them understand the hegemony of technology in our culture,[6] and they recognize that technological proficiency is an important cultural measure of success and integration. Many students feel uncomfortable with this measuring stick yet realize its apparent inevitability. In short, students often fear their own fear. One example of this fear is revealed in students' anxiety over the life-long learning that they know to be part of their rapidly approaching professional lives. Perversely, we found some solace in how closely the anxieties of students matched our own in this regard. Stacey Rex's articulation is particularly telling.

> My prediction for any future encounters with technology is parallel to that of the past in that I will have to practically force myself to become comfortable with it. . . . In fact, I cannot see any advantage to my "fear" of new technology.

Olivia Bartlett, one of the most sophisticated technology users in the MTU Publication Management class, expressed her apprehension in these words.

> I am scared to live in this technology age because by blinking an eye, it seems I have missed something new. . . . Technology is submerging us, choking us, and it never lets up. . . . [College life] is just a warm up routine for the real world, where I will have to undergo a life long learning if I want to keep a job in the technology field.

---

[6]For a fascinating social and philosophical treatment of humans' relationships to institutions in Western culture, see Anthony Giddens' *Central Problems in Social Theory: Action, Structure, and Contradiction in Social Analysis.*

Although some students relish the prospect of life-long technological learning, most of them feel at least some reluctance toward the professional regimen that technological hegemony preordains for them.

LESSONS LEARNED AND NEXT STEPS

Clearly, and not surprisingly, students will continue to come to our English Studies classes with a number of learning strategies and views about technology. Some of their attitudes and approaches will be unfamiliar and uncomfortable to us, and many of the attitudes will be unacknowledged or unarticulated. Throughout this chapter, we have hinted at some implications of new technological fluencies and capabilities, multiple modes of learning, and the range of attitudes that students bring to the English classroom, yet questions such as the following remain unanswered:

- What can we do with the lessons learned with students in these technology autobiographies?
- How can we incorporate students' views and abilities in an on-going way in our creation of new technology-rich literacy classes?

Although we are not in a position to offer any conclusive answers to these questions, we can, based on our observations, suggest several productive strategies for teachers. First, teachers must admit that observations of student technological attitudes, literacy practices, and expectations should inform, to some extent, our class planning for the foreseeable future. It is the contention of the chapter authors that students should be a more robust part of that planning.

How we integrate students into our course planning will depend, obviously, upon the institutional contexts in which we and our students labor. For example, in small, cohesive programs, it may be easier to predict which students will enroll in particular courses. Teachers and students often become well acquainted in such programs; it may even be practical to collect technology autobiographies from students as they enter the program, and to publish those documents on a website or make them available in a central repository accessible to teachers of upper-division courses. On the other hand, large programs that enroll many part-time or nontraditional students may find it more difficult to predict enrollments or determine which students will turn up in a given semester.

In addition, teachers will certainly have to challenge students' research capabilities as they become increasingly dependent on and expert in technologies such as surfing the web, evaluating sources, and constructing arguments in that realm. Not only should students know and value the paper-based research literacy skills prevalent in English studies, we should understand and value—and take advantage of—their special skills.

Many students have the ability to design, create, manipulate, and transfer files, music, and video around on the Internet and incorporate those media into classroom compositions. In Karla Kitalong's Fall semester 2000 honors composition courses, for example, three of eight groups assigned to present a ten-minute skit chose the medium of video; what the videos lacked in technical quality, they made up for in rhetorical sophistication. Seth Jacobs, another Fall 2000 honors student, followed up his technology autobiography with a community study detailing his participation in a hip-hop musical group. Although the members of the group are now scattered at colleges around the country, they continue to mix music and produce CDs. Each records his portion of the song and transmits it via the Internet to the group member who is studying digital media, because he has access to a high-quality audio mixer in his school's production lab. Without the technology autobiography, Kitalong would not have known about Seth's interest and skill in music production. He returned to her class for the second semester, giving her an opportunity to incorporate his expertise into her course planning.

English teachers wrestle with the problem of finding reasonable and equitable ways to incorporate a wide variety of media into the "composing" that goes on in our classes. Can our class projects, for instance, take advantage of a student's access to a digital video-editing suite? Can our assignments remain flexible enough to accommodate any media to which the course participants, both teachers and students, have access? And, in our grading, can we remain "fair" to those students who lack access or haven't yet learned to use technologies? Will the least fluent students in this diverse mix of experiences and expertise be given the lowest grades despite our best intentions?

It is our intention—although not yet our smoothly integrated habit—that our classes take advantage of any literacies that the students bring to the table, in addition to those with which teachers walk into the classroom. In order to accomplish this collaborative planning with students who enroll in our classes, we might need to ask more of one of the most established and often conservative institutional practices in our schools: the registration process. We might ask the registrar to initiate early planning mechanisms that go beyond imposing prerequisites—

minimal standards to which students must adhere. Effective planning mechanisms for collaboratively designed literacy courses need to allow us to survey ahead of time students' technological proclivities, access levels, interests, and levels of ambivalence and to take those survey results into account in our course development. Electronic registration makes this process somewhat easier. At UCF and Michigan Tech, teachers who know how to use the web-based registration database can preview the list of students enrolled in their classes. But teachers are typically among the last employees to receive the often extensive training necessary to use such resources. And gaining access to a list of names probably won't help with planning general education courses, except in the smallest of institutions.

Lacking effective mechanisms by which to assess the students' technological abilities in advance of the semester, other ways of leveling the playing field are available. For instance, some of the experiential diversity we face in our classes might be alleviated if we call upon the most sophisticated technology users to lead workshops that allow those who haven't been exposed to technologies in the past—whether students or teachers—to be taught by those who have.

During the fall semester of 1999, when Karla Kitalong was assigned to teach a graphic design course for technical communication majors at the University of Central Florida. She recognized her own shortcomings: For one thing, she had never before taught a graphic design class. Moreover, as a newcomer to UCF, she was unfamiliar with both the technical communication curriculum and the program's computer lab. To help compensate for her own limitations, Kitalong assigned students to prepare "mini-teaches"—20-minute instructional modules—covering particular tools used by visual designers of technical documents. The mini-teaches correlated with specific chapters in the course text to help students learn necessary technologies in a timely fashion.

In reflecting on the assignment, Kitalong concluded that the workshops would have been more effective had the students conducted a significant audience analysis in order to target the demonstrations toward the contextualized needs of their fellow students in the course. Technology autobiographies could have been assigned early in the term, both to acquaint Kitalong with the experiences and needs of her 23 students, and to give her an introduction to their perception of the technical communication curriculum.

Can technology-training sessions—including the research, planning, and supporting document production that they entail—legitimately "count" as part of students' grades? Indeed they can, as Kitalong's experience shows, but such course components must be collaboratively developed with the students, and should take advantage not only of their previous experience, but also of the learning needs of the class, and of the "surgical strike" and other learning tendencies that many students prefer.

Some of these planning mechanisms—review of technology autobiographies, collaborative design of assignments, flexibility in how course goals and assignments are enacted—are available to us now. Others depend upon the vagaries of institutional contexts. In closing, we reiterate our conviction that teachers are obliged to find ways to engage students in course design and planning because such engagement encourages participatory citizenship. If we expect students to respond honestly and openly in their technology autobiographies and to take our educational efforts seriously, we should be prepared to demonstrate to them how their work influences the class in which they are enrolled, and to a greater extent, classes we teach in the future. If we can somehow place students at the beginning, middle, and end of our course-designing process, we will have made a powerful first step toward engaging them in a form of participatory citizenship.

The authors invite potential collaborators to join us in designing and enacting future inter-institutional literacy-based projects. We are particularly interested in working with students and teachers from K-12 districts, community colleges, and schools with historically underrepresented populations. We are further interested in additional applications of the technology autobiography assignment.

Karla Saari Kitalong - kitalong@pegasus.cc.ucf.edu
Dickie Selfe - rselfe@mtu.edu
Michael Moore - mmoore@mtu.edu

WORKS CITED

Aristotle, *Politics*. cited in Johnson.
Brandt, Deborah. "Accumulating Literacy: Writing and Learning to Write in the Twentieth Century," *College English* 57 (1995): 649-668.
———. *Literacy as Involvement: The Acts of Writers, Readers, and Texts*. Carbondale: Southern Illinois UP, 1990.
Bravo, Ellen. "The Hazards of Leaving Out the Users." In *Participatory Design: Principles and Practices*. Eds. Douglas Schuler and Namioka Aki. Hillsdale, NJ: Erlbaum, 1993. 3-11.

Eldred, Janet Carey, and Peter Mortensen. "Reading Literacy Narratives." *College English* 54 (1992): 512–539.

Giddens, Anthony. *Central Problems in Social Theory: Action, Structure and Contradiction in Social Analysis*. Berkeley: U of California P, 1979.

Johnson, Robert R. *User-Centered Technology: A Rhetorical Theory for Computers and Other Mundane Artifacts*. Albany: SUNY Press, 1998.

Mead, Margaret. *Culture and Commitment: A Study of the Generation Gap*. Garden City, NY: Natural History Press/Doubleday and Company, 1970.

Miller, Richard. "The Arts of Complicity: Pragmatism and the Culture of Schooling." *College English* 61 (1998): 10–28.

Moore, Michael R. "Adapting to a Digital Culture: Technical Writing in a Networked Classroom." *Interactive Learning: Vignettes from America's Most Wired Campuses*. Ed. David G. Brown. Bolton, MA: Anker, 1999. 226–228

——. "Reading, Agency, and Participatory Pedagogy: Recent Titles in Technical Communication." *Reader: Essays in Reader-Oriented Theory, Criticism, and Pedagogy* Fall 1999: 62-76.

Moran, Charles and Cynthia L. Selfe. "Teaching English Across the Technology/Wealth Gap." *English Journal 88* (1999): 48–55.

Nardi, Bonnie A. and Vicki L. O'Day. *Information Ecologies: Using Technology with Heart*. Cambridge, MA: The MIT Press, 1999.

Selfe, Cynthia L. "Technology and Literacy: A Story About the Perils of Not Paying Attention." *College Composition and Communication* 50 (1999): 411–436.

Selfe, Richard. *Critical, Technical Literacy Practices in and Around Technology-Rich Communication Facilities*. Diss. Michigan Technological U, 1997.

Soliday, Mary. "Translating Self and Difference Through Literacy Narratives." *College English* 56 (1994): 511–526

Tapscott, Don. *Growing Up Digital: The Rise of the Net Generation*. New York: McGraw-Hill, 1998.

13

CRAZY QUILTS
Piecing Together Collaborative Research

Katherine Fischer
Clarke College

with

Chris Bailey, Aaron J. Brown, Jennifer Dondlinger, Joe
Doolittle, Jacqueline Kerkeman, Rosemarie Schneider,
Elizabeth Serflek, and Pam Smith[1]

*What happens when students and teacher abandon that which they
have held sacred in writing research—tenets of the carefully formed thesis, singularly written argument, "proven" conclusion? What happens
when, worse yet, neither students nor teacher has a clue at the beginning of the project what research will lead to? Throw all this pandemo-
nium into a melting pot of html and quilting and there's no telling what
is likely to happen! This chapter describes the work of a second-semes-
ter FYC course in which students collaborated to create a web text from
the individual papers they had written during the first semester. This
activity fostered four conditions important to modern research writing:
a shared writing environment, associative and metaphorical thinking,
a heightened sense of audience, and reduced authorial control.*

---

[1]All students noted in this essay participated in Honors Colloquium: Voices
From Nature at Clarke College in Dubuque, Iowa, 1998-1999. They generously have given their permission for the use of their work and have collaborated
with me on the writing of this essay. I am most grateful to them for the many
things they taught me through this project and for allowing me to write about
them. Their webtext may be viewed at http://keller.clarke.edu/~honcoll/.

FLANNEL AND VELVETS

In crazy quilt years, we'd just bring whatever we could find. Got rid of my husband's favorite shirt that way—all green and orange with yellow waves running through it—awful as a shirt but quite splendid as part of a quilt. All the same, you should have heard him squawk, "TILDY, what did you do with my shirt?" These quilts didn't look as elegant as those we made out of carefully patterned yards of cotton cloth, but they sure kept us in stitches during the making. I'm sure glad the museum invited the Queen Bees to display our half-century of quilts for the exhibit.

"Yes, you'll each bring the research papers you wrote first semester and patch them together on the Web," I explained to students in our two-semester composition class. Their original first-semester papers were individually written thesis/support compositions rooted in research done by teams. Quite obviously, they already knew how to write traditional academic research, but these papers lacked meaning beyond the stencil of thesis-fill-in-conclusion. These papers took no risks. I knew the students could deliver more. I hoped they could actually pull up their chairs to the table of scholarship and *contribute to* rather than simply *repeat* the conversations. Second semester, I hoped, they'd unite these separate pieces on the quilter's frame collaboratively and move beyond traditional research papers.

It seems inauthentic to expect first-year students to so immediately assume voices of authority typical of such research papers. They are, after all, new to writing at such levels of authority, new to thinking beyond encyclopedic snippets patched together with formulaic transitions, and quite often the halls of academe intimidate them. Given postmodern theory, fostering only the loner, single-voiced paper is also counterproductive to negotiated learning. Among all the kinds of academic writing we do, research should be the *most* shared and dialogic task we perform (interviewing experts, quoting other texts, arguing or agreeing with others, etc.), yet we pretend that it is not a shared space; thus we raise questions of plagiarism and stolen ideas (Howard, and Lunsford and West). Traditional first-year student research writing too often reads like "an assignment" rather than like the energetic offspring of those engaged in the need to explore and the desire to learn.

Yet to satisfy our college's expectation, first-term students wrote individual research papers employing multiple sources and documentation. Far from engaging in a loner exercise, however, they worked in research teams exchanging information and divvying up subtopics.

Discussing in class and filling one another's e-mail/voicemail, they also shared research across teams. Out of this very cooperative learning environment, they returned to their garrets to hammer out single-authored papers—with the exception of Jacqueline and Chris, who sat together at the keyboard from Word One.

The academic norm for writing research privileges airtight theses nailed down by numerous textual references, footnotes, and truckloads of Aristotelian logic. It favors linear sequencing of information leading up to conclusions with which readers must agree. Otherwise, students are taught, they have failed as writers. Once the conclusion is reached in such papers, the learning ends—for both reader and writer. Many of their first-term papers fit this model and Rosemarie even went so far as to proclaim, "Just let me work alone. Teams and collaboration drive me crazy."

I make a distinction here between "collaborated" and "cooperative" writing. In this first adventure with students, I strove for *collaborated* and ended up with *cooperative*. The first, I believe, is more multi-authored from the start, more shared, more successful in achieving a higher degree of shared authorship and revision. The latter involves teamwork and cooperation, but the work remains at once individual, although shared through "links." The writer's signature remains intact. Collaborated writing, however, is that which results in the authors wondering afterward "what did I write?" versus "what did a classmate write?" versus "what did *we* write?"[2]

PIECING IT TOGETHER

See this piece? The stitches are tidy, even. They make the different colors and patterns blend. It came out of one of the stitcher's uniforms. She quit work once she had children, so she didn't need the nursing whites anymore. And this one over here, the gray-green patch, it came from my husband's World War II uniform. Wasn't

---

[2]Linking from this essay written at the conclusion of the "Dirt on the Disk Drive" project, in the following term a new class of students moved into much more "collaborated" writing. For this project, "Back to the Future" (which focused on millennium and futurist studies) students never wrote individual papers. From the start they worked together writing paragraphs and links and creating a grand bulletin board in the Writing Lab of "boodrows," their name for chunks of text. They strung yarn from boodrow to boodrow linking their collaborated texts and later moved the entire works to the electronic space on the Web (http://www.clarke.edu/honors/colloquium/2000/index.htm.

any use to him any more, thank goodness. You English teachers
have pages to write and to read. We quilters "read" the fabric.
The squares of our pajamas, the pieces from our kids' shirts, our
husband's trousers. These are our pages.

As an advocate of alternate writing in composition classes
(along with people like Bishop, Heilker, and Starkey), I also wanted students to explore more Montaignian ways of writing research. Writing
that allows for letter-writing and storytelling, that makes room for multiple voices, and that asks questions rather than always serving up conclusions, I believed, might be more conducive to actual learning, to taking risks. Hypertextualizing their individual papers on the World Wide
Web would coax students into more teamwork, I hoped, because they
would have to connect their independent texts. In short, they would
attempt to stitch their single patches together to form their own crazy
quilt.

Informed by theorizing on the nature of collaboration, team
writing, and collective intelligence (Ede and Lunsford, Yancey and
Spooner, etc.) I hoped, too, that students might discover new ways of
shaping research—even their heretofore-individual papers. But I discovered that our crazy quilt process was more complicated, messier, more
haphazard, and far less under teacherly control than I'd found in the
past. "Create a Web text in which you connect your individual papers,"
I invited. Beyond this, I offered no design for co-ordinating, hyper-writ-
ing, and blending their research. Such a blueprint, I worried, might
restrict students to my design resulting in papers snipped to fit and
patched together with perfunctory and very visible duct tape. They
would lay out their paragraphs, reshape the fabric to fit, and add newly
multi-authored text to fill in. Normally, I have a fairly good idea of the
scope, labor, and potential papers that will result in assigning research.
But with this project, I knew as little as students did (or less). Excerpted
from their first online "chat" negotiation of linking together, students
commented:

Aaron J. Brown:
Ok, let the funfest begin. My research is on Midwestern
culture's relationship to the land. I see tie-ins with Joe
and whoever's doing the Native American paper. Who
else wants to sign on?

Jacqueline Kerkman:
We discuss geothermal energy in the Midwest.

Jennifer Dondlinger:
Mine is about the New Madrid earthquake in the Midwest in 1811.

Jacqueline Kerkman:
I see some major connection, geothermal energy is all about fault lines!

Pam K. Smith:
Joe, our papers both deal with land issues and legislation—How are we going to save farmland? How are we going to save national parks?

Jacqueline Kerkman:
Hey, Lizzy, maybe we could link because we talk about alternative energy and you talk about alternative medicine.

Elizabeth Serflek:
My paper deals with herbs used for medicinal purposes and, Pam, if your parks have plants, there's linkage.

Rose Schneider:
This free association is weird. People are going to see some links and ask "what the heck?"

Chris Bailey:
Here's a link, there's a link—everywhere a link, link.

Through ongoing discussions, students revised their original papers, coordinating with one another multi-authored swatches of text between papers, introductions, and explanatory texts; they added features such as an e-mail link for readers' response to the group and a "Genesis" page revealing their original discussions collaborating online. The initially odd swatches opened new edges. When they saw a purple plaid butting up against a puce stripe, they had to question the integrity and beauty of the quilt more carefully. Evidence of their original papers was still apparent, but most underwent major upheaval in order to contribute to the needs of the group text. Students decided, however, to keep their own voices and styles rather than to adopt a standard because, "we want to sound like ourselves." The student "paper" below represents one possible reading of "Dirt on the Disk Drive." As with all multifariously linked web projects, "Dirt" could be read hundreds of ways depending on the links selected. "Click," "return," and "scroll" indicate the reader's choice in navigating the text. (Links to sites outside student writing appear underlined but not emboldened.)

*   *   *

DIRT IN THE DISK DRIVE

We focused our research on the theme of "The Real Dirt." We traveled through archeological digs and ancient Native American rites to discover how the land offers preservation of the body after death and homeopathic remedies used by healers of the living. We researched everything from the history of land legislation, land ownership, and the National Parks to eco-feminism, family farms, and alternative energy sources. From the field of linguistics, we questioned how language affects our attitude toward land environmentalism.

We invite you, dear reader, to stroll the landscape of this research, to explore links, to scoop handfuls of information and check them for soil quality, to till your own thoughts on these issues, and to join us as land-rovers over the hills and valleys of scholarship.

"Big Problems for Small Farms"
by Joe Doolittle

I have no problem saying the family
farm should be
DO YOU?

"Dirty Words: Propoganda in Environmental Literature".

by Rosemarie Schneider

The word "dirt" should be eliminated from English!

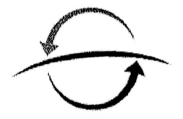

"Geothermal Energy: The Alternative of the Future"
by Christopher Bailey
and Jacqueline Kerkman

Fossil fuels are being burned faster than dinosaurs are becoming coal.

"Dr. Chemical, Dr. Earth: Remedies from Native AmericanCultures"

by Elizabeth Serflek

A tree curing backaches?

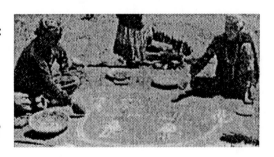

"The Great Plains in Midwestern Culture"
by Aaron J. Brown

What do Bob Dylan and Joe McCarthy have in Common?
The Midwestern Essence!

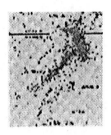

"Shake, Rattle, 'N Roll: The New Madrid
Fault, Past and Present"

by Jennifer Dondlinger

Do you think, "We don't get earthquakes
in the Midwest?"
WRONG!

"National Parks or National Problems"
by Pam Smith

Would you like to visit a national park?
GO NOW!

click

> When you think of <u>California</u>, you probably conjure up images of
> warm sunny beaches, palm trees, the Pacific Ocean, blondes in biki-
> nis, muscle men, the Beach Boys, Hollywood, and, of course, earth-
> quakes. One of the most infamous earthquakes to rock California hit
> on <u>April 18, 1906</u> with the strongest tremor measuring 8.3 on the
> Richter scale (Cherny, 1996). This quake was responsible for a **<u>fire</u>**
> that burned uncontrollably in San Francisco for three days and two
> nights.

click

> **<u>Fires</u>** are yet another component of the controversy of natural regu-
> lation. During the 1988 Yellowstone fires, official let them burn in
> accordance with the principles of natural regulation (<u>National Park
> Service Fire in the National Parks, 1</u>)

return to <u>earthquakes</u>

Various other major earthquakes dot California's shaky history and are expected to continue into the future (Lowell, 1996). As a result, California has developed and implemented earthquake safety measures to prevent losses (U.S. Geological Survey Circular, 1990). **<u>The Plate Tectonics</u> <u>theory</u>** explains the causes of an earthquake.

click

Geothermal energy is available wherever the earth's large oceanic and crystal plates slide apart. This is based on the idea of **<u>plate tectonics.</u>** The earth is made up of huge plates of rock floating on molten rock and magma. These plates do not fit together perfectly.

or click <u>theory</u>

Not only do these connotations and hidden meanings influence thinking, they can determine it! I have done extensive reading on linguistic **<u>theories </u>**and according to Sapir-Whorf hypothesis, the words we use determine the way we think (Crystal 15). Mr. Editor, you could help save our children from impure thoughts forced on their minds whenever they hear the word *dirty*!

return to <u>plate tectonics</u>

When the energy crisis hit America in the 1970's, people scrambled to find ways to conserve energy. They produced smaller cars, drove less, and turned down thermostats. They started to examine **<u>alternative energy sources</u>**.

click

Why is <u>alternative</u> medicine becoming so popular? Wolf notes that "In some instances, individuals suffering from chronic aliments become disenchanted with Western medicine's ability to help them cope. . ." According to Dr. Zimmerman, Director of anthropology at the University of South Dakota, Native Americans used poplar bark to cure <u>**headaches.**</u>

click

Also giving the family farmer a <u>**headache**</u> is the way the United States handles trading policy. U.S. corn exports are down 30% because nations we generally trade with do not have a large demand for American crops right now. . . This topic's impact is very important to me. My great-great-grandfather <u>**settled the land**</u> where I live now, and I am a descendent of a long line of family farmers.

click

Farmers <u>**settling**</u> in the western and southern plains tore up the plains to grow crops foreign to the <u>**land**</u>, such as wheat and corn. In 1935, the first major dust storm of the Dust Bowl occurred (Worchester 10). The storms were actually enhanced by agricultural practices of farmers in this region (5). If Oklahoma farmers had simply waited out the storm instead of persistently plowing at the onset, the costly operation of repairing the land would have been averted. Granted, the problem of massive unemployment due to the loss of farming jobs would have been equally daunting. (5)

To see the plight of modern family farms, see <u>Joe Doolittle's paper</u>.

scroll to beginning of Great Plains

Today the sun will rise on the American Great Plains. Amber light will streak across the prairie, over the flat land and around the scarce hills. It will dart through the wind-swept wild grass and domesticated corn and wheat. The same **sun** has charted this same path every morning for million of years and today will be no different. Yet the people who live on this land they call the Great Plains may wake feeling quite a bit different than their ancestors who settled the prairie only a few centuries ago.

click

A bear meanders across the road several hundred yards in front of your slowly moving vehicle. The **sun** shines in such a way that it seems the mountains above you go on forever. This pristine image of our nation's national parks is unfortunately getting harder to find. Several of the National Park Service's duties currently include managing the daily needs of the national parks, expanding the system, communicating the significance of American heritage, and preserving the land for enjoyment by **future generations**. (Hartzog, 95)

click

I'm sure, Mr. Editor, that you will be hailed as a prophet and savior of English from the degradation that has befallen it if you implement a few of my modest proposals. If even one person of note takes the first step, the path will be open to the elimination of all the nasty, rude, vulgar and disgusting words. . . It would be a return to innocence for both our language and our culture. I'm sure **future generations** will thank you.

*   *   *

PATTERNS

If you look at it this way, it looks like a ship coming into port. But if you spread it out this way, you'll see a cow entering the barn. However you see it, this quilt is all the grander for the many patches and ideas we each brought to it. Right now you might be thinking, "Old Tildy is a nutcase," but just you wait and see. Next time you visit the exhibit, I'll bet you'll see the moon, the sun, and the stars in it, yourself!

With their incessant tendency to make associative links, I can hear these students coaxing even now, "Wouldn't it be cool if you said something about **future generations** for comp. students, Katie?" Although educational uses of HTML/Web are fairly recent, much of what it does is not really new. Readers have always been able to jump from page to page after all, and multiple-voiced essays do exist on paper. Yet we found the medium fosters more strongly four main conditions conducive to more modern research writing: (1) shared writing environment; (2) use of associative and metaphorical thinking; (3) heightened sense of audience; (4) lessening of authorial control.

(1) Students engaged in a cooperative writing environment made more possible (2) by the necessity of thinking in associative, non-linear ways to form links. Because they shared one another's links, students immediately realized the need to revise text, often cowriting; they gained a sense of group ownership of the project. Many like Rosemarie—who reframed research into a letter to the Editor from an Orwellian teacher proposing censorship—changed their original papers significantly to coordinate with others in "acts of accommodation" as Mortensen and Kirsch suggest (561). Seeing how links juxtaposed their varying texts, Jennifer juxtaposed historical paragraphs within her own text relaying flood victims' accounts alongside paragraphs of informational text: "A bunch of us were talking—it could be like one of those 'Lewis and Clark' documentaries."

Some like Elizabeth developed metaphorical links between papers (alternative headache remedies linking to farmers' headaches over government controls). Within his own paper, Aaron linked Bob Dylan and Senator Joseph McCarthy as Midwesterners shaped by prairie culture. In assisting students through research obstacles, teachers often tell them to come up with other key words, to consider a multitude of other ways to connect to information; hyperlinking research reiterates this process.

(3) Because their work was published on the Web and because (4) readers could choose links, students gained a heightened sense of audience; furthermore they came to terms with a shift in authorial control, echoing the findings of Penrose and Geisler. Relinquishing authorial control via button links ran the gamut from Rosemarie and Pam, who offered numerous graphic buttons and highlighted words, to Aaron, whose button links were carefully restricted to fellow students: "**for Joe Doolittle's paper, click here**." Discussing how their project more closely resembled a magazine in which readers flip back and forth among articles and ads, students grew comfortable with the electronic options. They also quickly discovered that they could offer readers more accurate access rather than merely the quoted and paraphrased passages of sources; now they could link readers directly to original sources such as the National Park Service site.

Because compositions on the Web are only a button-click away from beer banners, the MTV homepage, and Congressional hearings, students found their research situated in a more expansive environment than just academe. They consternated over including graphics and controlling links—where to give readers more or less choice. This loss of authorial control was threatening to some such as Jennifer, who commented, "Knowing someone may link out of my paper and never come back is a bit disheartening." Others thought they may actually gain readers because of links. Joe's research focused on the plight of the family farm. In his reflection essay of one reader's journey, he imitates the reader reluctant to read about farms: "Agriculture? Why do I keep landing in this paper! Who'd want to read THAT?" only to later conclude, "Hey, now that I've landed in here, this farming stuff isn't so bad."

Answering Lunsford and Ede's call for students to learn "to interrogate the discourses of schooling" (177), Chris claims, "It's almost impossible to read any individual paper from beginning to end. Eventually you'll click and be swept away from one writer's idea into a new one. Good! Let learning and reading center around the *reader* instead of the *writer*." By engaging in research writing quilted on the Web as a lively collaborative activity, students gained that which poet Walt Whitman reminds us of in describing a dimpled spider. As the spider flings out gossamer thread after gossamer thread, Whitman writes, his goal is "Only to connect, oh my soul."

WORKS CITED

Bishop, Wendy. *Elements of Alternate Style*. Portsmouth, NH: Boynton/Cook, 1997.

Ede, Lisa and Andrea Lunsford. *Singular Text/Plural Authors: Perspectives on Collaborative Writing*. Carbondale: Southern Illinois UP, 1990.

Heilker, Paul. *The Essay*. Urbana, IL: NCTE, 1996.

Howard, Rebecca Moore. "Plagiarisms, Authorships, and the Academic Death Penalty." *College English* 57.7 (1995): 788-806.

Lunsford, Andrea, and Lisa Ede. "Representing Audience: 'Successful' Discourse and Disciplinary Critique." *CCC* 47.2 (1996): 167-179.

Lunsford, Andrea, and Susan West. "Intellectual Property and Composition Studies," *CCC* 47.3 (1996): 383-411.

Mortensen, Peter, and Gesa E. Kirsch. "On Authority in the Study of Writing." *CCC* 44.4 (1993): 556-72.

Penrose, Ann M. and Cheryl Geisler. "Reading and Writing Without Authority." *CCC* 45.4 (1994): 505-520.

Starkey, David. *Teaching Writing Creatively*. Portsmouth: Boynton/Cook, 1998.

Yancey, Kathleen Blake, and Michael Spooner. "A Single Good Mind: Collaboration, Cooperation, and the Writing Self." *CCC* 49.1 (1998): 45-62.

14

WEB-BASED PEER REVIEW

An Opportunity for Conversation

Daniel Anderson
University of North Carolina—Chapel Hill

Investigation of ways of responding to student writing over the years suggests that readers should avoid error hunting and provide feedback that is "conversational." Responses to writing should prompt authors to reflect on and practice opportunities for serious rewriting. In addition, peer-driven response should allow student reviewers to enjoy the benefits of reflection on higher-order writing concerns. This article discusses implications for peer review when carried out using a Web-based review platform in a first-year writing class. Here, Web-based reviews shift attention away from surface-level writing concerns, and the public nature of the Web-based review platform impacts the peer response experience. Evaluations of the Web-based exercise indicate that students saw themselves as participants in a public act of communication that heightened their engagement as writers and reviewers. The online environment both influences the peer review process and prompts writing instructors to reflect on how such technologies impact familiar activities of readers and writers.

Richard Straub highlights the strengths of responding to student writing with "conversational" commentary in "Teacher Response as Conversation: More than Casual Talk, an Exploration." Straub suggests that conversational response can prove useful in facilitating "comments that dramatize the presence of a reader, keep a good deal of control over the writing in the hands of the writer, and lead students back into the chaos of revision—three goals that have come to dominate our talk about responding to student writing" (391). Straub is discussing teacher response to student work, but he also places conversational response within a framework for developing literacy that extends beyond the student writer and teacher authority. Straub quotes Deborah Brandt in his observation that

> When teachers treat their responses as a conversation—not just feedback—they model for students how readers and writers muster and manage language, metacommunicative cues, and context in order to create meaning. They provide the kind of knowledge about texts and text-making that Brandt finds crucial to literacy learning, by giving students "not merely experience with texts but ample access to other people who read and write and who will show you why and how they do it" (6). Teachers who make their comments part of a larger conversation with the student do not view the text as an autonomous artifact; they view the text as a meeting place for writers and readers, a "public social reality," a means for intersubjective dialogue. (392)

One such public forum for conversational response is the Web-based peer review platform. The peer review platform can be seen as an emerging kind of "meeting place" where conversations between readers and writers occur. I discuss a peer review exercise and offer interpretations based on the reviews written by students and responses to survey questions. The Web-based peer review platform may facilitate guided readings of papers and shift attention away from surface-level writing concerns. Additionally, the public nature of the review platform may impact the peer response experience.

The peer review platform can be read as both offering benefits and raising concerns. Familiar benefits of face-to-face peer response play out in the exchanges that take place using the online review platform.[1] At the same time, a key tension emerges between a "conversa-

---

[1]Over the years, the usefulness of peer response has been argued to the point that the process is now almost naturalized into writing pedagogies. Building community, liberating students, providing audiences for writers, and delivering facilitative feedback are only some of benefits peer response can claim.

tional ideal" for peer response and the more directive comments submitted to the online review platform. This tension plays out (and in some ways may originate) in the prompts designed to guide the review process, prompts that seem able to guide readings of papers, but that may be overly directive as well. Finally, it is possible to view tensions between conversational and directive readings as in some ways related to the "read only" format of the online review platform.

This last point is crucial because increasingly teachers find themselves called upon to conduct electronic peer review exercises or compose electronic responses. The experiences discussed here suggest that the online review environment influences the activities of readers and writers. Further, platforms for electronic response (and other online, learning environments) are quickly becoming standardized, conventionalized, naturalized. In concluding, then, this article details responses and revisions to the peer review platform itself. By looking at the peer review platform as a kind of draft in need of reading, perhaps we can begin a useful conversation about online peer review environments for writing instructors working in "the late age of print."

The peer review exercise discussed here took place in a first-year composition course taught during the summer of 1999 at the University of North Carolina at Chapel Hill. Prior to conducting the peer reviews, students developed a research question, explored topics in the social sciences, and conducted interviews. They then composed first drafts of papers that articulated a research question, contained and documented evidence from readings and interviews, and followed appropriate guidelines for formatting in the discipline. Students were also given explicit instructions for conducting the peer review assignment that discussed reviews as an opportunity to show rather than tell peers about opportunities for rewriting and stressed the importance of avoiding "error-hunting" while reviewing.[2]

The exercise was carried out using a Web-based peer review platform designed to facilitate paper sharing and response. Creating

---

Common tracings of these themes emerge in writings about community such as Kenneth Bruffee's "Collaborative Learning and the Conversation of Mankind," in manifestos such as Peter Elbow's *Writing Without Teachers*, in specific discussion of peer review practices such as Ronald Barron's "What I Wish I Had Known about Peer Response Groups but Didn't," and in guides to response and assessment such as Edward White's *Assigning, Responding, Evaluating: A Writing Teacher's Guide.*

[2]For more on showing and telling in responses to writing, see Peter Elbow's *Writing Without Teachers*. For more on avoiding error hunting, see Erika Lindemann's *A Rhetoric for Writing Teachers*, especially Chapter fourteen.

such a peer review platform begins with an instructor developing a set of prompts that will guide the peer review. The instructor has the option of composing her own prompts or choosing prompts from a menu. Once an instructor has chosen or written a set of prompts to guide the review, she submits a Web form and a peer review platform for the exercise is created.[3] The platform used for the assignment discussed in this paper is shown in Figure 14.1.

Figure 14.1 has been annotated with three numbers to better explain the functionality of the peer review platform. Annotation 1 indicates the "Submit a Paper" button at the top of the review platform. Selecting the "Submit a Paper" button loads a form into the left-hand frame of the browser window where participants paste the text of their papers to be submitted for review.[4] Once a paper has been submitted, it

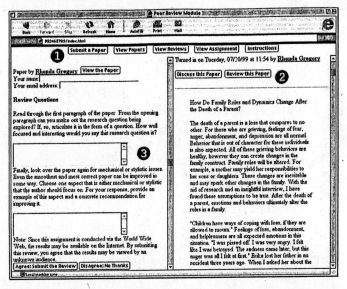

---

[3]The peer review platform is one of many online learning environments developed by the Studio for Instructional Technologies and English Studies at UNC, Chapel Hill (you can see and use the latest version of the peer review platform at http://sites.unc.edu/tools/pr2.0).

[4]Pasting text to be reviewed into the peer review platform results in the loss of formatting elements such as italicized and boldfaced type. Whereas the loss of formatting poses real problems in many situations, the "pasted text" form of review offered two benefits: (1) it simplified logistics a great deal, virtually overcoming elements of disruption posed by other electronic review methods (see Irvin Peckham's "If It Ain't Broke, Why Fix It?: Disruptive and Constructive Computer-Mediated Response Group Practices"), and (2) it focused attention away from surface-level writing concerns.

will be linked to a list that will be loaded into the platform by selecting the "View Papers" button. A paper submitted by a student is displayed in the frame on the right-hand side of the browser window.

Annotation 2 shows some of the review options available once a paper has been submitted. Selecting the "Discuss this Paper" button opens an asynchronous discussion forum associated with each paper where participants can engage one another in open-ended conversation. Selecting the "Review this Paper" button loads the form seen in the left-hand frame of the browser window. The form contains the prompts that the instructor selected or composed when initially creating the platform, as indicated by annotation 3. (This form has been edited for the screen shot.) Reviewers refer to the paper in the right-hand frame while responding to the prompts in the left-hand frame. When a reader selects the "Submit the Review" button, her review will be added to a list reviews and linked to the bottom of the paper being reviewed.

Students reviewed the papers of partners in collaborative groups of three or four that were established at the beginning of the course. They conducted their peer reviews outside of class over the course of several days using the review prompt function of the online peer review platform. After all the members of the group had offered reviews, the instructor read and commented on the papers using the review platform. On average, each paper submitted to the platform was reviewed three times. The assignment concluded with revisions of papers based on the comments authors had received.

Before continuing, I must offer a familiar disclaimer. The responses discussed here represent a single class that conducted peer reviews using only the Web-based platform. The survey given to peer review participants should not be seen as generating authoritative data from which to draw conclusions, and the length of this piece does not allow me to address numerous responses and counter- and cross-currents that flow from them. In short, my claims here merely articulate an interpretation of the assignment that can be used to facilitate discussion of the online peer review platform and online learning environments. Further, in retrospect, I now see that the prompts used to guide the peer review exercise warrant as much investigation as do the responses to them.

The initial prompt in the Peer Review platform called for reviewers to identify and articulate the research question explored in the paper:

> Read through the first paragraph of the paper. From the opening paragraph can you make out the research question being

explored? If, so, articulate it in the form of a question. How well focused and interesting would you say this research question is?

This prompt (and the others used in the exercise) can be seen as guiding a reading of the paper and as eliciting a specific response from reviewers. Here we might begin to trace a tension between generating reviews that express the general impressions of interested readers and those that provide specific recommendations for writers. In Nancy's Sommers' influential "Responding to Student Writing," we may see such a tension already emerging in recommendations both to avoid focusing on "accidents of discourse" (150) and to offer comments "anchored in the particulars of the students' texts" (152).

Responses to this prompt that were able to pinpoint a clear research question tended to simply state their success or articulate the question in the response. Alternatively, responses that had more difficulty identifying the research question, tended to be more directive or to try to develop a possibility for a question to be used:

> Your examples are good because they really give the reader something to think about. The biggest problem I see is your research question is not stated clearly. If I had to guess what your research topic is about, I would say, What are some burdens that parents face after becoming a parent? You should clearly state this in your paper. Overall this is good research topic.[5]

This response by Connie Galles suggests the conversational reader Straub recommends: "If I had to guess. . . ." It also seems to avoid the "vague" directives that concern Sommers by offering a specific suggestion for revision. Still, the response may be viewed as overly directive in its recommendation to "clearly state this" in your paper. Perhaps a review prompt that focused on the research question but asked participants to discuss their impressions or pose a question for the original author might have helped respondents to offer specific advice in less directive ways.[6]

The second review prompt was meant to guide a reading of the entire paper with an eye toward spotting problems with organization:

---

[5]Responses represent informal writing situations and are reproduced verbatim with the students' permission.

[6]In "Peer Response that Works," Jane Schaffer advocates posing questions to the author as a part of response: "Questions . . . spur writers to substantial revision and improvement. They provide a ready-made springboard for invention and elaboration that the statement format does not" (82).

Now read the entire paper. Take notes if you need to. Track the organization of each section of the paper. Record what the sections are generally about and say something about how well they relate to the overall research question. Next, look at how well the sections transition from one to another. Next, look at the coherence of each section. Are there some sections where the focus drifts? For your response, chart the movement of the paper from section to section and list any problems with the transitions or the coherence of the sections that you find.

Responses to this prompt indicated that reviewers were able to carry on the guided reading during a more extensive review of the entire composition. With few exceptions, all responses detailed the paragraph-by-paragraph development of the paper. However, not all of the responses went on to discuss transitions between paragraphs and fewer than half of the responses touched on the coherence of paragraphs specifically.

Again, as much at issue as the responses is the construction of the review prompt. The diminished focus on transitions and coherence may indicate that the conflation of all of these concerns in a single prompt is overwhelming. Whereas reviewers no doubt give attention to all of these issues as they read and some papers demonstrate fewer problems with transitions and coherence, more careful separation of these concerns may have benefited the organizational reading. Here it seems as if instructors creating review assignments might draw upon a less-is-more philosophy. Rather than including an organizational prompt as one of four concerns in the overall review exercise, a single review exercise covering organization that includes prompts geared toward mapping ideas, exploring transitions, and looking for coherence might lead to more productive guided readings.

Further, the review prompt may be seen as overly directive. The prompt asks reviewers to "track," "record," "chart," and "list" characteristics of the paper's organization. Clearly, the prompt diverges sharply from a conversational ideal. In some ways, this divergence may be attributed to the tension between guiding readings (or revisions) and opening avenues for conversation. Some of this tension can be seen in Straub's advocating response strategies that "provide direction for the student's revision [without taking] control over the writing or establish[ing] a strict agenda for that revision" (389-90).[7]

---

[7]For more reflection on tensions and potential prejudices in Straub's conversational conception of review, see "Surprised by Response: Student, Teacher, Editor, Reviewer," by Louise Wetherbee Phelps.

Still, it is possible that the Web-based nature of the peer review platform amplified tendencies toward creating directive review prompts. In general, both prompts and responses can be seen as influenced by the need to conduct the review process through the online platform, especially by the inability of respondents to comment directly on papers under review. Unlike printed or word processor copies that allow specific markup, or electronic review options such as e-mail or discussion forums that allow reviewers to embed commentary within the text of a paper, the peer review platform used in this exercise established papers as "read-only" artifacts. The inability to interact directly with the text may have contributed to the more directive review prompts and responses.

However, we should also consider the ways in which the read-only nature of the peer review platform may have positively impacted the reviewing process.[8] Another prompt asked readers to make a recommendation about one surface-level concern in the papers under review. Lucas Barnhill's response was typical in its generic recommendations:

> I would suggest to limit the use of commas in your paper. Sentences with a three of four commas can sometimes lose the reader's attention. I would suggest breaking the sentences down into two or three individual sentences, which would also add length if needed.

The impulse to "add length" is a bit humorous, but the recommendation to concentrate on a single aspect of the writing is likely to benefit the author by revealing a problem habit that can be addressed to improve her writing over the long run. In many ways, the nature of the peer review platform here is beneficial in its limiting respondents' abilities to pick and choose errors for comment. In some instances, reviewers made efforts at "pasting in specifics," excerpting problem sections of the papers and critiquing or offering suggestions for revision. However, the trend was for students to make blanket recommendations about an aspect of the composition that could be addressed in an overall revision.

After conducting the peer review exercise, participants were given a Web-based survey asking them about their impressions of the experience. In most cases, responses seemed to support the sense that,

---

[8]See "Developing Sound Tutor Training" by Lee-Ann M. Kastman Breuch and Sam J. Racine for more on evaluating online review environments on their own terms.

although perhaps overly directive, the review prompts were valuable in guiding readings. Karen Silas noted, "As I read the papers over and over, to look at one aspect of the writing at a time, I become a more careful reader." Karen also suggested that the review prompts were effective in promoting a more careful reading:

> I find the review questions to be very useful. They help me focus and pay more attention to different aspects. I read the papers more carefully and think on them more to be able to make recommendations instead of just telling where the problem is.

Although these observations suggest that the peer review platform was successful in its ability to promote guided readings, it bears noting that this is facility not limited to electronic reviews. At the same time, it would be worthwhile to investigate ways in which the side-by-side placement of the papers and the review prompts in the frames within the Web browser window may serve to foreground the importance of the prompts during a reading.

Responses by participants also suggest that the peer review platform affected the ability of reviewers to concentrate on surface-level concerns. Two responses promoted the use of paper as superior to readings conducted on screen, preferring to make notes "on the paper, which can't be done on the web. . . ." However, it is possible that this limitation also allowed reviewers to make nonintrusive comments and to concentrate on higher-level writing concerns. Brenda Salazar put it this way:

> reading papers over the web makes me look harder for things to correct on a paper because normally i just look for gramatically errors, which is a pain in the butt to correct over the web. therefore i have been looking more at organization and coherence of a paper. this has helped me realize how the way i have been editing before, is not really editing.

What might be read as complaint also reveals the potential power of the peer review platform in reducing reviewers' ability to error-hunt and shifting their attention to more organizational concerns. Karen concurred: "Since we don't have the chance to write on the papers, we can only mention the most important problems that the writer can focus on."

Finally, the public nature of the Web-based peer review platform may have influenced review activities. In many ways the peer review platform actualized the kind of public "meeting place for writers and readers" lauded by Straub. In addition to making available all of the papers composed by members of a class, the peer review platform collects all of the reviews composed by respondents. Jennifer Brown suggests that this archival ability offered benefits beyond convenience:

> It is very convienent to give advice over the web because you can go back and refer to it at any time. it also allows us to read others papers and see the responses which might also help us in our own papers. when i responed to others' papers it make me aware of things that i should check on in my paper to see if it needs improvement in that same area.

The majority of responses suggest that drawing on the collective expertise represented by the archived papers and reviews in the platform lead to a beneficial awareness of writing issues. As Sahala Pruven put it,

> I have learned a lot about structure from reading my partners papers. I thought that I would have to adhere to the five paragraph rule. I noticed that with some of the other papers, it was just more effective to put some points together in one paragraph. I was also confused before about whether I was including my quotations in the correct way. I've found from reading the other papers that I have done a good job.

Andrea Carr's response detailed similar moments of self-assessment sparked by performing reviews of papers and a heightened appreciation of ownership in terms of writing: "I have really learned about the style of others writing. You are constantly taught that there is a certain form to follow when writing. These people have taken this form and made it their own." Ownership is in many ways central to issues of responding to text, as Lil Brannon and C. H. Knoblauch pointed out long ago:

> incentive is vital to improvement and also . . . linked crucially to the belief that one's writing will be read earnestly. Since teachers do not grant student writers the authority that ordinarily justifies serious reading, they tend to undervalue student efforts to communicate what they have to say in the way they wish to say it. (159)

John Duncan suggests that the peer review exercise may have contributed to a sense that the writing process is a serious public act: "I like the peer reviews mainly because I enjoy seeing how others respond to my writing. I like seeing and hearing how they respond. This helps me figure out what works and what doesn't." Robert Montegue indicated the peer response exercise helped him develop a sense of audience expectations: "I have learned that clear, concise language makes all of the difference between having the information and getting it across, and just having the information. Other people have expectations. If I do not meet their expectations, then they are likely to reject all of my work."

Will Nesbitt connected the public nature of the Web with a sense of openness in the review process: "I feel that you are probably more honest because you don't know who will read your feedback. That makes you want to give the best opinion that you have." Brenda Salazar also associated the peer review exercise with honesty: "hmmm, i think i have had to read papers more carefully. and giving critiques is a little easier because normally i am a bit nervous to correct things, or say 'i think this is bad' to a persons face, its less personnal doing it over the web. allows me to be more honest." While two responses argued that face-to-face exchanges would have been preferable, the majority of responses suggested that the public nature of the exercise was beneficial to the review process.[9]

A LATE AGE OF PRINT REVISION

When I discussed the Web-based peer review platform with colleagues, they frequently recommended revisions that would allow participants to comment more directly on the papers under consideration. Instructors also offered feedback requesting that direct interaction with the text be added to the platform. In response to these comments, I revised the peer review platform to enable reviewers to link comments to papers on a paragraph-by-paragraph basis. The paragraph commenting function can be seen in Figure 14.2.

Annotation 1 in the figure indicates an icon for selecting the paragraph review function. Selecting the icon opens the review form

---

[9]Comparing the online peer review platform to face-to-face options is a key concern that I am unable to address in this limited space. One of the two responses recommending face-to-face peer review suggested that there was a lack of "back and forth" exchange during the peer review exercise. If conversational exchange is a valuable component of response, this observation as well as the overall relationship between online and face-to-face options for peer review warrant further investigation.

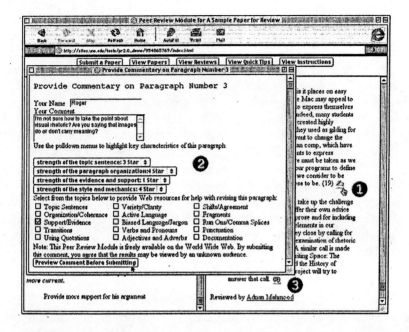

indicated by annotation 2. Annotation 2 also shows some of the paragraph review functionality, including the ability to rate paragraphs and to suggest resources in a number of writing categories. Selecting the check boxes will incorporate links to Web-based resources in the comment that is linked to the paragraph. Annotation 3 shows a paragraph that has been commented on, as indicated by the comment balloon icon. Selecting the comment icon will display commentary in a pop-up window; this commentary can itself be commented on by the author of the paper or subsequent readers.

The design and functionality of the new platform represent a revision based upon the feedback of readers. But what do we really know about reading online learning environments such as the peer review platform? What criteria should we use to evaluate their effectiveness? If we use criteria highlighting increased functionality as measures of success we may view the revised platform as an improvement but, in the process, miss a larger point. The interpretations offered in this article are tentative, but still, the possibility that the read-only format of the original peer review platform promoted attention to higher-level writing concerns is compelling. Could it be that the less-sophisticated first draft of the platform is better suited for peer review exercises? It's something we need to consider. What does seem clear is that the form and functionality of the online environment influence the experiences of participants using it.

At the same time, though, if we read online, learning environments from the perspective of a limited pedagogical agenda—even something as worthwhile as wanting to promote higher-level reading and revision—we limit their applicability in other areas of composition and teaching. We limit an instructor's flexibility and options. Worse, we limit an instructor's role as a respondent to online, learning environments. We read the electronic, learning environment out of context, ignoring the role of student and instructor, classroom and institutional environments, and the choices connected to these contexts. An online, learning environment such as the one discussed here both represents a nonneutral platform that influences activity and a malleable resource to be adapted to an individual's goals and contexts.

This article merely scratches the surface as a statement concerning online peer review. I'd also like to discuss the ways in which more conversational avenues might be built into the platform; ways in which the authors of papers might be brought into the online peer review process; the significance of some respondents' desire to conduct face-to-face reviews; the role of foregrounding prompts in the interface design of the peer review platform; issues of collaboration and conflict in the peer review exercise; comparisons with other online peer review environments; best practices for instructors and respondents using online peer review environments; and a host of other concerns. I raise these issues here, at the last minute, looking forward to others' responses, knowing that although my "writing space" is closing, the spaces for reading and talking about online learning environments are just beginning to open.

WORKS CITED

Barron, Ronald. "What I Wish I Had Known about Peer Response Groups but Didn't." *English Journal* 80.5 (1991): 24–34.

Brannon, Lil and C. H. Knoblauch. "On Students' Rights to Their Own Texts: A Model of Teacher Response." *College Composition and Communication* 33 (May 1982): 157-66.

Bruffee, Kenneth A. "Collaborative Learning and the Conversation of Mankind." *College English* 46 (November 1984): 635-52.

Elbow, Peter. *Writing Without Teachers.* 2nd ed. New York: Oxford UP, 1998.

Kastman Breuch, Lee-Ann M. and Sam J. Racine. "Developing Sound Tutor Training for Online Writing Centers: Creating Productive Peer Reviewers." *Computers and Composition* 17 (2000): 245-63.

Lindemann, Erika. *A Rhetoric for Writing Teachers*. 3rd ed. New York: Oxford UP, 1995.

Peckham, Irvin. "If It Ain't Broke, Why Fix It?: Disruptive and Constructive Computer-Mediated Response Group Practices." *Computers and Composition* 13 (1996): 327-39.

Phelps, Louise Wetherbee. "Surprised by Response: Student, Teacher, Editor, Reviewer." *Journal of Advanced Composition* 18.2 (1998): 247-73.

Schaffer, Jane. "Peer Response that Works." *Journal of Teaching Writing* 15.1 (1996): 81-90.

Sommers, Nancy I. "Responding to Student Writing." *College Composition and Communication* 32 (May 1982): 148-56.

Straub, Richard. "Teacher Response as Conversation: More than Casual Talk, an Exploration." *Rhetoric Review* 14 (1996): 274-98.

White, Edward M. *Assigning, Responding, Evaluating: A Writing Teacher's Guide*. 3rd ed. Boston: Bedford/St. Martin's, 1999.

III

TEACHING/WRITING...

...for ACADEMICS,
AGENCIES,
and other AUDIENCES

15

WRITING BEYOND THE CLASS

Jonathan Anderson
Carol Peterson Haviland
Charles Williams
California State University—San Bernardino

Engaging students in "writing that keeps on writing" is one characteristic of useful teaching, say this chapter's authors, a professor and two M.A. in English Composition students. They support their assertion as they describe a contemporary composition theory paper that the two students wrote collaboratively and then the four projects that emerged as the three "kept on writing": two conference panels, one thesis, and one book chapter. Even as they celebrate writing that continues rather than ends discourse, they note the risks both faculty and students take when they assign and produce alternative discourses that challenge rather than reproduce academic norms.

"Don't fret about tying everything up in your course papers," Charles Cooper commented during the first week of a graduate course Carol took on writing across the curriculum. "Instead, select an issue you want to learn about, use your paper to wrestle with that issue, and conclude by telling us what you've done and learned and where you want to go next."

"I learned in a different way as I wrote that paper," Carol says. "Because I felt freed from the pressure to make a final pronouncement, I expected to keep thinking about the topic after the course ended, and I did just that. The ways disciplines and pedagogies intersect to shape the academic discourse faculty members expect their students to produce is still a major research thread for me. Unfortunately, Cooper's invitation was not the norm in my doctoral program, but since taking it, I've continued to believe that one way to make teaching writing good is to help students engage in writing that continues after the specific class assignment or even the full course has been completed." Together, we (Carol, Jonathan, and Charles) present one writing assignment that "kept on writing." We follow its path beyond the course in which it originated, and we situate our project within others' calls for similar writing.

The course is an introduction to contemporary composition theory in an M.A. in English Composition program at California State University, San Bernardino, a diverse, 14,000-student campus in Southern California. Along with keeping reader/writer journals and making class presentations on their reading and writing, students were asked to complete one major paper: an investigation of one contemporary composition issue. The writing excerpted from two students' (Charles and Jonathan) collaborative paper, coupled with their instructor's (Carol) and their reflection on that project as well as several subsequent projects the three worked on together, illustrates one specific class assignment as it "keeps on writing."

Early in the quarter, the class read Lisa Delpit's essay "The Silenced Dialogue: Power and Pedagogy in Educating Other People's Children," and almost immediately they began to argue, but no one as intensely as Charles and Jonathan. The two kept at each other, both during and after class, sometimes dialogically but more often talking past each other, wondering how someone who seemed so intelligent could be so obtuse. "You have to help students resist easy answers; they learn nothing when they just follow the rules," Jonathan argued. "But I agree with Delpit. When no one explains the rules, how can students follow them, much less challenge them?" Charles retorted. Then, several class meetings later, the two proposed writing their course paper collaboratively, something neither had done before. "We were kind of nervous," they recalled. "We had read collaborative theories, and we had worked on projects with others before, but we hadn't written a major course paper collaboratively, certainly not one that would decide our grades and not with someone we thought was dead wrong on the issue. We worried about whether we could write a coherent collaborative paper and especially whether we could write anything approaching a complete paper in ten weeks."

However, Carol encouraged them to try, offering to share some of the risks they were taking and to help them make their collaboration work for rather than against them in their course grades. "I was a bit nervous about what their paper might look like," Carol recalls. "I knew that both of them were bright and would work hard, but in ten weeks it was likely that their paper might not look like most finished papers. It was likely to raise more questions than it answered, and, if they took the risks I hoped they would take, some readers might see it as a naïve piece of graduate work. I was torn. I knew how much I had learned from Cooper's course—both about disciplines, pedagogies, and genres and about the ways I hoped to teach—so I wanted them to take on this project. But I also wondered how I'd feel if one of my colleagues saw their paper as an example of the work students in my grad classes produced. Finally, I decided to take that risk with them; we all needed to act on what we espoused theoretically."

So Charles and Jonathan began to write, and Carol began to hope that she hadn't set all three of them up for disappointment. Early in their paper, Jonathan wrote:

> What I had learned from my experiences as a successful writer in many genres was that writing was about pushing at whatever boundaries were in place. Successful writers succeeded because of their ability to add something new to the discussion, to push at accepted ways of thinking, structuring, and speaking. Thus, when it comes my time to teach students how to write, my mission seems clear; not only am I going to allow students to push against the boundaries of accepted discourse, I am going to push them in that direction as well. When Charles proposed that we teach the styles and structures of the academy as the primary way to prepare students for success both within and outside of the academy, my gut reaction was to shut him down, dismiss his argument. What I heard him saying was that students needed to mimic the values and assumptions of the academy in order to become successful writers, that by digesting, unquestioningly, the standards of the academy, these students would become good writers.

In contrast, Charles wrote:

> I have always had a feeling of being trapped between two worlds: one consists of cultural elements that entail a history and identity of self (a sense of family and love), while the other demands for me to accept a process of diffusion from the dominant culture that

I cannot ignore because my ability to accommodate may determine my survival. In many ways, I see my life as what Mary Louise Pratt calls a "contact zone," an arena where cultures clash and grapple for supremacy, and I don't think I'm unique in this. In fact, I heard many students worry about the same problem. So when Jonathan and I first talked about academic discourse, I felt as though he was only seeing the stylistic features and was ignoring the fact that within the academy's discourse, like within any discourse, there are unique ways of valuing, evaluating and constructing knowledge. I questioned his position because I felt he was ignoring the complexities of the process of an individual actually appropriating a new discourse, especially when this involves new ways of seeing and discussing the world that may be contradicting a more familiar discourse.

But as their paper continued, the two began to listen to each other more carefully, to try to understand what might make an otherwise intelligent sounding person speak "so foolishly." Wrote Jonathan,

As I listened, it became harder to argue, and at this point a change began to occur in me. I felt my initially polarized view begin to weaken. A very simple yet profound awareness began to chip away at the foundation of my assumptions. I had been assuming, it seems, that writers were coming to the writing classroom with the same abilities, needs, and desires that I had come with. Clearly, something had to give. As my position began to give, I felt the need to restructure or redefine myself in several ways, looking at the various uses writing had in my life and in the lives of others. What had I learned from the academy that was useful, and what had I discarded? Several times in my internal debate, I had the feeling that my ability to push at the limits of academic discourse was what gave me the desire to keep writing. It was this ability to contribute something new that allowed me the personal space and drive, hence, the need to continue expressing myself in text. At the same time, it became clear that understanding the rules of the game gave me an advantage. Thus, I began to see some validity in the moves Charles wanted to make in the classroom.

Charles countered:

Undeniably, one of the reasons I had arrived at my position is because of my personal experiences at attempting to appropriate the right discourse for the right situation. I think this is a clear concern for any minority within a color-conscious society. Negotiating for position within this type of environment is so complex that I cannot imagine doing so with a degree of success unless one has identified some patterns for survival. As a middle-class African American, those patterns have come from direct instruction and observations of those like me who have gained some level of comfort and success within the world. I am reminded of W.E.B. DuBois' essay "The Talented Tenth," where he argued that it was the responsibility of educated African Americans to model and live as examples for the rest of this community in order to assist them in overcoming the horrors of slavery. This idea of modeling or following examples has been important in my own construction of patterns of survival. In my personal life as well as in other events that have played a significant part in who I am, I have noticed the value of being "put on," or clued in, to the appropriate discourse; undoubtedly this has shaped the way I approach academic discourse as a teacher.

However, just listening to each other only moved them both to uncertainty. They wrote together:

> To teach only the dominant paradigm is to indoctrinate and disallow students the chance to define writing on their own terms since they are forced into patterns of thinking that may be foreign and work against their own intentions. But not to teach the dominant paradigm is equally problematic because then voice, style, and structures of power remain a mystery. Either way, we may push our students into places they may not need or want to go. This echoes our parents' words "this is for your own good," as if we ultimately know what is best for our students—and yet we must act.

The two then moved into a more complex understanding of collaboration as they wrote:

> To make progress on these issues, it is inevitable that we now step out of our respective positions and let them inform each other. To do this we must begin by looking for relationships between the differences and use these relationships to constructively push the boundaries of our positions. We see the need to expand our perceptions of academic discourse to include the space for agency.

Their collaboration began to incorporate Cooper's invitation as they continued:

> The tendency, however, is to value consensus or resolution. As we attempt to incorporate multiple ways of knowing, dissensus can help us question and not just search for answers. Thus, exploring something for the sake of exploration becomes as or even more important than where one ends up.

Their collaboration was rich, and they had thoughtfully situated themselves within Delpit's and each other's texts—and they had run out of time. After offering a tentative position on academic discourse and agency, they concluded:

> Although our pedagogies still remain very different from each other, our positions have been altered by the discussion, which is exactly what we both ultimately hope to accomplish with the relationship between our students and the university.

"We were pretty nervous," they recall, "about handing in this paper. We knew that our understandings of the issues Delpit raises were rich and complex, and we had much clearer ideas about how we wanted to approach the first-year composition classes we were planning to TA in. But in many ways our paper seemed like the least sophisticated piece we'd ever written. We were glad for what we had learned, but we worried that even though Carol was pretty cool about rewarding learning, she'd be disappointed in what we had produced and our grades would mirror that disappointment."

"And I was disappointed on first reading," Carol notes. "I had had both of them in earlier classes and had seen the complicated, graceful writing they could produce. This paper was nothing like that. But it was something else—it was a terrific beginning. I could see them at the same place with the academic discourse quandary that I had been years earlier with WAC questions in Cooper's class. So, I gave them an 'A,' acknowledging what they *had* done and some of the places I hoped that they would continue to go—and offered to continue writing with them—and I hoped that none of my colleagues would think I'd gone soft before my tenure review came up the following year."

If the story ended here, it would offer some nice support for student-centered curricula and a few insightful excerpts from a useful but not profound paper. But it doesn't. Rather, Charles' and Jonathan's paper was indeed the preamble for their continuing thinking and writing—together, with Carol, and independently. The three of them continued to tug at the issues of academic discourse and agency and to argue about how first-year composition courses might be constructed. And these conversations led to an even fuller delivery of Cooper's challenge to consider the fruit that unbound assignments can bear: producing writing that keeps going.

The following year, the three, along with two other graduate students, presented panel discussions at two conferences: the Pacific Coast Writing Centers Association Conference at Washington State University ("Writing Centers as Passing Agents: What Kinds of Tents Shall We Weave?") and CCCC in Atlanta ("'Passing' Freshman Composition: Making Norms, Secrets, and Students Visible"). In these panels, they situated their exploration of agency, resistance, and discourse conventions within "passing" literature such as that of Nella Larsen. Charles then wrote his MA thesis, "Challenging the Boundaries of Academic Discourse," a topic he plans to explore further during his doctoral study. For Jonathan, the topic infiltrated his two-year stint teaching high school English. There he struggled to reconcile a school district's press to raise students' standardized test scores, with parents' demands that their students "succeed," with adolescents' flipping between wanting to fit in and to reject anyone's norms, and with his own concerns for pushing students to interrogate boundaries without allocating too much of his or his students' lives to dressings down in a principal's office. As he now returns to further graduate work and university teaching, he continues to work seriously on these questions as he designs writing assignments for his students and writes for his own graduate classes. Carol continues to wrestle in her teaching of undergraduate and graduate composition courses as well as in her writing center, writing-across-the-curriculum, and writing program administrator roles with the competing demands for regulatory and liberatory pedagogies. And the writing continues.

When Carol asked Jonathan and Charles to collaborate on this chapter and to use their course paper for the core, they were appalled. They argued that because this course had come at the end of their graduate school tenure, their text in print might make them look "really stupid" and forever shear them of whatever academic reputations they had established. "Until we took this class," Jonathan commented, "We had pretty well forged an understanding of academic writing through our experiences with our undergraduate majors and two years of graduate work. We had very definite and educated understandings of what writing was, and both of us were preparing to use those understandings as we stepped from our lives as grad students into those as composition instructors. Thus, you weren't just asking us to do something new; instead you were asking us to rewrite three years of graduate practice and our whole undergraduate experience."

Jonathan continued, "Much of the collaborative theory we had studied had had very little to do with what we practiced in our grad classes; in most, we had one shot and one shot only to get it right. To pull someone else into that process—a process intimate enough to do only behind closed doors, hermetically sealed against the frustrations and complexities of anything more—felt like hunting sparrows with a .22. We had a lot at stake when we agreed to write that paper, and I think that we have a lot at stake in this chapter. You asked us to take considerable risks in the class, and now you are asking us to take even bigger risks in publishing that exploratory writing." Carol concurred: "You are correct; I asked you to take risks then, not being sure myself that the whole project wouldn't crumble, that I hadn't set two excellent students up to test my idea at their expense. And even now, I worry that what we are advocating isn't simply a mindless celebration of process."

Despite our misgivings, we agreed to write the chapter. In fact, Charles commented, "This was a significant experience for us because it helped us see how instructors wrestle with the same issues. Also, such an intense positioning of ourselves intellectually established a precedent for the way we would engage in other issues; that is, the fleshing out of our opinions on this issue helped us to locate ourselves more clearly in other issues as well. So, I guess we will come across as neither smug nor not too bright if we can articulate this way of thinking about writing as more than process for process' sake."

We begin by reading our own observations alongside a report of the CCCC Dissertation Consortium's insightful critique of rhetoric and composition's dissertation traditions, a critique that locates our questions and Delpit's in another high-stakes arena familiar to many composition faculty.

First, the Consortium, a group of current dissertators, recent PhDs and dissertation advisers, poses its question: "The question is why aren't dissertation committees allowing composition and rhetoric students to write innovative, tradition-challenging dissertations? No, scratch that. The question is why aren't dissertation committees ENCOURAGING composition and rhetoric students to write innovative, tradition-challenging dissertations?" (441).

Two Consortium members note that reworking the "almost painfully familiar" form of "one introductory chapter, three discussion/explication/criticism body chapters, and one conclusion chapter" creates confidence for both student writers and faculty readers" (442). All participants know what they are doing. For students, even the traditional dissertation can be terrifying, so thinking about alternative forms sometimes seems ludicrous, and usually the information traditional dissertations generate is useful for the student writers. In addition, another Consortium member reports that faculty members do value traditional work because they feel responsible for teaching students conventions, for helping them write "solid, get-a-job" dissertations (443). She adds that even professors who use alternative discourse in their own writing step back with their students, saying that students need to establish their own academic credentials and status before they can write the ways they want (447).

A fourth member, observes, however, that it is not composition's ever improving narratives that make it an important intellectual discipline. Rather, he says, it is "that it composes new beginnings" (441). Yet, as another member notes, "when we experiment with structure and style, we experience different, sometimes 'new,' selves *and* identities. Maybe this is what scares people about 'alternative' dissertations. We are not just revising the way we look at academic writing, we are revising who we are, who we can be, as women and men, writers, and academics"(443). Describing her decision about her own dissertation, she continues: "After several dead-end sessions in my library carrel (hands dutifully typing one way, head and heart wandering elsewhere), I decided I simply could not do it. I could not adequately represent the feminist content, the spirit of the class, in the structures and styles I was used to" (447). However, as others warn, just deciding to write alternatively and to risk rejection doesn't solve all of the dissertators' problems: having no models to consult may free them of constraints, but it also may jettison them into nothing recognizable (447-48).

The Consortium summarizes its challenges: "We speak as if we are certain of the views and requirements of others (but what if we are not?). We speak as if we ourselves have no investment in these norms we feel bound to uphold (but what if we do?). Most disturbing, we speak as if, given another reality, a little more power, a few more available models, we really would encourage experimentation in our students' and dissertation advisee's texts (but what if we would not?)" (451).

David Bleich and William Covino confirm the reticence that lurks in the Dissertation Consortium critique as well as in our own reflections. Bleich notes that the ways we resist mixing the "sacred" texts of authorized writers with the common texts of students shape writing pedagogies as "direct instruction" (118). "This pedagogy," he argues, "is the opposite of the interactive, intersubjective pedagogy that accompanies the exchanges through which we acquire language to begin with" (119). In *The Art of Wondering,* Covino asserts that "In even the most enlightened composition class," all other concerns become subordinated to "finishing" (128-29). Thus he calls for writing that continues rather than ends the discourse, that avoids rather than intends closure, and that trades ambiguity for certainty, investigation for preservation, counterinduction for conclusions. Writing that encourages students to maintain thoughtful uncertainty is what ought to count, he concludes, for it is this writing that prizes the places of puzzlement and disequilibrium in rhetoric (120-31).

Urging faculty members to help students "build mysteries," Robert Davis and Mark Shadle offer a range of alternatives to one of the most traditional academic forms, the "modernist research paper." At the outset, they note the practical aim of suggesting new choices, but they also note the theoretical value of alternative discourse forms that move away "from the modernist ideal of expertise, detachment, and certainty, and toward a new valuation of uncertainty, passionate exploration, and mystery." These moves, Davis and Shadle believe, increase rhetorical sophistication as they lead students to a rhetorical flexibility that accounts for multiple genres, medias, disciplines, and cultures, that look carefully at "the false oppositions prevalent in composition studies and academic culture" (418).

It is this kind of teaching of writing—the teaching that encourages students to see school writing as worth extending beyond their immediate classroom assignments, that helps them do through language what they want to do—that we hope this chapter represents. Without limiting Jacqueline Jones Royster's CCCC 2001 bold challenges to traditional academic discourse, we want to follow her lead in seeing alternative discourses not as invasions but as already present—just unrecognized by many in power. Indeed, as she said, the discourses themselves are less alternative than the assumptions academics have made about appropriate discourse.

For Carol this means working hard to build on the progress her department is making in reimagining the M.A. thesis in English Composition. However, as she notes, "Charles says that he gained the ability and confidence to take these risks after he knew 'the rules.' This means that faculty need to work carefully to unveil existing conventions without constraining students' ability to create alternatives." Charles says, "Carol encouraged me to take lots of risks with my thesis, and I did take some, but just reading and writing for as many M.A. classes as I have has already reshaped me. It is so much easier and safer to just follow the rules now that I know them. As I think about doctoral work and whether I want to take ten years to write my dissertation, I'm really torn. I hope that I'll be strong enough to keep looking for new spaces, both to be true to myself and to stay the way I want to be when I teach students like myself." Jonathan, fresh from the straits of teaching high school says, "Look out when I write my thesis! After all of the claims I've made, I just can't write in a cage, and I have to figure out how to find acceptable writing ground without silencing my own dissensus or that of my students." Carol responds, "I can hardly wait. Jonathan will indeed challenge our graduate committee's views of M.A. theses. I hope that we will see the possibilities he offers and help him contextualize them for himself and for the students he will continue to teach. I hope that we will encourage him and them to keep on writing."

We thank Charles Cooper, who started this venture for us, and we want to accept Royster's charge to use writers, not unexamined systems, as our anchors as we interrogate the primacy of the traditional academic essay. When Royster challenges to design writing assignments that help students do through language what they want to do, leading to a more fully textured view of academic discourse, she encourages us to take risks as writers, students, faculty, and administrators and to see good writing as more than final projects in individual classes.

WORKS CITED

Bleich, David. "The Materiality of Language and the Pedagogy of Exchange." *Pedagogy: Critical Approaches to Teaching Literature, Language, Composition, and Culture* 1:2 (2001): 117-141.

Covino, William A. *The Art of Wondering: A Revisionist Return to the History of Rhetoric.* Portsmouth, NH: Boynton/Cook, 1988.

Davis, Robert, and Mark Shadle. "'Building a Mystery': Alternative Research Writing and the Academic Act of Seeking." *CCC* 51.3 (Feb. 2000): 417-446.

Delpit, Lisa D. "The Silenced Dialogue: Power and Pedagogy in Educating Other People's Children." *Harvard Educational Review* 58.3 (Aug. 1988): 289-98.

The Dissertation Consortium. "Interchanges: Challenging Tradition: A Conversation abo+t Reimagining the Dissertation in Rhetoric and Composition." *CCCC* 52.3 (Feb. 2001): 441-454.

Larsen, Nella. *"Quicksand"* and *"Passing."* Ed. Deborah E. McDowell. New Brunswick, NJ: Rutgers UP, 1986.

Royster, Jacqueline Jones, Patricia Bizzell, and Peter Elbow. "The Future of College Composition: Impacts of Alternative Discourses on Standard English." Conference on College Composition and Communication. Adam's Mark Hotel, Denver. 16 Mar. 2001.

16

DISCOURSE COMMUNITY SERVICE

An Advanced Composition Course

Jane Carducci
Gary Eddy
Winona State University

Our service-learning approach to a sophomore-level English class, Advanced Expository Writing, asks students to create documents in collaboration with local groups. One group of Women's Studies students, whose work we present in detail, constructed a program for social awareness and used the available media as a platform for their community service. In their self-evaluations, students often report new-found awareness that their writing matters; they also report both academic and intellectual development. But the greatest reward of the project, for the students and ourselves, is the pride taken in a project they've designed and accomplished. The instructor who takes a service-learning approach to composition must anticipate the ethics, responsibilities, and consequences of the work. In response to these concerns, we speak to our experience at a medium-sized institution in a small community, and we provide cautions and suggestions for those interested in adopting a service-learning approach to their writing classrooms. The risks are worthwhile: such work can help inspire meaningful change for students, teachers, institutions, and communities.

In the long-standing absence of a formal writing-in-the-disciplines requirement, our sophomore-level English 210 class, Advanced Expository Writing, has long been required by so many departments at Winona State University that we've tended to think of it as our college's *de facto* one-stop Writing-Across-the-Curriculum program. But this institutional context—a writing classroom populated by prospective teachers, nurses, social workers, psychologists, creative writers, paralegals, and biologists—provides a two-fold opportunity for students. Early essays in the course ask students to study and model the discourse of their major fields. The second opportunity calls students to engage critically in public discourse for the community service writing project.

In her valuable introduction to the subject,[1] Laura Julier describes two main approaches to service-learning in the writing course. One immerses students in community service (say, volunteering in soup kitchens) and asks them to use writing to reflect on their experiences in the context of larger social issues. The other, the approach we take, asks

---

[1]Julier's essay is a useful introduction to the pedagogical approaches and the research in the field. Readers interested in adopting or adapting service-learning pedagogy will find her bibliography especially useful. In addition, we recommend the following resources for consideration in constructing such courses:

> Adler-Kassner, Linda, Robert Crooks and Ann Watters. *Writing the Community*. Urbana, IL:AAHE/NCTE, 1997. Presents an array of approaches and theoretical perspectives.
> National Council of Teachers of English. *The Service-Learning in Composition homepage*. <http://www.ncte.org/service/>. A resource for teachers, researchers, and community partners interested in connecting writing instruction to community action.

The following may be used as course texts in a service-learning writing course:

> Watters, Ann and Marjorie Ford. *Writing for Change: A Community Reader*. NY: McGraw-Hill, 1995. A compelling collection of essays; each chapter ends with a service writing assignment and example.
> ———. *A Guide for Change: Resources for Implementing Community Service Writing*. NY: McGraw-Hill, 1995. A useful rhetoric and list of student forms and activities as well as detailed examples and analysis of student work. * Klooster, David and Patricia Bloem. *The Writer's Community*. New York: St. Martin's, 1995. Sound rhetoric on writing in various discourse communities.

Other rhetorics and readings relevant to such courses include Collins, *Community Writing;* Carter and Gradin, *Writing as Reflective Action;* Ervin, *Public Literacy;* Trimbur, *The Call to Write;* Loeb, *The Soul of a Citizen;* Coles, *The Call of Service;* Hatch, *Arguing in Communities;* Flower, *Problem-Solving Strategies for Writing in College and Community;* and/or Ervin, *Public Literacy*.

students to create documents in collaboration with service groups, applying their skills in direct service to the communities and organizations the students themselves choose. More specifically, for this project, students identify a social issue that motivates them first to act; second, they locate a community group who addresses that issue; and third, they research and compose a related argumentative essay. Because student interests may intersect, this course encourages students to cooperate in researching, editing, and other duties. The four students whose collaboration we discuss and present later in this chapter were taking the course as part of the Women's Studies minor and found their sponsor through the Women's Resource Center in Winona. They were, thus, able to combine both goals of the course at once and to make writing a valuable agent for change, problem solving, and community improvement. What they gain from this service-learning approach is first-hand knowledge of the ways in which writing happens in the world and must be responsible to the world.

By the time students reach this sophomore-level writing class, they should have mastered the requirements in first-year English. For the most part, students can engage in more sophisticated rhetorical analysis and application. Indeed, the goals of this class (as stated in our class policy sheet) indicate that, at this point, students ought to be trained as writers, and the course will further develop their critical reading, thinking, and writing skills. We have supplemented the community service writing project with a variety of other types of writing: research essays on their chosen area of felt need, analytical and argumentative essays on public issues, defenses of controversial books, and essays that analyze the academic discourse of their major. The capstone experience is the final project embodying Paulo Freire's praxis of critical literacy: posing a problem, deriving the felt need, adopting a solution, acting, and reflecting on the action in pursuit of further problems and actions. In fact, "reflection on service experiences is almost universally understood as essential to service-learning" (Julier 141). Our assignment asks students to identify a need for written documents in the community, research that area, produce a research paper and the document(s) the organization requires, and, finally, reflect on that experience as writers and as citizens.

Moreover, the goals of this class call on students to become familiar with the discourse in their field of study and apply their understanding of rhetoric in both public and academic spheres. They analyze, for example, acceptable evidence, writer/reader relations, language/syntax, and organization/format as they join the academic conversation in their community. This process, as in the Burkean parlor, is ongoing, and students begin *en medias res*. As Klooster and Bloem note, most students seem to learn the language of their academic communities like they learned to speak as children: they listen quietly to others speak and then experiment with strategies until somehow the rules sink in (41). Therefore, we encourage a more active investigation and practice in the community and genre of their choice. In preparation for the final project, we ask students to apply this process of investigating discourse communities to public discourse as part of their final project:

> Students will seek out groups on campus or in the community that have a tangible need for written documents, research the area of need, and produce the document[s] that the organization requires. The project constitutes 40% of your final grade for the class; therefore, it should be a substantial body of writing, and it is to include the following:

> 1. **A Journal** (from each individual), including (1) a log of attendance, date, and hours involved; (2) objective description of your experience; and (3) subjective reflection. The latter should address these questions: What does the experience mean for you? What knowledge or skills did you acquire today? What did you learn about yourself? Note: your journal supplies important evidence of what you are learning from your experience; it is also a very important source of information for writing your Final Project Report.
> 2. **Documents** (a collaborative effort), depending upon the rhetorical context and community needs. The documents will be evaluated for their rhetorical effectiveness (including layout, text, and presentation); their correctness and completeness; their representation of the community group; and their presentation (unless otherwise specified beforehand, all documents will be camera-ready). Documents must comprise the equivalent of 15 (3800 words) pages of formal, polished prose.
> 3. **Assessment Essay** (a collaborative composition), which will be evaluated on the quality of the discussion of the process of the project; the depth of your reflection on the value of the activity for you and for the service organization; the uses to which you have put the content of the course and the skills it imparts; the voice and style of the essay (it is, after all, a personal essay); the effectiveness of the essay's organization; and the effectiveness of expression (in terms of its style, usage, and correctness).

Keely Berge, Alison Betts, Sandy Filla, and Britt Johnson were all Women's Studies minors interested in educating the community about Rohypnol, the date rape drug. They made their first connection with the local Women's Resource Center, an organization that was eager to sponsor them. For further information, the students also contacted other sources including the State of Minnesota Department of Human Services, Students Against Sexual Assault (SASA), local bar owners, and the Department of Criminal Records in Winona for reported cases of date-rape. They began by taking pictures for posters, which they hung at sites on and off campus. They researched and wrote an article about Rohypnol for the Advocate, the newsletter of the Women's Resource Center. Among the many documents this group produced for their project was the news article that follows, published in our university newspaper, *The Winonan*:

Four WSU students wage war against Rohypnol, the "rape drug"
By Alison Betts [with Britt Johnson, Sandy Filla, and Keely Berge

Four Winona State University students are trying to inform women that rape is now as easy as dropping a pill into a drink. Alison Betts, Britt Johnson, Sandy Filla, and Keely Berge are working with the Women's Resource Center to inform females in the Winona area about the drug Rohypnol.

"We have got big plans on what we are going to do in this community; hopefully by the time we are done every woman will be informed."
Johnson said.

Rohypnol, also known as "roofies" or "the forget pill" is illegally used and is becoming more common in southern states and now in southern Minnesota. Betts, Johnson, Filla, and Berge have been in contact with the Women's Resource Center who has mentioned cases in Winona where this pill may have been used in assaults.

Rohypnol is typically used medicinally for purposes of insomnia, because it is a type of anesthetic. However, it is not used for that in the United States; in fact, it is no longer marketed in this country.

"It is only being misused here in the United States, and what is allowing this misuse to continue is that the public is not informed about how dangerous it can be," Johnson stated.

Rohypnol is associated with date rape and is sometimes called the "date rape" drug. The pill is odorless and tasteless and can be slipped into a drink causing the victim to pass out, which can lead to sexual assault.

"It is extremely worrisome, if the victim doesn't know that she has been given this drug. She and her friends may just think she is drunk, " Johnson continued.

Pharmaceutical reports state that Rohypnol's effects can be seen or felt approximately two hours after its administration. It can cause sedation and psychomotor impairment, headaches, dizziness, and gastrointestinal pain.

"When a woman is affected by this drug she is the perfect prey for her attacker. She can either black out or become almost paralyzed, making it easy for her to be assaulted, sometimes without her knowledge," Berge said.

"What we are trying to do is put up informative posters in women's bathrooms and to supply dorm R.A.s with informational packets to inform their female residents," Filla said.

Betts, Johnson, Filla, and Berge have had several meetings with the Women's Resource Center and are now coordinating their efforts to get this project started.

"Our main goal is to spark awareness within the community. Ultimately, we want to be able to arm women with the information that can lead to prevention," says Johnson.

"We have read personal encounters of women who have been victims of rape that were given this drug. One particular story has motivated us. She was assaulted while under the influence of Rohypnol, and since the traces of this drug only remain in the system for 20-30 hours it was too hard to prove in court, allowing her attacker to go free. Since this enormous disappointment she has been writing to government officials to try to make the penalties for possession of the drug stiffer," said Berge.

The government has begun to take action against the misuse of this drug. On March 5, 1996, the U.S. Customs Service banned its importation. Also, President Clinton recently signed a bill that could add up to 20 years onto a sentence if there is use of an anesthetic drug during an assault.

"It is being imported mainly from Mexico, and it is becoming a major college concern for Southern campuses. Another reason why it is becoming so widespread is because it is relatively cheap: one pill ranges in cost from $1-$8," Filla said.

The Drug Enforcement Agency has made more than 2,000 seizures in 32 states, and is in the process of reclassifying the drug to stiffen penalties for its possession.

"Government is a critical part of ending this new 'style' of sexual assault. However, it is extremely important to let women know that they need to watch out for themselves. I see women leaving their drinks alone at bars all the time, only to return later and finish them. We need to be more careful and protect ourselves," said Johnson.

For now these students say they want to send a message to women, *"Keep your eyes on your drink!"*

This group of Women's Studies students defined and participated in the social program and the rhetoric of their discourse community, constructed a program for social awareness, and used the available media as a platform for their community service. One goal for this class, then, is, through the final project, to offer students a place to ease into discourse communities, a safe place to listen, speak quietly, and experiment with strategies as they join the on-going conversations in their fields. Students are immersed in a language-rich environment and are encouraged "to understand the systems that comprise the diverse discourse communities in which [they] find themselves" (Lindemann 296). And by understanding these systems, students can participate in them and eventually work for change. Students involved in these projects thus come to see that writing is a valuable agent for change, problem solving, and community improvement, not just another research paper that nobody but the teacher will read. The success of this project and dozens of others rests in trusting the students to understand and come to address the social changes they feel most pressing for themselves and those around them. Our role as instructors is to guide their entry into the discourse of their disciplines and into the public discourses that, in turn, guide positive social change.

When colleagues question—and even become alarmed at—the notion of turning over all the responsibility for this project to the students, we can only reassure them that doing so has worked well for us. From the conception of the project to its completion, students understand the faith and confidence we have in them and respond accordingly. They *want* the project to succeed. Paulo Freire's conviction of faith—that "trusting the people is the indispensable precondition for revolutionary change" (46)—is well supported by our experience. Because our students choose the organization or cause they wish to work for, they become more invested in the success of the project.

Our trust in the group of Women's Studies students who contributed the above article was clearly warranted. And they were able to see their impact on the community, to see that writing happens in the world and is responsible to the world. At that time, the staff at the Women's Resource Center (WRC) was concerned about the entry of the date-rape drug, Rohypnol in the area. Under the sponsorship of the WRC, then, these students launched an information blitz against this drug. Their resources and audience included suspected victims, the director of the WRC, police officers, bar owners, and other students. They also addressed, at different moments and in different venues, the Feminist Issues Committee on campus, the State Department of Human Services, the Minneapolis Prevention Resource, and the National Drug Hotline. Further research included both the public and the university libraries.

This considerable research surfaced in several documents the group composed for their completed publicity packet. They hung a series of posters in women's restrooms on campus and around town; they produced a pamphlet used at the WRC, summarizing their findings and offering tips to avoid Rohypnol; they wrote an article for the school newspaper (included above) and a ten-page research paper about the drug for the class. The students used their skills in discourse analysis to define and practice writing in the news writing community. Their work was further recognized when a local reporter picked up on their project, interviewed them, and wrote an article that appeared on the front page of our city newspaper, *The Winona Daily News*, in timely fashion—on New Year's Eve.

Clearly, these students made a sizeable contribution to women's lives in this community. But evaluating their projects can seem daunting. Because every project is different, evaluation poses many challenges, but we resolve these, too, by empowering students. They have a great deal of control over their group evaluation because of their project journals that record their legwork, insights, and obstacles. They also write a sustained evaluation of their process, project, and learning, and they evaluate their fellow group members as part of the final grade for the project. And we have the project itself to grade for rhetorical effectiveness and its realization of the course—and the community group's—goals.

But it can be difficult to compare projects. Students may choose to, say, write a fraternity constitution and promote its annual charity drive. Others may end up revising the STD brochures for the local clinic. One project has significantly more social impact, but both fall within the project purview. What has to keep us honest, finally, are the course goals. But we may acknowledge—as the students themselves often do during our last class project sharing—that the more public the project, the greater the risk to students. And those challenges, too, must be part of the final evaluation.

In their self-evaluations, students often talk about their newfound awareness that their writing matters. For example, a group of history majors who worked with the Winona County Historical Society wrote, "We found this project interesting because we were out in the community and not confined to the classroom. . . . We usually present our material only to fellow history majors, but this project's audience was the entire community." A group of sociology students who wrote a grant proposal for Grace Place, a Christian home for single, pregnant women, told us, "Our group enjoyed this project because we liked being able to work hands on in the Winona community for the benefit of someone else rather than writing yet another dispassionate term paper."

Besides contributing to the community, students find other benefits as well. They are also exposed to the ever-present politics in the organization, an important part in the workings of any system. A sociology student who focused on Rational Recovery, an alternative to Alcoholics Anonymous, said, "My eyes were really opened to the reality of our health care system. It surprised me that one group such as A.A. has become such a powerful force not only in our health care system, but in our government."

Students also have the opportunity to learn about themselves. Ilona McGuiness confirms that service work in her course aims to help students "articulate their personal values" (5). For example, psychology majors who, uncertain about their direction, prepared a report and brochure for the psychology department about the Psy.D. degree. They commented: "The most beneficial aspect of this project was that we were able to learn about ourselves in the process." And, in the process of learning about themselves, students can discover that they are marketable. For example, in a project for the English department, some of our English majors researched and put together a report, "What can you do with an English major?" They felt reassured about their future: "We know that we can expect to be in demand for our writing and communication skills after college. . . . This experience has left us more confident about our futures."

But the greatest reward of the project, for the students and ourselves, is the pride students take in a project they've designed and accomplished. As they testify in the following, the group who wrote the Rohypnol project were very proud of their work:

> Although all of us could already understand the feeling of satisfaction that comes from finishing a tough project, this one was somehow different. It is an even richer feeling of satisfaction to know that our research and hard work will bring an awareness to much of the community about the drug Rohypnol. It is not far fetched to believe that the four of us have succeeded in preventing women from undergoing the trauma of rape. If we help just one woman, our work will be well worth it.

Clearly, they now recognize the connection between rhetoric and change and can see how their writing works in the world.

It would be irresponsible of us to imply, however, that such change can occur without risk—for either the students or for the practitioners of service-learning pedagogy. The instructor who takes on a community service writing project must accept a set of risks: Will the community groups actually participate and give students meaningful work? Will I eventually run out of community groups and resources?

Do I run any risks with community groups? What are the risks for students? Is the workload manageable? Does this pedagogical innovation affect my professional status?

In response to these we can only speak to our experience at a medium-sized institution (7,000 undergrads) in a smallish community (28,000) that has a notable history of social and environmental responsibility. Although it retains many conservative values that one might expect from a rural Midwestern town, it also has a long-standing mandatory recycling program and a deep appreciation for environmental issues due, perhaps, to its being bordered by a National Wildlife Refuge.

We try to assuage the difficulties the students face in contacting service organizations by providing each student with a letter of introduction; this letter assures the organizations that this is an offer of a free writing intern for a semester and that they can negotiate the dimensions of the project with individual students. In some instances students have had to fall back on community service work—say, participating in after-school programs for latch-key kids—and writing about the experience in terms of their estimation of its value to themselves, the group, and its clientele. They will also provide journals that are more introspective and developmental than the logs we usually require of students. In other cases, students may have found that a group wanted them merely to compose a letter. The students performed that task and then went on to find another group.

In our small community, we have found, with two of us teaching two sections of the course each semester, that after a while the projects do get smaller. Some of the most popular organizations, the Women's Resource Center, for example, could not afford to update their publicity brochures every few months, but they also came up with more complex and challenging assignments (revising the advocate training handbook, grant writing). In some cases, as with writing goals and mission statements with a group, students do not produce big documents but have negotiated a collaborative writing process that has challenged all they know about syntax, vocabulary, and rhetorical audience. Sometimes, we just have to look at the whole experience, not just the page count. Of course, those in larger communities should find this to be less of an issue.

Do we run risks from the groups themselves? Possibly, but that has not been our experience. Because organizations have control over the product and have the resources of peer review in class and our final review before anything is submitted, organizations tend to be pleased to have the load off their necks and desks. A survey of the literature reveals a skepticism based on an us/them dichotomy: middle-class students helping the "needy" poor. We address these issues in course dialogue, but manage to avoid most conflicts in practice: our students are serving the organization and have, in most cases, little contact with clientele who may resent their intrusions.

The risks to students include time management, problems with collaboration (with the organization and within a student group), and shifting timelines. For the first and last of these, we enforce an early start. By the third week of class, we demand status reports and often meet in individual conferences with students to get them and keep them on track. Problems with collaboration between students and community groups usually amount to difficulty in making and keeping contact. Student persistence, too, is rewarded as part of their project logs. We have yet to have the kinds of personal clashes between students and community groups that we fear most. Maybe it's "Minnesota Nice," but students seem to pride themselves on professional demeanor and most folks in the community see the project as a valuable service. Finally, for problems within groups, we meet regularly with groups and base a part of the grade on collaborative success.

As for professional status questions for service-learning practitioners, pedagogical change always entails professional risks. However, these risks may be minimized by helping any departmental or administrative faculty reviewers to appreciate the many dimensions of the assignment. It not only aids student growth in several academic ways, but also provides them with professional work samples that may enhance their employability or their work in their majors. It also supports the habits of community service upon which a sound democratic society is based. In addition, it can count as part of an instructor's own service to the community and an enhancement of the university's image. Finally, it is an important part of any teaching portfolio to include samples of student work and keep a running list of the organizations served and the projects accomplished. After even a single semester, the record will probably strike most colleagues and administrators as impressive.

In some cases, such work can even help inspire, or at least inform, meaningful institutional change. At our university, our most recent revision of our general education program now includes a "contemporary citizenship" requirement at or above the sophomore level. The service-learning writing course we describe here has now been renamed, "Writing in Communities." It will serve as an elective fulfilling the requirement, focusing more exclusively, as the course description reads, on "the study and practice of writing as a means of participation in a diverse, democratic, and literate society," and fostering "development of students' ability to understand and use writing as a means of ethical decision-making, community activism, and civic collaboration." The new course further provides a practical and theoretical link with the developing writing-in-the-disciplines courses soon to be required in every program, and it has more recently become a required course in our English Department's writing major.

So as our students, through their education at WSU, prepare for citizenship, scholarship, and the world of work, this project offers them the opportunity to be what Klooster and Bloem call "professionals-in-training." In addition to their experience as participatory citizens, students are thus exposed to the politics and negotiations of organizations and collaborative work. Self-discovery is an important benefit, and students can gain confidence in their marketability. This project gives them real-world experience as they learn the language of their discourse community and have been responsive to various voices within it. They know that theirs is not the last word in the ongoing polylogue, but, as Burke notes, they have entered the conversation and they have learned the power of their writing.

WORKS CITED

Burke, Kenneth. *The Philosophy of Literary Form: Studies in Symbolic Action.* 2nd ed. Baton Rouge: Louisiana State UP, 1967.

Freire, Paulo. *Pedagogy of the Oppressed.* New York: Seabury, 1968.

Julier, Laura. "Community Service Pedagogy." *A Guide to Composition Pedagogies.* Eds. Gary Tate, Amy Rupier, and Kurt Schick. New York: Oxford, 2001.

Klooster, David and Patricia Bloem. *The Writer's Community.* New York: St. Martin's, 1995.

Lindemann, Erika. "Three Views of English." *College English* 57:3 (March 1995): 287-302.

McGuiness, Ilona M. "Educating for Participation and Democracy: Service-Learning in the Writing Classroom." *The Scholarship of Teaching* 1.2. (1995): 3-12.

17

WRITING WITH THE JONNYCAKE CENTER

Libby Miles
University of Rhode Island

This chapter describes a student-initiated project written with and for a nonprofit community support agency for an advanced writing course. As a class, students crafted the criteria for appropriate community-based writing projects, and one particular group of four students chose to focus their efforts on The Jonnycake Center in Peace Dale, Rhode Island. The framework of the course demanded that students practice writing as a form of social action, as collaboration, as the means toward inquiry, as a technology, and as design. What follows is a description of the sequence leading to the final project and an analysis of both the collaborative decision-making process and the written texts these students produced, exploring both the richness of writing as social action and the complications of evaluating such writing.

"Jonnycake" is not a typo: it is a culinary treat indigenous to southern Rhode Island. Made of local stone-ground white cornmeal, Jonnycakes are cooked on the griddle much as one would prepare a pancake. Thinner than pancakes, they are coarse—even gritty. They are a fabulous local phenomenon.

So, too, is the Jonnycake Center. It is located in the heart of Peace Dale—a village within the township of South Kingstown (which also houses the University of Rhode Island). Gritty, as former New England milltowns can be, Peace Dale is generally considered the "wrong" side of the tracks. Jonnycake's central location on the Peace Dale rotary is adjacent to subsidized housing and the center's primary constituents. As a resident of Peace Dale for the past three years, I've admired their work; as a teacher, however, I have just begun to understand fully the effectiveness of this local treasure. For that, I thank the students in my Advanced Writing for Community Service class (Fall 2001) who became the Jonnycake Center's most vocal advocates on campus: Amanda Heryla, Rachel Horton, Jim Ridolfo, and Eric Venet.

PEDAGOGICAL ASSUMPTIONS

No matter what level writing course I teach (from first-year writing through graduate seminars in rhetoric), five key assumptions about what writing *should* be drive my course design. I insert them here as they appeared in my most recent syllabus for my Advanced Writing for Community Service course. What I haven't said below is, perhaps, the most important piece for me: that writing instruction happens best when I get to learn from my students, from their interests and abilities, and from the considerable energy they bring to our conversation. For that reason, most of the community clients with whom we work in this class are identified by the students in the class.

1. *Writing as a social action*: Writing never happens without a context and a community. It arises from social situations, it interacts with other texts (explicitly or implicitly), and it has consequences. The writing you do in this class will be in response to needs in the URI or greater Rhode Island community—you find the need, you research the range of appropriate responses, you create texts that live on beyond the scope of this class.
2. *Writing as a collaborative enterprise*: The whole is often greater than the sum of its parts. Therefore, the final two projects in this course revolve around writing in teams for clients. Collaboration in this class means offering productive feedback, making strategic decisions together, dividing responsibilities, building on one another's strengths to produce something better than any individual effort one person might have

produced. Outside of academic settings, most writing you will do throughout your life will be collaborative to some extent; this class offers an environment to figure out how to collaborate well.

3. *Writing as a form of inquiry*: Merely writing down what you already know doesn't do much good for you or for anyone else. Accordingly, this class approaches writing as a way to learn more, to gain insight, to deepen your understanding of something familiar. To that end, each project involves research—some firsthand, some reflective, some based on more traditional print (library) sources, some based on the observations and reflections of others.

4. *Writing as a technology*: As you can see, this class is meeting in a computer lab—one form of technology with which we will grow increasingly comfortable. But writing is also a technology itself, something that allows a structure for other things to happen. We will work together toward making the most of our technological opportunities.

5. *Writing as more than words on a page*: Because visual literacy has become a critical tool in today's world, we will also focus on the visual impact of the way your writing is presented. We will work on document design with every project, using the textbook as a starting point. You will be required to design several different formats for your projects, you will integrate visuals and graphics with your texts, and you will try your hand at "visual invention" exercises as part of your research.

Although the growing service-learning scholarly community might quibble with whether or not my course fits *their* categorizations of legitimate service-learning, this class does count at my own institution because of its focus on experiential learning and critical reflection through curricular connections with the local community beyond the university. More than anything, however, I place student expertise and experience at the center of the course. For that reason, I fall well outside the sphere of service-learning courses that focus on a theme (literacy, immigration, hunger) or that work only for one preplanned organization set up by the teacher. (For more on these categorizations, see in particular Adler-Kassner, Crooks and Watters, 1997; Deans, 2000; Schutz and Gere, 1998; and many others).

In this piece, I describe in some detail the context of the class and the pedagogical goals because those issues constrain what "successful" writing will be. This is a class with unlimited choices, and therefore, unlimited opportunity for wrong turns. Each student grapples with understanding several different rhetorical situations, all of which call for different genre selections, different research paths, different stylistic and tone choices. Thus, the choices they make can sometimes be more "successful" than the piece of writing they eventually produce.

NAVIGATING THE CLASS

As the syllabus materials on the web site indicate, success in this class demands that students make all the major decisions about their writing projects throughout the semester. In order to create the "products" described below, each team of students completes a series of complex sequences to create a client-driven student-designed community service project. The sequence begins with the initial research into several potential project sites; each student creates at least two visually compelling one-page fact sheets about the organization they are thinking of proposing. Explorations for the fact sheets generate class-wide criteria for what we will consider "good" writing projects and "worthy" clients. By the end of a week-long discussion, this class decided that the best clients would have immediate and effective local impact, should not carry any particular "ideological baggage" from affiliation with religious organizations (their terms, not mine—and sadly, this knocked out our local chapter of Habitat for Humanity), and should seem to really *need* clear-cut help from URI students.

When all students in the class present their fact sheets, each writer can see which ones engender the most excitement and which elicit the most resistance. For example, two students independently chose Peace Dale's Jonnycake Center, and each was able to support the other's fact sheet presentation. On the other hand, the writer who presented on behalf of the DARE program opened a fascinating, rich, and highly contentious conversation (face-to-face and on our class discussion board) about the merits of this police-sponsored school program. As students debated the effectiveness of DARE, compared it with other drug-resistance programs, theorized about governmental intervention, and ultimately rejected DARE as an appropriate client for this class, the writer of that fact sheet learned much about the values and assumptions of his immediate audience: his classmates. For my purposes, the DARE conversation sparked a terrific set of criteria that described successful local programs, and the class adopted them as guidelines.

With the feedback of the entire class, and with the new criteria in hand, each student crafted a proposal to the class justifying the choice of client and tentatively offering a writing-specific project that would grow from the particular needs of that client. Those proposals were distributed to the class and voted on. Students ranked those projects they most wanted to do, and the groups were formed for the remainder of the semester.

One final wrinkle in the course was that each group was given a modest budget from the URI Feinstein Center for Service Learning to use in their final projects. Choosing what to do with this money provided an extra opportunity for reflection and analysis.

THE JONNYCAKE PACKET

The student writing in this chapter is, in fact, a packet of collaboratively-produced far-ranging materials addressing a range of audiences for a variety of purposes. Amanda, Rachel, Jim, and Eric turned in a packet of materials including the following:

Distributed to the Jonnycake Center (all presented in print and supplied on a disk):

- Donation solicitation letter for local businesses
- Donation solicitation letter for nationally based organizations with Peace Dale connections
- Fact sheet insert about the Jonnycake Center
- "Why give" insert
- Address list for local businesses to send donation letter
- User instructions for the above

Distributed to the URI Feinstein Center for Service Learning:

- Letter with corrections for the Clearinghouse for Volunteers web site entry for the Jonnycake Center
- Informational binder titled "The Jonnycake Center: Why You Should Volunteer"
- Flyers to be distributed to URI 101 teachers and students (URI 101 is a 1-credit class introducing students to the university, which has a required service-learning component)
- Posters to be hung around campus urging students to volunteer during off-peak times

Distributed to me:

- A team report reflecting on what they had done and why
- Copies of everything distributed elsewhere

Most of the full packet appears in the webbed materials accompanying this book, but I share with you samples from each student below.

TEAM PLAYERS AMANDA AND RACHEL

Amanda, a student-athlete and English major, and Rachel, a full-time waitress and business student, decided that obtaining more money for the Jonnycake Center would be their top priority. As they indicate in their cover note to me, they drafted two versions of a solicitation letter—one to locally owned businesses, and the other for those local companies owned by national corporations (see webbed materials for their cover note). Here, then, is one of their letters.

[Salutation]:

For the past twenty-six years, the Jonnycake Center has been serving underprivileged families in the Peace Dale area. As it becomes more and more difficult for many working families to provide for themselves, the Jonnycake Center has services such as a stocked food pantry, emergency and holiday food baskets, the sale of used clothing and home supplies, clothing and housing vouchers, funds for necessary bills that would otherwise go unpaid, and welcoming new families to the Peace Dale area.

Unfortunately, this marks the first year that the Jonnycake Center was denied state grant money that it has been receiving in past years, in order for said money to be transferred to another state department. Because of this, the money that we have been using to help others is no longer available.

This is where you can help. As a non-profit organization, the Jonnycake Center relies on the generosity of others to help aid underprivileged families in the area. Any donation that you can provide will be greatly appreciated, not only by the Jonnycake Center, but by the families of the Peace Dale area as well.

Thank you,
[signature]

This letter nicely typifies a strong collaboration between English and business majors. The organization of the letter frontloads the many positive accomplishments of the Jonnycake Center, while saving the "bad news" for the second paragraph. The tone throughout is respectful, professional. The writers vary their sentence length, speaking directly to their audience at the end. The local angle is emphasized in every paragraph. I even find the occasional slippage of parallelism effective, in that it keeps this letter from seeming too glossy, too contrived.

JIM-THE-PHILOSOPHER

Jim, a recent transfer and philosophy major, was the course's most prolific poster in online discussions, and our most careful reader. His first few writing assignments showed less comfort with writing, and no sense of document design whatsoever. When his idea of a Jonnycake Center web site fell through, he became the group's main on-site researcher and client liaison. His first-hand experiences at the Jonnycake Center showed him a serious lack of volunteer labor, which he and Eric addressed with their parts of the project. After a visit to our Clearinghouse for Volunteers, Jim decided that Jonnycake was not well represented in their materials. In a project I feared would be too much of a stretch for someone who seemed not to be spatially-inclined, Jim proceeded to create an informational binder designed to recruit more volunteers from URI (images from the binder are available in the webbed materials).

On a particularly effective page, Jim combines several elements. First, there is a picture of the Jonnycake Center's neighborhood—a sharp visual statement that the Peace Dale rotary and flats is *not* a scary-looking place at all (pictures of the center permeate his document). In a shaded box next to the picture, Jim stresses the local nature of the support Jonnycake provides. A two-column item offers reasons for volunteering, nicely summarized and reinforced in a shaded box with four bulleted points:

- Only three short miles away
- Volunteer with friends
- Get to know the local community
- Make a difference

His appeals are clearly to students, and he organizes them in the order he thinks will be most compelling to his colleagues.

IN-YOUR-FACE ERIC

The final member of the team is Eric, the computer science major. Also disappointed by the collapse of the web site project, Eric nonetheless persisted vociferously in his belief that URI students would all be better people if they just worked at the Jonnycake Center for a day. He embraced that as his personal mission and pursued his agenda with gusto. Eric quickly became the master of the in-your-face document, and he found a genre that would suit his approach. In addition to crafting impassioned prose that infuses some of the other documents, Eric also created a series of posters to hang around campus at times when the center was most in need of volunteer labor. Although some border on noblesse oblige (a motivating factor for some students), others are just eye-catching enough to make people stop and react.

Example 1:

REMEMBER MOM TELLING YOU TO EAT YOUR DINNER BECAUSE THERE WERE PEOPLE STARVING IN OTHER COUNTRIES?

MOM DIDN'T KNOW THAT THE HUNGRY ARE RIGHT NEXT DOOR.

WANT TO HELP?

[Jonnycake Center logo and address]

Example 2:

EVER BEEN HUNGRY?

EVER BEEN HUNGRY AND NOT HAVE ENOUGH MONEY FOR FOOD?

EVER HAD TO CHOOSE BETWEEN HEATING YOUR HOUSE OR PUTTING FOOD ON THE DINNER TABLE?

WANT TO HELP THOSE WHO HAVE TO MAKE SUCH A CHOICE?

[Jonnycake Center logo and address]

With these posters, Eric blends what he has learned about hunger and poverty with catchphrases from popular culture, and he builds on what he knows of the attitudes and assumptions shared by his audience of fellow URI students.

WHAT MAKES *THIS* WRITING "GOOD"

Through the students, I met Pat Whitford, the director of the Jonnycake Center. I consider this project a success in part because *her* feedback was positive: she liked the interaction with the students, and she actually *uses* the materials they created for her (good product with ongoing production). Further, these students did work that Pat knew she needed to get around to doing, but daily crises inevitably kept her from completing them. She felt they helped make her more effective in her job, and their work showed an understanding of and sensitivity to the local culture. Thus, as a teacher I appreciated these students' good researching processes, their sensitive outreach, and their positive town-gown linkages.

Why else did I like this project so much? At one level, the sheer volume of it was impressive. And the range of products they created was more vast than I would have imagined at the start of the semester. Most importantly, though, this team of four very different students labored all semester to navigate several complex rhetorical situations in the space of one project. As gratifying as its bulk was, however, the strength of this project was in its appropriateness for its multiple audiences. Without question, this writing is good because of the complexity with which these four students navigated their range of rhetorical situations.

For example, the students initially wanted to do a webbed component, preferably a web site. Their research with the client moved them in different directions, and early on they discovered that their desire to do Web work did not match the needs of the client. The Jonnycake Center's constituents generally don't have Web access, for one thing. Additionally, they found out that too glossy an electronic presence would undercut the Center's local ethos. So much for their initial proposal. As their teacher, I felt part of this team's success was in their ability to regroup and devise a more appropriate alternative project. Further, they realized that writing in the late age of print does not always automatically mean digital writing. They learned about instances in which webbed projects might not make good sense.

By the standards of a collaborative project, the Jonnycake packet may not appear to have succeeded. After all, the group splintered off into separate subprojects aimed at different audiences for different purposes. However, looking at the language choices in all of the documents (see the webbed materials), reveals authorship lines that are marvelously blurry. The same phrases show up in several documents, as each member of the group helped revise and redesign every portion. Something that worked well in one document was shared, lifted, and modified in another. Clearly, these students practiced revising in strong and subtle ways appropriate to their rhetorical situations.

To be honest, I suspect they split into multiple projects for several reasons. In their end-of-semester reflections, they all *claim* to have chosen individual subprojects because they saw it as a way to "get even more accomplished" for their client. I think, however, members of this group in particular had a difficult task in negotiating different personality types, learning styles, majors, attendance patterns, and academic abilities. Splitting apart did allow them to get more done, just as it allowed each group member to shine and grow in different ways—in the spirit of the course, to each according to his or her needs.

The writing practices these students regularly navigate and the range of options from which they have to choose speaks to the heart of teaching writing in the late age of print. With their collaborative work, they practiced and examined different approaches to individual, corporate, and group authorship. With their genre selections, they practiced and examined several forms in print and electronically. With their stylistic choices, they practiced and examined language variation in different discourse communities. With their organizational patterns and document design, they practiced and examined textual impact on different audiences. And finally, with their budget, they practiced and examined working within specific material conditions.

In fact, their monetary choices make a fitting coda to this exploration of their class. Although Amanda, Rachel, Jim, and Eric produced copious amounts of documents, any of which might have been reproduced and circulated with the help of their budget, these students left the choice to the Jonnycake Center. Convinced that their client held the most expertise and had the greatest understanding of their local knowledge, the team chose to hand the materials over to the director of the center, and they used their budget for a donation. As they said in their reports to me, Pat knew best where the money was most needed, and they felt confident that she should determine whether the priority would be starting a donation campaign, or recruiting more volunteers, or writing somebody a check to pay their oil bill during an unusually cold December.

That decision, too—honoring local knowledge and the expertise of a member of the community—contributes to my sense of the Jonnycake Center project as effective writing and learning.

WORKS CITED

Adler-Kassner, Linda, Robert Crooks and Ann Watters, Eds. *Writing the Community: Concepts and Models for Service-Learning in Composition.* Urbana, IL: AAHE/NCTE, 1997.

Deans, Thomas. *Writing Partnerships: Service-Learning in Composition.* Urbana, IL: NCTE, 2000.

Schutz, Aaron and Anne Ruggles Gere. "Service Learning and English Studies: Rethinking 'Public' Service." *College English* 60 (1998): 129-49.

18

SPECIAL TEXTS AND SPECIAL NEEDS

A Closer Look at Electronic Community

Christine Hult
Utah State University

In too many instances, writing pedagogy has lost sight of where writing is headed in this age of technology (and the "late age of print"). We do our students a disservice when we ignore electronic writing and instead privilege print writing. Not only are the writing processes changed in an electronic classroom with a postmodern writing pedagogy, so are the products. This web site or "Cybertext" assignment for upper-division English majors at the University of Hawaii-Manoa shows clearly how the writing processes of the students working collaboratively to construct a web site are radically different from those of a solitary writer composing alone in a garret. The writing products themselves are drastically different as well—they are hypertextual, multivocal, multigenre, and graphically intensive. They convey meaning through not just text but delivery and design as well. In essence, the writing products themselves display postmodern values of diversity and multivocality.

Writing teachers interested in computers in the classroom have been speculating for more than a decade about the ways in which network pedagogy is changing the teaching of writing. These teachers have rede-

·fined the work of composition to include an emphasis on the building of community and the communal construction of knowledge. Handa states that "as writing teachers and perhaps even more importantly as humanists, we see that the computer offers immense possibilities for restructuring relations in both our classes and society" (xvii). In their essay in Handa's collection, Barker and Kemp call this restructuring of relationships a "postmodern pedagogy." They state that "a postmodern writing pedagogy represents a structured attempt to combine the realities of current social and economic conditions with instruction that emphasizes the communal aspect of knowledge making" (2).

Of course, in 1990 when Handa's collection appeared, the writers were talking about networked computers (LANs), not the Internet. The advent of the Internet and its ubiquitous presence in our lives underscores even more strongly the need for writing teachers to foster the development of writing communities in their classes. As Cooper points out, "Like all writing (and language use), electronic writing responds to cultural changes . . . writing online sets up a different rhetorical situation and encourages different writing strategies than writing for print technology does" (141). Computer classrooms today are often hybrids that combine face-to-face classes with online extensions of the classroom through Internet technologies such as e-mail, discussion forums, or other Web course tools. Or, increasingly, modern writing classrooms may be entirely virtual, with no face-to-face component at all. Students in these 21st century classrooms are learning to read and write with media that were unheard of even a decade ago. It is incumbent upon writing teachers in the new millennium to help our students become intelligent users and producers of these media.

While on a teaching exchange during the Fall semester of 2000, I taught a course for upper-division English majors at the University of Hawaii-Manoa. The course, titled "Rhetoric, Composition, and Computers," is offered at UH annually to introduce majors to new, computer-based writing environments. My focus is on an assignment written for this course, a group-constructed web site or "Cybertext," because this assignment exemplifies my efforts to implement a postmodern writing pedagogy based on community and the communal construction of knowledge.

I taught the course in a networked computer classroom, but I also extended the classroom's traditional boundaries via the Web, resulting in a hybrid course with both face-to-face and online components. Students met face-to-face in class twice weekly and continued their course work throughout the rest of the week online. I set up the class using the *SyllaBase™* online classroom as a Web course environment.[1] Using *SyllaBase*, I was able to include for my students in one convenient Web location all of the online features that helped to make our class a community, including threaded discussions and chat rooms, a hypertext syllabus and weekly bulletins, class assignments, homework upload, online resources and references, and an online portfolio for student work. Below is the course description included on the syllabus:

> English 307 is a writing course that combines necessary academic writing practice (argument and research) with the use of computers for writing and for information access. By the end of the term, you will know how to use computers to write a hypertext document. Electronic writing in hypertext allows you to construct information in a format that is infinitely flexible in a writing space that is manipulated to suit the purpose of the writer as well as the needs of the reader. Hypertext facilitates a multi-genre and collaborative approach to writing because layers of the document can employ different genres and voices. You should come to understand the changing nature of rhetoric as you practice your own writing with computers. You will also be able to write a creative text, if you wish (essay, fiction, or poetry), taking advantage of the power of computers to publish your work. Specific requirements and deadlines will be provided as needed.

You can see in this course description the way I have outlined a postmodern writing pedagogy: I assume that the students will take a collaborative approach to their writing and that they will be able to experiment with different genres and voices as they construct knowledge together. As Palmquist et al., discovered in their *Transitions* study, I have also found that students in electronic classrooms spend the bulk of their time actually writing and sharing writing rather than listening to the teacher talk about writing (as is often the case in traditional writing classrooms). I further assume that they will become familiar with new media and new writing spaces at the same time as they are learning about the rhetoric of these new writing environments.

There are four major assignments for this course: (1) A hyperpoem (in which students create a hypertext using a poem of their choice); (2) A persuasive piece (in which students write a hypertext that seeks to persuade an audience that "something is not what it seems to be"); (3) A researched argument piece (a multipage, linked hypertext that argues a position on a "cyber" topic); and (4) A cybertext (a col-

---

[1]For more information about the *SyllaBase* Web classroom environment, see the following URL: http://www.3gb.com.

laborative web site developed for a service organization of the students' choosing). The fourth assignment will be the focus because it provides the most specific example of the collaborative knowledge making and connection to community so important in postmodern pedagogy.

I decided to use this final assignment as a way for our own classroom community to extend out to the community at large through a service-learning project. Writing for the Web provides a natural and logical way to extend the boundaries of the traditional classroom. About halfway through the semester, students began to think about what service organizations they would like to work with to develop a web site for that organization. Four projects were mutually decided on: a web site for a wheelchair sports organization and for a local preschool, and two web sites for public housing projects in connection with a technology outreach grant sponsored by local colleges, including UH. My example comes from group one's web site for Wheelchair Sports Hawaii.

Brian Kajiyama, a special needs student and a member of Wheelchair Sports Hawaii, had approached me via e-mail several months prior to the semester with a request to join the class from home. Brian was unable to come to the UH campus every day for classes, so I arranged for him to attend my class via the *SyllaBase* chat room. Either a note-taker provided by the Disabilities Service Center or another student in the class communicated with Brian in the *SyllaBase* chat room during class time. Neither I nor the other students in the class ever met Brian in person. However, he was a fully participating and vital member of the class through his presence and participation on the Web.

Students expressed their preferences for groups, and I assigned them to either their first or second choice. When the groups met for the first time, they negotiated who would fill which role or roles. Depending on the number of group members, some needed to assume more than one role. I have found that when arranging for group projects, it helps the students to have a sense of all of the tasks that they will need to accomplish before their project is completed and to assign specific roles to each individual in the group. Of course, these roles do not end up being rigidly adhered to—rather, roles become blurred as the students construct knowledge communally. Not too surprisingly, group one chose Brian to be their group leader as well as the liaison with the Wheelchair Sports organization.

Below is the assignment outline from the course syllabus. Part One outlines the group roles for which each group assumed responsibility. Part Two describes the group activities to be accomplished during the project. My comments below *[bracketed and in italics]* describe how this assignment illustrates a postmodern writing pedagogy.

GROUP ASSIGNMENTS FOR CYBERTEXT WEB SITE
You will work together in groups of 4-5 to write a web site on a topic of your group's choice related to: 1) Wheelchair Sports web Site, 2) Preschool Project, 3) Palolo Valley Web Site, 4) Kuhio Park Terrace web Site.

I. GROUP ROLE ASSIGNMENTS: Combine roles as necessary depending upon the size of your group.

[Students must negotiate their own group roles. This always engenders a great deal of discussion and sorting out of group members' relative skills. Each person becomes an important contributor to the collaborative project. They all feel ownership for the project.]

YOUR GROUP'S NAME:
GROUP LEADER: The group leader is responsible for making sure that everything is done in a timely fashion. The group leader, in consultation with group members, will assign specific writing tasks (see number 2 below) and is responsible for seeing that these are completed. Every group member must report at least weekly to the group leader as to their progress. The group leader will evaluate all members of the group (and the teacher will consider very strongly this evaluation as she grades the project). The group leader will post WEEKLY updates of the groups' progress on the group's Discussion Forum in *SyllaBase*.

LIAISON: The liaison is responsible for setting up any meetings or interviews with the community or individuals for whom a Web site is being developed. The liaison should arrange for several in the group to personally meet with individuals, to set up meetings with any project coordinators, e.g., Dr. Zuern and Dr. Kirkpatrick, and to be sure the lines of communication between students and community are maintained productively.

[The need for both a group leader and liaison shows that this assignment is postmodern: it assumes that students will take responsibility for their own work—rather than relying solely on the teacher. Cooper cites Shor's Frierian model "where the teacher is 'a problem-poser who leads a critical dialogue in class . . . which sends a hopeful message to students . . .; it encourages their achievement by encouraging their aspirations. They are treated as responsible, capable human beings who should expect to do a lot and do it well'" (Shor as cited by Cooper 158).]

LIBRARIAN: The librarian is responsible for the sources and the links for your web site. The librarian will catalog each relevant web site or print source into an extensive bibliography for your group's project. The librarian will be responsible for making sure that URLs are correct and that all links on your web site work. The librarian is also responsible for the correct format for bibliographical information at your web site.

WEBMASTER: The webmaster is responsible for putting together all of the written pieces supplied by the individuals in the group into a cohesive web site. [Individuals are responsible for putting their own writing into basic HTML format.] The webmaster will lead the group in storyboarding their site. The webmaster, working with the lab consultant and/or Dr. Hult, will post the group's work onto the class web site.

PUBLISHER: The publisher is responsible for the format and "look" of the final web site. The publisher must ensure that everything about the site is perfect—no spelling or grammatical errors, etc. All fonts, headers, graphic colors, etc., must be made consistent for the web site. The publisher has the final say about when something is ready to be "published" at the group's site.

[The librarian, Webmaster, publisher, and graphics coordinator roles show that the task of writing for the Web encompasses many additional, and perhaps new, skills with which students will need to become familiar. Within any given group, students with differing computer skills can find something they are good at doing.]

GRAPHICS COORDINATOR: The graphics coordinator is responsible for gathering and posting graphics to be used at the site. The graphics coordinator must ensure that each graphic is appropriate in size and memory so that it doesn't take too long to load. The graphics coordinator must ensure that all links to graphics are working correctly. Working with the publisher and the webmaster, the graphics coordinator will ensure that the site is visually appealing, adjusting colors and fonts as necessary for visual coherence.

[An additional postmodern characteristic is that the assignment shatters our traditional image of the solitary writer: "The image of the secluded writer is a Romantic notion, outworn and suspect . . . . We live in an age where the individual must learn to balance between valuing self and working with others; today we acknowledge that students learn as much from each other as they do from us" (Handa xix). Faigley also speculates about the same phenomenon; he says that dissolving boundaries of time and space by making writing public in electronic spaces also helps to dissipate this romantic notion of independently constructed knowledge (191).]

II. GROUP ACTIVITIES

1. Meet with your group and assign a role for everybody in the group. When you have assigned the roles, post to your group's Discussion Forum. All of the roles are equally important in order for the group to come up with a successful project. In addition to evaluations by the group leader, every group member will also evaluate the work of the others in the group. I can't stress enough how important it is that this be a team project. One of the most-desired qualities for hiring as cited by employers is the "ability to problem solve in a group or team." This is a skill everybody can learn.

[Skills learned in this project transfer directly to the workplace and to the projects that writers today often complete across time and space.]

2. Each group member is responsible for writing one extensive piece (at least one "page" on the web site). The individual pieces could be evaluative, informative, critical, etc., but should relate somehow to the topic of your group. Individual pieces may be in any genre: poetry, song lyrics, essay, story, news release, letter, etc. Each individual piece should be signed with the author's by-line as identification.

[Figure 18.1 shows an example of the tasks that group one decided on for the individually-authored contributions to the web site.]

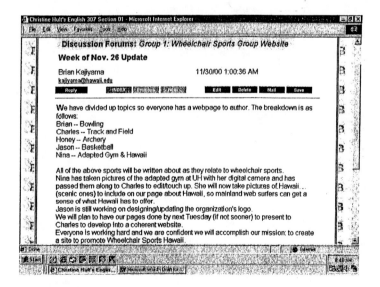

Fig. 18.1. Brian's Discussion Post about Group Task.

3. Use your group's discussion forum and file sharing as a place to share ideas/collaborate as you build your web site.

4. Each group member will be given a grade by the teacher, based on evaluations by the group leader, individuals within the group, and my own assessment of your contribution to the project.

[Even the grading of the project is communally based, as the responsibility for evaluation is shared by the teacher and the students.]

Following the group assignment instructions as outlined above, the four groups began to work on their web sites.[2] They contacted the service organization with whom they would work and even made numerous site visits as appropriate. Each day in class, the groups met collaboratively to discuss their progress, conduct Internet research, and review model Web sites on which to base their web designs. Group one met with Brian in their group chat room during class time. As Brian describes it below, this was not always an orderly, or quiet, process, but in the end they thoroughly enjoyed working with each other and they were able to construct a congenial working community:

> I'm aware that we were the only group who was "noisy and laughing all the time" (I got this info through my group members) and people would think we were only goofing off. I want to stress that my group worked extremely hard on this project and I am very happy that we were able to create an environment where it wasn't just a serious atmosphere but rather a situation where everyone got along and was comfortable with each other to laugh and have fun. That in itself makes me feel that I accomplished my goal. Everyone enjoyed being a part of the group and took great pride in the product we produced.

Figure 18.2 shows the splash screen for the Wheelchair Sports Hawaii web site. Notice that there are several linked pages listed on the index to the left side of the screen. These links are repeated again at the bottom of the screen (not pictured) to allow for multiple navigational points. The linked pages, each researched and written by a different student in the group, include information on the major sports sponsored by the parent organization: archery, basketball, bowling, and track and field. The other two major links, University of Hawaii and State of

2 To see all four of the groups' web sites, please go to the following URL: http://english.usu.edu/faculty/chult/Fall2000/English307/cybertext

Hawaii, were included at the organization's request because their members wanted to use the site for both informational and public relations purposes. The University of Hawaii link tells about the adaptive gym that is available to special needs athletes. The State of Hawaii link is a promotional and informational link about the state. The final link, Contacts, makes it possible for anyone visiting the site to contact the parent organization. It also tells about any sponsored events that are upcoming for the organization.

The group that researched, designed, and wrote this web site has clearly achieved the course objectives of constructing a Web document that is multigenre, collaborative, graphically appealing, and hypertextual. They show a rhetorical sophistication that takes into account issues of audience, purpose, and persona. Carolyn Miller argues that "rhetoric should take seriously its social grounding" so that rhetorical communities will have the overt intention of purposeful action (as cited by Gurak 12). A collaborative web site that eventually is turned over to a service organization is a perfect example of such action. Gurak also points out that of the three modes of appeal in classical rhetoric (logos, ethos, pathos), ethos takes on a tremendously important role in cyber-

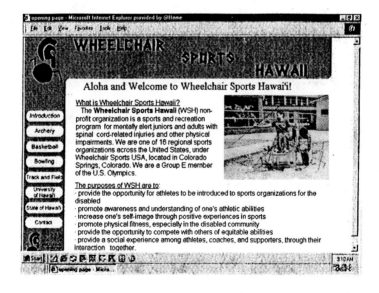

Fig. 18.2. Splash Page for Wheelchair Sports Hawai'i

communities. She states that "group ethos has been noted by Michael Halloran (1982), who suggests that 'the word ethos has both an individual and collective meaning'" (as cited in Gurak 14). Group ethos was considered very carefully by group one as they talked about the audience, purpose, and persona they wished to display in their web site:

Audience. To ensure that they were meeting the needs of their audience, the group members interviewed several of the Wheelchair Sports members via e-mail. They also used Brian, a member of the organization, as an informational source. Whenever they had a draft page on the Web, they sent a copy to the organization for their approval. They determined that the audience was two-fold: members of the organization and prospective members or interested outside parties.

Purpose. The purpose of the site, as articulated by the organization, was to both promote the organization through a Web presence and to provide current group members with information. When the web site was presented to the organization, they accepted it with pride and gratitude. They felt that the organization's purposes had been well represented by the site. It was informational as well as graphically appealing.

Persona. The group was especially sensitive to the need for portraying the organization in a positive and inviting way. Everything from the design of the new logo to the graphics included on the site were intended to reflect a positive persona. As Kress points out, in electronic texts, "the visual is taking over many of the functions of written language" (68). What this means for Web writing is that graphics must be selected in a way that they enhance the meaning of the text. This group uses that fact to their advantage.

During the semester, the class often discussed what makes a good Web page. We used as our guidelines the eight principles outlined in an article by Roy Tennant of the University of California-Berkeley. I introduced these principles to the class because I felt they articulated succinctly what I had found in several other Web authoring guidebooks. The principles were also used in peer reviews of each others' web sites while they were under construction. As students in my class were learning about writing for the Web, they were at the same time exploring together postmodern values of communal construction of knowledge, as these values are inherent in the classroom environment itself and are echoed in the structure and content of their actual responses to the class assignments.

Below is a summary of four of the most important of those principles, along with my critical interpretation for the assignment from the Wheelchair Sports group as it relates to postmodernism:

Rule #1: Design is secondary to content. I emphasized throughout the semester that students needed to pay attention to the writing of their Web pages (both what is said and how it is presented), not just the design or construction of the web site. When reading the Wheelchair Sports web site, you will see that students were careful to write succinctly and correctly, knowing that what they wrote would ultimately be published. Gurak states that, in addition to ethos being tremendously important in cybercommunities, delivery takes on increased importance as well. How writers present their content on a Web page might be considered to be "delivery" in the classical sense, that is, how one delivers a speech. Gurak quotes Bolter (1993) who suggests that "electronic writing compels us to reconsider the classical concept of delivery" (as cited in Gurak 15). As Gurak explains it, delivery is "now bound up in the *medium* of distribution. Delivery in cyberspace means multiple, simultaneous transmissions of messages across great distances and without regard for time" (15). Students in this group were cognizant of the impact of "publishing" their writing in this way—of the ethos that they would portray and of the effectiveness of their delivery to their target audience. This multiplicity of delivery is also a feature of postmodernism because it makes possible communication with a great diversity of people and cultures.

Rule #4: Abolish linear thinking. We talked about this principle many times in class. When writing for the Web, students had to think in terms of the changing nature of texts and of writing spaces. As Bolter (1991) states, "Electronic writing emphasizes the impermanence and changeability of text, and it tends to reduce the distance between author and reader by turning the reader into an author" (3). Students had to understand that they were not able to lead a reader in a linear fashion through a sequentially formed argument. Rather, they had to write hypertextually, weaving together graphics and texts in a way that each reader could reconstruct him or herself (idiosyncratically). They grew to appreciate first-hand Bolter's maxim that "unlike the space of the printed book, the computer's writing space can represent any relationships that can be defined as the interplay of pointers and elements. Multiple relationships pose no special problem. . . . This multiplicity and abstraction already render the electronic writing space more flexible than its predecessors" (21). Students came to value this flexibility because it gave them leave to explore their own unique voices within the context of a collaborative project. By focusing on hypertext, our class emphasized many of the multivocal values of postmodernism.

Rule #5: Avoid "chunkitis." As the students constructed their web sites, they were careful that each link would lead to information that was valuable rather than treating anything as worthy of a link (chunkitis). These links are the major "topics" that Bolter (1991) describes as the linchpins in any text's structure: "Writing in topics is not a replacement for writing with words; the writer must eventually attend to the details of his or her prose" (17). The students limited the number of links (topics) to those that their audience would find the most useful. And they developed each "topic" with words and details: each page that you visit at this site contains writing that is comprehensive enough to give you adequate information on the topic being covered. Along with the text, the students also provide visual representations in their graphics that help to illustrate the topic under discussion. This rule is important in a postmodern pedagogy because, even though writers cannot know how their audience will ultimately construct their texts, they need to provide the readers with enough raw material to make the individual topics discussed meaningful and rich.

Rule #8: Consider a diversity of users and purposes. This rule expands upon Rule #4 (Abolish Linear Thinking) because it also emphasizes the fact that when delivering a hypertext to an audience, students are writing for readers who might have differing purposes and needs, readers who will ultimately create their own "texts" out of the hypertext—once again, an essential value in a postmodern pedagogy. This group did an excellent job of providing readers with a hypertext structure that had multiple access points and clear navigation. The students were careful to think about their multiple audiences, including outsiders who might want more information about Hawaii in general, when they decided on pages to include at the site. They also provided for multiple navigation points so readers could read the information in any order they desired. For example, in Figure 18.3 notice the "click here to learn more" link. This link allows readers to decide how much information on this subject they desire.

I have included the above description of the changing nature of texts from my assignment because I think it also illustrates basic principles of postmodernism. As articulated by Cooper, "Postmodernism is, above all, a response to our own increased awareness of the great diversity in human cultures, a diversity that calls into question the possibility of any 'universal' or 'privileged' perspective and that thus values the juxtaposition of different perspectives and different voices and the contemplation of connections rather than a subordinated structure of ideas that achieves a unified voice and a conclusive perspective" (142).

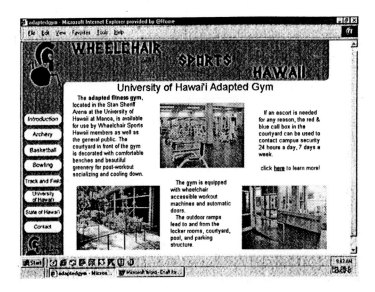

Fig. 18.3. The Adaptive Gym at the University of Hawai'i

In too many instances, writing pedagogy has lost sight of where writing is headed in this age of technology (and the "late age of print"). We do our students a disservice when we ignore electronic writing and instead privilege print writing. Not only are the writing processes changed in an electronic classroom with a postmodern writing pedagogy, so are the products. This writing assignment shows clearly how the writing processes of the students working collaboratively to construct a web site are radically different from those of a solitary writer composing alone in a garret. The writing products themselves are drastically different as well—they are hypertextual, multivocal, multigenre, and graphically intensive. They convey meaning through not just text but delivery and design as well. In essence, the writing products themselves display postmodern values of diversity and multivocality.

The changes in the roles of teachers and students are also readily apparent. The postmodern classroom is more collaborative, more community-focused, more communal in its knowledge construction. Furthermore, as I have shown in this example, many of the rhetorical principles we are so familiar with in print writing are equally important in electronic texts: for example, principles of audience, purpose, and persona. But, along with reinforcing those principles in the cybercommunity, we also need to help students to understand and become fluent in the new electronic media. They need to read and write Web texts to become both critical "readers" of new media and excellent writers in electronic genres.

As well as having individuals learn to write in these new genres, we need to stress the community aspects of writing. Writing as a basis for forming communities has become even more important in the computer age, particularly in the postmodern writing classroom. By using electronic communications, we are able to build and sustain communities that are geographically separated from each other. It is feasible to connect the larger community to the classroom community. What made this project possible was the need for it in the community at large (the "service" in the service-learning component). The web site would look very different if its audience weren't real. Web sites allow more connections between the classroom and the community than are typically possible.

Not the least of the important lessons from this class experience is the positive impact of Brian, a special needs student, on the classroom community as a whole and on his group in particular. We all learned so much from his participation. According to his own description, Brian has trouble forming words to communicate verbally. But, he's an absolute whiz on the computer: he has found that typing at a keyboard has transformed his own communication possibilities. I'd like to close with the description, in Brian's words, of what the class meant to him:

> Thanks again for all your help throughout the semester. It's truly been a blast, and the class didn't seem like work at all. At the same time I really felt like I learned a lot about online communications, technological issues, and I became a stronger writer as well. It's rare to be disappointed that a semester is ending, but with this class it was so enjoyable I'll definitely miss it. Even though I wasn't present in class, I felt I was a presence within, as everyone accepted me as just another classmate. Again I thank you for everything. Aloha, Brian

WORKS CITED

Barker, Thomas T., and Fred O. Kemp. "Network Theory: A Postmodern Pedagogy for the Writing Classroom." *Computers and Community*. Ed. Carolyn Handa. Portsmouth, NH: Boynton/Cook, 1990. 1-27.

Bolter, Jay David. *Writing Space: The Computer, Hypertext, and the History of Writing.* Hillsdale, NJ: Erlbaum, 1991.

Bolter, Jay David. "Hypertext and the Rhetorical Canons." *Essays on Rhetorical Memory and Delivery.* Ed. J. F. Reynolds. Hillsdale, NJ: Erlbaum, 1993. 97–111.

Cooper, Marilyn. "Postmodern Pedagogy in Electronic Conversations." *Passions, Pedagogies, and 21st Century Technologies.* Eds. Gail E. Hawisher and Cynthia L. Selfe. Logan: Utah State UP, 1999. 140-160.

Faigley, Lester. *Fragments of Rationality: Postmodernity and the Subject of Composition.* Pittsburgh, PA: Pittsburgh UP, 1992.

Gurak, Laura J. *Persuasion and Privacy in Cyberspace.* New Haven: Yale UP, 1997.

Halloran, S. Michael. "Aristotle's Concept of Ethos, or If Not His Somebody Else's." *Rhetoric Review* 1.1 (1982): 58-63.

Handa, Carolyn. "Introduction." *Computers and Community.* Ed. Carolyn Handa. Portsmouth, NH: Boynton/Cook, 1990. xvii-xxii.

Kress, Gunther. "'English' at the Crossroads: Rethinking Curricula of Communication in the Context of the Turn to the Visual." *Passions, Pedagogies, and 21st Century Technologies.* Eds. Gail E. Hawisher and Cynthia L. Selfe. Logan: Utah State UP, 1999. 66-88.

Palmquist, Mike, Kate Kiefer, James Hartvigsen, and Barbara Godlew. *Transitions: Teaching Writing in Computer-Supported and Traditional Classrooms.* Greenwich, CT: Ablex, 1998.

Shor, Ira. *Empowering Education: Critical Teaching for Social Change.* Chicago: U of Chicago P, 1992.

Tennant, Roy. "Web Sites By Design: How to Avoid a 'Pile of Pages.'" *Syllabus: Technology for Education* 11.1 (August, 1997): 49–50.

19

GOOD TEACHING AND GOOD WRITING

Practices in Public Life and Rhetorical Ethics

Lisa Toner

University of Kentucky

Teachers' notions of "good writing" must recognize students' development of authority as a hypertextual and casuistic negotiation of pedagogical goals and projects and lives beyond class. Students' openness to others' views evolves through writing several assignments, not just through a single research paper or persuasive essay. An examination of one student's process of constructing situated rhetorical authority within and despite consensus and dissensus shows how the student's rhetorical ethic broadens from an individual-based reasoning to a community-oriented one, from absolute freedom to reasoned responsibility, from ignoring to reflecting her vulnerable position in unequal and diverse power relations, and from certainty to ambivalence about peers' commitment to their views. A good writing teacher respects and facilitates students' struggles of constructing voice in a constrained agency and helps students avoid the paralysis that comes with recognizing the legitimacy of others' critique.

In the late age of print, "good writing" cannot be conceptualized simply as a text that argues the "right" opinion in the "right" way. The age of simulacra with MOOs and MUDs, sound-byte campaigning and internet advertising, calls for an understanding of "good writing" that cannot be limited to either the formal correctness of a text's features or the absolute ethical rightness of its views. Rather, the notion of good writing—in traditional as well as the computer-integrated writing classes—must be expanded. A good writing class must be expanded to recognize students' hypertextual and casuistic construction of authority as a negotiation among course goals, projects, and assignments and activities of their public lives beyond class. This calls for a change in the way we view good teaching of writing.

Moreover, permeation of traditional classroom boundaries made possible in computer-integrated writing classrooms coincides with an increasing concern for writing teachers to foster students' participation in public life. Both radical and more traditional theorists in composition argue that good teaching in a postmodern age fosters students' responsible or engaged citizenship. On the radical side, a decade and a half ago, John Timbur proposed that using a "critical" or Habermasian approach to collaborative learning can help students identify and transform discursive techniques that mask difference and disagreement about cultural values, knowledge, and power relations (612–6130. Arguing for a "non-foundational authority" (671), Patricia Bizzell urged writing teachers to take up their roles as "orators" (672) by creating assignments and classroom dialogue that "can collectively generate trustworthy knowledge and beliefs conductive to the common good" (671). Explaining the complementary relationship between cultural studies and rhetoric, James Berlin maintained that a composition pedagogy based in students' resistance to hegemonic discourse practices and their participation in democratic dialogue will enable them to "resolve disputes peacefully, as an alternative to armed conflict" ("Collapsing" 116). On the more traditional side, a decade and a half ago, James Kinneavy emphasized the centrality of *kairos* in a writing curriculum dedicated to promoting student writers' development as ethically and politically responsible professionals and citizens (98–103). At about the same time, Eugene Garver suggested that teaching writing promotes skill in "deliberation" and "practical reasoning" needed by an effective citizenry (68–69). In a more conservative line of thinking, in the early 1990s, Sandra Stotsky argued that teaching students the principles and practices undergirding academic writing can advance "a student's moral character as a citizen" (798).

The pedagogy I describe in this article situates the "good" writing teacher in the late age of print as a facilitator of students' development of authority by engaging them in the decision-making and policy concerns within local or campus communities. Having students write to relevant decision makers about policies that govern their campus lives (e.g., dormitory visitation policies, cafeteria meal plans, or participation in campus clubs) positions them to write with a conscious authority that emerges regardless of the ultimate effectiveness of their texts in bringing about specific actual changes, though these are to be hoped for, urged, and celebrated.

Enabling students to compose all kinds of texts—from analytical to persuasive to self-exploratory—can foster situated, respectful self-assertion that avoids overstatement and remains open to growth, revision, and critique. Students' openness to others' views develops through writing several assignments, not just a single research paper or persuasive essay. For example, in my first-year writing course I have assigned a sequence of analytical, critical essays that ask students to choose a campus or local issue and speculate upon the positions of various groups affected by it. This assignment sequence was originally designed by Karin Evans and Joanne Addison as part of the developmental writing curriculum at Purdue University. Many of my students choose to write about the university's dormitory visitation policy, which allows no visitors (including parents) to rooms before noon daily or after midnight on weeknights and two a.m. on weekends. As would be expected, most students find this policy very restrictive and unfair, and they argue that it treats them as children instead of responsible adults. Freshmen in particular adopt this argument easily, in part because a required weekly first-year seminar emphasizes taking responsibility in their academic and social lives.

Students acknowledge that the policy results in part from Roman Catholic teaching against premarital sex,. as well as parents' (i.e., tuition-payers') concerns. Students also quickly point out gender bias in the policy's implementation: a twenty-four hour guard protects entrance to the women's dorms, whereas student workers supervise the front doors of men's dorms only after six o'clock in the evening.

Four essay projects build upon each other. First, a problem description written by students identifies a campus or local issue students believe should be examined, then discusses its context, and justifies research about it. A second paper speculates about economic, social, political, legal, ethical, and personal interests of each group involved in or affected by the issue; therefore, students are required to write as both community members and disinterested mediators. A third paper discusses results of a survey of the opinions of one of the relevant groups, typically students. Survey results usually complicate and broaden students' beliefs about consensus within their own group of supposedly like-minded peers and lay groundwork for openness towards other groups' concerns.

Finally, drawing upon insights from previous papers and anticipating critique of their recommendations, students write letters to a campus decision maker in which they advocate specific actions on the issue. This letter thus requires students to construct situated rhetorical authority within and despite consensus and dissensus. In particular, students struggle with the responsibilities of representing others' views. Anna Freeman's writing as a non-Catholic in a Catholic institution exemplifies one effort to assert authority within oppositional discourse.

Anna Freeman
Problem Statement

One of the major problems at Wheeling Jesuit University is the visitation policy. The problem with the visitation policy is that it is more of an inconvience [sic] than it is helpful. It is causing more issues to arise for the people involved.

The policy was meant to build security. The administrations hope was to lower theft and abuse rates. Unfortunately, the policy is not really effective. These things still occur at similar rates, and in some situations they are happening more often.

One of the biggest flaws with the policy is that because students can not stay in the opposite sexs' room as long as they like, they are then forced to find other places.

Quite possibly these alternate places are ones that most students are unfamiliar with. And most likely have little or no security. Thus causing many problems to elevate.

Another dilemma facing the policies' potential success is that it may be to confining for students of this age. Many residents feel that they are not in need of this type of discipline. They feel that it is unrealistic to attempt to shelter them from real life aspects.

Similarly, most students think that since they are paying to reside there they should be in charge of their own life. And that they should be responsible for any effects of consequences steaming from these privileges.

In the late age of print, Anna's rhetorical authority must go beyond mere self-assertion to respect for the difference of others. Her authority emerges in the ways she writes about the views of those groups of people with whom she might not only disagree but who, like the teacher, may hold some form of institutional power over her. As the semester progresses, Anna's writing evidences Trimbur's expectation that students can recognize "how differences in interest produce conflicts that may in fact block communication and prohibit the development of consensus (611). Opinions and facts Anna decides to include and omit from her final arguments indicate her difficulties in achieving Bizzell's objective "to engage [students] in a rhetorical process that can collectively generate trustworthy knowledge and beliefs conducive to the common good—knowledge and beliefs to displace the repressive ideologies an unjust social order would inscribe in the skepticl world" (671). In addition, Anna's writing shows her occupation of what Dale Bauer describes as "[t]he ambivalent space of this signing" of "public and private voices" and attempts, in Bauer's words, "to negotiate that opposition in order to speak a multiplicity of voices into the cultural dialogue" (388). Taken as a whole, Anna's writing articulates a postmodern rhetorical ethic, which, James Porter explains, is not to be understood simply as a static, unconflicted set of ethical principles to be applied to a text (233), as traditional philosophical conceptions of ethics and civic thinking (e.g., Stotsky) hold. Rather, he proposes, rhetorical ethics is articulated casuistically and hypertextually through the writing process.

From this first writing to her last, Anna's writing about the dorm visitation policy evidences limited achievement of my pedagogical objectives through changes in attitudes, appeals, and arguments supporting her views. Having engaged with other students' and her instructor's comments throughout the semester, Anna writes her final letter in a way that respects divergent views more than does her problem statement. Although Anna continues to oppose, even resent, the visitation policy, her writing at the end of the semester reflects an important development in her struggle for self-assertion amid divergent views and conflicting claims of responsible authority.

Dear Director of Campus Life,
My name is Anna Freeman and I am a freshman at Wheeling Jesuit University. During my time as a resident on this campus, I have noticed an extreme controversy in peoples' opinion on the effectiveness of the existing visitation policy. As a student and a resident of Wheeling Jesuit University, I am very concerned, as I'm sure you are also, about the welfare of student life within this institution. My inquiry is, could campus life conduct an investigation into the views concerning the present visitation policy and its effectiveness?

Due to my survey results, most of my speculations about the policy have been confirmed. The problem does not seem to be in having a visitation policy. In fact, most students like the idea of having some type of visitation policy as a form of security. The dilemma begins with the effects of the present policy on all the groups involved. I understand that living in a community setting causes many unusual circumstances to arise, therefore, I'm sure it is extremely difficult to install a policy that will please everyone involved. But the most important issue involved is, is the existing policy working? Most students feel that it is not.

The policy seems to have many problems that you may not even be aware are occurring. Due to my research on the topic, I realize that this is a very complex situation to try to understand. Hence, I will try to break the aspects down into specific interests. The first interest affected by the policy is the students and their families' economic situation. The policy indirectly causes them extra expenses such as hotel and automobile fees. The policy forces visitation at certain hours, which may not be accessible to those involved. For example, families are then forced to drive extra miles which rack up gas and other automobile costs. Along with this, there are hotel costs due to long drives back and forth between cities.

Second, the legal interests of students rights are being ignored. The majority of these rights consist of the fact that they are legal adults, therefore, legally responsible for their actions. This aspect of the policy offends students. It makes them feel like they are being treated like children. The students feel that if their parents trust them to leave home and move on in their new life, then the school should also respect their maturity. Also, in any other area of behavior students would be held accountable, so what is the difference?

The next aspect of the policy that is affecting students' lives in a negative way deals with the social issues. I think its quite obvious that the policy, because of its definate hours, is affecting the students' and their families' and friends' social life because it restricts them from the amount of time they want to spend together. Due to conflicting college student schedules, along with their families' and friends' schedules, it is difficult to adhere to such a strict deadline for visitation.

Similarly, the ignorance of students private affairs has caused much frustration. For the students, whether male or female, the policy greatly affects their personal life because they do not have the opportunity to do what they need or want to do at the times they are available. With school, studying, and part time jobs, it is hard to accomplish all things during a set time everyday. The family is also being greatly affected in this way because they are not allowed to visit with each other at their available times. Some families are far apart for long periods of time, and in consideration of this, they should not be confined to a set group of hours. These groups feel that the administration has been apathetic about their personal interests because it does not affect them directly. This makes families feel very unwelcome. Economically, however, parents' and students' personal concerns could directly affect the school because if they are not satisfied with the schools' concern for them they may pursue an education elsewhere.

The final aspect of the students concern about the effectiveness of the policy, concerns religion. Is the policy influenced by the fact that this is a Jesuit institution? I think we all realize that many non-Catholics attend Wheeling Jesuit University and if the policy is influenced by the school being Catholic, then how will this affect the non-Catholics? Should they be forced to abide by these standards even though they do not have the same beliefs simply because they attend a Jesuit school? Can the administration force a set religious standard on non-Catholics because it is a private institution?

As I stated earlier, it is practically impossible to perfect the policy, yet there is room for improvement. Maybe the administration could experiment with possible solutions and see each ones effects. For example, one possibility would be to try twenty four hour visitation on the weekends or only one day per weekend.

Although this is not a complete solution, it is at least a compromise. The students' would then feel as if the administration cared about their position. I do understand, that in attempt to alter the policy, it will create more work for you. I have faith that although it may cause some imposition, you will realize that the well being of the students should be the number one concern of this institution. Thank you for giving me the time to discuss this dilemma with you.

Sincerely, Anna Freeman

On the whole, Anna's arguments about the campus visitation policy articulate not so much changes in her basic position against the policy but struggles to assert herself respectfully in relation to constraining viewpoints, attitudes, and concerns from others. The initial problem statement, in which her teacher is the primary audience, speaks mainly from the perspective of students by appealing to respect for their freedom as individuals. In contrast, Anna's argument to a decision maker reveals her position as one of negotiating obligations to others, such as teachers, boyfriends and girlfriends, and parents. Her letter voices disagreements and conflicts about enforcement of the policy and integrates shared concerns about ensuring dorm residents' safety. In this way, Anna's letter broadens her rhetorical ethic from an individual-based reasoning to a community-oriented one and shifts her authority from that of an autonomous agent whose freedom is "discipline[d]" by a policy to one whose freedom is constrained by conflicting obligations, which she began feeling more acutely as the semester progressed. Anna's rhetorical authority at the end of the semester positions her as a member of not only one community but several.

Anna's more broadly situated rhetorical authority speaks more justly than does her problem statement to her position in unequal and diverse power relations. Between writing the initial problem statement and the final letter, Anna reconceptualizes the policy from being a "problem" that fails to meet the concerns of a particular group (students) to a "dilemma" that negotiates inadequately these competing concerns that Anna herself and the college as an institution must choose among. In order to speak to the policy's inadequacy for each of these groups, Anna revises her reference to its limitations from being stated simply as a "biggest flaw," which takes the perspective solely of students controlled by the policy, to being more broadly explained as "a very complex situation to understand," a statement that accommodates more fully the conflicting viewpoints that she must negotiate in asserting her viewpoint. Importantly, Anna's authority is most constrained where the differences between herself and the institution are most evidently closed to dialogue. At a midsemester conference with me, Anna emphasized her religious difference from the Jesuitness privileged by the university's name: she is "not Catholic." In her letter, this difference, constrained by nonnegotiability, takes the form of rhetorical questions.

Anna's rhetorical-ethical development was partially shaped and encouraged by my comments on her writing throughout the semester, as well as in-class explanations about how to develop persuasive appeals, fulfill assignment objectives, and critique peers' drafts. Each stage of the writing process asked Anna to consider multiple viewpoints on the issue and points of contention. For instance, in response to Anna's problem statement, I asked her to address, in my words, "weaknesses [in the policy] related to administrative concerns" and to explain "both the 'helpful' and 'inconvenient' effects of the policy." I advised her to survey administrators, as well as students, for their views on the policy and to ask respondents if they felt that the policy should be "changed or abolished." These responses direct Anna to take a more qualified stance towards her critique in the final assignment.

My comments on Anna's third paper also prompt her to anticipate and respond to challenges of those who might disagree with her claims, values, and, hence, authority. In response to this paper, in which Anna considered the religious, economic, and legal interests that might inform the policy, I suggested that her questions about the rightful role of a Catholic view in regulating the behavior of non-Catholic students be asserted as "statements about the non-Catholic groups' view." However, I also identified the institution's probable response to these questions by stating that the "argument may be made that in deciding to go to a Catholic school, students should expect to at least encounter those views a lot in policies." I also added that "This is, of course, a highly debated topic, even here [at WJU]." These comments prompt Anna to anticipate responses of others who might disagree with her claims. Unfortunately, my comments did not enable Anna to have confidence in her situated authority by unambiguously asserting claims, instead of rhetorical questions, in her final letter.

The broadening of Anna's rhetorical ethic from the initial problem statement to the final letter does not ideally fulfill my objectives. Both the initial statement and the letter emphasize hardships of those controlled by the policy rather than the ineffectiveness or inappropriateness of that control. Anna's stance is, therefore, more complaining than persuasive and, although it might change policy makers' perceptions of the complexities of student life, it might also further reinforce perceptions about how well the policy is working to help students manage "conflicting schedules." Most significant, I think, is what I learned as a teacher from Anna's struggle for a situated rhetorical authority. Her constant emphasizing that the policy is "difficult to adhere to" and that "it is hard to accomplish all things during a set time everyday" points the importance of respecting students' differences and their difficulties in attaining credibility as adults while "feel[ing] like they are being treated like children" and simultaneously "need[ing] or want[ing] to" accommodate others' concerns. This balancing act was difficult for Anna, and no doubt for all our students. Though she did complete both fall and spring semesters, Anna did not return to Wheeling Jesuit the following year.

I would also characterize Anna's broadened rhetorical ethic and situated authority as less than ideal in honesty. The argument of her letter occludes the fact that through her survey results Anna came to recognize students as being less responsible and mature in dealing with this policy issue than she would have hoped for or believed. In an earlier report, Anna had acknowledged that her survey results showed that "many students are unwilling to help in the decision making process of the policy" and that "This concept was a bit surprising to me because I assumed most students would be eager to help alter the policy so that it would be more of a benefit to them." In that paper, she had speculated that students' lack of enthusiasm for participating in a policy reconsideration might result from their lack of time, "laziness," or belief that "their opinion does not count." Only the last of these student perspectives appears in her letter, which, therefore, remains silent on a key factor constraining her call for action.

In addition, Anna's situated authority only approximates conviction and requires the readers of her letter to draw conclusions from her queries. In her problem statement, Anna had forthrightly asserted that students "should be responsible for any effects or consequences st[r]eaming from these privileges" of a less restrictive visitation policy. But in the final letter, she asks less assuredly: "in any other area of behavior students would be held accountable, so what is the difference?" This question indicates less dishonesty than newly forming ambivalence about students' commitment to taking responsibility for their lives, an ambivalence that mitigates her self-assertion. As is the case with nonnegotiable values, Anna's rhetorical authority is reduced to rhetorical questioning of others who do not affirm her position.

Teaching writing in the late age of print, I see myself as a facilitator and mediator in Anna's often frustrating, sometimes tedious, sometimes murky process of rhetorical-ethical development. If my goal were simply to enable students to write well-constructed persuasive texts, assigning simply the persuasive letter would be all that would be necessary. However, as writing teacher, my role is to help students to work through the stresses of constructing voice in a constrained agency. Students' speaking for others while speaking for themselves situates their agency within a dialogue shaped by and about them. Helping students deal with the frustrations of fairly expressing others' views prevents a paralyzing relativism (Paine) that comes with recognizing the legitimacy of others' critique.

Students come to our classes from increasingly diverse backgrounds and are familiar with digital discourses such as e-mail and Web writing, which challenges writing teachers to rethink first-year composition as a "transition" course. A course often required for students to bring their writing skills up to snuff for other courses, composition is a rare learning event in which students provide much of the significant content, opinions, and information. What students and others write for the course is concrete information they take with them at the end of the semester.

Writing teachers can create and maximize pedagogical opportunities when both the subject written about (Anna's views, values, and experiences) and the writing subject (Anna as writer) coincide. Because a writing course is "about" students' writing and "about" themselves as Lester Faigley describes (119–128), teachers can help students negotiate rhetorical authority among conflicting discourses and adapt their rhetorical ethics despite partiality. As Bizzell argues, hypocritical moments, in which a writer recognizes contradictions in his or her basic beliefs, problematize individual rhetorical authority (672). Such moments put a writer at the interface between a self-centered rhetorical ethic and other-oriented public life that begs taking responsibility for one's assumptions, exclusions, and relatedness to various communities.

WORKS CITED

Bauer, Dale M. "The Other 'F' Word: The Feminist in the Classroom." *College English* 52 (1990): 385-396.

Bauer, Dale M., and Susan C. Jarratt. "Feminist Sophistics: Teaching with an Attitude." *Changing Classroom Practices: Resources for Literary and Cultural Studies.* Ed. David B. Downing. Urbana, IL: National Council of Teachers of English, 1994.

Berlin, James A. "Composition and Cultural Studies." *Composition and Resistance.* Eds. C. Mark Hurlbert and Michael Blitz. Portsmouth, NH: Boynton/Cook, 1991. 47-57.

—. "Composition Studies and Cultural Studies: Collapsing Boundaries." *Into the Field: Sites of Composition Studies.* Ed. Anne Ruggles Gere. New York: MLA, 1993. 99-116.

Bizzell, Patricia. "Beyond Anti-Foundationalism to Rhetorical Authority: Problems Defining 'Cultural Literacy'." *College English* 52 (1990): 661-75.

Garver, Eugene. "Teaching Writing and Teaching Virtue." *The Journal of Business Communication* 22 (1985): 51-73.

Faigley, Lester. *Fragments of Rationality: Postmodernity and the Subject of Composition.* Pittsburgh: UP, 1992.

Hairston, Maxine. "Diversity, Ideology, and Teaching Writing." *College Composition and Communication* 43 (1992): 179-193.

Kinneavy, James L. "Kairos: A Neglected Concept in Classical Rhetoric." *Rhetoric and Praxis: The Contribution of Classical Rhetoric to Practical Reasoning.* Ed. Jean Dietz Moss. Washington, DC: Catholic University of America P, 1986. 79-105.

Paine, Charles. "Relativism, Radical Pedagogy, and the Ideology of Paralysis." *College English* 51 (1989): 557-70.

Porter, James E. "Developing a Postmodern Ethics of Rhetoric and Composition." Eds. Theresa Enos and Stuart C. Brown. *Defining the New Rhetorics.* Newbury Park: Sage, 1993. 207-226.

Stotsky, Sandra. "Conceptualizing Writing as Moral and Civic Thinking." *College English* 54 (1992): 794-808.

Trimbur, John. "Consensus and Difference in Collaborative Learning." *College English* 51 (1989): 602-16.

20

WHY WRITE, AND TO WHOM?

Revisiting Concepts of Audience and Purpose

Susan Lang
Texas Tech University

Creating good writers is more than increasing the proportion of media, adopting the right ideology, or valuing correctness appropriately. Rather, Lang asserts, her goals are to help students at all levels become accomplished information managers and adept readers of multiple audiences. She uses a sophomore technical communication course to illustrate the complexities of these two aims, noting that faculty members, particularly as they become more experienced, rely on their own implicit definitions, leaving students to grapple with defining good writing by instructor and course rather than explicit rubrics.

Contemporary writing teachers face a difficult task. Students walk into our classes having been taught to write from a variety of perspectives—expressivist, cognitivist, social constructivist, whole language, and current-traditional rhetoric—but without an understanding of what they are doing and why they should care. They have been given so many implicit definitions of what good writing is during their careers that they begin to define writing by instructor and course, rather than by any other consideration. And they still aren't sure how to write well.

Complicating matters for students is the fact that assessment rubrics often vary depending on the assignment, course, or instructor. In the past two decades, another variable has entered into assessment of student work. Use of new media, including ever more complex word processors, HTML editors, graphics, video, and audio applications has become of increasing importance to some writing instructors, sometimes so much so that occasionally we find ourselves falling into the habit of defining good writing by the proportions of media contained in it. That is, our own fascination with hypertext writing and web publishing can sometimes overshadow our sense of what makes a document effective for a specific audience when we assess students' assignments that rely, to some extent, on these media. Additionally, we may sometimes find ourselves commenting to such an extent on the content of a student's paper that students see us as arguing with their ideological stance rather than the effectiveness of the document. Finally, within the field of rhetoric and composition, we still disagree about the relative value of "correctness," as applied to grammatical and mechanical conventions, even about the definition of the term, or if such a term even belongs in our classrooms.

If it is true that composition as a field has reinvented itself repeatedly in the last three decades, so have our assessment instruments. Not surprisingly, in our effort to extract and combine what we find useful in various pedagogical theories into those assessments, we run the risk of giving students apparently contradictory advice. What we most often overlook are what I'll term the rhetorical essentials of audience and purpose. As James Porter explains, "Composition and rhetoric texts have long advised writers and speakers to 'consider your audience'" (ix). However, all too often, students still end up writing for the teacher or for some vague notion of the term "audience" using an equally vague purpose. In the classroom, instructors are reluctant to engage students in the intricate discussion of audience offered by, among others, Roland Barthes, Mikhail Bakhtin, Wolfgang Iser, Jonathan Culler, and Michel Foucault. Rather than conceive of an audience as a dynamic contributor to an interpretive act, we prefer to keep the concept of audience manageable in terms of whom we think our students are capable of writing for.

So what, then, are instructors to do in integrating these rhetorical concepts of audience and purpose into the writing classroom? My first governing precept in designing writing assignments for any course, whether it be first-year composition, introductory technical communication, or a graduate seminar, is that I want to create *good writers*, rather than good writing. The difference is crucial. Good writers, even excellent writers, can write rather badly on occasion. So, if my goal is to develop good writers, at the outset of the course I discuss this goal with my students and explain what I believe a good writer to be. A good writer is one who can, first and foremost, *manage information and knowledge*. As Richard Barry observes, "information management is important because it facilitates intellectual or logical control over information assets, a *sine qua non* for effective management of information toward strategic ends." Although some may object to the discussion of information as an asset, to our writing students, it is. Regardless of whether we teach basic writers, in-service workshops for writing teachers at the K-12 or postsecondary level, or graduate students, the writing tasks that we demand of our students require that they be able to identify and articulate intellectual relationships between pieces of information. Second, a good writer understands that much of writing is reader-, or user-, centered (see Johnson). As Porter and others have observed, talking about audience in a writing class is, of course, nothing new, but a level of detail in that thinking that considers (1) the number and types of audiences external to the writer for each document, and (2) the portions of the document for whom the primary audience is the writer herself, extends our conventional treatment of the term in ways that our students seem to grasp more readily than before.

My agenda, then, as a writing instructor is to work with students at all levels to emphasize the importance of these concepts—information management and reader-centered writing. By starting with these two concepts, I have a foundation upon which I can build any number of discussions and assignments, whether the work be for a first-year composition class, a technical communication class, or a graduate course in rhetorical analysis or visual rhetoric.

To better illustrate how this rhetorically based agenda works across a variety of levels even within a single assignment, I will describe how I invoke this agenda in a sophomore-level technical communication course, which is required of technical communication majors and acts as a service course for many departments across the university. The course is designed to introduce students to the fundamentals of writing professional and business documents; the only prerequisites are ENGL 1301 and 1302, the first-year composition sequence. The assignment I have selected for inclusion here is one of the first I assign—the revision of a letter written by an apartment manager to the complex's tenants. It is assigned during the second week of class; students have just completed a shorter revision assignment of an advertisement, and will start the following week on a résumé. The assignment itself has two parts: the first is a memo written by the students in which they provide a full rhetorical analysis of the letter. This first portion demands that students recognize the role of readers or users in this communicative act. Thus, they are asked in this initial portion of the assignment to examine the letter and to compose a memo in which they discuss in detail the following elements. Whereas the top-level bullets identify common rhetorical concerns, the subordinate listings attempt to move the students to a more comprehensive understanding of the communicative situation, one that compels students to consciously consider the readers' or users' concerns.

- purpose of the document
  - beyond identifying the overarching purpose of the document, students examine the text for subordinate, possibly conflicting purposes and attempt to articulate a relationship between them.
- intended and possible audiences for this memo (e.g. those who may or may not have violated one or more of the policies discussed in the letter)
  - beyond identifying the audiences, students place themselves into the context of the reader to approximate the mindset of the audiences prior to reading the letter, which requires students to consider such items as when/where the letter is distributed, at what time it will most likely be read, and whether or not the target audience will even read the text if distributed in one particular way as opposed to another.
- information conveyed
  - beyond examining the letter's content, students must consider whether all of the contents are appropriately placed in a single document, given the writer's purpose; whether some information is unnecessary in any context; whether the writer includes too much or too little information for the audience(s).
- tone of the letter
  - beyond simply identifying the dominant tone (and recognizing that the tone changes at different points in the piece), students must explain how the tone and content interact as audiences read and respond to the document. Additionally, students consider whether the tone contributes to the communication of contextual purposes— those not necessarily spelled out in the document but still conveyed to the audiences via the tone of the piece.

- document design and grammar/mechanics of the piece
  - most students assume that this final issue is no more than identifying errors and editing them appropriately. However, beyond simple identification, students consider *how* their perception of the writer is influenced by the presence of these errors—how the *ethos* of the writer rises and falls based on choices made in document design, as well as in matters of grammar and mechanics.

The second part is an actual revision of the letter, in which students apply the results of the analysis. Having spent a significant amount of time examining the document from the audience's perspective, they now don the hat of the writer, take what they have gleaned from their analysis, and represent that knowledge in the writing of a new document or documents. This quick shifting of roles is an integral part of the assignment, as it shows the students how readers and writers approach a document with often vastly disparate contexts that influence the communicative act. It also gives students an opportunity to wrestle with the management of information at both the content and cognitive levels. By this I mean that students must grapple with questions regarding the reorganization and appropriateness of the content as well as issues involving the context and reception of the document. Students find that a simple cut and paste of a paragraph or sentence, or even the changing of a single word, may influence or alter the entire effect of the document upon a reader or readers. This is further complicated by the fact that a particular revision, which may help one audience, may hinder the reception by another. Suddenly, students find that they are engaging in what we often call higher-level thinking as they learn to negotiate these rhetorical conflicts. They also find out how difficult it can be to implement their understanding of the effects of the unrevised document into their revision of it. They can conceptualize the transferability of the information gathered and understood in the rhetorical analysis, but managing and implementing this knowledge poses yet another important challenge that moves students beyond the usual expectations of many assignments.

Parts one and two weigh equally in my evaluation of the assignment. I want to see if students are, at this early juncture of the course, able to recognize in a piece of writing the problems another writer has encountered with reader-centered writing and information management; I also want to see if they can articulate the ways in which the formal characteristics of the document (design, mechanics, etc.) influence the way in which the document is received. Finally, I want to see how well the recognition and articulation of problems in the text influences the students' revision of the document. In other words, can they put their observations into practice?

The following is a portion of one student's analysis of the audience:

> This letter is intended for the residents of the apartment who are just arriving home from either work or school in the early evening. They are probably tired and not in the mood for harshness. The head of the household will be the one to receive this document. Because they just got home for the evening, they are probably in a rush to change clothes, eat, or just relax and most likely will only glance at the sheet on their door before throwing it away.

In this response, the student has clearly moved beyond simple identification of the audience and has started to consider in more detail the reading situation of the intended audience(s). Although she does not differentiate between specific audiences, that is, those who may actually be a target of one portion of the original letter, she does recognize that the audience has a context different from the writer's and that that context will influence how the reader reacts to the text. In addition, the student already perceives that the form of delivery—a sheet of paper attached to every apartment tenant's door—will also affect the interpretation of the document, as it is not apt to be taken as seriously as a personally addressed letter that one receives through the mail, or even the same letter with the tenant's apartment number written on it.

In this excerpt, the student discusses problems with the tone of the document and how this tone could affect a reader's interpretation:

> The author misuses pathos in that he/she is very degrading to the residents. For example, the author asks the residents if they have enough insurance to cover the complex if a fire were to break out. This seems like a way that a parent would address a child, but by no means should a professional address others in this manner. He shows [a] lack of credibility when he states that he will call the towing company instead of clearing cars. . . .

We see here that the student has not only identified particular characteristics of the author's tone, but she has also been able to identify and categorize tone as it is used in different communicative situations. Although the student resorts to analogy and comparison to define the tone of the letter, her ability to move toward a definition and description of an anticipated tone for a particular situation is crucial and will serve this student well when she begins to revise the letter. At this point, I would encourage the student to think about additional ways of describing more subtle variations in the letter's tone such as sarcastic, patronizing, or antagonistic so as to assist the student in developing a more sophisticated understanding of tonal variation.

The student's concern with tone, which was evident in her analysis, transferred to her revision of the letter. The original document, a hybrid memo/letter, contained no salutation whatsoever. The student's revised version began with the salutation "Dear valued resident." This single change alone transformed the document from a rant into an act of professional communication.

The student's second paragraph, which follows a brief introduction, addresses a parking problem at the complex. Whereas the original contained such lines as "Residents, we have been over the parking situation over and over, if you or your guests get towed, don't call me" as well as "The next time I am called to clear out the cars to avoid being towed because it is blocking a door or driveway at Furrs, I promise, I will call the tow truck myself," the student's revision illustrates a far different approach:

> The first issue which we must cover involves those of you who are parking on the west side of Furr's Cafeteria. Please be cautious of where you are parking in that particular area. Be sure that we do not block the delivery entrance at Furr's. All vehicles that are improperly parked will be towed by the Furr's management. Please be sure to remind your guests of this policy. We would hate for them to have their vehicles towed.

The student has abandoned the confrontational rhetoric of the original document, preferring instead to develop a sense of shared community with the residents as evidenced by her use of the first person "we." Although the original author also used "we" in discussing the parking situation ("We have had a good relationship with Furrs for along[sic] time . . ."), this use is designed to share the blame among all residents rather than to create a common purpose. Additionally, the student's revision allows the author to serve as an advocate for the residents. One can construe from the original document that its author is more concerned with keeping the restaurant management happy, as well as maintaining a distinct hierarchical relationship with residents.

Whereas this student's analysis and revision pay particular attention to matters of audience and tone, they tend to subordinate concerns of purpose, content, and document design. That is not to say that the student ignored the issues. Her revision rid the original document of many misplaced or redundant sentences and actually added information not contained in the original document. This added information served the student's goal of using the document as a community-building device and thus left readers with a more positive interpretation and response. Implicit in these revisions is a concern with purpose in particular; however, other matters of content as well as those of document design remained unaddressed. For example, nowhere in the student's analysis or revision do we find significant attention given to the fact that the original letter treats five separate issues (parking, smoke detectors, rent payments, trash disposal, and balcony cleanliness). It is highly probable that few, if any, residents need to address all of these problems. A few other students in their analyses noted that a personal note to the violators of some policies or posted notices near the complex office, rent drop-box, and even on the manager's apartment door might be more effective ways of communicating management's concerns.

Clearly, no single document is capable of meeting every need of every possible reader. And clearly, no single assignment or course, for that matter, can prepare students for every potential writing situation or medium. However, assignments such as the one discussed here can go a long way toward giving students an understanding of those concepts that serve as the cognitive artifacts that they will take with them, refine, and further develop as they are faced with additional academic and professional writing tasks. After completing this assignment, students spend the remaining twelve weeks of the semester applying these fundamental concepts to a wide variety of writing situations. Students write individually and collaboratively and become increasingly aware of the complex interactions that occur in a writing situation.

The terms *information management* and *reader-centered* can be understood and applied on many levels, in any context. However, within the context of a composition or technical communication course, they need to be understood by students as words that do not simply replace the old standbys of organization, structure, audience and so on. Rather, these terms need to be taught and understood as dynamic systems in and of themselves. Invoking these dynamic systems creates a type of writing instruction that analyzes and produces written communication as multidimensional entities in all media, both print and electronic-based. Our challenge is to ensure that we define effective writing in ways that are comprehensible to our students but that do not compromise the complexity inherent in each writing situation.

Special thanks are due to Dr. Sam Dragga, who supplied the original letter for this assignment.

Rite Properties
7001 S. Loop 289 A 107
LUBBOCK, TEXAS 79425
Office (805) 555-1329

September 5, 2000

TO: ALL PLAZA RESIDENTS

FROM: The Management

SUBJECT: towing

Effective today, September 5, 2000, FURRS CAFETERIA will tow any Plaza residents vehicles or Plaza visitor vehicles that park on the south end of their parking lot on the west side of their building. One visitor vehicle from Plaza was parked directly in front of the cafeteria's back door, blocking the way for a big delivery truck coming in this morning, consequently, no on e may park over there any more. Residents, we have been over the parking situation over and over, if you or your guests get towed, don't call me. I've put out several newsletters or spoke with individuals about the parking. It is your responsibility to tell your guests where to park. We have had a good relationship with Furrs for along time, but when we get in the way, everyone must pay the price. Stop and think where you park, is it going to be in someones way in the morning? The next time I am called to clear out the cars to avoid being towed because it is blocking a door or a driveway at Furrs, I promise, I will call the tow truck myself.

We have also been changing the filters and checking the smoke alarm batteries this week and lo' and behold, there are those of you that are removing or tampering with your smoke alarms!

Repeatedly we have told you not to take the battery out of your smoke alarm. IT IS AGAINST THE LAW. Do you have enough insurance to cover all your home's contents in addition to all the contents of several other homes if a fire breaks out in your apartment and because you have no battery in your smoke alarm, no one was warned before it was too late. When your alarm beeps, it means you need a new battery, we have as I have repeatedly told you have batteries in the office. Come and get the new battery or call and place a work order. There is absolutely no excuse that can be justified for removing or tampering with any part of the smoke alarm that I will accept. If we didn't have an alarm in your apartment and you had a fire, you would immediately blame us, do we get to blame you when you have removed the battery or tampered with the alarm? Each of you that had removed your alarm will be fine $25.00 which is clearly stated and had been explained in several newsletters.

In addition, do not bring rent payments to my home, I do not have a receipt book at my home and I will not return to the office to make on after the office has closed.

This month, several residents put cash in the drop slot of the office, do not do this, for your protection and ours. Get a money order, they can be purchased at any convenience store for .19¢. When you pay by case, bring the exact amount of your rent to the office, we do not keep change at the office, if you do not have the correct amount, any amount that is over, will be credited to next month's rent, we will not make change.

Please do not hand me your rent in cash while I am standing outside in the courtyard, without having a receipt book, this is not a good policy.

Again, it is your responsibility for telling guests where to park. You know how it feels to come in and there are parking spaces because they are filled with guests. I constantly see the same guests parking on the the lot, the lot is posted for resident parking with all others towed, I have threatened to tow in the past, but once again, it has gotten out of hand and we are almost full and it takes every space on the lot just so our residents are allowed to park on the lot. Effective today, all non stickered vehicles will be towed with no advance warning. When this happens, perhaps you will want to pay the towing charge to your guest since you did not tell them where to park.

When your guests vehicles get towed, please do not contact me. There will be a sticker telling them exactly where to get in touch with the wrecker service to retrieve their vehicle.

Once again there is trash being left outside apartments overnight and during the day. Please, we take prospective residents thru the courtyard nearly every day and it is very embarrassing to have to pass other peoples trash. If you can't carry it out, leave it in your house until you can. It will be greatly appreciated.

Finally, please move all the mops that are hanging on balconies and on the pool fence. A good place to put a wet mop is in the water heater closet. It is warm in there and the mop will dry very quickly.

WORKS CITED

Bakhtin, Mikhail. *The Dialogic Imagination: Four Essays.* Trans. M Holquist and C. Emerson, Ed. M. Holquist. Austin: U of Texas P, 1981.

Barry, Richard E. "Making the Distinctions Between Information Management and Records Management" 5 May 2001. <http://www.rbarry.com/IMT-ARM1/IMT-ARM1.html> January 1996.

Barthes, Roland. "The Death of the Author." *Image—Music—Text.* Trans. Stephen Heath. New York: Hill and Wang, 1977. 142–148.

Culler, Jonathan. On Deconstruction." *Theory and Criticism after Structuralism.* Ithaca: Cornell UP, 1982.

Foucault, Michel. "What is an Author?" *The Foucault Reader.* Ed. Paul Rabinow. New York: Pantheon-Random, 1984. 76–100.

Iser, Wolfgang. *The Range of Interpretation.* New York: Columbia UP, 2000.

Johnson, Robert R. *User-Centered Technology: A Rhetorical Theory for Computers and Other Mundane Artifacts.* Albany: SUNY Press, 1998.

Porter, James E. *Audience and Rhetoric.* Englewood Cliffs, NJ: Prentice Hall, 1992.

21

REINVENTING COMMUNITY

Steve Parks
Lori Shorr
Temple University

Writing programs need to be linked to local community needs. Providing students with such a writing experience allows them to develop a collective sense of their identity as well as an increased ability to think through what a collective response might require. In fact, we believe that creating a context in which such critical engagement actually matters makes for students who read essays more carefully, gain a sense of purpose in their written responses, understand the reasons for certain theoretical distinctions, and believe that something is at stake in the production of knowledge.

Every time a student sits down to write for us, he has to invent the university for the occasion—invent the university, that is, or a branch of it, like history or anthropology or economics or English. The student has to learn to speak our language, to speak as we do, to try on the peculiar ways of knowing, selecting, evaluating, reporting, concluding, and arguing that define the discourse of *our community*. Or perhaps I should say the various discourses of *our community*, since it is in the nature of a liberal arts education that a student, after the first year or two, must learn to try on a variety of voices and interpretive schemes—to write, for example, as a literary critic one day and as an experimental psychologist the next; to work within fields where the rules governing the presentation of examples or the development of an argument are both distinct and, even to a professional mysterious.

David Bartholomae, "Inventing the University"
(emphasis ours)

Often, when discussing teaching, community is narrowly defined as those students in our classroom, perhaps in our program, and less often, within our particular college. In the following chapter, we would like to consider how our community might be better defined as a dialogue between our students, our writing program, and our neighboring citizens and organizations. Part of our work as writing teachers, then, should be to ask students to explore how the university interacts with their home community and how university-based intellectuals should act as responsible members of the neighborhood communities in which they exist. It is this dialogue between the academic and the community, we believe, that helps students position themselves as writer of valuable texts and helps them to see writing

For that reason, we believe pedagogical practices and writing programs should be developed in concert not only with the different partners across the curriculum, but also with the surrounding community as well.[1] In fact, where and when certain issues come to dominate the political, cultural, and social workings of a community (such as abandoned properties or welfare reform), the writing program should serve as a conduit for building alliances among different literacy/policy organizations involved in seeking solutions. Such alliances can provide students not only with an institutional bridge between university and community, but can also provide a vision of what writing connected to collective action, to collection agency, means.

As a way to demonstrate the importance of such connections in creating student writing we would like to discuss a student paper produced through our community writing program, "Rigorous English Language Arts for All." At the end of the paper, we offer some general

---

[1]The development of this program took place within the larger context of work being done by Eli Goldblatt and Steve Parks in the development of our Writing Beyond the Curriculum program at Temple. For an accounting of this work, see Parks/Goldblatt, "Writing Beyond the Curriculum."

thoughts about the institutional work of creating community-based writing opportunities for our students.

In Philadelphia, the condition of the public schools is the dominant public policy issue. The creation of strong neighborhoods, job growth, and class mobility are all seen as connected to the possibility of effective public education. As with most urban centers, the public school system is in a state of crisis. For instance, the Philadelphia Public Schools are responsible for educating approximately 215,000 children a year. On the opening day of school this year, over 200 classrooms did not have teachers; 1,800 of the teachers were uncertified. Consequently, there were English teachers assigned to science classrooms. There were daily substitutes in core areas, such as mathematics, who could provide no continuity in instruction. This situation is further complicated by the diversity of the student population. In some clusters of schools around Temple, over 100 languages are represented. (In fact, in the schools surrounding Temple, the "minority" population is often well over 90%.) Many families are transient, living in Philadelphia only seasonally. As a consequence, the school population, teachers, and resources are under constant strain.

The results of this situation are dramatic. Focusing on the schools surrounding Temple University, a typical middle school might have 90 percent of the student population scoring below basic levels on district achievement tests. A typical comprehensive high school in Northern Philadelphia might begin with a first year class of 1,000 students. Six hundred might fail to pass ninth grade. Approximately 200 might graduate. Of those 200, a majority will continue onto college, often enrolled in transitional support programs or basic writing programs. Of those who go directly on to a four-year degree granting institution, the majority will choose to come to Temple.

We have learned that these students do not enroll at Temple to simply learn our language. They come with a strong sense of family and community obligation. The expectation is that they will bring the benefits of their education back to the community and to their schools. One indicator of this is the number of students involved in working with the community. For example, over 500 students per semester work as tutors in schools and community-based organizations. Through volunteer and work-study efforts, Temple students provide thousands of hours of service in community engagement.[2] Most of these students pass through

---

[2] For a listing of the community/school-based programs occurring at Temple, visit www.community.temple.edu. It should be noted that a cross-university inventory demonstrated 20,000 hours of community service was being generated every year by Temple students.

our entry-level writing courses. Yet our program, modeled on David Bartholomae's vision of academic discourse, was not providing opportunities for them to use that organic sense of the educational landscape to engage intellectually with the issues this work was surfacing or to enable them to intervene collectively for the benefit of others.

In the Temple University classroom, however, these structural and cultural narratives of community obligation became pedagogical issues. For although our students recognize the limitations of the public school system and wish to intervene, they do not always bring a systemic analysis to how they construct sentences or frame arguments. Reflecting on her Philadelphia high school experience, one first-year writing student, Anita, wrote:

> There was not much writing assigned to class, there was only allot of sentences to write and defining of words. If the writing assignments were assigned it was a one-page assignment. I wrote papers two and three pages long and got "A's" on them. My peers wrote one-page papers and got the same grades I did. So I thought that if they could write one page papers and get A's then I could do it to. From that point on, I put no time into my papers and I still passed. . . . Senior year was suppose to be a time of preparation for a post secondary education, I feel, as though Thomas Jefferson did not prepare me to take on a post secondary education. In my opinion I don't think its fair to us students that some teacher give out easy work to have a fast and easy year.[3]

To work with a student such as Anita in a writing class might require more than overcoming a resistance to academic discourse. The difficulty this writer faces concerns how her sentences cast the debate about education: her current analytical model places blame on individuals only (typically the teacher or the parents) or on low expectations (the easy "A"). A systemic analysis is not considered. Further, although she writes in the collective (us students), this collective does not seem empowered to change the situation. There is also no sense of how one might step in partnership with others and become an advocate for her education or the education of others. Being a student at Temple, she might ultimately see herself as a tutor in the schools, but this model might only reinforce her vision of the "benevolent individual."

To help this student to grow intellectually and as a writer would require something in addition to introducing her into the academy's

---

[3]All student and institutional names have been changes to protect privacy.

ways of speaking. Simply allowing the student to remain within a personalized view of her experience will not build a sense of collective agency from which she can become part of of a broader solution. Instead, the writing program should be providing her with not only a model that allows her to apply the rigors of academic study to the problem, but also connects her to the community from which the problem arose. Yet, for a writing program or a set of writing assignments to provide both moves, an introduction to academic discourse and a connection to the nonuniversity community, there has to be a programmatic reinvention of the student and the student paper. Such a program would attempt to see how the writing could be produced in concert and collaboration with the world from which the "student" came—the world before she was a university student, but a member of a network of community, cultural, and educational institutions that define a neighborhood and its aspirations.

In response to the situation, during the Fall of 2000, a team consisting of university administrators, college faculty, public school teachers, community activists, and educational consultants from Washington, D.C.,[4] met to create a program that would bring together writers from across the community around the aims of literacy instruction. Our particular focus at the outset was the writing instruction provided to middle school students in Philadelphia public schools. This emphasis was chosen in part because it was felt that grades 6 through 10 were where the seeds of Philadelphia's high drop out rate were sown. The tentative name of this program was "Rigorous English Language Arts for All." Here the "All" meant not just the students in public schools or in the university, but also the teachers, parents, and community members.

The actual plan was simple. Temple University would establish a service-learning component in their entry-level writing classes beginning with the 100 level courses and working back to basic writing

---

[4]This team consisted of Amy McNally, Stacy Johnson, Carlton Jordan, Rochelle Nicols Solomon, Bruce Campbell, and Bernie McGee. The fact that it was able to undertake such work was a result of a reform in our English Department that created "tracks" in the major. These reforms allowed our composition/rhetoric faculty to imagine an undergraduate curriculum stream that went beyond the first year. The Literacy, Language, and Rhetoric track committee consisted of many of the original figures in the first reform movement, Susan Wells, Eli Goldblatt, Dennis Lebofsky, as well as Muffy Siegal. Their support was instrumental in the narrative that follows.

courses.⁵ Students would be asked to study the debates around public education, the nature of literacy, and the history of their own education. In addition, they would provide literacy tutoring to middle school students through weekly visits to a public school. Teachers in the schools would receive professional development in integrating writing into their classrooms. Community and university tutors, acting as writing coaches, supplemented literacy instruction.

In creating a pedagogy for the university class, we intermixed a set of seemingly contradictory theories. We began with personal writing. Recent curricular alignment work with the Philadelphia public schools had shown that personal writing was the dominant writing genre assigned by teachers in schools, thus producing graduates who were unfamiliar with critical essay writing. Because we had many students from the public schools, this project, and its writing assignments, were produced to intervene in that cycle. This project and its writing assignments were produced to intervene in that cycle. Our goal was to demonstrate how the personal was part of a larger social/cultural process. So, the beginning of the course was modeled after the work of Paulo Freire and Ira Shor, where students used personal experience as a means to connect to larger systemic issues.

In line with strategies that Bartholomae and Petrosky present in *Facts, Artifacts, and Counterfacts*, students then engaged in a series of writing exercises in response to academic essays. In fact, the class began with Bartholomae's "Inventing the University" and moved on to academic writings by figures such as Keith Gilyard, Gloria Anzaldua, Lisa Delpit, and Glynda Hull, which further explored the social, economic, and political aspects of education. Through these essays, students were asked to think about how academic models reframed their personal experiences as the result of structural elements in public education— poor resources, for instance. Taking in the lessons of Linda Flower, we then used rhetorical models in the final section of the course and asked students to take this systemic analysis and use it to analyze their tutoring work at the school.

In addition to academic writing, students were asked to keep a double-entry journal (as framed by Ann Berthoff) of their responses to the writing of their middle school counterparts, to maintain a personal journal concerning their responses to working with the students. Out of this matrix of composition theories, literacy tutoring, and personal

---

⁵This year, we integrated this project into two sections of English 40: Introduction to Academic Discourse and two sections of English 50: College Composition. We expect to complete a full assessment of this project by 2002.

reflection, students gained a deeper understanding of academic writing—its context, goals, and limitations. The pedagogical move, then, was to shift the student from the personal to the collective and then to analyze his or her most recent personal experience in structural or collective terms.

In developing this course, we were also mindful of the need to make a service-learning course academically rigorous. Edward Zlotkowski has argued that the failure of such courses to be rigorously connected to traditional learning has hurt the credibility of service-learning. In part, the very nature of the middle school tutoring sessions, which required the middle school students to produce rigorous text-based writing, was an immediate connection to the class.[6] Students also gained a sense of rigorous writing by evaluating middle school writing and having to address public school assessment standards when working with the public school students.[7]

One insight of this project is the understanding that many of the distinctions made within composition studies about particular "schools" of thought get questioned when put in contact with a moment of community alliance and practice. Can this theory address this set of students? this community? this set of needs? Although there are important academic debates about the distinctions between the methods of Linda Flower and David Bartholomae, in the pedagogical moment, in this class, students learned to honor these theoretical distinctions within the pragmatic concerns of the context at hand. In fact, we believe creating a context in which such critical engagement actually matters makes for students who read the essays more carefully, gain a sense of purpose in their written responses, understand the reasons for certain theoretical distinctions, and believe that something is at stake in the production of knowledge.

As a way to demonstrate the results of this effort, we reproduce the following collaborative writing piece by two students in the class, both graduates of the Philadelphia public schools, Eliza and Shanea. As the final assignment for the term, we watched "Stand and Deliver," a 1980s film about Jaime Escalante, who successfully taught urban Hispanic working class students calculus. Working collaboratively with Eliza, Shanea drafted a paper that attempted to think through how these

---

[6]For an overview of service-learning work being done in composition, see Adler-Kassner.

[7]It should be noted that the Writing Program Administrators have developed a set of standards for what every first-year student should know about writing. The effect of these standards or the extent of their implementation is not yet clear.

issues are represented in popular culture. It is this paper that we would hold out as indicative of the aims of a reinvented writing program.

Films today about schools are taken to the extreme. I know one could say "well, that's just Hollywood" glitz, glamour, and simple solutions, and their right, but that damn sure does not mean that I half to buy into it. What I mean by films taking it to the extreme is that everything is over the top, the violence is magnified to quadruple what it really is. The problem seems to glide away smoothly and fairy tale endings are inevitable. The concept of one lone person coming in and turning everything around for the better is not realistic. People need support when they are trying to take huge strides in changing something that is messed up. I just wish "Hollywood" would realize that the days of one person coming in and carrying the load on his shoulders is just plain unrealistic.

In the film Stand and Deliver, the situation is deplorable, most of the teachers did not care about the students, teachers were teaching subjects they were not qualified to teach. The school was in disarray, and in need of paint, windows and a good cleaning. The students' appearances were sloppy or slutty. These attitudes were negative; they tended to be disrespectful, and full of themselves. . . .

In Stand and Deliver, the viewers noticed a lack of family support for the students. One students' mother told her daughter "boys don't like you if you are smart." How must that daughter of felt, and she still went on to pass the AP Calculus test. One student was a gangbanger who could not be seen with books by his homies. He was living with his sick grandmother and helping her get around to and from her doctor's visits. He still managed to come to class and ended up getting one of the highest marks on his AP exam. Another student was taking care of about four younger siblings, cooking dinner, playing the mother role and still found time to study in the dark. She was starting a new relationship, which was rocky and emotional but she kept up with her schoolwork. The movie showed the viewers what the students went through when they were accused of cheating.

Once the viewer is drawn in through the emotion into the drama, they hit them with a savor that rescues and saves the day. Wow? Is this really what American's want to see? (Yes.)

In most films there is one tough guy or gal who doesn't take any shit and gets the students in line. They get the masses to believe in them and gaining their confidence through their forceful actions. In most cases they half to crack a few skulls and then they are looked up to. Sometimes, they can gain the confidence of the students by being an expert in their fields and being able to demonstrate their knowledge. In almost every movie the teacher has a strong, vibrant personality and they have leadership qualities.

I think that Anzaldua would like what is going on.in "Stand and Deliver." This teacher was bilingual and so were all of his students. In his class both languages were spoken and nothing was wrong with that. The teacher was Hispanic and so it was like second nature to him to speak Spanish in his classroom. This is Anzaldua's ideal class structure. I think she would agree that that is the best way to teach. The only problem would be that it is not done on purpose, this type of learning situation was not going on in every class. Anzaldua may think, well it's a start and you half to start somewhere. If people see this bilingual teacher is doing well then maybe it could be a mandatory requirement in other subject areas and other schools.

A film on the [middle school we visited this term] could actually make a good documentary, but not a Hollywood blockbuster. The documentary could start out with our first visit when we came to meet the facility and students. That first day I think even the tutors were a bit nervous. As time went on the tutors and the students formed relationships with one another and the students were actually excited to show their work to the tutors. This boosted the confidence levels of the tutors and the students. I think showing the work the students did the first day and then what they did close to the last day would be a huge improvement. This type of documentary would generate more people wanting to come and tutor at the school, and possibly donate money.

In a way, it would follow "Hollywood" success model. The students were saved by a group of college students who came in to help them and they did make a difference. The only difference would be that it would half to show a group effort not a lone beer-drinking cowboy [figure like Jaime Escalante]. There was not one person who came in and taught all the students to write better alone. It would half to be a shown through the eyes of every tutor, on the days that were hard for them to make it and the days were they did exceptional with one or two students.

The sad part of the film would half to be all the countless other students who do not receive any extra help at all. The other students who do not even learn how to write papers at all. The lack of teacher's assistants on a daily basis is something that the public schools seriously need. The overall lack of funding which is depriving these students of the basic utensils to have a good education. The fact is that, yes we made a difference, but what about the rest of them?

As with all beginning writers, it is possible to examine the paper for error. Eliza and Shanea consistently write "half to" instead of "have to." Certainly, there are areas where the rhetoric of "transitions," "topic sentence," or "controlling idea" would be useful. Yet, they also bring the reading to bear on the argument, successfully summarize the film, and bring both texts to bear on the social text they have been asked to critique. Finally, it is important to notice the sense of agency in this paper and how it bespeaks a collective consciousness about the ability to confront social injustice. In contrast to service-learning projects studied by Bruce Herzberg, where students remained locked in personal salvation narratives, these students write, "The concept of one lone person coming in and turning everything around for the better is not realistic. People need support when they are trying to take huge strides in changing something that is messed up."

Earlier when examining the work of Anita, who reflected on her educational experience, we commented upon the fact that it was the sentence-level work of her writing that was determining her sense of political action. In the work of Shanea and Eliza, what emerges through the sentences is a sense of being part of the collective, which brings together the many voices of a community—academic, personal, political, positioned against the mainstream narratives of heroic reform. Through dialoguing with both academic and nonacademic texts, university and nonuniversity sites, a systemic vision of writing and its role in social change has been created. Neither the academy nor the community has been left behind; they have been conjoined.

Here, then, we return to our argument about seeing student writing and pedagogy within an institutional/community context. For what is equally important about the work of Shanea and Eliza, is the fact it occurred within a larger program modeling how such collective work can exist. The students were aware of the work being done by teachers to overcome structural/educational difficulties. They could use public school standards to understand how the writing of middle school students was improving. And, as importantly, they were able to use academic theorists to judge the political and ethical goals of those standards. It is the combination of these forces that enabled the insight of the above paper to occur.

From this position, students can learn that political change can be achieved through the hard work of coalition building and always reminding ourselves of those excluded. If a writing program can wed the study of academic discourse to community concerns and the possibility of structural understandings and collective action, we believe it will not only reinvent the potential work of students, but will also ultimately reinvent the goals of the university.

Notably, at the end of the term, both Shanea and Eliza continued to tutor and work at the middle school.[8]

*   *   *

At the outset of this chapter, we invoked Bartholomae's "Inventing the University" and his concern with bringing students into "our community." We are not dismissing its call for students to learn academic discourse. Instead, we have tried to show that any definition of the academy must necessarily involve integrating its mission with the streets that produce our students and the citizens that surround the campus. We have been arguing for an interpretation of "our community" that actually implies families, neighborhoods, local organizations. To that extent, we are merely carrying out an implicit desire of academic discourse—to join with other local discourses in the examination of important community issues.

We hope to continue to imagine our writing program as a response to the insights and needs of our students and neighbors. By imagining our role as a conduit between the academy and the community, we can continually recognize the need to be vigilant not only in the work we ask students to perform but also about the context of that work as well. We can continue to recognize the need to build true partnerships that will allow the development of a common agenda. Only within that framework will our students continue to produce the best work not only for themselves, but for others as well.[9]

---

[8]It is also important to note that when this college course was first offered, seven students enrolled. By its third offering, over 25 students enrolled. The combined drop-out rate in all of the classes is only about four students. Each class has also voted to expand the number of tutoring sessions in the middle schools, often at the cost of increased writing assignments to insure required reading assignments are covered.

[9]Since the writing of this article two important developments are worth noting. First, all of the Philadelphia public schools have been taken over by the state and our particular school was "given" to Edision Schools, Inc. to be privately managed. These changes added much to classroom discussion and student participation. Also Temple's writing program, in conjunction with the school district, will be making this writing partnership model permanent through the opening of a new writing center in the school. Three other universities and seven public schools will be following this model starting in the Fall of 2002. This effort will be funded by GEAR-UP.

WORKS CITED

Bartholomae, David. "Inventing the University." *Literacy: A Critical Sourcebook.* Eds. Ellen Cushman, Eugene R. Kingten, Barry Knoll, and Mike Rose. New York: Bedford/St. Martin's Press, 2001. 511-524.

Bartholomae, David and Tony Petrosky. *Facts, Artifacts, and Counterfacts: Theory and Method for a Reading and Writing Course.* Portsmouth, NH: Heinemann, 1986.

Delpit, Lisa. *Other People's Children: Cultural Conflict in the Classroom.* New York: New Press, 1995.

Freire, Paulo. *Pedagogy of the Oppressed.* New York: Seabury, 1970.

Freire, Paulo. *Education for Critical Consciousness.* New York: Seabury, 1973.

Peck, Wayne Campbell, Linda Flower, and Lorraine Higgins. "Community Literacy." *College Composition and Communication* (1995): 199-222.

Hertzberg, Bruce. "Community Service and Critical Teaching." *College Composition and Communication* (1994): 307-319

Parks, Stephen and Eli Goldblatt. "Writing Beyond the Curriculum: Fostering New Collaborations in Literacy." *College Composition and Communication* (2000): 584-604.

Shor, Ira. *Empowering Education: Critical Teaching for Social Change.* Chicago: University of Chicago P, 1992.

Sullivan, Frank, Arabella Lyon, Dennis Lebofksy, Susan Wells, and Eli Goldblatt. "Strong Composition, Strong Student Needs: Dialectics of Writing Program Reform." *College Composition and Communication* (1997): 372-391.

Zlotkowski, Edward, "A New Voice at the Table?: Linking Service Learning and the Academy." *Change* (1996) 21-27.

IV

TEACHING/WRITING. . .

. . . as RHETORIC,
READING,
and REVISION

22

FROM OPRAH TO ANDREA

The Ethos and Logos of Pathos

Rebecca Moore Howard
Syracuse University

Since the time of the Sophists, Western rhetoricians have debated the usefulness and legitimacy of pathos as a tool of argument. Teachers of composition and rhetoric need to adjust their instruction in argument to reflect the realities of what counts as effective argumentation online. There argument hybridizes popular rhetoric and academic rhetoric, creating new relationships between logos, ethos, and pathos. For example, Andrea Brooks, a student at Colgate University, an exclusive private liberal arts college, engaged in discussion with listserv participants at the other schools who may have assumed her to be a person of cloistered privilege. Andrea's posts advanced an argument in which both logos and ethos were part of, but subordinate to, pathos-evidenced claims. We may learn new principles of argumentation from our students' online arguments, where logos provides a superstructure for pathos, and ethos is derived from pathos. This configuration radically revises the received academic privileging of logos, with ethos an accepted means of argument and pathos a suspect one.

A college student goes online as part of her assigned coursework for an intermediate class in argument. With students from eleven other colleges, she debates the unfolding presidential campaign. She chooses to focus her attention on the campaign issue of welfare. In the listserv created for debate of the welfare issue, she makes contributions from time to time but gains little attention for her statements. When the talk turns to welfare fraud, she falls silent and angry. Finally she speaks, telling her own story of life as the daughter of a welfare recipient. The way she tells that story not only gains the immediate acclaim of the other listserv participants but also suggests how readily academic and popular rhetorics hybridize online. And it challenges 21st-century teachers of writing to recognize that technology is more than a new tool for writing; it is part of a literacy revolution that is changing the terms of rhetoric, changing the norms for what does and does not constitute effective argument. Specifically, Andrea Brooks' work in the Intercollegiate E-Democracy Project demonstrates the power of pathos in online arguments and the ways that logos and ethos online derive from rather than supersede pathos as a method of argument.

This reliance on pathos represents a significant divergence from academic taste in print arguments, where logos and ethos are required to validate an argument, whereas pathos can actually weaken it. Since the time of the Sophists, Western rhetoricians have debated the usefulness and legitimacy of pathos as a tool of argument. Associated with the body and thus with the excoriated feminine, pathos has been met with suspicion or even outright rejection among the intelligentsia,[1] who have instead preferred to ground their arguments in the logical and rational appeals associated with logos. In nineteenth-century literary culture, pathos was regarded as a tool not of argument but of solipsism: person-

---

[1]The connection between the body and the feminine is attested as early as Aristotle's *Politics,* which associated men with the mind (reason) and women with the body (emotion), and as recently as Emily Martin's finding that contemporary American health care systems represent women's bodies, in their cycles of menstruation, pregnancy, and menopause, as machines that fail, succeed, and break down (17-18). Nancy Duncan explains, "The materiality of our (women's) bodies is seen to exclude us from participating in an ideal of reason which 'knows no sex,' no embodied differences" (2). Pathos, because of its emotional bases, easily becomes associated with women's reasoning—or lack thereof. The consequences for rhetoric are significant, as Suzanne Clark explains: "In our culture, if you are emotional, you are irrational. Reason is associated with mind, and connotes a calm, studied, masculine approach to issues. Emotions are associated with the body and are thought to be superficial, dangerous, and feminine" (118).

al experience could not be shared with others but was useful only in forming one's own beliefs (see Winterowd).

Despite the continuation of this attitude in 20th-century academic culture, pathos has endured in popular culture as a powerful tool of persuasion, reaching its apogee in the vivid personal stories that form the sole basis of evidence for arguments on television talk shows such as Oprah Winfrey's *Got a story?* It can win an argument—but not the respect of academics.

Pathos matters, too, in online discourse. There the logos-dominated, print-based academic standards for argumentation have not prevailed; instead, online discourse tends to rely on the rhetorical conventions of popular culture. In cyberspace, pathos rules. Online newspapers have introduced chat sequences in which readers may comment on current events, and now even online academic publications such as the *Chronicle of Higher Education* offer opportunities for real-time, informal conversations among readers. With its fast pace of change,[2] its permeable forms and genres, and its independence from the regulations inscribed in writer's handbooks, the new medium causes the privileged forms of writing to shift, and those shifts, in turn, give rise to new models for writing.[3]

One such model is demonstrated by Andrea Brooks, a first-year college student who, in an email polylogue about the 1996 Presidential election, advanced an argument in which both logos and ethos (ethical appeals) were part of but subordinate to pathos-evidenced claims.

By the standards of the argument textbooks used in college writing classes, it would seem that when Brooks draws on personal experience for her argument about the issue of welfare in the 1996 presidential campaign, her argument is doomed to failure. Yet her audience—including the professors who taught the courses linked to the project—greeted her argument with acclaim. It is my belief that her pathos-based argument succeeded because it draws on a popular rhetoric in which pathos is privileged, not excoriated—a rhetoric that presently dominates electronic discourse, even the electronic discourse of academics.

Brooks defined her task in consultation with me. She was enrolled in my intermediate composition class in argument, and that class

---

[2]Even online language is changing quickly. When I first drafted this essay in 1997, I used the terms *on-line, postings,* and *listserve.* In my 2001 revision, these became *online, posts,* and *listserv.* These usages have become standard in an astonishingly brief time.

[3]See Killoran for an instructive exploration of the ways in which parody undermines logos online.

was electronically linked with composition, journalism, and ESL classes at twelve other institutions.[4] Students in all the classes were required to participate in at least one of eight topically organized listservs.

Brooks selected a listserv on welfare reform, where for several weeks she lurked—while complaining to me about what she character-ized as the uninformed, stupid posts she was reading on the list. I urged her to respond to those who were calling for the end of public welfare. One reason for her silence, she said, was that she didn't want to be "yelled at" by the others on the list. I countered that they needed to hear her point of view, even if they didn't like it.

During those weeks of lurking, Andrea Brooks was studying the assigned texts of my argument class: Lawler and Schaefer's collection of canonized American political rhetoric; Anthony Weston's compact overview of argument; and Rodrigues and Tuman's writer's handbook. In class we were talking about the relative values of logos, ethos, and pathos in academic discourse. Meanwhile, the participants on the wel-fare listserv recounted generic horror stories of welfare cheats.

On September 26, Brooks finally posted to the welfare listserv, urging that welfare reform efforts should consider multiple points of view. Her argument contains very little evidence of the sort that her textbooks had been privileging:

> I would like to address all of those out there who are saying that there are many people out there who are using and abusing the government. I agree with this, but I must play the devil's advocate and ask what about those who are not. Have any of you ever been on welfare? Do you have any idea of the added stress that comes along with it? You assume that everyone on welfare is just having a grand old time, depending on the dollars of taxpayers. Many people on welfare turned to this system as a transition ground. Welfare was talked of as a system aimed to help those in need. Has it done this, I say no. These people who turned to welfare thinking they would find help with paying for some of their bare necessities were sadly mistaken. If you think an $81 check, twice a month for a family of five is sufficient for survival in todays econ-omy, an economy in which the standard of living has increased drastically over the last ten years but whose minimum wage has just been slighty increased, you are sadly mistaken. Ok, this does not include food stamps but food alone can not possibly help

---

[4] A comprehensive description of the ongoing, electronically linked Intercollegiate E-Democracy Project is available at <http://caribou.cc. trin-coll.edu/prog_iedp/>. A detailed description of another course linked to the project is in Wall's essay.

someone become a fruitful and productive part of this society. We, as American college students seem to be looking at this whole issue from one point of view. In order to solve this problem, like any other problem, we must take into consideration the various points of view. I say this because, welfare recipients aren't of one type, they aren't derived from some select few. This wasn't a controlled experiment in which this group should be on welfare and that group shouldn't. I'm not sure if this nation will ever take the time to look at the positive side of any view. I say this after writing a paper on language in the presidential campaigns. I must end this by saying we must learn to be open minded if we plan to solve any of the many problems facing our "United States of America"!!!!!!!!!!

        -Andrea

        -Colgate

Brooks' first response was from a listserv participant at another school who agreed with the argument but who asked if Brooks had herself ever known a welfare recipient. (Because Brooks was enrolled at Colgate University, an exclusive private liberal arts college, listserv participants at the other schools might understandably have assumed her to be a person of cloistered privilege.) On October 2 Brooks responded to that question, providing the evidence that had been missing from her earlier post. This second post demonstrates an interesting mix of rhetorical techniques that hybridize conventions of academic and popular argument:

[T]o answer your question, yes I have been on welfare, actually my mom has and she still is. Not because she wants to be, but because when she goes out to look for jobs and they ask her about her past experience, she can only tell them about the work she did before getting on welfare. Then they ask her why she hasn't had a job and she says because she hasn't been able to get one since she's been on welfare. It's like they won't give her the job because she doesn't have experience but she can't get the experience because she can't get a job. And no, she doesn't drive a nice car. Actually, she has never had a car in her entire life. That's because she uses her AFDC checks to put food on our table and a few decent clothes on our back (and I don't mean name brand, I've never had the luxury of wearing anything except Caldor, Kmart, and Salvation Army Thriftshop clothing until I decided to get a job at Burger King). Some of you may say, "Well why doesn't your mom get a job at BK?" Well she tried that but working ten to fifteen hours a week (that's the most hours they ever gave her in a given week) isn't enough to support her and her children, get all of the bills paid and put oik in the tank for heat during the winter. As a student, my job at BK was hardly enough to pay all of my senior dues, buy my cap and gown, go to the senior awards dinner at which I was getting an award but stil had to pay, let alone pay dues for all of the activities (in which I got involved so that colleges would be more likely to accept me and offer me some financial aid so I could go to college), and get a somewhat decent dress for my senior prom.

I am happy to say that in Schenectady, where my family currently resides, they have recently established a program called America Works. this program is specifically for people on welfare. it is a job training program that runs for I believe 8 weeks and trains you in interviewing skills and all of that type of stuff. My mother has recently enrolled in this program and is trying her best to get off of welfare. I must let you all know that I do believe that we need to change the welfare program, but until programs like America Works are established all over, it would be detremental to our economy just to take people off of welfare with no type of preparation for the real world.

We must also think about why people turned to wlefare in the first place. If we deal with those problems first, then we can go back and try to figure out a way to reform the welfare system. The problem with welfare is not just one big old problem. It is a series of problems that have fed off of one another and gotten to a point of no return.

I hope I answered some of your questions about my personal connection to welfare.
　　　　 –Andrea
　　　　 –Colgate

This post single-handedly stopped the listserv discussion of welfare cheating; instead, talk on the list briefly turned to the eloquence and persuasiveness of Brooks' argument. Andrea Brooks actually received several pieces of online fan mail from listserv participants. Eventually the listserv returned to its opposition to welfare, but this time without the red herring of welfare fraud. One person in one post had succeeded in redefining the terms of the listserv debate.

How she did it is a fascinating question. Clearly in this post Brooks is not adhering to all the principles of good argument advanced in my class; she did not, for example, spell check her post. I had asserted that a spell check was needed for authorial ethos, and Andrea adhered to that principle in print but not online. Nor in this post does she adduce support from external authoritative sources, a standard tactic of academic argument, and one endorsed in her textbook (Weston 28-36) and practiced by her in the print texts she produced for my class. Instead, she bases her argument in pathos, in an emotionally charged personal experience—one that quashed her opposition. When the term was over and the teachers of the linked Intercollegiate E-Democracy classes met together, they argued that Brooks' post was based on ethos—the authority of personal experience vividly recounted—or on logos. I wondered whether I had incorrectly analyzed the argument; whether we shared common definitions of the terms; or whether the terms are actually useful for analyzing arguments. I also wondered whether my colleagues' perspectives might reflect the low esteem in which academic discourse holds pathos: they liked Brooks' post; therefore, it couldn't be based in pathos.

I remain convinced of my analysis. Brooks' is an argument based in pathos, the power of personal narrative that inevitably elicits shame in the listserv participants who had been blithely denouncing hypothetical or apocryphal welfare cheaters. She does indeed gain a powerful ethos from her argument, but the argument renders rather than draws on ethos; it is intrinsic rather than extrinsic ethos, generated by rather than marshaled for the argument. Until the October 2 post, no one on the welfare listserv had paid serious attention to Brooks' contributions, even though her September 26 post contained details of life on welfare.

And indeed, Brooks is logical in her October 2 entry: she accounts for possible opposing points of view and explains why they are inadequate. But the ethos is a product of the argument, and the logos is subordinate to the pathetic appeal. Like the candidates in that presidential election who chose talk shows as a primary campaign venue, there to tell family stories of tragedy and triumph, Brooks demonstrates pathos as an effective means of persuasion. Unlike those presidential candidates, Brooks welds the pathetic appeal to a logical superstructure. Brooks' argument, though brief, is not a sound bite. It does not universalize her personal experience, and it provides a logos-based superstructure. In sum, Andrea Brooks' October 2 post offers a model for argument in the late age of print.

It should reassure those of us who worry that electronic media will destroy print culture values. Writing in 1988, Kathleen Hall Jamieson announces, "What we traditionally knew as eloquence cannot survive this new environment intact" (ix). As evidence for that assertion, she traces the demise of the political campaign speech, from one to two hours in the nineteenth century to four minutes in 1984 (10-13). Since 1988, Americans have become accustomed to the sound bite, and candidates' appearances on talk shows have replaced the sustained argument of a campaign speech. The online discourse of e-mail and chat rooms is similarly attenuated. In this environment, the extended logos-based argument disappears, replaced by pathos-based discourse that too often recalls the solipsism that W. Ross Winterowd attributes to Emerson: it is personal narrative that is of lasting value only to the narrator.

The demise of elaborated, considered argument should fill us with alarm. As Sharon Crowley points out, argument is an essential tool of a democratic society (1-18); it is the means whereby agreement can be reached. And as Jamieson points out, logos-based argument is on the wane, replaced by binary oppositions that do not move audiences toward consensus (11). Argument—indeed, rhetoric itself—arose as a means of establishing and maintaining democratic government. Rhetoric's possibilities for persuasion were quickly apparent to the emerging democracies in Gorgias' Mediterranean (Enos 49). The democratic rhetoric of Gorgias, Lincoln, and Roosevelt is one of extended argument, not sound bites. In lamentable contrast, community members today, impelled by passing emotions untested by argument, reach decisions to which they feel no commitment. Such ephemeral decisions lack the conviction essential for implementing enduring public policy.

What makes teaching good in the late age of print is the courage to face these facts and to adjust democratic rhetoric so that, even in the new media, it can contribute to shared understandings and common purpose. Andrea Brooks' post to a listserv conversation on October 2, 1996, offers one model of how this might be accomplished. Brooks' argument is brief, fueled by pathos; but unlike the personal narratives of talk shows and the sound bites of cyberflames, it is a considered argument that logically accounts for audience and for opposition, intrinsically building the arguer's ethos as itself an authoritative and ethical source. I cannot take credit for Brooks' tactics; they are her own blend of the rhetorics of popular culture and print culture. But from them I can learn something about how to teach digitized rhetoric in the twenty-first century. Suzanne Clark worries, "[A] strong barrier against acknowledging pathos, a barrier marked by . . . anxieties about sentimentality, works to keep academic argument from being powerful or effective in the public arena" (101). Teaching cyberrhetoric with Brooks' post as a model, rhetoricians can overcome these anxieties and teach students how to contribute to constructive public discourse online.

Writing in 1994, Stuart Moulthrop comments on Jay David Bolter's 1991 *Writing Space*. Bolter describes "our historical moment as 'the late age of print,'" believing that hypertext will undo print linearity, but Moulthrop predicts that our future is not hypertext but the relays between it and linear print (302-316). Moulthrop's focus is linearity versus hypertextuality, but in our current literacy revolution, many other aspects of rhetoric and discourse are at stake as well. Relays between the print and online environments breed hybrid discourses, of which Andrea Brooks' rhetorical strategies online are one example. The challenge now is for writing teachers to comprehend, practice, and abet these new rhetorics.

WORKS CITED

Aristotle. *The Politics of Aristotle*. Ed. and Trans. Ernest Barker. New York: Oxford UP, 1946, 1958.

Bolter, Jay David. *Writing Space: The Computer, Hypertext, and the History of Writing*. Hillsdale, NJ: Erlbaum, 1991.

Clark, Suzanne. "Rhetoric, Social Construction, and Gender: Is It Bad to Be Sentimental?" *Writing Theory and Critical Theory*. Eds. John Clifford and John Schilb. New York: Modern Language Association, 1994. 96-108.

Crowley, Sharon. *Ancient Rhetorics for Contemporary Students*. New York: MacMillan, 1994.

Duncan, Nancy. "(Re)placings." *Bodyspace: Destabilizing Geographies of Gender and Sexuality*. Ed. Nancy Duncan. New York: Routledge, 1996. 1-12.

Enos, Richard Leo. *Greek Rhetoric before Aristotle*. Prospect Heights, IL: Waveland P, 1993.

Jamieson, Kathleen Hall. *Eloquence in an Electronic Age: The Transformation of Political Speechmaking*. New York: Oxford UP, 1988.

Killoran, John B. "@ home among the .coms: Virtual Rhetoric in the Agora of the Web." *Alternative Rhetorics: Challenges to the Rhetorical Tradition*. Eds. Laura Gray-Rosendale and Sibylle Gruber. Carbondale: Southern Illinois UP, 2001. 127-144.

Lawler, Peter Augustine and Robert Martin Schaefer, eds. *American Political Rhetoric: A Reader*. 2nd ed. Savage, MD: Rowman & Littlefield, 1990.

Martin, Emily. "The New Culture of Health: Gender and the Immune System in America." *Bodily Boundaries, Sexualised Genders and Medical Discourses*. Eds. Marion de Ras and Victoria Grace. Palmerston, New Zealand: Dunmore, 1997. 17-26.

Moulthrop, Stuart. "Rhizome and Resistance: Hypertext and the Dreams of a New Culture." *Hyper/Text/Theory*. Ed. George P. Landow. Baltimore: Johns Hopkins UP, 1994. 299-319.

Rodrigues, Dawn, and Myron C. Tuman. *Writing Essentials*. New York: W.W. Norton, 1996.

Wall, Beverly. "Political Rhetoric and the Media." *Coming of Age: The Advanced Writing Curriculum*. Eds. Linda K. Shamoon, Rebecca Moore Howard, Sandra Jamieson, and Robert A. Schwegler. Portsmouth, NH: Heinemann Boynton/Cook, 2000. 124, <file:///shamoon/wall.html>.

Weston, Anthony. *A Rulebook for Arguments*. 2nd ed. Indianapolis: Hackett, 1992.

Winterowd, W. Ross. "Emerson and the Death of Pathos." *JAC* 16.1 (1996): 27-40.

23

TECHNOLOGY IN THE HIGH SCHOOLS

Aunt Polly's Answer to High-Tech Tom Sawyers

Betty Eidenier
Orange High School, Hillsborough, North Carolina

To address a high school technology plan that requires both teachers and students to be computer literate, our English Department created a technology research pacing guide. In tenth grade, a complex interdisciplinary English-world history writing project, one that uses internet research to answer essential questions by means of narrative, assures that students gain competency in using technology, reduces problems with plagiarism, and enhances creativity in response. One student composed a short narrative about Mansa Musa, trade, and cultural artifacts; she relied upon sources including art museums, historical web pages, and African cultural pages. This involved assignment is perfect for today's technology: the students really enjoy using their imagination to create a world of historical fiction, and, for the class as a whole, the project teaches teamwork, editing, writing for an audience, and quality control, all "real world" expectations at which our students become extremely capable.

Orange High School, where I am fortunate to teach writing and literature, may be the premier high school for technology in North Carolina.
We were the first school to have a technology plan that requires both
teachers and students to be computer literate in word processing and
internet research; our students regularly use probes in science classes,
create spreadsheets and Power Point presentations, and register for
courses on computer. Despite this rich environment at school, and
despite the North Carolina requirement for all eighth graders to pass
computer competency tests, there is some disparity in access to computers that creates a disadvantage for some students.

To address this disparity, our English Department created a pacing guide for research projects that assures that all students use technology for research. Ninth graders complete I-SEARCH papers that include
using internet sources for information. In tenth grade, the focus is on
creating classroom presentations of research done for interdisciplinary
studies. Primary research, interviews, and site visits are included in
eleventh grade projects that are presented to parents and friends. The
senior research projects are in-depth studies that culminate in presentations to the public, and that include a senior portfolio.

Because our rural public school of 1700 students is close to
Duke University, UNC-Chapel Hill, and the Research Triangle Park,
many of our parents are employed in technological research and development. IBM, CISCO, NORTEL, and other companies provide
resources for our students to complete coursework that leads directly to
jobs in the computer industry. Our students and teachers often win
recognition for excellence in computer technology.

With the mandate from the curriculum, the support of the
teachers, the expectations of the parents, and the wherewithal from the
community, our school places considerable emphasis on using technology in writing. But once you do that, a problem arises: how do teachers
get students to utilize the technology well?

Wily teenagers can subvert computer technology into a new
way to be Tom Sawyer. After reading too many suspicious "downloaded" reports, my colleague John Birkholz and I devised an answer
befitting Aunt Polly: a complex, dynamic, multifaceted, interdisciplinary
writing assignment using research to answer an essential question by
means of narrative—an assignment that defies prevarication, yet yields
creative invention of quite another sort.

In addition to deterring plagiarism, the assignment assures that
students use available technology to read and scan articles during
research on internet or CD-ROM resources and that students learn and
use desktop publishing. Students find resources, use e-mail to get per-

mission to quote from the resources, learn to copy and paste, scan, and download needed information, and establish links from one research paper to another within the class. As students gain competence in using technology, their writing becomes more audience-oriented and purposeful. They present research results clearly and creatively.

This particular assignment is an interdisciplinary world history-English 10 writing and research project that John and I wrote for our class study of African history and literature. From a time line of African history, students select a person or event of significance as a topic of research. In the example that follows, Katy has chosen to study Mansa Musa, ruler of the kingdom of Mali (1312-1332). Using internet resources and a variety of documents from libraries—both hard copy and electronic—the students research the topic. Katy relied on sources from AfricaNet (which, incidentally, was written by a fellow classmate working for the company); the Ackland Art Museum (http://www.unc.edu/depts/ackland); various web sites on both Africa in the Middle Ages and Mansa Musa; the UNC libraries; the school media center; and public libraries.

Student researchers like Katy face two challenges: first, winnowing down the immense amount of data available, and second, evaluating the sources their search yields. The process of selecting an essential question is, quite simply, the most important first step in the pilgrimage of research. Katy decided to focus on the essential question, "How did Mansa Musa's decision to make a pilgrimage to Mecca affect his people in Mali?" She read background world history assignments on Africa in the 1300s, she traveled to the Ackland Art Museum where she studied the *akua'ba*, and on the internet she found information about Mansa Musa and Islam. As she focused on the essential question, she gleaned information for the prewriting assignments required of the class. It's important to remember, however, how using the internet is radically different from using a traditional library: as Ellen Strenski notes, "a library sifts through and prearranges information for users through three or four means. . . . On the Internet, however, students are all on their own; all they have for help is their own perspicuity and robot software search engines to face a collection of information which differs in major ways from that in the traditional library" (225).

Although resources are rich, students need practical help navigating the internet sites. As they proceed through the potentially limitless resources of the Web, our students bear in mind that they must begin to focus on one essential question; otherwise, it would be impossible to sound the depths of what might be available yet limit the journey to the time given for the assignment. They must further develop the ability to evaluate the quality of the material their searches yield. As Strenski notes, "Students are increasingly snowed, in many senses, by the blizzard of undifferentiated data they encounter on any foray into online databases or the WWW. Without adequate guidance, they misuse inappropriate sources" (224). As writing teachers, we have to help them evaluate what they find. Although evaluating internet sources may not seem strictly analogous to the critical reading of literature, some of this work, Strenski points out, is indeed similar: in particular, helping students become "discerning readers able to exercise judgment by applying principles of inference and interpretation" (224).

During their research, the students complete four short essays— one each of persuasion, exposition, description, and personal narrative—that serve as the prewriting for the final presentation of research. The persuasive essay must address a question present during the historical period chosen for research. The expository essay concerns the culture, society, or historical episode studied in contrast to a comparative modern-day event. The description studies a work of art from the period. The personal narrative includes a decision made by a persona created by the student writer. Katy completed all aspects of the assignment, inspired by it to be creative as well as accurate in her writing. Her prewriting essays included not only a focus on Mansa Musa's decision to go to Mecca, but also a comparison of Islam to other religions practiced in Africa at the time, a description of the *akua'ba,* and an investigation of the way Mansa Musa conducted the government of his people. For each of these essays, she followed the writing process we use in all English classes (draft/peer review for content/revision/peer review for style/revision/peer review for mechanics/editing and proofreading) before having teachers evaluate her progress. She was writing to convey knowledge that she had worked hard to attain. For editors, she had available not only teachers but also peers engaged in similar studies.

These prewriting and research activities are crucial to students success. Erika Lindemann notes that "teachers often slight prewriting" (26); but the extensive internet searching and writing in multiple genres helped Katy complete what James Britton called "an essential part of the writing process": "explaining the matter to oneself" (28). Once the students have completed their research and prewriting, they present their findings in a manner that is totally original and unique: a work of historical fiction that is to be linked to other students' fiction in a giant web of discovery. Each student's story reports the research, links to another student's story and to another web site, and includes graphics that are either downloaded from the internet or scanned from originals (all with permission of site owners).

The ability to collaborate on knowledge-building projects is as important as the ability to develop an essential question. With the help of a project manager who loads all the stories onto a web site, the students publish and edit their historical research. This next phase of the project is accompanied by instruction on how to collaborate. The Research Triangle corporations that advise our school emphasize that their work is done in collaborative groups, and have clearly said that they would like for us to teach students how to work collaboratively using technology. Creating components of a larger product may be an industrial model, but one that works well for this project, as each student writes part of the whole web site of stories that is like a published book with many chapters. In this model, students must not only write for themselves, then, but for the other members of their communities. And teaching students to do so involves demonstrating to them that "they know something only when they can explain it in writing to the satisfaction of the community of their knowledgeable peers" (Bruffee 652). This kind of collaboration, even though determined by our corporate clients, offers more than workplace preparation: the social engagement of intellectual pursuits is made the center of students' educational development.

This particular class arrived at a compelling example of collaborative learning as a social construction of knowledge. They had decided to bind the stories each person was to write with a common thread. Because the topic was Africa, the students decided that a diamond should appear in each story, and that the students must collaborate to make the diamond pass from one story to another. At that point, Katy had to decide as a writer how best to include in her story the historical data, the *akua'ba*, and the diamond. She determined that the *akua'ba* was to be the focus of the story, created a situation in which Mansa Musa would become involved with the *akua'ba* just as he was preparing for his journey, and placed the diamond on the *akua'ba* as decoration. Her transition to another story in the web site was simple: as project manager, Katy also included graphics of an *akua'ba* as well as a link to a site for more information.

Although the Africa Story project is, unfortunately, no longer available online, the richness of the assignment is apparent in the story of "The Akua'ba's Diamond" by Katy Dunne:

> *"This is for you. It's a present. We have been married for one year."*
> *"It's beautiful, but what could I do with it? I can't possibly wear it."*
> *"It is yours. Do with it what you wish."*

Kala admired the diamond given to her by her husband. Only her husband could afford to give his wife such an extravagant gift, for he was Mansa Musa, ruler of the kingdom of Mali. For the time being, the diamond would have to stay in Kala's hut, where she kept her other precious possessions. Kala's hut had always been bigger and her things more extravagant than any of Mansa Musa's other wives. She always knew that she was his favorite, and this pleased her. She also knew that the other wives were jealous of her. She didn't usually mind, but sometimes she felt very alone. She missed her mother and sisters, and here she had no friends.

What Kala really wanted was a child. A daughter would give her someone to take care of, someone to occupy her, someone to love and to love back. Sadly, in the year that she had been married, she had been unable to carry a child. This was not only disappointing to her, but disappointing to Mansa Musa. One day he entered her hut, a serious expression on his face.

"I have decided to make an official pilgrimage to Mecca," he said. "I really believe that Islam is the true faith."

"That's wonderful! But why do you look so unhappy?"

"Since I have decided to accept the Muslim faith not only for myself, but for my people, I feel that I should set a good example. Do you—do you understand?"

Kala didn't know what to say. "You're skirting the issue. What is this about?"

"It is against Muslim law to have more than one wife," he said quickly. "You don't know how much I care about you, but, well, you haven't given me any children yet. It's very important for me to have an heir, so I must choose to keep a wife who will give me one, or more. I'm sorry."

Kala was stunned. She couldn't believe her ears. Especially since this was the same problem that had been upsetting her recently. "There must be something..." Kala trailed off. A long silence ensued. "I have an idea," she said hesitantly. "I know of a priest in one of the local villages. It is said that he can cure barren women. Maybe we can go talk to him."

Mansa Musa was silent. Finally, he consented. "All right, you can go. But we must be discreet. It would not be right for my wife to be seeing a witch doctor. I will send a servant to take you to the priest this evening."

When Kala arrived to see the priest, she was amazed. His hut was miniscule, half the size of her own. She stepped onto the bare dirt floor and looked around. The hut was only one room, and it looked like a shrine. There were candles decorating one whole wall, and small figurines populated every flat surface. The old priest only amplified the atmosphere. He was small and wiry, like the iron candle holders. His careworn face had the color and texture of a leather pouch, and the hair on his round head was sparse. In the long, brick-colored robe that brushed the tops of his bare feet, he looked like another of the statuettes in his hut.

"Welcome, my child," he said to Kala. "Come. Be seated. Have some tea, and we will see what can be done for you."

After the tea was drunk, Kala explained her problem. The little priest nodded, and every once in a while, he clucked his tongue; whether out of disapproval or sympathy, she was not sure. After she had finished, he sat silent for only a moment. Then, he jumped up and ran over to a table. He picked up a sculpted piece of akua'ba.

(At this point, Katy inserted a graphic of an akua'ba that she found at a museum web site. There is also a link to the web site.)

The priest told Kala the story of Akua, a woman who so desperately wanted a child. She had commissioned a doll similar to this one, and it gave her a daughter. He told Kala that she must treat the doll as she would a real baby. It must be carried, nursed, and even decorated with beads and other jewelry. Kala accepted the doll, and told the priest that her husband would send a servant with the fee the following day.

The next morning, Kala got up and carried the akua'ba with her to eat breakfast. She had decided to make some clay beads to put around its neck, when she remembered the diamond. It was the perfect size to adorn the head of her doll. That very morning, she set to work carving out a setting for the stone. As the weeks passed, Kala became more and more attached to the akua'ba. She slept with it on her sleeping mat and she even sang to it. She prayed every night for a child.

Meanwhile, Mansa Musa was praying, too. The date of the departure for Mecca was drawing near, and he dreaded choosing which wife he would keep. He knew he would regret any choice but Kala, but a child was very important to him. He had been trying to delay his pilgrimage for as long as possible by making hundreds of huge demands and preparations, but he could not postpone it any longer. He had already ordered 80 camels and 500 slaves. What more could he do?

"Rubaya, come here," he said.

"Yes, master. How may I serve you?"

"I've decided that each slave—yes, each slave must carry a golden staff on the pilgrimage."

"I'm sorry, sire. Do you mean all 500 slaves? It will take a long time to acquire 500 staffs."

"Yes, yes. All 500. We can wait," Mansa Musa said impatiently.

"Very well, sire," Rubaya said as he left the room.

"That should buy a little more time," Mansa Musa thought, "but that's all. I won't waste any more time or money on this trip."

A few weeks later, Kala approached her husband. He knew by the expression on her face exactly what she was going to tell him. She was with child. They were both so happy. Kala had never known such joy. Mansa Musa cancelled his order for 80 more camels and they left for Mecca the next week. Ten months later, Kala brought her daughter to the old priest. He told Kala to give the akua'ba to her daughter when she came of age, and her family would have healthy babies forever into the future. Kala was so grateful to the little man, she bid him ask anything of her.

"What I have already received is payment enough. I do not have need of anything else. I only ask that your husband allow me to keep my practice and not convert to Islam."

"Of course," Kala said. "I will do anything to repay you. My husband and I owe our happiness to your help. I am forever in your debt."

"Go, my child. Go and raise your daughter," were the priest's parting words.

Kala raised her daughter, who became beautiful and kind. Kala gave her the akua'ba and was blessed with a granddaughter.

Katy's story ends here, with a link to another student's narrative in which the diamond appears in a different century, revealing information about another historical personage.

It is obvious that Katy has done more work on this story than would have been required by an assignment to research one particular topic, and although a person reading the story does not learn all that there is to know about Mansa Musa or *akua'bas* or African culture of the 1300s, it is apparent that Katy has learned a great deal about them and will be happy—if the audience will click on the links—to show the way to find more. Best of all, the story has Katy's unique, original touch. She has taken care to be interesting ("sometimes she felt very alone," "he was small and wiry, like the iron candle holders"), to choose dialogue that indicates interrelationships, and to use vocabulary that is precise ("small figurines populated every surface").

The goals of the assignment have been met by research, prewriting, and story, which takes its place as part of the class's Africa story. The student selected and researched a topic for world history, during which Katy learned to use the internet as a research tool. She narrowed her research by means of placing her work within the context of an essential question. She wrote four types of essays, and for each essay she did content research and editing. She collaborated with other students to create links to stories and she collaborated with other Web site designers to create links to research. She has created an original work that is both satisfying in itself and strong in forwarding the larger class assignment.

Students engaged in this dynamic assignment cannot rely upon rote procedures of reporting research; they must do research and then analyze it themselves in order to achieve the tone and voice for their historical fiction. From the initial composition of the essential question that guides the study to the final product of an illustrated narrative, the student is engaged in thinking through the process as well as the implications of the research. Good writing of this nature is the result of recognizing that internet research requires students to learn specific skills, and that internet publishing makes possible complex assignments that are not beyond the capabilities of high school students and teachers who are willing to devote time to learn how to do it. Though the assignment is complex and not simple to choreograph, it provides multiple opportunities for teaching writing as a process (particularly prewriting skills), for finding and evaluating internet sources, and for working collaboratively on writing projects. Given the time and effort dedicated to these important features of writing, I have to hope that students like Katy will be well prepared for the analytical thinking that is essential to their college writing classes.

WORK CITED

Britton, James. *Language and Learning*. Portsmouth, NH: Boynton Cook, 1993.

Bruffee, Kenneth A. "Collaborative Learning and the 'Conversation of Mankind.'" *College English* 46 (1984): 635-52.

Lindemann, Erika. *A Rhetoric for Writing Teachers*. 3rd ed. New York: Oxford UP, 1995.

Strenski, Ellen. "Online Reading Between the Lines: Searching for and Evaluating Internet Information." *Assembly on Computers English Journal* 1.3 (1998): 56-69. Rpt. in *The Allyn and Bacon Sourcebook for College Writing Teachers*. Ed. James C. McDonald. New York: Allyn and Bacon, 2000. 223-33.

Further reading about using essential questions, creative writing, analysis of research, Internet use:

Burke, Jim. *The English Teacher's Companion*. Portsmouth, NH: Boynton/Cook, 1999.

Sizer, Theodore. *Horace's Hope: What Works for the American High School*. Boston: Mariner Books, 1996.

Tchudi, Stephen and Stephen Lafer. *The Interdisciplinary Teacher's Handbook: Integrating Teaching Across the Curriculum*. Portsmouth, NH: Boynton/Cook, 1996.

24

WRITING AROUND THE TEXT

A Network of Contexts, Opportunities, and Responses

J Paul Johnson
Winona (MN) State University

Because first-year students evidence a wide range of reading and writing abilities, our program's goals require that students "read challenging texts that reflect important cultural themes and demand critical thinking" and use that reading to improve and inform their writing. As an example, Sara Clendening's "Suffering in Silence" is presented in full: for the project, she read five books, posting numerous comments on each in online forums. As the semester progressed, her posts focused increasingly on the ways boys and girls are acculturated to develop discrete, unequal sets of beliefs and values, and, more particularly, how specific behaviors are rewarded for males and females. Posting regularly helped Sara rework her ideas into a successful, coherent analysis that works well within the constraints of a recognizable genre. Sara's work serves as a reminder that the experience of composing benefits greatly from critical reading and that it takes place in a rich network of textual transactions (whether the classroom itself includes computers or not). What a writing classroom can do best, in the "late age of print," is to provide students with what Chris Anson calls "the key roles" of composition: "opportunities and contexts for students who write" and "expert, principled response to that writing."

One of the many concerns that prompted this volume was based, not a little selfishly, on my own experience reading William Coles and James Vopat's *What Makes Writing Good: A Multiperspective* as a first-year graduate teaching assistant at the University of North Dakota in 1985. That volume was one of my very first introductions to the field, its contents informing much of my initial thinking about composition. In our introduction to this volume, my co-editors and I discuss some of the critiques weighed against *WMWG*, so I won't rehash them here. Instead, I want first to reflect on a small assignment that was posed to us in English 501, Composition Theory and Practice, a seminar required of all graduate assistants in the program, which we took concurrently with our first semester's teaching assignment. I hope that the anecdote will prompt some further reflections about the practice of reading student writing, for the focus of this essay will ultimately describe a pedagogy that immerses students in a rich network of contexts, opportunities, and responses for writing.

"Write your own chapter of *WMWG*," asked Libby Rankin, our new program administrator and course professor. "Provide a synopsis of your classroom assignment, the text of a successful student response, and your analysis of the student's work."

And so I did—dutifully. The assignment was much like one posed in *WMWG* by Erika Lindemann, Michael Holzman, James Britton, or Walker Gibson. My student's essay—a poetic reflection on her father's passing—was a moving elegy, brought to closure by a dramatized reading of one of her father's letters from abroad; my own analysis was deeply appreciative of the ways the student had orchestrated the sequence of narrative events to create suspense, develop character, and provide a meaningful resolution to her story. I was proud of my student's response to my assignment, as I was of mine to Prof. Rankin's.

I remember well the gist (if not the exact phrasing) of Prof. Rankin's response, even though the seminar is now more than fifteen years past. Her commentary moved, at least in part, something along these lines: "I find it interesting that in a seminar where we talk so much about composition theory and pedagogy, your own analysis of your student's writing reads just like a New-Critical explication of a literary text, pointing to its features, touting its virtues of unity, emphasis, and coherence, claiming for it a central, unchallenged meaning—and reaching conclusions based almost exclusively on the formal features of the text. So here are some questions for you to think about: How did your student accomplish this? Why did she write it? What does her work say about your teaching—and her learning?" she asked. My naïveté at the time probably kept me from feeling as humbled as I might have, but I found her comment instructive then, as I do now.

Prof. Rankin's critique pointed out to me a number of my assumptions about writing that had been inculcated, at least in part, by my earlier undergraduate study in English: that a text could (and should) be read by means of assessing its formal features, and, further, that writing could be taught simply and primarily by articulating those desired features for students. In the years since, spent nearly entirely teaching English at a relatively small state university, I've focused my teaching much less on the student text as a discrete, isolated unit and much more on the interplay of students' multiple opportunities for dialogic reading and writing. And particularly in the last half-decade or so, I've found that the increasingly universal access to the web helps occasion a much richer network of contexts, opportunities, and responses for my students' writing, in ways that encourage students to refine their thinking by interacting with other readers and writers in low-risk environments. It may seem blissfully obvious to say so, but a writing pedagogy can and should accomplish a great deal that simply can't be seen from a superficial review of an essay's formal features.

First-year students at my four-year undergraduate/master's-level institution (one delivering liberal arts, teaching, technical, and preprofessional programs) come to campus with a wide range of reading and writing abilities. Some, of course, were raised in literacy-rich environments and progressed through reading- and writing-intensive college-preparatory courses; others, meanwhile, had little more than the occasional interaction with the joys and demands of reading and writing. Our single required course, English 111: College Reading and Writing,[1] focuses on reading and writing arguments, and its key emphases (invention, research, rhetoric, collaboration, revisions, editing) will resonate with those familiar with the cognitive process and social construction movements of the 1970s and the 1980s. Many of our program's goals are parallel to those of the Council of Writing Program Administrators' Outcomes Statement. Others, though, are much more "local" in nature, evolving from years of departmental and institutional assessment pro-

---

[1]English 111 is a four-credit course in WSU's otherwise three-credit curriculum. It fulfills student's "Basic Skills" writing requirement in the University Studies (general education) program. Other writing-intensive coursework follows in subsequent years, with requirements fulfilled both within and outside the major. Every student is required to complete at least two Writing Flag courses in their major, but many other University Studies requirements and major and minor programs require additional writing of WSU students. For years, the first-year Basic Skills course was the only university-wide writing requirement—a curricular structure perpetuating the notion of writing as inherently remedial (and wholly the obligation of the English Department).

grams, issues, and discussions—in particular, those require that students "read challenging texts that reflect important cultural themes and demand critical thinking" and, further, that they use their reading in various ways to improve and inform their writing.

What we strive for, then, in our program is to encourage students to come to understand reading as far more crucial to their writing than the mere analysis of prose models of specific genres would intimate. I've never been completely comfortable with the presence (or absence) of reading as formulated by *The St. Martin's Guide to Writing* and various genre-based current-traditional rhetorics. In presenting readings primarily as prose models held up for rhetorical scrutiny, such textbooks perpetuate a false notion about reading: that one reads only to better understand (or practice, or emulate) writing. But writers read for countless other purposes, aims, and occasions: to develop ideas, to pursue notions, to construct knowledge. "Well-read" student writing, it follows, might well do much more than merely "display" the formal features of the genre; instead, it might demonstrate the student's developing understanding of course concepts, ability to use reading as a means of informing writing, and agility in formulating an argument based on a wide array of reading and writing experiences.

The primary assumption I'm working with is that "good writing"—to hark back to Coles and Vopat's original *WMWG* question—is prompted by, responsive to, and purposeful in, a rich network of textual interactions (oral/written, reading/writing, classroom/computer, teacher/student, student/student). What I aim for in my pedagogy, then—to revise the Coles/Vopat question for *Teaching/Writing in the Late Age of Print*—is to create and support that network via a complex web of contexts, opportunities, and responses for student writers. Even though by the late 1990s "using computers" in the teaching of writing had become less an unusual or transgressive act than a pragmatic a means of conducting one's business, my pedagogy was nonetheless greatly influenced by earlier scholarship about computers and writing. In particular, Fred Kemp and Thomas Barker's 1992 articulation of "network theory" gave me occasion to think through how the web might be used to develop the kind of network that provides for students what I suggest above. For Kemp and Barker, network theory encourages group knowledge that is negotiated and malleable, and emphasizes the textual transactions between students. In their scheme, networked computers thus serve as the agent for encouraging a communal understanding and sharing of texts and knowledge. In such classrooms, student exchanges take place via formal text, e-mail, and electronic discussions, with the advantages that such exchanges are both textual and retrievable, offering not only additional "writing practice" but also the convenience of easy access (1-3). A visitor to my English 111 classroom might not see computers per se, but would soon come to understand that our course web, with its links to readings, discussions, assignments, and work-in-progress, was crucial to the "network theory" that informs students' reading and writing.

Of course, I cannot in this short essay provide a full picture of all that that entire network of interaction includes; instead, I'll simply summarize a single formal writing assignment from the class, excerpt one student's response, and then provide some fuller context and analysis of the ways in which those "textual transactions" inform and motivate student writing. Truncated here, the assignment for the formal writing project, the last of the semester before the final portfolio, asks students to speculate about a topic raised in their prior course reading:

> This project requires you to write a carefully researched speculative analysis of any phenomenon suggested by your reading of Bernard Lefkowitz's *Our Guys* or Joan Jacobs Brumberg's *The Body Project*. Lefkowitz's book might inspire you to study gang rape, victims' rights, plea bargaining, homoeroticism, sex crimes by athletes, or rape trauma syndrome; Brumberg's, dieting, piercing, mentoring, "coming out," body "perfecting," "bad body fever," or "ovarian determinism." You will need to present some coherent, purposeful summary of the relevant sections of *Our Guys* or *The Body Project*; to articulate and defend a focused, analytical thesis; to use a variety of researched evidence to support clear, conspicuous claims—demonstrating both the subject's existence (and scope) and your analysis of its causes; and to make use of at least eight authoritative sources of correctly presented and documented research, with accurate paraphrase and quotation.[2]

What follows is one of a number of strong responses to the above assignment, this one, "Suffering in Silence," written by Sara Clendening, a first-year student, in the fall of 1999. For reasons of space alone, I've deleted two body paragraphs, ones that Sara allows are the least-developed of her claims. But the paper is otherwise (except for its reference list) presented in its entirety, for I wish to use it to engage some discus-

---

[2]This truncated version of the assignment emphasizes—too much so, to my thinking—the topic possibilities and formal requirements of the project. The full version, available on the course web, discusses the readings, genre, process, audience, and purpose in greater detail, and it should seem less prescriptive to readers.

sion of what kinds of reading and writing activities occur in the "network of textual transactions" surrounding the actual composition and submission of the paper itself.

> In 1995, a young woman identified only as Jane Doe filed a federal lawsuit against the University High School in Urbana, Illinois. A group of boys had assaulted her in January of 1993, unzipping her jeans, grabbing her breasts, trying to force their hands up her shirt, and exposing their buttocks and genitals to her and other students. For the next seventeen months, until the abuse finally forced her to leave the school, the same group of boys groped and taunted her (Loven, 1999).

> This case is unusual in one way only: Jane Doe reported the abuse. A national survey prepared by the American Association of University Women in 1993 reported that eighty-one percent of female public high school students said they were sexually harassed while in school (cited in Lefkowitz, 1997). Most high school females, then, experience verbal or physical sexual harassment. Only the fact that Jane Doe reported the abuse that she endured made her unique. In fact, only seven percent of the eighty-one percent who experienced sexual harassment reported the incident to an authority (Lefkowitz, 1997).

> In high schools all over the country, girls silently suffer harassment. Why is there a tendency for so few of the high school females sexual harassed to report the incidents? Several reasons compel girls to keep quiet about the cruelty.

> One reason involves the low self-esteem of adolescent girls, which drives them to want to be accepted. Also, the "hidden curriculum" learned in schools teaches girls to keep silent. Students learn to hold girls to higher expectations than boys. The last contributing factor to the girls' silence is the inability of teachers to react to the sexual harassment incidents they witness.

> [...]

> The hidden curriculum—a second major factor contributing to girls' reluctance to report sexual harassment—teaches boys and girls that boys are supposed to be dominant. Young boys learn that conquest of women is a man's role (Hyman & Rome, 1996). The conquest-of-women mentality makes boys unable to empathize with the girls' feelings. Gender equity specialists Myra and David Sadker found evidence of male dominance being taught in classrooms: boys dominated the class time, requiring more of the teacher's attention, asking more questions, and receiving praise for their academic skills. Girls, praised for obedience, learned submissiveness (cited in Orenstein, 1995). The differences in behavior of girls and boys in the classroom reinforce to girls that boys have power over them. Girls and boys are also taught that girls need to control their behavior where the boys cannot.

Another part of the hidden curriculum in schools teaches girls and boys the different sets of values tolerated by educators. In 1992, the American Association of University Women confirmed sex-role attitudes exist in classroom proceedings (cited in Anderson & Hayes, 1996). From an early age, teachers expect girls and boys to meet different expectations. For example, an observer in a seventh-grade classroom reported the following scene as the teacher handed out the class's grades:

"Dawn," said Mrs. Richter, the teacher, sharply, "for citizenship you're getting a B. You've been talking a lot and there have been a few outbursts." "Disruptive?" yells Nate from across the room, "She's not disruptive, I'm disruptive." "You've got that right," Mrs. Richter told him, laughing. When Nate's turn arrives, he also receives a disruptive mark for his citizenship comment. However, the pronouncement of his mark, relayed with an indulgent smile, conveys tolerance instead of the sharp criticism Dawn received for the same mark. (Orenstein, 1995)

Dawn thus is taught to behave quietly and respectfully in class, where Nate learns he can get away with obnoxious, loud behavior. The higher expectations placed on Dawn for conforming exemplify the mentality that "boys will be boys."

That old "boys will be boys" adage teaches girls that boys who act in an uncontrollable manner aren't responsible for controlling unacceptable behavior—even unacceptable sexual behavior. In the example above, Dawn learned Nate, as a boy, naturally behaved disruptively. Children carry this belief, taught at an early age, to the point where they believe boys can't help acting in a sexually harassing manner. Then the girls, instead standing up for themselves, write the harassment off as an inevitable behavior of males. For instance, Lefkowitz (1997) recounts an explanation illustrating the classic "boys will be boys" mentality, concerning the unspoken acceptance of certain girls displayed in having sex with a member of the jock group while the others watched. Said one Glen Ridge teen: "If I'd been the girl upstairs and these guys were spying on me, I'd have said: 'You scumbag.' But a lot of these girls would giggle or make a face and say, like the guys were just being a little naughty: 'Oh, you're a bad boy!'" (p.185). This mentality, along with teachers' apathy, causes girls to think that they have no alternative but to endure sexual harassment. Girls simply accept harassment as a part of life.

Orenstein (1995), of the American Association of University Women, concludes that some girls feel helpless against sexual harassment. "Middle-class and affluent girls in particular" often expect sexual harassment. The grabbing and teasing emphasize their submissive role in the classroom (where harassment usually occurs). The girls' belief that they

must control their sexuality, while boys are incapable of controlling theirs, is confirmed" (p.116-117). Without encouragement or support from the teachers, girls often don't possess the strength to stand up to sexual harassment. Instead, consistently harassed in front of teachers who over- look the behavior, they are discouraged from trying to end harassment and even come to believe the behavior is acceptable.
*   [...]*
*   Without a doubt, sexual harassment exists in today's schools, but most goes unreported. Instead, the victims silently suffer. Their silence comes from many sources: their need for acceptance; the message they receive from schools, believing they hold the responsibility to deal with wayward boys, even that they themselves cause harassment; or the belief that school teachers and administrators do not support them. However, the trend exists: half of surveyed students said they had been harassed in the classrooms (Orenstein, 1995). Steps to boost adolescent girls' self-esteem, efforts to stop teaching the "hidden curriculum," and more awareness and confrontation of sexual harassment in schools by teachers and administra- tors could go a long way in helping girls feel comfortable standing up for their rights.*

Sara's analysis offers readers much to consider. To begin from the vantage point of what we can see from the text itself, as a previous generation of readers had done in *What Makes Writing Good*, Sara con- structs an ethos of the concerned guardian of young women's physical and psychological well-being. She effectively delimits the scope of her paper to the evidence that supports her explicitly articulated thesis. She accommodates anticipated objections to her analysis. She selectively presents authoritative expertise, cases, and logic in support of her claims. And Sara's use of forecasts, transitions, summaries, and other cues (only some of which can be seen in this truncated version) guides readers through the careful scaffolding of her analysis.

Looked at from this perspective, as I might have for Prof. Rankin's seminar in 1985, focusing on the most readily apparent quali- ties of the text itself, Sara's composition seems almost paradigmatic of the late-20th century print literacy privileged by Myron Tuman in *Word Perfect* and later characterized as essentially modernist by Lester Faigley in *Fragments of Rationality*. After all, it is credited to a sole author. It is coherent and convincing, seeming to value features more associated with the modern (purpose, design, hierarchy) than with the postmodern (play, chance, anarchy), and presenting itself as finished and self-con- tained rather than as an in-progress, self-reflective, open performance. And for the most part, it seems to avoid conflicting evidence and exper- tise in order to assert its conclusions.

Critics of this "scaffolded" thesis form argue that its inculcation, with its thesis sentence, required topic sentences, and selective supporting details, can result in the naturalization of form at the expense of student development. Paul Heilker, for instance, laments students' writing habits that focus too exclusively on structure and form; he sees what he calls the scaffolding of the thesis/support form as closing, rather than opening students' minds, allowing them to organize information mechanically, simplistically, without embracing the complexities of difficult subjects and without engaging difficult and contradictory viewpoints (4). And, as William Zeiger noted a decade earlier, the perspective offered in thesis/support writing—the fixed, immutable, pseudo-objective stance laid out in the beginning, progressed through in the body, and reaffirmed in the conclusion—creates a "linear progression to a predetermined end," which allows for "one and only one conclusion" (456). These critics argue that slavish obeisance to the thesis/support form, in itself an essentially modern conceit based on the premise that form can be analyzed and technique mastered, can inhibit student learning.

I don't wish to argue that these kinds of concerns are groundless. Every writing teacher can cull up instances of students for whom slavish obeisance to form is the very definition of writing. What I wish to claim is that these concerns can be argued solely on the formal features of a given text, and that a claim based on such a limited perspective is, itself, suspect. It is true that from a distance—just, say, as one reads a chapter of *WMWG* or as one sees Sara's essay reprinted as an award-winner in our local Writing Center publication—claims about the "linear progressions" or "closed status" of the text seem warranted. What one cannot know from such a perspective, though, is much about the context, opportunities, or responses that inform the finished product. When one considers the amount and quality of reading, writing, and thinking that informed Sara's essay; or the multiple versions shared with colleagues, tutors, and teacher; or even the portfolio that would later present this essay as but one part of her larger body of work in the course, the concern that the form itself must necessarily limit the scope or depth of a student's thinking seems wholly unwarranted.

What one can't see from a mere reading of the published version of Sara's paper is the remarkable amount of reading, thinking, discussing, and writing—and learning—that informs and helps shape it. Aside from the 1,700 words and nine references that comprise Sara's final version of "Suffering in Silence," Sara read five books, posting numerous comments on each in the course site's online forums.[3] As the semester progressed,

---

[3]Students in this course read from a list of eight possible titles, ones selected in pairs that would provide models of the different genres students would write

Sara's posts focused increasingly more pointedly on the ways boys and girls—and later, young men and women—are acculturated to develop discrete, unequal sets of beliefs and values, and, more particularly, how specific behaviors are rewarded for males and females. In part, it was Sara's other reading for the course that allowed her to develop the notion of a "hidden curriculum," one she witnessed at work in her reading of Tobias Wolff, Esmeralda Santiago, and H. G. Bissinger, as well as the books by Joan Jacobs Brumberg and Bernard Lefkowitz mentioned in the assignment description. In the post that follows—one of nearly a dozen during the semester in which she explored the topic in the context of the course readings—Sara first began to articulate her thinking about the "hidden curriculum" of American education, this time in the context of Bissinger's *Friday Night Lights: A Town, a Team, and a Dream*:

Re: The Hidden Curriculum
From: Sara Clendening

The "hidden curriculum" that Permian students learn has nothing to do with education, but more of certain values. Permian students learn to have a great loyalty to their team, along with teamwork. Not only the football team, but the entire student body. The band, cheerleaders, and pepettes are a constant support to the team. The community rallies around the team through thick and thin. The students learn to stick together and be a constant support to the team. Another thing the students learn is conformity. Everyone is expected to support the team, everyone is expected to look at the football players with a certain reverence. Permian is about football, and not much else. Everyone is supposed to conform to this and adjust their life to mold around it. Permian students learn inequality. Not only is it mostly segregated, football players are treated better than all the other students in the classroom as well as socially. Whites are generalized to be rich, minorities poor. To these people, minorities were only useful in sports. Football players were given advantages in the classroom to encourage a passing grade, as well as unquestioned popularity in the school. No one questioned these principles, for inequality was a way of life in Odessa.

in even as they presented contested perspectives on potential subjects for student writing. To pass the course, every student needed to participate in at least four book forums (electronic discussions of each individual book on the course web), though to excel in the course, students needed to participate in five or more forums. Sara's reading for the course included (aside from at least 400 pages' worth of short essays and colleagues' work-in-progress) Wolff's *This Boy's Life*, Santiago's *When I Was Puerto Rican*, Bissinger's *Friday Night Lights*, Medved's *Hollywood vs. America*, Lefkowitz's *Our Guys*, and Brumberg's *The Body Project*.

Posting regularly in this and the other book forums on our course web helped Sara develop the ideas that were later critical to her analysis, as she was able, while posting, to address her colleagues' questions, test her rhetoric, and revise her position. As she later workshopped her draft of "Suffering in Silence," some colleagues contested her notions, prompting her to clarify her thinking; it was only after having done so that she attended to the careful structure of the claims with the kinds of organizational cues (the "scaffolding") that contribute to the essay's global coherence.

Sara's essay is, I think, a successful one, but not so much for its use of a traditional thesis/support form; nor did she approach the project with the kind of thinking that privileges the dictates of form to the extent of inhibiting the possibilities of the argument. I will allow that the traditional form probably contributed to the general perception among its readers that it was coherent and well argued. But more than anything, "Suffering in Silence" allowed Sara the opportunity to articulate and revise a notion that had been brewing all semester long, in a series of books, discussions, and postings. In doing so, she constructed her own ethos, and experimented with different kinds of evidence in order to manipulate logos and pathos to her own ends. What she was ultimately able to do well was to pull together disparate elements of the course into a successful, coherent analysis that works within the constraints of a recognizable genre. The readings for the course not only provided her a topic for critical analysis, but also the opportunity to discuss her tentative thinking in a text-rich, low-risk environment; the readings further served as models for the kinds of speculative analysis she was asked to do (albeit on a significantly smaller scale).

My presentation of Sara's work here should not be taken as an indication that I value it as an example of "what makes writing good" in its studious appropriation of a traditional form, however. Certainly, I hope that my analysis of student work here says more about the student's learning, and about my teaching, than did my project for Prof. Rankin's seminar in 1985. The sum of Sara's work on the project, from her private reading to her public discussions, from her early drafts and preliminary research to her final portfolio, should be taken (here at least) as an indication of what I hope that my pedagogy provides students. In this late age of print, I want the experience of composing to include (value, privilege, require) critical reading; to take place in a rich network of textual transactions (whether the classroom itself includes computers or not); to provide contexts that are rich in ideas, interlocutors, and responses; and to include opportunities to synthesize, reflect upon, and speculate about meaningful course readings, each of them in the context of the others. In short, in an increasingly technological culture, I want it to continue to provide students with what Chris Anson calls "the key roles" of composition: creating "opportunities and contexts for students who write" and providing "expert, principled response to that writing" (275).

WORKS CITED

Anson, Chris. "Distant Voices: Teaching Writing in a Culture of Technology." *College English* 61 (Jan. 1999): 261-80.

Axelrod, Rise B. and Charles Cooper. *The St. Martin's Guide to Writing*. Six editions. New York: St. Martin's, 1984, 1987, 1991, 1994, 1997, 2000.

Coles, William and James Vopat. *What Makes Writing Good: A Multiperspective*. Washington, DC: Heath, 1985.

Council of Writing Program Administrators. *WPA Outcomes Statement for First-Year Composition*. April, 2000. <http://www.english.ilstu.edu/Hesse/outcomes.html>

Faigley, Lester. *Fragments of Rationality: Postmodernity and the Subject of Composition*. Pittsburgh: Pittsburgh UP, 1992.

Heilker, Paul. *The Essay: Theory and Pedagogy for an Active Form*. Urbana, IL: NCTE, 1996.

Johnson, J Paul. *English 111 course site*. Winona, MN: Winona State University. Fall 1999. <http://course1.winona.msus. edu/pjohnson/e111>.

Kemp, Fred O. and Thomas T. Barker. "Network Theory: A Postmodern Pedagogy for the Writing Classroom." In *Computers and Community: Teaching Composition in the Twenty-First Century*. Ed. Carolyn Handa. Portsmouth, NH: Boynton Cook, 1992. 1-27.

Tuman, Myron. *Word Perfect: Literacy in the Computer Age*. Pittsburgh: UP, 1992.

Zeigler, William. "The Exploratory Essay: Enfranchising the Spirit of Inquiry in College Composition." *College English* 47 (1985): 454-66.

25

THE PERSONAL CHALLENGE OF ACADEMIC WRITING

Kathleen A. Welsch
Clarion University of Pennsylvania

This discussion of student writing engages the terms and arguments of the Bartholomae-Elbow conversation regarding the value of academic versus personal writing. The first-year rhetoric class that produced this piece of writing aimed to straddle this conversation. It aimed to teach students to resist traditional "academic" practice—to resist being written by the academy (Bartholomae)—and to develop a trust in themselves as writers with voices, ideas, and intentions—to experience themselves as writers (Elbow). The student essay considered here, "Et Lux in Tenebris Lucet/And the Light Shineth Into Darkness," clearly engages in the academic project of critiquing a text; however, it is the intellectual challenge of that pursuit that allows the writer to break free of "academic" writing and revel in voice, rhetorical awareness, and ownership of writing. The academic work of reading and discussing a text provided the student writer a way to talk about and to develop a rhetorical awareness that produces a kind of student writing that I would call "good." That is, writing that represents intellectual endeavor, self-reflective practice, development of the writer, and critique of the art of writing.

Writing as intellectual endeavor, critique of rhetorical traditions, pursuit of self-reflective practice, and occasion for a writer's development: these are elements of good writing, and all are evident in Michael's essay, "Et Lux in Tenebris Lucet /And the Light Shineth Into Darkness." Clearly Michael is engaged in the specific academic project of critiquing a text ("The Achievement of Desire" excerpted from Richard Rodriguez's *Hunger of Memory* in *Ways of Reading*). However, it is seeing the larger intellectual challenge of that pursuit that allows him to move beyond producing "academic" writing and to revel in his growing awareness of rhetorical possibilities, in taking the risks that such an awareness invites, in developing the voice that emerges when he takes ownership of his writing. Michael's combined critical stance and experimentation with voice and form produces an essay that straddles the Bartholomae-Elbow conversation.

Bartholomae's position is that academic writing is not static and, therefore, cannot be represented by any one form of writing. He proposes a writing class in which students develop both a critical awareness and a practice of writing as a site of power, tradition, and authority. Elbow counters that the roles of academic and writer are in conflict—that where academics value readers and what readers make of a text, writers value individual intention, voice, and experience. He proposes a writing class in which students learn to feel themselves as writers and imagine themselves at the center of discourse as a means of establishing their stances towards a subject and a reader. Michael's essay demonstrates the merit of both these positions as it moves beyond the either/or positioning that the Bartholomae-Elbow dichotomy often produces. Instead, he draws on and expands both positions as he accepts the intellectual challenge of the assignment and develops his own authority.

When I planned the course out of which Michael's essay was composed, I wanted to challenge students to both study and practice the "art of discourse," which I described in the course description as "the bringing together of thought, ideas from readings and discussions, outside sources, and the craft of composing in a 'design' that reflects intellectual engagement and, most importantly, provides the writer with a sense of accomplishment and satisfaction." Rather than guiding students dutifully through the production of an "academic" assignment, I hoped to lead them to experiment with what it might mean to resist traditional "academic" practice—to resist being written by the academy (Bartholomae)—and to develop a trust in themselves as writers with voices, ideas, intentions (Elbow). I wanted to help them imagine themselves as ready to think about the problems of writing. What might it mean to avoid being written by the academy—to resist modes, formulas, predictable narratives? To establish a voice, perspective, project of their own? To produce writing shaped by their thoughts rather than structural formulas or source material? What might it mean to pursue a project seriously rather than perform the perfunctory, mechanical exercise of completing an assignment for the assignment's sake? To produce writing that is interesting to both them and readers?

Engaging in a critique of academic, rhetorical traditions seemed an appropriate starting point for these students embarking on a four-year academic career at a liberal arts institution noted for its academic rigor and quality student body. And this was no typical first-year-composition course; it was a course entitled Rhetoric required of all English majors and honors students in the university. These were students well versed in academic conventions, who knew how to successfully produce clean, academic texts. For this reason, I wanted to offer them an opportunity to develop an awareness of the possibilities and limitations of language, the manner in which rhetorical traditions positioned them within the academy, and the ways in which they might choose to write within or against such traditions.

Similar to Michael's essay, then, this course also straddled the Bartholomae/ Elbow conversation. Our reading and discussion of course texts—student essays, some nineteenth-century materials, selections from *Ways of Reading*—focused on developing students' rhetorical awareness. I wanted students to engage in a critical conversation of texts: I wanted them to learn that "[r]eading is not simply a matter of hanging back and waiting for a piece, or its author, to tell [them] what the writing has to say" (Bartholomae and Petrosky 1). Rather than reading to honor or model published texts, I aimed for students to learn to critique a writer's work: investigate the nature of a writer's project, consider aspects of rhetorical decision making, and attend to the relationship between writer and source material. Students' growing awareness of the writer's work allowed them to establish their position in relation to a text and explore how they might respond with a project of their own. Their work responded to Bartholomae and Petrosky's invitation to "forge a reading" of a text, to cast it in their terms, to "put things together by writing" (4).

The critique of rhetorical and academic traditions positioned them to take themselves seriously as writers, not just assignment-doers, as they attended to their own ideas and use of language. Rather than being written by master tropes, *they* shaped their discourses; rather than reproducing standard texts, they drew on *their* personal knowledge and experience. Their writing was personal as it focused on their experiences as writers making choices, caring about how ideas were worded, following intentions, being aware of how what gets written can work against intentions or of where writers abandon responsibility by working off of assumptions or available narratives. Out of this work came their trust in themselves as writers, which is Elbow's goal, too. For these students, the experience of responding to and working with texts as equals was at times both harrowing and exhilarating because of the expectation that they had something of value to write—that they were not at the edge of the conversation and all the smart things had already been written.

The assignment that prompted Michael's essay was the second in a sequence titled "The Art of Discourse," which included readings from a nineteenth-century student writer, introductions to nineteenth-century and current composition textbooks, and readings by Richard Rodriguez, Adrienne Rich, Patricia Nelson Limerick, and Mary Louise Pratt. The Rodriguez assignment invited students to respond to an excerpt from *Hunger of Memory*, which focuses on Rodriguez's description of himself as a "scholarship boy." I had students begin by writing a series of short pieces as a means of working on their reading of the text, the writer's project, and their responses to it. They marked passages in the text and wrote about them; they wrote stories of their own to illustrate the commonality of Rodriguez's story; they revised their stories by pairing them with passages from the text that would allow them to resee/rethink their experiences from another perspective; again, drawing on story, they read against Rodriguez, explaining how his view might be a limited way of naming educational experience; and each class meeting found us in a discussion of their texts in conversation with Rodriguez's.

By the time students approached writing the essay, they were already engaged in the intellectual challenge of critiquing a text, a writer's project, and their own responses as writers and readers. Now they were being asked to consider the rhetorical strategy of using a source to frame a narrative: How does Rodriguez use Hoggart as a source and to what end? Just what is the relationship between a writer and a source? In responding to those questions, students needed to consider how they might maintain their own positions and voices while attempting to use a source to frame discussions of their own. It was an assignment for which students could not simply regurgitate the text, nor did it offer one correct, predictable response. In addition to being challenged to attend to Rodriguez's project (not its content or main points), the assignment also invited students to position themselves within the discussion by considering their experiences as students and writers who know something about "scholarship boys" and writing with sources. It was not an assignment with a clear and predictable path through it;

instead, students had to use writing to think through the questions and draw on their own imaginative forces.

Although one could imagine students taking a fairly traditional approach to this assignment (which some students did)—holding to a traditional essay structure, erasing complexity with a limited main point, reporting on Rodriguez rather than responding to him, or quoting him as an authority rather than engaging in a conversation with him—what impressed me about Michael's essay was his approach. He pursued the assignment as an intellectual endeavor, an opportunity to critique rhetorical traditions and engage in self-reflective practice, and an occasion to grow as a writer. The "design" of Michael's essay offers his readers a layered discussion of his encounter with the text. He doesn't allow its origin as an "assignment" to shape his sense of himself as a writer or his response to the text; instead, he actually writes his way through the limitations of "assignment" writing. Rather than open with the traditional introductory paragraph, he allows readers to see how he has come to find himself facing this assignment by recreating the student writer's dilemma. This is what he tells us:

> The classroom has that stale, hermetic smell of machine-produced coffee and cleaning agents. . . . Someone coughs from the other side of the circle. Will she get here?–perhaps she's sick. The door opens suddenly. . . . In an instant her pile of books are on the desk and we're ready to discuss. A frustrated murmur ripples the thick silence.
>
>   What of Rodriguez, anyway? What of his strife, his education, the rift, the loss? What of his essay? What of his sources? A volley of observations is tossed back and forth across the room. How are we to respond?

As he sits down later to ponder these questions in writing, he—like most students—finds himself staring at the "emptiness of a wordless [computer] screen," and it makes him feel "awful," frustrated, even "a little worried." "What should I be looking for?" he asks. And so he turns to "It That Must Be Obeyed: the sage advice of the dreaded god Wor" (*Ways of Reading*)—a typical academic and student response. After all, he has learned that textbooks are filled with information and written by professionals, so surely they must possess an authority greater than his. However, even though he knows these moves and sees that discussing the key words "success, education, parents, books" would fulfill the assignment, he can't see why he would want to do that. He tells the reader: "Trying to discuss.[those terms] in an interesting way would be like trying to conceal a German Shepard in my backpack;

it would take a lot of effort and people would wonder why the heck I would want to do it." As a writer/reader, he's reaching beyond easy answers, looking for a way to engage in composing his *own* reading of the text.

Michael's opening three paragraphs indicate that he has accepted the intellectual invitation of the assignment; he is invested in being more than an assignment-doer. His opening description of the classroom tensions and his isolation at the moment of composing offer his readers a portrait of the student writer's dilemma. His acknowledgment of the dilemma is the first step in his critique of rhetorical traditions. Michael moves beyond a traditional, academic approach that would honor Rodriguez and his use of Hoggart and accepts the challenge of investigating the relationship between writer and source, first, from his own experience as a writer working with Rodriguez as a source. Michael notices what sparks his interest, what appears as "a flash of relationship." He quotes the passage from Rodriguez that has captured his attention and then explains:

> THIS is a universal element, but not in the framework within which it was placed. Strip away the factors of class, race, setting, and personal circumstance. Voila!–something everyone can relate to: that mystical childhood before education when the world did not need to be explained.

At this point in his essay, Michael begins his conversation with the text. As he identifies what he considers a universal element in shared childhood experiences before education, he realizes he, too, has something to say about this. He includes a flashback to his own childhood, adds commentary, feels better that he had something to say. He's found a way into the text and his reading of it.

But what of the relationship between writer and sources in Rodriguez's project? I like Michael's honesty as he describes his uneasiness with block quotes, a feeling probably not uncommon to most students:

> Flipping through the essay, I realize that his block quotes make me uneasy. Perhaps I've associated source quotes with scholastic reading for too long. The indented square seemed to invite my eyes to bypass it, and at first I honored the temptation.

In light of this admission, it's evident that his taking the time to really read Hoggart's passages in relation to Rodriguez's project is a new experience. Michael learns that by not attending to the source of a key term like "scholarship boy"—a term used repeatedly throughout the essay, one on which the "entire essay practically pivots"—he cannot fully comprehend Rodriguez's argument. As a writer he realizes that this lack of attention obstructs his view of Rodriguez's project and what he might learn from it. Although it is not easy work ("The task of defining such a relationship frustrates me."), Michael's examination of Rodriguez's relationship with Hoggart reveals that the collaboration of writer and text can be the source of a meaningful project. His own work with sources in this essay leads him to an understanding of this relationship. He writes:

> I myself even cited sources in this very paper! Sources drawn from personal experience, true, but sources none the less. My entire fourth paragraph was supported by a flashback, and though it could have functioned without it, it added a completeness to the meaning that would not have existed had it not been present. . . . Rodriguez does the same; his entire essay practically pivots on Hoggart's terms. . . . Even in his title the loss is apparent. . . . He yearns for something beyond what he has experienced. . . . In Hoggart's terms, he has found a means of identifying it. . . . Rodriguez has mastered the source and still maintained his identity.

Where Michael once simply included sources in his writing, he now sees them differently: "[t]hey had seemed dry and lifeless before, more suited as a necessity than a bonus." And he certainly creates a bonus when he draws on the mat analogy from *Moby Dick* as a source for illustrating this new understanding. He explains:

> One strand represents necessity and its opposite free will, with chance guiding its tightness or looseness. So it must be with sources. One strand must be the story and the other the source, with the writer's creativity dictating how well they rely on one another.

I love moments like this in student writing where the imaginative leap is to another text. In this instance, Michael's connection to the personal is through his experience as a reader of *Moby Dick,* a text of personal significance to him because of his love for seafaring ships.

Michael's personal investment in making the assignment a project of his own creates a shift from task-oriented (academic) writing to authorship. Just as he writes that "Rodriguez has mastered his source and still maintained his identity," so has Michael. His essay combines the best of what usually are imagined as the incompatible opposites of academic and personal writing. Rather than follow "academic," formulaic constructions for the structure, content, and logic of the traditional essay, Michael creates an essay shaped by the pattern of his own thought process and interests. His essay echoes with his voice, creativity, and vision of himself as student writer: in his essay's opening classroom scenario, his focus as a reader ("Again I review."), his work as a writer ("I'm finding that the more I write the more I comprehend."), his use of metaphor ("The essay is a tree!"), his wry humor ("Don't they know it's too early to laugh?"), his excitement in the connections ("That's it!"), his attention to language and meaning ("I love that sentence."), his use of himself as a source. Every part of his essay shouts, "Listen to me! I have something to tell you!" in such a way that I can't help but stop to listen with interest and care. And yet his writing responds to a text, works through an idea, and offers a critique in ways that create a careful balance between author and source. His writing allows us to see a mind at work on the page.

Michael's title, "*Et Lux in Tenebris Lucet /And the Light Shineth Into Darkness*," captures the nature of his project: it's so academic (the Latin and its translation) and yet so creative (no "Rodriguez & Hoggart" or "My Response to Rodriguez" here). It aptly describes his understanding of his developing rhetorical awareness and his work as a writer. In his pursuit of the assignment's challenge, Michael shed light of his own making onto a subject he had little considered. He taught himself something about writers and sources and rhetorical traditions. His essay demonstrates how academic writing need not be imagined or practiced as lifeless and limiting. The light can shine in the darkness for a writer like Michael when he is aware of the power of rhetorical traditions and resists or uses them to create new possibilities.

But this takes understanding the personal as more than relating personal experience or being self-absorbed. It means understanding it in terms of the decisions a writer must make: establishing power over a text, challenging academic tradition, and investing oneself in a project. The willingness to risk the personal on this level in an academic endeavor creates the opportunity for voice, ownership of ideas, personal experience, and creativity in writing. Rather than be confined by limitations, Michael enacts a willingness to write toward possibilities as he designs a text-based essay that provides him with a sense of accomplishment and satisfaction. It's the type of student writing I enjoy reading: there is a writer at work here, conscious of his efforts, directing attention to his experience as a reader/writer as he tests the boundaries of rhetorical traditions.

WORKS CITED

Alderson, Michael. "*Et Lux in Tenebris Lucet* /And the Light Shineth Into Darkness." 5 October 1995.

Bartholomae, David. "Writing with Teachers: A Conversation with Peter Elbow." *College Composition and Communication* 46.1 (February 1995): 62–71.

Bartholomae, David and Anthony Petrosky. *Ways of Reading*. 3rd ed. Boston: Bedford Books of St. Martin's Press, 1993.

Elbow, Peter. "Being a Writer vs. Being an Academic: A Conflict in Goals." *College Composition and Communication* 46.1 (February 1995): 72–83.

26

TEACHING FOR LIFE

Application and Theory

Jeremy Ball
College of San Mateo
Judith Hawkins
California State University–San Bernardino

The apparent inability of many of our students to apply what they learn in our classes to other contexts has led us to develop a project-based learning system derived from Freire's pedagogy of "problem-posing education." This chapter describes our combined critical thinking (philosophy) and composition class (English) in which students participated in a semester-long mock trial. The trial provided a context more closely resembling real-life situations where teachers played consulting roles and students were confronted with thinking critically and writing well for purposes beyond isolated assignments. Students relied on each other online and in class to articulate their positions and to respond to the positions of other teams, which were posted on the Web weekly.

Education is the acquisition of the art of the utilization of knowledge.
—Alfred North Whitehead

THE PROBLEM: BATHTUB SWIMMING

You can't swim in a bathtub. The very structure prevents it. But if you needed to teach someone to swim, you could begin in a bathtub. You could demonstrate kicking, arm strokes, and breathing, making sure each skill is clearly understood. You could teach particular skills, collectively called swimming. But if your student fell off a boat into a lake or an ocean, would that student be able to swim? Probably not. Basic skills instructors in general and composition instructors in particular find themselves in a similar dilemma as they are being confronted with a very depressing empirical fact: most students don't seem to be using basic skills outside the immediate classroom context.

Moreover, they don't seem to be able to integrate the various basic skills they have accumulated into an organic whole and apply these skills in new ways in new situations. This poses problems for students—but also for instructors. All too often composition instructors' and critical thinking instructors' competence is challenged by other faculty who seriously question how their upper division students ever passed freshman composition and critical thinking classes. It appears that our students cannot swim in a lake or the ocean though they seemed to do fine in the bathtub.

This pitfall of education is not unfamiliar. Various theorists have warned about the consequences of the detachment of education from living. Whitehead comments:

> The solution that I am urging is to eradicate the fatal disconnection of subjects which kills the vitality of our modern curriculum. There is only one subject matter for education, and that is Life in all its manifestations. Instead of this single unity, we offer our children— Algebra, from which nothing follows; Geometry, from which nothing follows; Science, from which nothing follows; a Couple of Languages, never mastered, from which nothing follows; and lastly, . . . Literature, represented by plays of Shakespeare, with philological notes and short analysis of plot and character to be in substance committed to memory. Can such a list be said to represent Life? As it is now in the midst of the living of it? (Whitehead 19)

We must ask ourselves and show our students how our subjects are connected to this business of living. We must face the questions our students do not dare ask aloud: "Why do we have to learn this? What does this have to do with my life?" Without dealing with these often unanswered questions, students may learn to get by but fail to integrate what they can learn into life.

As a philosophy instructor and as a composition instructor, we have faced just this problem. Time and again we have passed students who—within the confines and isolation of the composition classroom and critical thinking classroom—performed well, accomplishing all the required assignments and doing well on exams. But these same students in upper division courses, and we suspect in their general lives, seem to have forgotten many of the writing skills and critical thinking skills they should have brought with them. We offer our students critical thinking, from which nothing follows, and composition, from which nothing follows. We must ask why?

John Dewey frames this problem stating:

> Almost everyone has had occasion to look back upon his school days and wonder what has become of the knowledge he was supposed to have amassed during his years of schooling. . . . These questions cannot be disposed of by saying that the subjects were not actually learned, for they were learned at least sufficiently to enable a student to pass examinations in them. One trouble is that the subject matter in question was learned in isolation; it was put, as it were, in a watertight compartment. When the question is asked, then, what has become of it, where has it gone to, the right answer is that it is still there in the special compartment in which it was originally stowed away. If exactly the same conditions recurred as those under which it was acquired, it would also recur and be available. But it was segregated when it was acquired and hence is so disconnected from the rest of experience that it is not available under the actual conditions of life. (Dewey 47-8)

This problem and its cause are well known. The challenge for educators interested in solving the problem is to develop and enact classroom structures that avoid this pitfall, classroom structures that weave learning into "the actual conditions of life" (Dewey 48). We need to find a practical application of this theory.

PROJECT-BASED INSTRUCTION: GOING TO THE LAKE

We asked ourselves what we wanted students to know and be able to do when they left our classes. We wanted students to learn particular skills and the appropriate context in which to employ those skills, and to develop self-responsibility and accountability for their own critical thinking and writing goals. To do this, we had to make their primary success or failure dependent upon their choices. They needed to know that their decisions mattered. They needed to see a clear cause-and-effect relationship between their critical thinking and writing and an audience's response to it in order to find their own motivation for thinking critically and writing well.

To achieve these goals, we began to investigate ways that we could change what we were doing in order to move students from the learning/knowing stage to the enacting/doing stage, where they would begin using the knowledge and independently implementing the skills we taught them. In particular, we wanted to:

- approximate closely real-life writing and critical thinking situations
- allow students to respond and answer to wider, more diverse audiences as they would in real-life writing situations
- cause students to confront various critical thinking and writing problems, the solutions to which would require them to seek out the skills necessary to complete the assignment
- cause students to remember and reapply independently critical thinking and writing skills

In order to achieve these goals, we wanted to teach students in an integrated environment. We recognized that their isolation occurred on two separate levels. First, within a particular critical thinking or writing class, skills are divided up into sequential chapters or skill segments. Students typically finish one set of isolated skills and then move on to the next. Second, within the context of the university, different skills are further sectioned off into different disciplines to be covered by different departments on campus. As our first step to teach students how to integrate basic skills, we decided to address the second form of isolation by integrating our composition and critical thinking classes into one two-quarter class. We considered various pedagogical methodologies and classroom structures that could help us address the first level of isolation and achieve our stated goals. These included teaching in a computer-facilitated classroom and using collaborative learning models, project-based learning, service learning projects, and "problem-posing" education.

Again, our ultimate goals were to get students to think critically and write well, and to apply these skills independently and appropriately after they left our classrooms. Having focused on this, the method we approached was to create "problem-posing" situations such as those discussed by Paulo Freire. Because Freire, like many other theorists who are aware of the pitfall, does not develop practical applications in his methodology, we applied his methodology to our combined classroom structure to achieve our goals. With Freire's "problem-posing education" as our primary methodology, we were able to address our goals by integrating a project-based, collaborative learning situation in a computer-facilitated classroom. Some of our best results were achieved with the project-based learning aspects of the course because it required collaborative learning and increased facility with computers. These most closely paralleled life situations in which students might find themselves after graduation. So here, we will focus on these aspects of our integrated experiment.

Instead of just giving students a writing assignment based on various readings and modeling how to do the various writing and thinking processes, we also wanted to create a course-long situation in which students needed to seek out and use the various thinking and writing skills independently in order to solve a thinking and writing problem. We needed a project that students jointly found compelling, so we moved toward a collaborative learning situation such as John Trimbur discusses: "Collaborative learning [incorporates] practices such as reader response, peer critiques, small writing groups, [and] joint writing projects" (87). His theories, based in part on John Dewey, reinforced our goals. According to Dewey, "the whole group . . . is held together by participating in common activities" (qtd. in Trimbur 92). From this type of foundation, we developed several project templates.

The first of several particular project templates we selected was a "mock trial." We asked the class to select a whole-course topic that could be argued in a courtroom setting and that also raised issues for exploration and debate. As a class,[1] they chose the topic and question "Should Prostitution Be Legalized in California?[2]" The class was then divided into three teams by drawing lots: the prosecution, the defense,

---

[1]Although we were at first apprehensive of such a problem-laden topic and uneasy about giving students control of the topic, students quickly allayed our fears. Each team independently divided up into subteams in order to research and explore different aspects of the issue, such as the history of the law, the medical issues, the moral aspects, the social considerations, and the constitutionality of the current law and situation of prostitution in California. Once excited about the topic and clear about the process, students went right to work.

[2]We realize that any topic, so long as it is complex enough and one that students prefer, could be worth exploring. Therefore, an instructor could use this particular project repeatedly over the years without repeating a topic. This benefits the instructor in that it places the instructor back in the position of learner, according to Freire, while still maintaining the role as an expert source on skills for students. But what is most important here is that this was a topic the class selected.

and the judges. The prosecution defended the current laws regarding prostitution in California, the defense argued for a change in law, and the judges evaluated evidence and arguments each subteam presented, advised and consulted with them to help them strengthen their positions, and arranged for the formal presentation of the case.

We set up an assignment schedule: first, both the prosecution and defense would construct a total of three arguments and three rebuttals on the issue. Each team then independently formed three subteams to complete one argument and one rebuttal for their position on the issue. After a period of open research, subteams sequentially posted their discovery material (research work in support of their positions) and arguments on a web page, one per week for six weeks. Second, the judges evaluated the posted discovery material and reviewed the arguments posted before giving written advice to each subteam on how to best develop their argument and present it. Subsequently, revision for each subteam became a matter of how to meet the demands of their own team, the constraints of the judges, and the counter-position of the opposing team. Because of these constraints, revision became a natural reflex to their audience's response; students saw exactly why revision was necessary.

This is where things became fun for us.

The students displaced us as the "authorities" in the class as they began to look to audience response as a motivation to revise. Instead, we became their expert resources, their midwife-coaches. We were not the ones who were the initial or solitary judges of whether or not the writing was working. Subteam and team members as well as the other students in class became primary readers. As we were thusly replaced, we began guiding and coaching them. We were there as resources for them, to coach them through the difficult process of developing the issue as a whole class. These students had a far more diverse audience that placed on them multiple expectations.

First, students had to answer to their subteams, and their subteams had to answer to the team as a whole. This made the students responsible for their work in an acute way: their peers were depending on them, and if they failed to perform, the pressure would not end at the end of class; it would follow them back to the dorms. Second, they had a team of neutral spectators who were going over the work with a fine-toothed comb—the judges. As such, they received much external, often contradictory advice, on what they ought to do to improve. They needed to discriminate to find useful advice. And third, they had an adversarial audience in the opposing team who were searching for weaknesses in the argument that could be exploited in their refutation.

We, the instructors, had become their allies in the writing journey as opposed to their adversaries and judges.

Audience also became a motivating factor for students because discovery materials, arguments, rebuttals, and reviews were posted on web pages. These arguments and rebuttals were not just presented to a few peers or even the rest of the class or the rest of the campus; students' potential audience became every human being with a computer. Also, once students' work was posted, most class members often saw postings long before we had a chance to take a look at them. This moved students' perceptions of audience beyond the norm of instructors only. Students began to care what people would think about what they were writing rather than only what their instructors would think.

SPECIFIC EXAMPLE: JUMPING IN

Often as subteams revised their positions, we sat with them, asking them to articulate the position upon which the team had agreed. Our questions helped them narrow their focus. Then we pointed to critical thinking or composition problems and asked them what they wanted to do. Our goal was to help them discover their own writing and thinking problems and successes as well as to teach them how to learn independently and interdependently.

The prosecution team supporting current California law was the first to present their argument on the social effect of prostitution. Their first draft (which here includes all their first draft errors) was posted on February 1, 1999:

In American society the right to privacy is dear to all. Found between the lines of the 1st, 2nd, 3rd, 4th, 5th, and 9th amendments, privacy is seen as a Constitutional right. Everyone in America has the right to privacy, however as soon as it impedes others' rights, there must be intervention in order to protect the rights inherent in the Constitution. When there is a crime taking place, there is victim. Although defenders of prostitution would argue that prostitution is not a crime, this is not true. There are victims. Therefore it is a crime.

Is it not a crime to, in the privacy of your own home, commit suicide? The instant one becomes a danger to himself or anyone else, he is breaking the law. The legalization of prostitution would affect many individuals along with the standards in society Americans have accepted and chosen to respect. The harm that the legalization of prostitution would cause far outweigh the benefits.

One of the most basic and important things to the human race would be affected of prostitution were legalized Although you may scoff at the idea of prostitution violating nature, that's exactly what is occurring when you put a monetary value on something as important as intimacy. There's more to sex than a dollar amount.

Prostitution also affects the idea of a monogamous relationship and may cause the breakup of marriages. The family unit is the basic building block of society as we know it. Prostitution has the potential to cause destruction to families and who in their right mind would argue that this would be beneficial? Also, statistics show that those who are married are less likely to break the law in a criminal manner.

Statistics show that only 15 .7% of all inmates (nationwide) were currently married. The amount of divorced was similar 15 .6% and those widowed only included 1 .4%. The total percentage of inmates who were never married is 58.6% In conclusion, the percentage of inmates who were unmarried, widowed, or divorced, that is, not part of a family unit as we would prefer, is 75. 6%(>-jail inmate statistics 1996, national).

Statistics also prove that more inmates come from homes where they were not raised by both parents.

Although 60 .4°/o of those jailed were raised by a single parent or other relatives, only 39% of all inmates were raised by both parents. (JBID)

Therefore evident that the results of prostitution would potential cause harm to society, but also the individual. If I may step away from statistics for a moment and plead to your humanity.

Imagine yourself having a daughter. Would you even want to imagine her becoming a prostitute? And don't you think there's a reason why "slut" is a derogatory term? Compared to a waitress, a profession is which one also serves others, prostitution is a much less worthy profession, is it not?

When you rook around, you see people—not objects, people. With the legalization of prostitution, people have the potential of becoming objects of capital gain. Prostitutes become instruments of production and commerce. They become dehumanized. Defenders of prostitution would argue that the country could tax prostitutes and benefit the economy. But do we really want to tax something as sacred as intimacy? Do we want to tax people just as items in the supermarket are taxed? It becomes a consumer/product interaction?

Humans were once sold as objects. This goes greatly against the precepts of society—"all are created equal." For this reason, slavery was abolished. Prostitution almost resembles slave trade. Whether consensual or not, it is still the selling of a human being as an instrument of production. Consent does not make it right. With or without consent, it still goes against the precepts of our society, our government, our human nature. We do not intend to tell people what to do. But we also do not want to be responsible for promoting prostitution, something deemed immoral by most religions, by making it legal. If the legalization of prostitution is not beneficial to our society, then why would anyone want to change the current law, which maintains that in the state of California, prostitution is illegal?

In class, response to this first presentation was lively and boisterous, and it focused on the argument and not the arguers. Responses were specific and to the point. They called this subteam's argument into question. Members of the defense team asked the prosecution subteam to define "family." Also the defense team asked how prostitution could cause "destruction to families," saying the cause-and-effect relationship needed to be established. Judges questioned the clarity and focus of the argument.

Written responses to this first draft followed in a few days. This is one of the defense's subteam's response:

The prosecution discusses the Right to Privacy in the first argument. They show it in a three-step pattern, which is as follows. The A to B to C pattern does not flow well and needs to be explained more. As far as we understand the pattern in A prostitution breaks up a home, B broken homes lead to criminals and C prostitution causes crime. The A to B, B to C, and therefore the A to C pattern is unclear and broken. The way they all tie in together needs to be explained better.

The Right to Privacy does not apply because prostitution is illegal and there is a crime being committed. It may be your property but the laws still apply in your house.

The statistics do not apply to this argument. The valid statistic that is missing that would apply would be exactly how many criminals had families broken by prostitution.

An unstable home does not necessarily mean that it was a home that was broken by prostitution.

> Relevant statistics are needed or explanations of how the statistic stated apply. In addition, the slavery right was a bad example. A slave does not choose to go into slavery whereas prostitutes choose to go into prostitution.

These comments served as a wake-up call for revision for the prosecution subteam. Although we could see several more problems, we did not jump in but let the dynamics of the class's written responses motivate this subteam. We remained available, offered general suggestions and support, and let teams know they could come to us for specific help and advice on developing their papers. This prosecution subteam did just that.

Whereas their final draft differed dramatically from this first draft in several ways, the revision process was slower than they expected because they were working as a team, they were learning about revision as they were doing it, and they had many decisions to make about their argument. First, they chose one of the many points they tried to corral together in their first draft and eventually developed that one point into a whole argument: "Prostitution has the potential to cause destruction to families."

The second draft shows that they are beginning to develop this idea:

> Marriage is just the stepping stone to that building block of society know as the family unit. This legalization of prostitution would be a threat to that unit as we know it. It is apparent that in the 90's that unit is already in danger—but why should we add to that danger by legalizing prostitution?

During the next few weeks when this subteam came to our offices, we echoed the defense team's questions to their original presentation by asking them to tell us what constituted a family and what their research on families led them to understand about families. After some brainstorming and further discussion, they hand-wrote this draft as they began defining family:

> A family is "any team of people closely related by blood as in parents, children, aunts, uncles. Or a team of persons who form a household under 1 head." This team is brought together by heads of the household—the parents. Because there is no blood relation between the parents there must be a deep, close, personal knowledge of friendship with other. This relation is called intimacy.

Next, we asked this subteam how family relates to society, how the breakup of the family leads to the breakdown of society, and how prostitution is related to these processes, again echoing the judges and defense team's first comments, which this prosecution subteam raised with us. From this discussion, they produced this free write during an office-hour conference:

> Intimacy leads to committal intimacy and that leads to marriage vows. These are the foundation of the marriage & monogamous relationship of the parents. ~~If one goes outside of these foundations for sex following these foundations . . . is sex~~ If one goes outside of the foundation for sex it is saying that there is no purpose for the foundation—breaking it. If this is broken then the union is no longer needed. This union is the beginning of the family unit + if it is broken then so is the family. . . . Prostitution provides sex who the foundational beginnings + therefore leads to the break down of the family unit. And [the family] is the foundation of society.

Because this subteam was courageous enough to post their first draft and present their argument first, they received the fervor of the other teams' evaluations. Knowing and caring about their audience and knowing their work could to be published in its blemished state motivated these students to learn to control their arguments quickly and enthusiastically.

CONCLUSION: READY FOR THE OCEAN

The structure of this project-based class radically altered our function as instructors in the classroom and these students' perceptions about critical thinking and writing. In the typical lecture or discussion classroom, we disseminate information and then check students for retention. Most of the time we struggle to teach our various skills to our students, and we feel the need to prod them into some motivated state. But in the context of this class, although the content was the same, the situation was very different. Our role was that of midwife-coach. We spent class time helping students frame and solve the various thinking and writing problems they confronted during the whole project. As such, we taught the same skills, but now we did it because students were coming to us and asking for the information we usually struggle to get them motivated to learn. Here, because students were tied to the outcome of their work and actively sought out skills that would help their work succeed, they became active learners in an active learning situation.

Additionally, the whole course project functioned as a collaborative effort, the sum of which is greater than its individual members could have produced. At the end of the course, they held a public debate juried by members of the audience: other professors, family, friends, and peers. Also they presented the web pages they had written, designed, and built during the course. As they left class on that final day, their work was not "round-filed." They had put their knowledge to good use and had something to show for it. Their collaborative endeavors were archived on their university web site.

WORKS CITED

Dewey, John. *Experience and Education.* New York: Collier Books, 1938.

Freire, Paulo. *Education for Critical Consciousness.* New York: Seabury Press, 1973.

———. *Pedagogy of the Oppressed.* Trans. M. Bergman Ramos. New York: Continuum, 1992.

Trimbur, John. "Collaborative Learning and Teaching Writing." *Perspectives on Research and Scholarship in Composition.* Eds. Ben W. McClelland and Timothy R. Donovan. New York: MLA, 1985.

Whitehead, Alfred North. *The Aims of Education and Other Essays.* New York: The New American Library, 1949.

27

"TO MAKE ONESELF HEARD AND FELT, TO SIGNIFY" [1]

Jeffrey R. Galin
Florida Atlantic University

This chapter explores a set of e-mail exchanges between a student and a teacher in an upper-division intensive reading and writing class that enabled both to reflect on their assumptions about learning, teaching, and social change. The class, designed as a broad-based discussion on the social, political, economic, and ideological underpinnings of literacy and teaching practices within the United States, provides a rich context for discussing these reflections. I provide a glimpse into the critical teaching, reading, and writing practices that I value—writing as thinking, reflection, and social self-awareness—and how my expectations are enacted in assignments, responses to student work, and negotiation of class work with students. The chapter focuses in particular on a reader response heuristic that served as the basis for the e-mail exchange and that best demonstrates how I use critical reading practices to stimulate class discussion and reflective writing.

---

[1]This title is a quotation from Charles Schuster's "The Ideology of Literacy: A Bakhtinian Perspective" in which he is defining what he means by "literacy" (227).

Date: Fri, 02 Mar 2001 15:30:23 -0500 (EST)
From: VLeproso@aol.com
Subject: ira shore, galin rhetoric class
To: jgalin@fau.edu, KarB17@aol.com, dannibrowne@hotmail.
com, reallayla@hotmail.com

*This is Ricardo. Let's talk. The passage on page 12, second full
paragraph, not only helped me understand where this author is
going with his pedagogy, but it also helped me understand where
our class is going with it. Taking into account that Mr. Shore is
paraphrasing Mr. Vygotsky's views, nonetheless, this democratic
approach to the classroom, teacher-student relationship, is quite
radical to me. "Again, one key departure is that all participants in
a critical process become redeveloped as democratic agents and
social critics. Critical teaching is not a one-way development, not
'something done for students or to them' for their own good."*

In his typically no-nonsense manner, Ricardo has identified the
passage in Ira Shor's opening chapter of *Critical Literacy in Action* that
marks possibly the most important moment of the author's argument,
speaks most directly to Ricardo, and best challenges me as a teacher to
reflect on my praxis. His statement was meant to provoke an online
conversation that I had asked my upper division Studies in Rhetoric and
Writing: Literacy class to hold while I was away. I was surprised and
excited by Ricardo's post. It had the promise of laying open Shor's complex argument quickly and in ways that reflected critically on our class
structure. I responded by encouraging him to "Help us understand this
packed quotation." I continued, "What are the implications of students
becoming 'redeveloped as democratic agents and social critics?'" After a
few lines about the chapter in general, I posed a question to the rest of
the class: "Do you follow what Ricardo means when he says that the
passage he [sic] helps him understand 'where our class is going'? could
we talk about this point a bit over e-mail before Monday's class?"
(Galin 02 Mar.). In the end, the other three students in the class did not
pick up the challenge, and Ricardo and I were left to continue in private
e-mail. Nonetheless, this set of exchanges provides an opportunity for
both Ricardo and me to reflect on my course and my teaching. In the
process of contextualizing and discussing these reflections, I explore
how my expectations are enacted in assignments, responses to student
work, and negotiation of class work with students. This exchange also
demonstrates the kind of vested writing that I most value, writing as
thinking, reflection, and social self-awareness. I focus in particular on a
reader response heuristic that I use in all writing classes, which served as

the basis for our e-mail exchange and which best demonstrates how I use critical reading practices to stimulate class discussion and reflective writing.

All but one of the students who registered for my Studies in Rhetoric and Writing: Literacy class did so within the five days before classes began. As a new, upper-division class being taught by a professor new to the department, its low enrollment reflected the unknowns. The department chair allowed the class to "make" because it was new, because it fulfilled the requirements for a course in the Writing and Rhetoric track for English majors and for Advanced Expository Writing in the teacher certification program, and because he knew how eager I was to teach it. Much of the reading we would do informed my own teaching practices and grounded a chapter of my dissertation. This class would enable students to theorize teaching in a range of cultural contexts and, more than any other class I have taught, enable me to reexamine my praxis, what Ira Shor defines as "reflective action"—theorizing practice/practicing theory (15).

In the flyer I posted to entice students to take the class, I wrote:

> If you are considering being a teacher in the primary or secondary schools, college, or a community literacy program, this course is a must for you. If you consider going into public policy or the social sciences or if you are simply a concerned citizen, this class will provide you with the kind of critical take on literacy in American culture that will enable you to participate in a wide range of critical and cultural debates that shape our national agendas.

My aim was to provide a broad base for discussing the social, political, economic, and ideological underpinnings of literacy and teaching practices within the United States, to encourage these upper-division students to reflect critically on the assumptions they brought to these discussions, and to lay out a roadmap for the teaching they would do after they received their degrees. I set up the sixteen-week syllabus with about 20 pages of reading due per class meeting, four one-page, single-spaced reader responses, two large writing projects, and two in-class exams.

Of the 15,500 students enrolled on the Boca Raton campus of Florida Atlantic University, about a third were taking a full class load and also working. Although the demographics of the school are changing, it is still primarily a commuter campus and ranked as a Research II university. Because the University is growing by about 700 students per year, there are buildings going up all over campus. Departments like English that manage large general education courses have nearly doubled in size over the past decade. Upper-division students at FAU have grown comfortable with a lecture format for content classes, but my Literacy class posed a different model, one that expected a high degree of close, critical reading, daily class-wide discussions, and critical reflection on the uses of and assumptions about literacy in American culture.

For the first four weeks of the class, I asked students to come prepared to talk about historical representations of literacy in the works of Goody, Watt, Ong, Scribner, Cole, Pattison, and Havelock. We also studied a few historical documents such as the 1975 *Newsweek* article, "Why Johnny Can't Write," and the 1983 report, *A Nation at Risk*. We generally started our discussions with someone reading from a reader response or by looking for the landmark claims of the arguments, how the author supported and structured those claims, and how each new article spoke to previous ones. When I handed out the first formal writing assignment in the fifth week, an ethnographic research paper, I told the students that I expected them to have already mapped out the arguments of the articles before our discussions. We began spending most of our time exploring how the articles were speaking to each other by examining their underlying assumptions. By the eighth week in early March, when Ricardo posted his message on Shor, we had reached the midpoint of the term. Names and theories of literacy were no longer unfamiliar terrain. And students were studying for an exam for which they had submitted questions that they developed from our readings. At this moment, for Ricardo, Ira Shor provided the opportunity to make some important connections that I was eager to understand.

In my initial response to Ricardo, I had asked, "What are the implications of students becoming 'redeveloped as democratic agents and social critics'?" He replied:

> that through the mastery of language [the student] can begin to participate critically in the world that he inhabits. instead of accepting precepts and mandates of the ruling minority, the democratic-agent can express the experience of the majority. change is a key issue in this article in that through language one can define himself in society and even redefine his role in it. (03 Mar.)

Although I was still unclear what Ricardo meant by "the mastery of language," "change," and how he could "define himself in society and even redefine his role in it," I was struck by his conviction that students could and should play a role in the classroom other than being passive recipients of information. Only a few weeks before, Ricardo had come to my office to say he was considering dropping my class because he was unsure whether he would be able to meet my expectations. A couple of other students had already dropped the class before the first formal assignment was due (six weeks into the class) because of course overloads, personal reasons, and the quantity and quality of work I expected the students to perform. Because of his earlier reservations, the confidence and promise evident in Ricardo's analysis of these first two e-mail posts surprised me.

We had been working with complex arguments nearly every class period, and I had sent out late the previous week over e-mail the set of compiled study questions for the upcoming midterm that I had collected from the class, modified/edited, and supplemented with questions of my own. Later that week, students would have to select one of three questions that I chose from the study list on which to write an in-class essay. In addition, I returned their first formal writing assignments the Monday after Ricardo sent his first two e-mail responses. Students had performed ethnographic research in a local community, studying a form of literacy and discussing how the literacy reflected its social contexts. They all had worked hard on these papers, but my portfolio evaluation procedures and the complexity of the assignment guaranteed the need for revision.

In the fourth week, a student had asked me why I would not tell the class how to interpret the articles. I responded that I aimed to facilitate discussion and help students develop strategies for critical reading but that it was their responsibility to engage the readings in meaningful ways. The same student responded, "But that's not what other teachers do. They tell us what we need to know." I explained that I would not be testing them on "what they needed to know" but on what they were "able to do" with the materials we read. Everything in the class was geared to this purpose.

In all previous course descriptions for writing that I have taught since beginning my PhD program at the University of Pittsburgh in 1988, I have included a version of the following statement:

> You will find first and foremost that the assignments of this course are designed to encourage you to reimagine the work of reading and writing as opportunities to develop new ways of seeing, knowing, and making meaning. They are designed as invitations for you to question habitual ways of thinking, to move beyond obvious responses, and to develop your own strategies of posing questions about the reading, writing, and thinking you do.

Such "strong reading"[2] practices require students to construct readings of complex texts and position themselves as respondents in relationship to the arguments they encounter. Although this passage did not appear in the syllabus for my Literacies class, its work was implied throughout.[3] During the second week of class, I handed out a reader response assignment that students would use at least four times during the term on class readings of their choice before we discussed them. It asks students to perform four basic steps: (1) identify and quote the most important or interesting passage in the article; (2) offer a close reading of the passage by paying attention to its specific terms and phrases; (3) demonstrate why they interpreted the passage as they did by drawing on associations from their own experiences; and (4) use the first three parts of the assignment to help the rest of the class better understand the author's article as a whole and larger issues we have discussed thus far.

The process of selecting the passage for analysis encourages students to read critically and carefully and to vest themselves in an examination of the article from the vantage point of a single passage. The close reading of the passage requires that students not just paraphrase but work closely with specific terms and phrases and cite other spots in the article where those terms and phrases were first defined or discussed. The examples from students' experiences need to be chosen carefully to externalize assumptions that normally remain unspoken. And the focus on the passage as a window into the overall argument and larger issues helps students contextualize their analyses, examine argument structures, and synthesize their readings of the article for themselves and others.

The original idea for this reader response heuristic came from one that David Bleich explains in *Readings and Feelings;* however, I have shifted the emphasis from personal—"subjective"—readings to public ones. Rather than asking students to draw on associations from

---

[2]This emphasis on self-reflective reading, writing, and thinking practices grew directly out of my training a the University of Pittsburgh. Strong readers, according to David Bartholomae and Anthony Petrosky, must take responsibility for constructing meaning within the texts that they read (*Ways of Reading* 8). Louise Rosenblatt describes this negotiated process in *Literature as Exploration* as transactional in nature (27-8). "The meaning is forged from reading the essay, to be sure, but it is determined by what you do with the essay, by the connections you can make and your explanation of why those connections are important, and by your account" of what authors are saying as they lay out their claims (Bartholomae and Petrosky 8).

[3]I have already revised my syllabus to include this statement for future classes.

their life experiences to interpret readings for themselves, I ask them to draw from their experiences to make visible to others the assumptions they bring to the materials they read and thereby help readers follow how they arrived at their interpretations. Thus, I am less interested in Bleich's notion of "subjective reading" than I am in Gerald Graff's and James Paul Gee's assertions that we, as educators, have a responsibility to our students to enable theory to "break out" in our classrooms.[4] The final step of the heuristic is by far the most important. By resituating the passage and its interpretations within the context of the article's overall argument and other texts we have read, students position themselves to speak back with some degree of authority. The process of writing the reader response becomes the process of constructing a reading that serves as the basis for class discussion, which in turn helps students pre-draft stages of papers drawing upon the readings.

In first-year composition classes, I ask students to respond to all primary readings in this way, although sometimes they do this work in class. For the Literacies class, I asked that at least one reader response be completed by the end of the third week and the others at their convenience, before we discussed the pieces in class. Similar to the questions I asked of Ricardo in his e-mail posts, my feedback and check, check-plus, check-minus grading scheme for reader responses are designed to reinforce the literate practices students need to perform in this kind of close reading.

When I saw Ricardo in class on Monday after our e-mail exchange, I encouraged him to continue working on his responses to my questions, particularly how Shor's argument had helped him better understand our class. At the time, neither one of us was imagining our exchanges as a means toward a reader response, but he did eventually fulfill the criteria for a successful response. The next day, just three days before our midterm, I received the following post:

Date: Mon, 05 Mar 2001 21:29:50 -0500 (EST)
From: VLeproso@aol.com
Subject: Re: ricardo
To: jgalin@fau.edu

---

[4]Graff explains that theory breaks out when "the kind of reflective discourse about practices that was generated when a consensus that was once taken for granted in a community breaks down"(32). Gee goes a step further by asserting that every person in a society has an "obligation to (try to) explicate . . . any theory that is (largely) tacit and either removed or deferred when there is reason to believe that the theory advantages oneself or one's group over other people or other groups" (Gee 20).

> *This is in response to how i think the class serves the means to democratization of the students. This class is structured so that each student applies oneself in the lesson, that is to say, we as students have to work at this democratic discourse. The instructor is not going to spoon feed the student the knowledge, or dictate it;however, this application of the dialogic discourse is in effect constructing a relevant knowledge base and means for discussion. In Ira Shore's essay he state on page 12 that the difference between his critical literacy and Vygotsky's is that critical literacy reconstructs and develops all parties involved, but Vyogtsky's model focuses only on the development of the student. I see this as a premise, Ira Shore's model, of where this class is going, in that, the class' participants are becoming agents of the democratization of the classroom. First we study complex arguments and discuss them in class, and then we build our expertise in literacy criticism: hence this reflects in an authorial voice when we answer questions. Will this actually happen in the class is a question already answered. yes, it has. Will this experience serve us in the future when teaching our own class? yes. I myself, think that this class, although the lack of commitment by some is evident, will come to reflect that the notion of democracy as being a privilege or easily attainable is a false assumption. What the structure of this class has shown me is that democracy is something that one works very hard at, and that one must participate diligently in to maintain it. "The literacy process, as cultural action for freedom, is an act of knowledge in which the learner assumes the role knowing subject in dialogue with the educator," as Paulo Freire puts it, to view the subject as vessel to be filled by the word is erroneous thinking, but that the subject, the learner, forms a base of knowledge in which allows one to critically interact with the educator, this is in essence the role of democracy in the classroom. Ricardo. Sorry, Jeff about being a little long winded, but i really had a lot to say. i hope i said it clearly. this, of course, is a complex issue. see you on wednesday. (Mar 05)*

In his explanation of Shor's term "democratization of students," Ricardo has made a keen insight into his own learning processes and my teaching practices. Although his statement may seem obvious, few students ever realize that they "have to work at this democratic discourse." By work here, Ricardo is not referring to the assimilation of information. He is referring to methods of reading such as those that John Clifford describes in "Enacting a Critical Literacy"—an article we read a week later. Clifford explains that no method of reading is natural: students are taught to read specific texts in specific ways. We all are. We are taught either to look to authorities for a text's meaning or to look inward; we are taught to be passive or active, involved or detached. Therefore, if responses are encouraged, students begin to realize that their interpretations are, in fact, intimately connected to their world's, to experiences, to gender and race, to the social contingencies we are all enmeshed in. (259)

Although Ricardo is drawing upon Paulo Freire's explanation of the banking model for education, his notion of "spoon feeding" reflects Clifford's explanation of looking "to authorities for a text's meaning." Because we are all "taught" to read either passively or actively, if students are spoon-fed, they will not assume the responsibility of active reading themselves. Furthermore, as in Clifford's example of double-entry journaling, Ricardo's response to my question demonstrates the ways in which his "interpretations are, in fact, intimately connected to [his] world," in this case our class.

Ricardo goes on in this longer post to draw upon Mikhail Bakhtin's theories of communicative discourse. He explains that active reading, which the class fosters, builds "dialogic discourse," and "this application of the dialogic discourse is in effect constructing a relevant knowledge base and means for discussion." Numerous times over our first eight weeks, I made references to Mikhail Bakhtin's theories of "utterance" and "dialogics" as ways to explain Charles Schuster's definition of literacy, which I quote in my course description. In "Discourse in Life and Discourse in Art," Bakhtin explains that the extraverbal context of the utterance involves the specific physical context, common knowledge of the speakers, and common evaluation of the situation under consideration (Bakhtin, 396). Schuster uses this notion of utterance in "The Ideology of Literacy: A Bakhtinian Perspective" to suggest that we can only be literate if we share these extraverbal contexts in order to get heard. "Literacy," says Schuster, "is the power to be able to make oneself heard and felt, to signify. Literacy is the way in which we make ourselves meaningful not only to others but through the other to ourselves" (227). I explain this passage in my course description, saying "that literacy is the power to speak and be heard across cultural boundaries" and that "we make ourselves meaningful by communicating ideas to others, but more importantly by acknowledging that meaning travels through others and then reflects back to ourselves." In Ricardo's e-mail message to me, his explanation of dialogic discourse and its ability to construct a knowledge base for discussion is somewhat cryptic because he has not made explicit the extraverbal information that he and I share, which includes both Bakhtin and Schuster.

After his comment on dialogic discourse, Ricardo returns to the passage that he cited in his first post to distinguish between Vyogtsky's cognitivist model for learning and that of Ira Shor. Shor explains, "a critical writing class is the zone where teachers invite students to move into deepening interrogations of knowledge in its global contexts." He continues,

> the main differences between critical literacy as I propose it here and Vygotsky's zone of proximal development are first that critical literacy is an activity that reconstructs and develops *all* parties involved, pulling teachers forward as well as students (whereas Vygotsky focused on student development), and second dissident politics is foregrounded in a critical literacy program, inviting democratic relations in class and democratic action outside class (whereas Vygotsky did not foreground power relations as the social context for learning). (12)

Ricardo's understanding of the class structure and the passage are accurate, even if his interpretations of Shor's points are not fully articulated. In what seems to be an obvious omission, Ricardo does not directly address my role as the teacher, a move that puzzled me and encouraged me, upon reflection, to look at my practices more closely. He says that he sees how our class fulfills Shor's model of critical literacy because "the class' participants are becoming agents of the democratization of the classroom." He explains this process as opportunities students have to speak with authority in all class discussions when he says, "First we study complex arguments and discuss them in class, and then we build our expertise in literacy criticism: hence this reflects in an authorial voice when we answer questions." The "authorial voice" here is another reference to Bakhtin and the process of dialogics that enable voices from many strata of society to unmask authorial discourse, thereby revealing the ideological assumptions represented by the dialogue.

What he has left unsaid, however, interests me most of all. In taking a closer look at my praxis in light of our exchange, I notice several things that I had not considered before. Although I had never fancied myself as the kind of radical pedagogue that Shor describes, I have made numerous efforts to "invite democratic relations in" the class. Ricardo has made me realize that my reader response assignment, as scripted as it is, does invite students to speak from their world perspectives even as they are grounded in the authorial discourse of the text. It also invites students to select the texts to which they most want to respond. The ethnographic assignment, which I have used in all levels of composition classes, provides an opportunity for students to examine literacies that affect their own lives but that also move "into deepening interrogations of knowledge in its global contexts." The assignment also provides me with insight into the "needs, conditions, speech habits, and perceptions of the students," which I then use to help design activities and integrate in my own expertise (Shor 12). Like Shor suggests, I am working to learn "how to design the course *with* the students (co-governance)." My students also contributed to the development of class exams and shared responsibility for developing the final class project. And the class syllabus is modified often to respond to student needs and class goals. Finally, nearly all class discussions begin with the students. They either read from their reader responses or take us to key passages that they have identified for us to discuss.

Ricardo does point out a level of dissident politics that my class fosters as he addresses how the course will apply to dialogic praxis in his future work. He asks, "[w]ill this experience serve us in the future when teaching our own class? Yes." But, again, he leaves unspoken whether dissident politics play a role in our class. I said to him in a subsequent discussion in my office that I did not foreground dissident politics in my own class as much as Shor would expect. As I reflect further, I do not believe I have yet learned all that I need to know for effective co-governance of my classes.

Like Ricardo, I realize just how much effort is involved in maintaining consistent democratic values within the academy. In the final, pivotal move of his e-mail message, he explains how the structure of my class has shown him that "democracy is something that one works very hard at, and that one must participate diligently in to maintain it." Ricardo has in fact worked hard. He assumed the responsibility of reading Shor's chapter in my absence and responded online when his classmates were devoting their time to studying for the exam and other concerns. His efforts explain the jibe he gave the class about their "lack of commitment." He has demonstrated his ability to identify a passage in Shor's long and complex chapter that both spoke to the text and his experiences in ways that helped him reveal his interpretation and assumptions to his classmates. He positioned his initial statement so that theory could break out over these issues, which provoked me into dialogue with him and helped me reflect on my praxis in ways that I have not before.

He closes his final e-mail response by citing a passage from a previous class reading, Freire's "The Adult Literacy Process as Cultural

Action for Freedom and Education and Conscientização." He interprets Freire concluding,

> as Freire puts it, to view the subject as vessel to be filled by the word is erroneous thinking, but that the subject, the learner, forms a base of knowledge in which allows one to critically interact with the educator, this is in essence the role of democracy in the class-room.

Starting with that first e-mail post, Ricardo asserted his role as a co-teacher, and, in my responses to him, I asserted my role as a co-learner of our class. Our ongoing exchanges during the remainder of the class and beyond lead me to believe that he will continue to interact critically with educators in future classes and other social contexts. I have had a chance to witness how my aims for teaching have been meaningful not only to Ricardo but also through him to myself. My next challenges are to find ways to extend the work he and I have begun to other students and other classes.

WORKS CITED

Bakhtin, Mikhail. "Discourse in Life and Discourse in Art (Concerning Sociological Poetics)." *Contemporary Literary Criticism: Literary and Cultural Studies*. 2nd ed. Eds. Robert Con Davis and Ronald Schleifer. New York: Longman, 1989.

Bartholomae, David and Anthony Petrosky. "Introduction." *Ways of Reading*. New York: St. Martin's Press, 1987.

Bleich, David. *Readings and Feelings: An Introduction to Subjective Criticism*. Urbana, IL: National Council of Teachers of English, 1975.

Clifford, John. "Enacting Critical Literacy." *The Right to Literacy*. Eds. Andrea Lunsford, Helene Moglen and James Slevin. New York: MLA, 1990. 254–261.

Galin, Jeffrey R. "Syllabus." *English 1101: College Writing I*, 2000. Florida Atlantic University. 4 Apr. 2001 <http://www.english.fau.edu/faculty/galin/classes/1101f00/syllabus.htm>.

———. "RE: ira shore, galin rhetoric class." E-mail to Kari, Danielle, Layla, and Ricardo. 02 Mar 2001.

Gee, James Paul. *Social Linguistics and Literacies: Ideology in Discourses*. 2nd ed. London: Taylor & Francis, 1996.

Graff, Gerald. "Debate the Canon in Class." *Harper's*, Apr. 1991. 31-32ff.

Rosenblatt, Louise M. *Literature as Exploration*. 4th ed. New York: MLA, 1976.

Schuster, Charles. "The Ideology of Illiteracy: A Bakhtinian Perspective." *The Right to Literacy*. Eds. Andrea Lunsford, Helene Moglen and James Slevin. New York: MLA, 1990, 225-232.

Shor, Ira. *Critical Literacy in Action: Writing Words, Changing Worlds*. Portsmouth, NH: Boynton/Cook, 1999.

Vazquez, Ricardo Marcello "ira shor, galin rhetoric class." E-mail to Kari, Danielle, Layla, and Jeffrey. 02 Mar 2001.

——. "Re: ira shore, galin rhetoric class." E-mail to Kari, Danielle, Layla, and Jeffrey. 03 Mar. 2001.

——. "Re: ricardo." E-mail to Jeffrey. 05 Mar. 2001.

28

RHETORICAL BURSTS
IN THE LATE AGE OF PRINT

Helen Rothschild Ewald
Iowa State University

Course architecture can encourage agency in first-year writing courses by inviting students to participate in ways commonly reserved for teachers. This chapter focuses on a class magazine assignment that features students acting not only as contributing writers but also as editors, designers, and reviewers. It argues that teachers have to look to the culture and, specifically, to the students' cultural spaces to understand how to start bridging the gap between the students' tacit knowledge of how texts work and the teacher's specialized knowledge of how academic writing works.

In the final chapter of *Assuming the Positions: Cultural Pedagogy and the Politics of Commonplace Writing*, Susan Miller remarks that "Bursts of rhetorically prescribed literary imitation fill many pages of this collection" (254). Such bursts represent for Miller a "heroic" attempt of writers to redefine authorship in terms of commonplace texts, first recognized by Aristotle and in later centuries labeled as "low" modes of writing by various rhetoricians. Occupying the space between *belles lettres* and text acts that are culturally not assigned authorship, low modes include texts such as daily menus posted on a signboard outside a restaurant or employment application forms or instructions for assembling a mail order item. These bursts of rhetorically prescribed efforts to which Miller refers, in fact, represent a heritage that may well culminate in "late age of print" commonplace writings such as diaries, letters sent via snail mail, scribbled notes posted on refrigerators, and, ironically, the types of writing we assign in first-year writing classes.

Although I have become increasingly sanguine concerning the function of generic modes or conventions in writing and the important role imitation of such conventions plays in literacy training, I still tend to approach first-year writing classes from the perspective of helping students "find an effective way of saying what they want to say." This impulse is represented in the assignment that informs my discussion below. This assignment, a class magazine, can be best understood as part of a course architecture designed to encourage student agency in authorship. By *course architecture*, I mean

> the management of assignments and activities that make up the day-to-day functioning of the class and, in particular, the ways in which classroom assignments and activities encourage or discourage interaction among disciplinary knowledge and students' varied knowledge and experiences. (see *Mutuality* 68)

By *agency* I mean "both the ability to interpret events as well as the ability to influence, change, or redirect them within a specific situation" ("Exploring Agency" 343). The class magazine assignment itself entails not only the requirement that each student will write for the magazine, but also the expectation that each student will serve in staff positions, such as editor, graphic designer, peer reviewer, or producer.

Students assume agency in their roles both as staff members and as writers. As staff members, students are responsible for generating and circulating tough but fair criteria for submitting manuscripts and for participating in the review and acceptance of those manuscripts. In so doing, students take their tacit knowledge of magazines as a genre and apply this knowledge to decide what their section of the magazine will include. Students explicitly express this tacit understanding in their calls for contributions and in the examples they bring in for potential student contributors to view and to follow. As staff, students also commonly generate "themes" for their magazine sections. Furthermore, students make sure that the writing submitted meets the course requirement that the magazine focus on *academic writing*. Students' interpretation of what constitutes academic writing, however, is usually quite broad and can include the expected essays and analyses, as well as interviews, book and media reviews, feature stories and other reportage, and other commonplace writing to which Miller refers. Students are also responsible for formatting the magazine and participating in other aspects of its production. As writers, students are responsible for meeting student-generated criteria in a timely fashion. As they meet these criteria, students concurrently decide how they will fulfill the course requirements of contributing at least 5-7 pages of approved text to each issue; students can write one five-page piece, or, say, one two-page piece and one three-page piece for each issue in question. As contributors, class members are expected to write more than one draft of their submissions and to make every effort to fulfill the expectations articulated in calls for contributions, to follow suggestions of the peer reviewers, and to adhere to the schedule set forth by magazine staff members.

The actual submission I cite here was written in our first-year, first-semester composition course (English 104) here at Iowa State University, a land grant institution with about 26,000 students. In addition to having a large first-year English program, the English Department at Iowa State offers a BA in English and a BS in Technical Communication, MAs in Linguistics, Literature, and Rhetoric, Composition, and Professional Communication, and a PhD in Rhetoric and Professional Communication. The department had recently instituted a TA training program in which senior staff, such as myself, taught first-year courses and, in the process, mentored several TAs, who, during their first semester, observed classes, taught selected lessons in their mentor's classes, and interacted with students. The bulk of first-year writing courses are taught in computer labs. Students can, and many do, place out of English 104 by virtue of SAT or ACT scores and a writing sample given during orientation.

In contributing this assignment to the magazine, the student, Markeeta Keyes, addressed a "call for contributions" posted by student staff for "current events" following the theme of "music." For this issue, students had designated that movie, software, and especially CD reviews as well as feature articles, music video reports, and current events were needed. Markeeta responded to a call for a "current events" discussion under the general theme of "music." She focused on Internet resources and benefited from on-line peer review of drafts of her manuscript. She submitted a final article entitled "The Death of Tupac Amaru Shakur." The article consisted of both factual information on Shakur's life and, as announced by Markeeta, "my own personal viewpoints about the topics Tupac rapped about and even his own life compared to that of present day youth."

Markeeta's agency with this submission is reflected not only in her choice of assignment and of topic but also in her interweaving of factual and personal detail in her submitted account, as her opening sentences show:

> Tupac Amaru Shakur was called a gangsta rapper by critics, because of his explicit lyrics and his violent history. But to his fans 2pac was a rap artist who could put reality into rhythm and song, and make a person sympathize with his situation, or connect the meaning of their own life struggles. To 2pac's fans he was like a guiding light, a man who had suffered many of the hardships and troubles of everyday youth, from drugs, to living in poverty, being fatherless, and a parent on drugs, and he showed that he could survive. For the youth of today, he was a sign that they could suffer and struggle and still be successful in life.

Later in her article, Markeeta reveals her own system of values when she asserts,

> His lyrics no doubt were full of much demeanor towards women, and much hate which epitomized his childhood, but as he grew . . . his maturity began to show. He was planning on building a safe house for trouble teens, his belief in God was outspoken, and marriage was even on his agenda.

Such interweaving continues as she comments:

> It was also very hard for Tupac to accept the fact that he was fatherless and this made it harder for him to feel like a man. He said this in a Vibe magazine May issue, "It made me bitter seeing all those other niggas' with fathers gettin' answers to questions that I have. Even now I still don't get'em."

Following the researched biographical information on Tupac, Markeeta concludes her account with a mix of opinion and fact consistent with the rest of her piece:

> Unfortunately Tupac is no longer with us, but his words of wisdom and his experiences from his own life will live with us forev-

er. Tupac Amaru Shakur, one of the most successful rappers in the year 2000, was critically shot on Saturday, September 7, 1996.

Markeeta's contribution was judged a success by the student editors and, after some revision required by peer reviewers, printed in the class magazine.

This course architecture invites students to participate in some ways commonly reserved for teachers. Namely, the class magazine assignment fosters student agency in areas such as:

- task definition—as staff members, determining the way the section of the magazine will look; and, as writers, deciding what their contribution(s) will be;
- paper evaluation—as staff members, articulating criteria for contributions and peer reviewing manuscripts accordingly; and, as writers, revising drafts for publication according to student-generated criteria and comments;
- genre description—as staff members, describing the range of submissions needed in calls for manuscripts and providing examples of wanted contributions; and, as writers, deciding what writing strategies will fulfill staff expectations (Markeeta, for example, decided that a mix of personal and researched information was appropriate);
- assignment logistics—as staff members, setting up deadlines for drafts, times for peer review sessions, meetings for production, and so on; and, as writers, determining how to meet the 5-7 page requirement in the submissions for each issue.

I believe that students as writers can, through such course architecture, actually learn to recognize what text plans work best to express "what a student has to say" while still meeting various conventional expectations regarding text in print. In this case, expectations were set forth in specific submission guidelines drafted by the students as editors, working to put together this section of the magazine issue. These expectations, as I am quick to point out to the class, represent tacit understandings of how various types of writing for magazines work and of how well the individual contributions meet those expectations. These expectations also represent the literacies that students bring to the table in this writing class. To encourage student participation, I generally serve as more of a consultant than a teacher during class sessions, and most of the "direct teaching" on my part takes place opportunistically or inductively. This is not to say, however, that I believe that writing cannot be taught.

In *Paralogic Rhetoric: A Theory of Communicative Interaction,* Thomas Kent explains the futility of Edward Corbett's frustration as he contemplates what he sees as the impossibilities of teaching writing.

> Corbett's uneasiness derives, I believe, from his stalwart but mis-guided conviction that writing can be taught. He presupposes that writing—and probably reading, too—constitutes a body of knowl-edge, or a skill, or a process that may be codified in some way and then taught to others. Of course, I have been arguing throughout this book that discourse production and reception cannot be reduced to discrete processes, systems, or methodologies and, as a result, cannot be taught. (157)

It has been my experience, however, that English 104 students, rather than thinking writing cannot be taught, often are convinced that writing cannot be learned. What my the student-run magazine assignment does for teachers is to free their syllabi from the expectation that reducing writing to discrete processes is the key to teaching writing (e.g., "today we will learn about thesis sentences" or "today we will practice using outside sources"); what the student-run magazine assignment does for the students is free them from the idea that they don't know anything or haven't learned anything about writing. The student-run magazine pro-vides an occasion for writing that invites students to parlay their own lit-eracies into a publication that represents what this writing community knows about writing, about the world, and about finished texts. Because students, mentors, and teachers in this class bring different literacies to the table, the environment fairly crackles with mutuality in knowledge making.[1] In "Tupac," Markeeta blends what she knows about Tupac from her personal background, home community, and national reports and in this way creates meaning from a [then] current event.

But, if course architecture that depends on students bringing their own literacies to the table is to continue in such first-year writing courses, teachers not only will have to help students redefine their per-ceptions of what constitutes discourse, but they also will have to seek to redefine their own. That is, teachers will have to look to the culture and, specifically, to the students' cultural spaces, to understand where to start in bridging the gap between students' tacit knowledge of how texts

---

[1]See *Mutuality in the Rhetoric and Composition Classroom* for further dis-cussion of course architecture and mutuality. See also the sometimes ironic outcome of not consistently honoring the strategies discussed here in "A Tangled Web of Discourses: On Post-Process Pedagogy and Communicative Interaction."

work and teachers' specialized knowledge of how academic writing works. And, at this point in our culture, students' tacit knowledge includes—for better or worse—an understanding how electronic discourses work. If we accept Dewey's claim that the acquisition of new knowledge depends on links to what students already know, then the course architecture of any given course *must* continue to depend on students bringing their own knowledge to the table. And, in today's culture, there is no "if" to including in that knowledge an understanding of electronic discourses.

Any move to incorporate students' knowledge of electronic texts in teaching academic writing is, of course, fraught with difficulties. In one sense, these difficulties resemble those basic writing teachers have long experienced in trying to translate students' facility with oral discourse into knowledge about how to construct written texts. Orality and literacy, when defined as the ability to read and write, may share common ground, but one is not the other. This said, orality has never been the threat to text-based literacies that digital and visual literacies represent. The dangerous nature of digital and visual literacies, however, does not change the fact that writing teachers, in the end, will do well to access students' understanding of electronic discourses in teaching text-based academic discourse. The danger these digital and visual literacies pose to text-based literacies can indeed be productively understood within a Deweyan framework, where a "strategy of reconciling traditionally opposed forces by showing ways in which they cooperate and interact" is central (see Fishman and McCarthy 16). Ironically, accessing the students' tacit knowledge of digital and visual literacies will in most cases enable mutuality, if only because many students tend to know more about surfing the net and constructing web pages than do their technologically beleaguered instructors. In fact, I must admit that the class magazine of my 104 students has transformed itself into a web-based anthology for my 105 honors sections (http://www.public.iastate.edu/~rhetoric/). This move, however, did not dramatically change the nature of the academic discourse itself. In fact, the class anthology on the web featured writing that, textually, more closely conformed to traditional expectations of academic and professional discourse than did the contributions to the 104 magazine. With the potential audience of student peers, other university personages, and—perhaps most importantly—parents, the 105 students mined their past knowledge of school writing to display the admittedly conservative strategies for writing that underpinned my course: line of argument, specific support, and focus. These strategies were operational in both academic and professional writing options in the syllabus. In short, the bursts of rhetorically based writing on line did not break new textual ground.

Our "escape" in 105H from any redefinition of academic writing, however, might represent a missed opportunity. And I'm happy to report that it's an opportunity that I did not miss on the graduate level, when one of my students wanted to submit an "electronic dissertation." In this instance, we successfully redefined what "dissertation" meant at Iowa State. In addition, I, frankly, don't see electronic discourses as the death knell of text-based discourses, any more than "low modes of writing" have marked the passing of *belles lettres*. (At least, the "electronic office" has, in my experience, generated more paper/text rather than less.) The challenge, to use Davidson's language, is to recognize the potential of all types of discourse knowledge in our prior theories to create a passing theories about academic discourse that work for teachers and students alike in this late age of print.

WORKS CITED

Davidson, Donald. "A Nice Derangement of Epitaphs." *Truth and Interpretation: Perspectives on the Philosophy of Donald Davidson*. Ed. Ernest Le Pore. New York: Blackwell, 1986. 433-46.

Ewald, Helen Rothschild and David L. Wallace. "Exploring Agency in Classroom Discourse or, Should David have Told his Story?" *College Composition and Communication* 45.3 (October 1994): 342-368.

___. "A Tangled Web of Discourses: On Post-Process Pedagogy and Communicative Interaction." *Post-Process Theory: New Directions for Composition Research*. Ed. Thomas Kent. Carbondale: Southern Illinois UP, 1999. 116-31.

Fishman, Stephen M. and Lucille McCarthy. *John Dewey and the Challenge of Classroom Practice*. New York: Teachers College P, 1998.

Kent, Thomas. *Paralogic Rhetoric: A Theory of Communicative Interaction*. Lewisburg: Bucknell UP, 1993.

Miller, Susan. *Assuming the Positions: Cultural Pedagogy and the Politics of Commonplace Writing*. Pittsburgh: U of Pittsburgh P, 1998.

Wallace, David L. and Helen Rothschild Ewald. *Mutuality in the Rhetoric and Composition Classroom*. Carbondale: Southern Illinois UP, 2000.

29

UNDERSTANDING DIFFICULTIES
A Heuristic

Mariolina Rizzi Salvatori
University of Pittsburgh

"Understanding Difficulties: A Heuristic" is a theoretical reflection on a particular teaching experience. The context for the experience is a freshman composition course titled "Writing About/Through Poetry." The chapter examines the texts students produced in response to a particular assignment (the "Difficulty Paper") that required them to confront and to reflect on some of the difficulties they encountered as they read selected contemporary American poems. This particular teaching and learning experience suggests that what students often identify as a reading difficulty may be instead their incipient, not-yet articulated, recognition of the particular demands the text they are reading is making on them.

p.s. Lest my "Difficulty Paper" assignment be turned into a "teaching tip," I urge readers to pay attention not so much to what I do as to why I do it: my theoretical understanding of what reading and writing are, their interconnectedness, and the cultural and institutional context that make my work possible.

You can expect to write regularly in this course. In preparation for
class discussion and writing assignments, you will write short (1/2
to 1 page) "difficulty papers": these are papers in which you identify and begin to hypothesize the reasons for any possible difficulty
you might be experiencing as you read a poem. Each week, you
will write a difficulty paper on one or more of the assigned poems.
Each week, I will select one or two of them as unusual or representative examples of the readings you produce. I will photocopy,
distribute, and use them to ground our discussions. My goal, in
doing so, is to move all of us from judging a difficulty as a reader's
inability to understand a text to discerning in it a reader's incipient
awareness of the particular "demands" imposed by the
language/structure/style/content of a text.

The excerpt above is from my course description for a freshman
composition course titled "Writing About/Through Poetry." The use of
reading in composition courses, in fact teaching writing through reading,
is something that I have argued for and written about since my first foray
into the field of composition (Salvatori 1983, 1986, 1996). And the use
of poetry to teach sentence boundary, paraphrase, coordination, subordi-
nation and other formal aspects of writing, is a regular practice of mine.
But focusing an entire term of freshman composition on poetry is something I had never done before 1994. The conceptualization of this particular required freshman composition course came about "by accident,"
the result of and compromise for a scheduling difficulty. When, because
of a breakdown in communication with the advising office, the "Writing
About/Through Poetry" course I had proposed to teach at a more
advanced level did not register enough students, the director of our composition program suggested I adapt the work I had already planned to
the needs and demands of the freshman writing class.[1]

I still remember the collective gasp and the palpable dismay of
the 22 students packed in the small rectangular smoldering classroom
on a late August afternoon. I was fully aware of and uneasy about the

[1] I want to make sure that neither the director of composition's decision, or
my compliance with it, be misread. Although I have alluded to the "acciden-
tal" genesis of the course, there was nothing improvised or off the cuff about
teaching it. When Joseph Harris asked me to do it, and I accepted, we both
knew that it could and would be responsibly done. I am theoretically and ethically opposed to constructions of teaching that rely on a teacher's improvisa-
tion. For a discussion of this issue and its historical antecedents, see my
Pedagogy: Disturbing History, 1819-1929. For several theoretical reflections
on teaching and the teaching of teaching, see *Reader: Essays in Reader-
Oriented Theory, Criticism, and Pedagogy.* 33/34 (Spring/Fall 1995).

double jeopardy they had been put in (and my own complicity with it). They were taking a required course in composition and, as if that were not bad enough, they were told on the first day of class that they were going to read and write about poetry, a genre not too many students seem to appreciate (at least in many classrooms). When I read the course description to them and elaborated on it, the tension seemed to ease a bit. Yet, at the end of class, a small contingent of students came to tell me that they were going to change sections. Graciously, one of them wanted me to know that poetry, not I, was driving him away.

Next class they were all there, some of them quite despondent. All the other sections of freshman composition were closed: they had no immediate way out. I wondered what went through the minds of those who had openly announced their displeasure. Could I ever earn their trust? I worried. Over the Labor Day weekend, I looked at the writing they had produced in class in response to the "diagnostic" (a brief history of themselves as readers) and at my class notes.

Quite a few, indeed more than those who had made it public, affirmed their dislike of poetry. But, as I had noticed on prior occasions, what my students systematically presented as indictments of the genre, or admissions of their shortcomings as readers, struck me as plausible and insightful readings. In fact, what they cited as the reasons for their dislikes were actually enumerations of foundational formal, rhetorical, and structural features of the genre, or descriptions of responses activated by those very features. I decided then that the "difficulty paper" assignment (a strategy I have devised and have used over the years when I want to pinpoint and textualize otherwise invisible moments of difficulty in reading, writing, thinking)[2] should systematically function as the spine of this course. The first paragraph of the detailed syllabus they received on the second day of class (see "Course Description, Cont'd") briefly describes this assignment, its rationale and function.

Let me turn now to the kind of work this approach can make possible. Here are four different responses to the difficulty paper assignment. They describe the difficulties four students experienced with particular poems. The texts they are responding to can be found in the Poulin edition of *Contemporary American Poetry*, but they can be easily found in other anthologies as well. I should emphasize that in my courses I regularly use student responses to this assignment to begin and to ground our collaborative explorations and theorizations of reading and writing. Texts like the ones I reproduce here are written before class discussion, without any suggestion from me beyond the prompts of the dif-

[2]For an early articulation of my work with "difficulty," and the scholarly texts that shaped it, see my "Toward a Hermeneutics of Difficulty."

ficulty paper assignment. This practice enables me to hold back, to pay close attention to features of texts that students find difficult, and to turn them into opportunities for recursive thinking, for hermeneutic reflections.[3]

September 12, 1994

The selection of poems I just read seem to be related by the fact that they all integrate forces of nature. The poems make the subject of the poem seem helpless when contrasted with the forces of maturing, snow, and darkness. The poems have an ominous mood to them, making one feel small compared to the huge world surrounding him.

One poem that gave me trouble is "The Hermit" by Robert Bly. The poem begins in a frightening way, as if something is falling uncontrollably. I feel I must read it quickly as if darkness is enveloping me. My difficulty comes in the last line, when "they" see a hermit and want to sail into "joyful death." The poem begins with such an uneasy feeling to it, and suddenly the mood becomes soothing with talk of death.

Another poem that causes me difficulty is "Looking into the Tide Pool" by Robert Bly. Bly begins by portraying the tide pool as a tranquil, innocent body of water "clear, tiny white-shell people on the bottom, asking nothing, not even directions." The seaweed just moves slowly back

---

[3]In the Composition Program at the University of Pittsburgh it is common practice to discuss theoretical issues of reading and writing by focusing on the writing students produce in response to our course assignments. At the beginning of the term, teachers circulate a form that (1) briefly explains the use of student papers, (2) gives students the option to deny consent to publicly discuss their writing, and (3) promises that their writing will be discussed anonymously.

In every class I teach, undergraduate or graduate, I begin by upholding the convention of anonymity. (But invariably, after a couple of weeks, students begin revealing and reclaiming their authorship in class discussions. I always look forward to this moment: it marks, for me, students' investment in the work they are doing, and their trust toward their classmates and teacher.)

Consonant with this convention, in this chapter I do not disclose the names of the authors of the papers. The names (actually "first names," a convention I have argued against since I wrote this piece) I chose to refer to them are actually the names of people I dearly love—family members. I do this, and make it public, to signal that although it is their *texts* I discuss, the four women who produced these texts are still very real and dear to me. For this piece, I had to get in touch with them six years after the fact, to obtain their consent to publish. On that occasion, I was moved by their graciousness, and by that of their parents, who gave me their current addresses. I am deeply grateful.

and forth. Bly reverses the mood by writing "the heeler sings wildly, shouting to Jesus and his dead mother." I do not understand how this fits into the poem.

The common confusion I had in regard to all poems is the poet's decision to reverse the flow of the poem quickly. Many begin in an uneasy way and suddenly change to an unlifting mood. Or, the poem begins calmly and quickly becomes uneasy. In general, though, I feel I have a good understanding of the poems and found enjoyment in them.

October 17, 1994

When I read the poem "Those Winter Days" by Robert Hayden, I was confused by the last two lines and how they related to the rest of the poem. The entire poem had a very rough and harsh tone, except for the last two lines in which he mentions the word "love." I did not comprehend how these two different ideas or feelings were connected.

The poet discussed his father throughout this poem. When I first read the poem, I only saw the rough qualities of his father. Hayden used many distinct and very descriptive words in order for the reader to attain this image. He used the phrase "cracked hands that ached / from labor" to show how hard his father worked. Hayden also described his fear of the "chronic angers" in his house. These descriptions did not give me an image of love as it is mentioned in the last line.

Then I discovered that this poet is talking about love throughout the whole poem, even in the first two stanzas. Although, this love is a different kind of love than the obvious. His father shows his family an indirect love. He did not come out and display his affections, but he rather did the necessary things that this person took for granted. He went to work in the most severe weather to provide for his family. He woke up extra early to make the house warm. When I looked at the term love in this manner I understood the connection better. He did so many things for this person and his family, but nobody realized that these things were his way of expressing love.

October 18, 1994

I found "The Mirror" by Louise Gluck to be a very interesting poem. When I read it through the first couple of times, I knew I missed something at the beginning (or did not read the words in the right manner) because the line "needing to show me how you scrape the flesh away" didn't make much sense. I also felt I was not grasping the meaning of the poem after the first readings.

I re-read the poem many times, and concentrated mainly on the first lines because I felt I was missing something, and I was.

It was in the way I was reading lines through three and four. I was reading "why do you not love / but cut yourself" as the speaker asking the man shaving why he did not love her, but I found if I paused after "cut" and not at the end of the third line, I got a totally different meaning. She was asking him why he didn't love himself. I realized that this was exactly what I was missing in the earlier readings, and the poem fit together much better.

I believe that because the man who is shaving is "beautiful," the speaker thinks he should love himself and is perplexed because he is mutilating himself, purposely, in front of her. She begins to think that he is doing it as a way of expressing himself. After making this connection, the eighth line which gave me trouble before actually became the line which pulled the whole poem together for me.

The man is scraping his flesh away to reveal to his friend that he is not the perfect man she thinks he is.

He is trying to show her that he, indeed, has problems and troubles, but keeps them "under his skin" because he knows he would not be "desirable" to her if she knew.

October 24, 1994

I found all of this week's poems particularly difficult. I could not begin to find meaning in them. I tried to use the techniques that were always helpful to me, but I still could not understand them.

Looking at a "Poem," by Donald Justice, I discovered many obscurities, for example: throughout the poem, the poet seems to be putting down the purpose of reading poetry. He says that people begin to vanish as soon as they begin to read a poem. They do not totally go into the depth of the poem. Instead they hope that the poem is soon over because they do not want to study it. Justice also says that the reader cannot and should not understand the poem. Doesn't this appear a little confusing? All this time I thought poetry was meaningful and symbolic, and then this poet goes and contradicts everything that I thought poetry was.

It just surprised me in such a way that I really began to wonder if I had misinterpreted this poem; however I remembered what I had just read in Crossman's essay. In the essay it stated that the reader does in fact make meaning. By this statement I can assume that my interpreta-

tion is the meaning that I believe this poem generates. Even with this resolved, I still am dumbfounded as to why a poet would write so carelessly and harshly against his profession.

After reading the bibliography section about Justice, I had a clearer image of what he wrote about in his poems. One of his characteristics is "loss" and "his profound acceptance of human condition as he finds it." Once I read this information, I began to make a connection with the poem. I believe he wrote this poem to bring out both of the previous points. He informs us how we generally look at poetry boring and non-informative. Think about this, though; he writes about loss. He tells the reader how he/she, generally, reacts to poetry. From this information I concluded that he wants people to realize that by looking at poetry in this way, the reader is only hurting him/herself. It is the reader's loss, since he/she does not want to open his/her mind and venture into poetry. By writing how we, the readers, look at poetry, I believe he has made me more aware of the loss that many people experience.

In response to his "profound acceptance of human condition as he finds it," I believe he also wrote this poem to show the readers that he is aware of the fact that not all of them enjoy poetry. I think it is important to take note that he is not critical of those who do not have a sense for poems. As part of the loss that the reader experiences he also experiences a loss. He is unable to share his thoughts with another person, particularly the reader. Fortunately he is able to accept the way people look at poetry, and he is able to write about it without criticizing the individual readers.

In my course description, I usually mention only two functions of the difficulty papers (identification of difficulty and reflexive engagements with it). But they serve other functions as well. They offer what composition theorist Ann E. Berthoff, drawing from I. A. Richards (who with C. S. Pierce and Suzanne Lange constitutes the philosophical triad that most shaped her thinking) would call an "assisted invitation."[4] They urge students to do "demanding work," but they go

---

[4]In *The Making of Meaning*, Ann E. Berthoff writes: "When we offer what I call, after I. A. Richards, 'assisted invitations' to students to use their minds in looking at things, we're also exercising the capacity to form concepts. Perception is not something that comes first and then we get ideas; perception is itself a construing, an interpretation, a making of meaning, a composing" (37). Actually, although Ann Berthoff gives credit to Richards' conceptualization of "assisted invitations," I see Richards' approach to teaching as often punitive and condescending. Berthoff's articulation of the work teachers must learn to do with their students is enabling in ways that Richards' is not.

beyond the hortatory move.[5] They provide them with procedures that teach them to look at, to acknowledge, even to name, the kind of work that a specific text demands of them as readers.[6]

Consider these four difficulty papers; consider how uncannily they record and map out the work each reader might do beyond what she has already done. The difficulty each reader identifies is, in part, a function of her assumptions about interpretation in general, and interpretation of poetry in particular. What deserves notice is that what the student identifies as her difficulty in understanding the poem, as something that, she thinks, prevents her from making sense of it, can be for a trained reader "an understanding difficulty," that is, a difficulty that marks an understanding of the kind of work the text activates and opens up for interpretation.

---

[5]hortatory, adj. "Characterized by or given to exhortation or strong urging." *The American Heritage Dictionary*. Here is an example of what I call the hortatory mode: "We read deeply for varied reasons, most of them familiar: that we cannot know enough people profoundly enough; that we need to know ourselves better; that we require knowledge, not just of self and others, but of the way things are. Yet the strongest, most authentic motive for deep reading of the now much-abused traditional canon is the search for a difficult pleasure. I am not exactly an erotics-of-reading purveyor, and a pleasurable difficulty seems to me a plausible definition of the Sublime, but a higher pleasure remains the reader's quest. There is reader's Sublime, and it seems the only secular transcendence we can ever attain, except for the even more precarious transcendence we call "falling in love." "I urge you to find what truly comes near to you, that can be used for weighing and for considering. Read deeply, not to believe, not to accept, not to contradict, but to learn to share in that one nature that writes and reads." Harold Bloom, *How to Read and Why* 28-29.

I feel compelled to ask, to whom is Bloom's eloquent advice addressed? How would students who have been "trained" to think of difficulties as impediments, or failures to understand, respond to Bloom's hortatory teaching? How might they experience its eloquence? I am not trying to make light of Bloom's "difficult pleasures." What I am suggesting is that teachers' enthusiasm and exhortations will not, cannot, by themselves, produce these effects in students, unless students are already culturally and educationally predisposed to them. (And this is not an indictment of students.) But teachers can, and should, make sure more students experience the pleasure of this accomplishment, by devising appropriate strategies that can enable them to perceive difficulties' potential for understanding.

[6]As a matter of theoretical coherence, I do not identify difficulties for my students. When students identify their own difficulties, their acts of identification set up for them and their teachers an area of investigation and a process of inquiry that will vary according to who they are, their reflexivity about their

As I read these difficulty papers, again, after several years, I am struck by the immediacy with which each student provisionally captures through her writing the features of the poems her reading has actualized. "Pia," the author of the first paper, reads the cluster of assigned poems in terms of "the forces of nature" and of the mood of helplessness they evoke when they are contrasted with the smallness of the individual in relation "to the huge world surrounding him." And then she focuses on two specific poems, and identifies the difficulty they pose for her, in terms of "the poet's decision to reverse the flow of the poem so quickly." Particularly striking, I think, is Pia's materialization of that ominous feeling. She makes fear palpable: "The poem begins in a frightening way, as if something is falling uncontrollably. I feel I must read it quickly because it seems as if darkness is enveloping me." In spite of her confusion, the student claims in the last line that she has a good understanding of the poem(s). What does "good understanding" mean in this context? This is a place in the difficulty paper where the teacher could profitably intervene, asking questions that put the student in a position to hypothesize and reflect on the reasons why the poet might have planned the sudden turn, and why she finds the turn disorienting. And this is the place in the difficulty paper where the student might begin to reconceive her difficulty as an interpretive key. Writing later in the term, the authors of the other papers demonstrate a trained ability to endure the difficulty, to trace and then retrace it, reading it for interpretive directions. "Olga," the second student, reads and rereads the poem, returning to, rather than moving away from, the moment of difficulty. As she reflects on it, she discovers in a "pause," an absence, a moment of suspended activity, a structural feature, a way of coming to terms with what Louise Glück's poem might possibly mean. "And then the eighth line which gave me trouble before actually became the line which pulled the whole poem together for me": this is a sign of remarkable prosodic sophistication; it is in the rhythm, in the movement of verses, that Olga finds her clue for understanding the poem.

Like the first, the third student, "Giulia," reads for connections, for "consistency building." The mention of "love" in a poem that she thinks is characterized by a rough and harsh tone, surprises her at first, until she understands what she claims the narrator and his family did not understand: that what this father with "cracked hands that

cultural location, reading practices, poetic forms, their assumptions about teaching and learning. Thus the work that a student's identification of difficulties sets in motion can more effectively attend to his or her specific needs and abilities. The challenge for teachers is to orchestrate collective discussions out of individual needs and observations.

ached/from labor" gives his family is "indirect love." (The student mis-quotes the title: "Those Winter Days" rather than "Those Winter Sundays," a trace of a misreading her teacher can lead her to reflect on so as to open up a space for revision.)

"Franca," the fourth student, discovers that the techniques that have proven helpful to her so far do not clear up the obscurities of Donald Justice's "Poem." Even Robert Crossman's assertion that "the reader does in fact make meaning" (which she seems to take as license to construct *any* meaning), does not satisfy her. And so she deploys a different strategy: she looks for help in the biographical notes. Therein she reads about Justice's exploration of "loss" and his "profound accep-tance of the human condition." Through these two themes she makes an effective connection with the poem, which allows her finally to con-struct this layered understanding of the "loss" of which the poem speaks. It is a loss that one definition alone cannot quite capture: it is the loss of readers who look at poetry as boring and uninformative; the loss of the poet who cannot share his thoughts with unreceptive readers; and then there is a kind of productive loss, one that effects some changes: it is the poet's "letting go" of what he expects of readers, which leads to his "acceptance" of the "human" (educational?) condi-tion: the fact that not all readers enjoy poetry.

*　　*　　*

Why, when students are introduced to difficult texts, do so many of them assume they are justified in turning away from them? Why is it that to name a text as difficult seems to trigger, in many stu-dents, disengaged, dismissive, patronizing, even chastising responses? (And there is also, the "I am not smart enough to do this kind of work" response, which always wounds me deeply.) Actually, I think these responses are not surprising. Students' (and teachers') consistent and persistent avoidance of difficulties, particularly in entry-level courses, bespeaks the effects of educational approaches that, by streamlining and providing answers for difficulties, nurture continuous dependence on a hierarchy of experts, most of whom are unwilling or unable to share with others the processes that enabled them to acquire and amass their cultural capital.

What I find startling, arresting, year after year, is that some of the students who believe, or have been led to believe, that they are not fluent, sophisticated, readers are precisely the ones who demonstrate a remarkable awareness of textual bumps, irregularities, twists, devia-tions from or transgressions of rules—linguistic, conceptual, structural. And what I find equally startling and arresting is that some of the students who believe or have been trained to believe that they are fluent and sophisticated readers, glide right over those features, and turn them into prompts to display and give notice of a kind of knowledge that, in many cases, is formulaic, prepackaged, static. They will praise that author for his or her "excellent use of language," "intelligent use of metaphors," and so on, jettisoning their comments into grandiose, universal conclusions.

As I think of the Hirschian proposition according to which (cultural) literacy produces knowledge/understanding and the underlying proposition that (cultural) illiteracy produces lack of knowledge/ understanding, I see a theoretical chiasmus connecting the items in the two series obliquely and reversibly.[7] This chiasmus reminds me of and makes me rediscover, through the work of my students, the force, and the sagacity of theories of reading, and of epistemologies, that posit the potential blocking, impeding, static effect of knowledge, or of certain knowledges, or at least of certain ways of utilizing knowledge(s). It also reminds me that knowledges that block the possibility of imagining alternative ways of knowing produce forms of not easily detected illiteracy.

As a corollary to this, however, and most relevant to my argument, the theoretical chiasmus above also suggests that what in certain contexts or within certain educational approaches can be defined as a lack of knowledge or of understanding, symptomatic of a certain kind of illiteracy (I am thinking of students unschooled in literary conventions), can be seen instead as a form of knowledge, of understanding. It is a form of literacy that is not only activated by a specific literary convention, but also mirrors back, and makes visible, the intellectual moves the convention invokes and relies on. When readers learn strategies that enable them to reflect on and to account for the structuration of those moves, as Pia, Olga, Giulia, and Franca are learning to do, they begin to construct and to tap into difficulty as a rich pool of knowledges that a construction of difficulty as shortcoming, inadequacy, shameful error, places beyond a learner's reach.

WORKS CITED

Berthoff, Ann E. *The Making of Meaning.* New York: Boynton/Cook, 1981.

---

[7]See E. D. Hirsch, *Cultural Literacy: What Every American Needs to Know,* 1987.

Bloom Harold. *How to Read and Why.* New York: Scribner, 2000.

Hirsch, E.D. *Cultural Literacy.* Boston: Houghton Mifflin, 1987.

Salvatori, Mariolina. "Reading and Writing a Text: Correlations Between Reading and Writing Patterns." *College English* 45 (Nov. 1983): 657-66.

——. "The Pedagogical Implications of Reader-Response Theory." *Reader: Essays in Reader-Oriented Theory, Criticism, and Pedagogy* (1986): 1-19.

——. "Conversation with Texts: Reading in the Teaching of Composition." *College English* (April 1996): 440-54.

——. "Toward a Hermeneutics of Difficulty." *Audits of Meaning: A Festschrift in Honor of Ann E. Berthoff.* Ed. Louise Z. Smith. Upper Montclair, NJ: Boynton, 1988. 80-95.

——. and Paul Kameen. "'The Teaching of Teaching': Theoretical Reflections." *Reader* 34/35 (1995): 103-124.

——. *Pedagogy: Disturbing History, 1819-1929.* Pittsburgh: U of Pittsburgh P, 1996.

30

AFTERWORD:
COMPOSITION'S EMERGENT
DISCIPLINARY IDENTITY
Aims, Patterns, Problems, and Possibilities

> It is in the writing we have students practice and the values of writing we hope to instill—the ways we read, evaluate, respond to, and talk about the work of our students—that we most clearly define ourselves as teachers and characterize our courses in composition.
> Rick Straub, "Teaching Writing as Writing; Teaching Students as Student Writers"

In *A Teaching Subject: Composition* Since 1966, Joseph Harris stated that his aim was to discuss a series of metaphors that have marked "composition as a teaching subject—as a loose set of practices, concerns, issues, and problems having to do with how writing gets taught" rather than "composition as a knowledge-making discipline" (x-xi). Like others in the 1990s who distanced themselves from projects such as Stephen North's *The Making of Knowledge in Composition*, Harris acknowledges his own disciplinary professionalization even as he worries that it might "come at the cost of the close ties to teaching that are what give so much work in the field its political and intellectual edge" (xi). *Teaching/Writing in the Late Age of Print* works to reconnect theory and practice and thus offers an opportunity to explore a complex representation of composition's emerging disciplinary identity as well as some of the questions it now faces.

The 29 chapters and accompanying online teaching materials that constitute *TWLAP* provide a demographic cross-section of institutions, faculty, and classes. Of the twelve large Research I institutions (>18,000), two are technical universities. Also represented are seven medium-sized state universities (9,000-17,000), three small state colleges (3,000-8,000), four small liberal arts universities, one upper-division two-year college, and one high school. Nearly half of our contributors are recent PhDs, twelve are established scholars, two are adjuncts, one a teaching assistant, and one a veteran high school teacher. Nearly two-thirds of the chapters represent first-year writing classes, although a range of other classes are represented as well: six upper division, three honors, two sophomore, two graduate, one basic writing, and one high school class.

No dominant model emerges from the collection of chapters; nevertheless, their convergent—and sometimes competing—practices provide a compelling set of data for analysis. In the sections that follow, we examine, first, the theoretical aims of the chapters, using James Berlin's 1985 taxonomy of expressionist, cognitive, and social epistemic rhetorics.[1] Second, we study their *discourse,* articulating their structural oppositions and common metaphors. And third, we consider the specific *problems* our contributors pose as they describe their teaching and administrative work. These analyses, we suggest, demonstrate that compositionists today share enough in terms of their aims, discursive patterns, and identified problems to characterize a disciplinary identity— but a different kind of disciplinary identity than traditional expectations

---

[1]For James Berlin, cognitive rhetoric was "heir apparent of current-traditional rhetoric" ("Rhetoric and Ideology" 11). We use that former term as did Berlin: to imply that the ultimate aim of both was similar in the conservatism of the underlying epistemology. Here, our references to the aims of cognitive rhetoric include those of current traditionalism. Like Berlin, we find both to share an epistemological aim, if not a pedagogical method. However, the clear distinctions between the pedagogical components of each may make such a conflation seem surprising to some readers. For example, current traditionalism's product-oriented focus on generic conventions contrasts, rather obviously, with cognitivism's more research-informed and process-oriented approach to invention heuristics. In a few cases, we have retained the use of the term "current-traditionalism" to refer to classroom practices clearly aligned with its assumptions (and not with those of cognitivism). Yet we claim, like Berlin, that the two share essentially indistinguishable epistemological aims.

might lead us to expect. They also pose a set of common challenges as they point to our discipline's new roles and responsibilities.

THEORETICAL AIMS

Given the broad-ranging discussions of postmodern teaching practices, the many chapters that integrate computer technologies, and the near absence of process-writing discourse in *TWLAP*, we were surprised to discover how aptly Berlin's analysis still describes the practices represented in the volume. Other scholars (notably Richard Fulkerson and Lester Faigley), have charted the aims of composition theory in different ways, yet it remains Berlin's analysis that grounds most disciplinary discussions. The clear labels Berlin assigned, however, have become blurred or bundled in telling ways.

The striking ascendancy of cognitive approaches to writing instruction in the studies of Linda Flower, John Hayes, James Britton, and Janet Emig in the 1970s and early 1980s played an important role in Berlin's distinctions among expressionist (now more commonly called expressivist), cognitive, and social epistemic rhetorics. Furthermore, Berlin's argument that the ideologies of expressivism and cognitivism were inferior to those of social epistemicism led him to isolate the characteristics of each, setting them apart from and against each other. However, our use of his terms has little to do with promoting a particular kind of program or set of practices. Rather, we use these terms to describe the aims of these richly intersecting teaching practices, including particularly the extensions and complications of what Berlin called social epistemic rhetoric, which emphasizes the social nature of knowledge, locating its construction in the interactions among dynamic communities of discourse.

Berlin's critique of expressivism is by now well known. He acknowledged that expressivism values the use of dialectic (a Platonic conception) in encouraging writers to interact in dialogue with others, but he argued that its focus is clearly on the development of personal visions that demand an "original" use of language. Although expressive writing as an end in itself plays a minor role in *TWLAP*'s chapters, nearly a third are concerned with personal narrative and a quarter with voice and tone. More than half state directly that a central goal of the classes they describe is to motivate students to vest themselves in their work. Several chapters note the importance of authentic assignments for authentic audiences. And at least one, Rick Straub's, sees its mission as emphasizing personal writing that helps "students gain a practical understanding of writing as a way of thinking, a means of discovery, an act of saying something—really saying something—to someone else and adding to the community's storehouse of knowledge" (15). Straub wants his students to use what Berlin called "[a]uthentic self-expression" that leads to "authentic self-experience for both the writer and the reader ("Rhetoric and Ideology" 16).

Unlike Berlin's representation of expressivism, where practitioners assigned personal writing as a form of self-discovery and self-empowerment, faculty like Straub situate their expectations of students in broader disciplinary contexts. Straub's discomfort with such easy labels reveals the ways that they overdetermine other significant institutional, social, and ideological aspects of teaching. For example, he carefully describes the ways his expressivism addresses broader expectations of his university community:

> I am looking to encourage students to craft a casual voice, name their ideas sharply and evocatively—in Emerson's words, to attach their words to things—and give substance to their key statements. Later, we'll do more with the overall shape and form of their writing, in time, more with arrangement and sentence structure, and, by the end of the course, more and more with correctness. We'll look increasingly, in other words, to do more to shape their writing into formal, full-fledged essays. (20)

Straub's discomfort with reductive labels is not surprising, given Berlin's critique of expressivist and cognitive rhetorics. Straub's uneasiness with these terms motivates him to describe his teaching as working in "the space between process and product pedagogies and between expressivist and social constructionist approaches to teaching writing" (17). Students in his classes write a sequence of personal essays that emphasize "exploration and reflection" on a "common general subject, in the manner of William Coles and David Bartholomae . . ." (16). Straub is not unique in recognizing how choosing terms and theories both reveals and constrains one's work.

Preferring new metaphors, other writers such as Richard Miller avoid specifying such terms or even citing disciplinary influences. Yet closer analysis reveals the aims that inform their work. Miller states, "'Engagement,' 'conversation,' 'connection': these are the words I rely on in my teaching; they are the metaphors that point to the kind of writing I value most—speculative, deliberative, meditative writing" (76). He wants "students to produce writing that moves from here to there, writing that teaches as it goes" (76). Miller positions his work squarely in contrast to current-traditional pedagogies that yield the unengaged and unengaging prose that William Coles called "theme writing" in The *Plural I—And After*.[2] The difficulty with such an approach, particularly for those new to the teaching of composition, is that it suggests that everyone knows why Miller has chosen these metaphors and how they situate his work. Miller's claim could look as if it is speaking from transcendent truths formulated upon what new teachers often are so hungry to find—"what works."

Nonetheless, this writing that "teaches as it goes" is the kind of work that David Bartholomae, Patricia Bizzell, and others were advocating in the mid-1980s, work that Berlin suggests has "moved firmly in the ranks of the epistemic category," but that "conceives composing in personal terms, as the expression of an isolated self attempting to come to grips with an alien and recalcitrant world" (*Rhetoric and Reality* 185). We can see this pattern emerge out of the assignment to which Miller's student, Rachel, responded. Miller wants students to realize when "the question of how one reads and why one reads" begins to matter. He explains, "The relatively impersonal work of reading books for class moved close to home as the links between one's reading habits, one's upbringing, and one's cosmology started to line up" (77). It is no surprise that he would choose a paper in which Rachel, an orthodox Jewish housewife and mother of four, uses Carlo Ginzberg's *The Cheese and the Worms* to examine how her own faith informs the ways she reads and constructs her world.

Unlike Straub, Miller does not situate his teaching between social constructionism and expressivism. His epistemic aim is not to have students just "learn *about* theory" but to "do theory." Yet, Miller also desires that his students use "[a]uthentic self-expression," which leads to "authentic self-experience for both the writer and the reader" (Berlin, "Rhetoric and Ideology" 16). And, he values Rachel and her work for her ability to reconsider her experience in light of the assigned material, "to demonstrate her command of the assigned approach," to note the "limits of that approach's explanatory power," and to do all of this work "in prose that is simultaneously lucid and thoughtful" (82).

---

[2]William Coles explains in describing Assignment 1 for his course: "Please try to bear in mind that the issue in this paper is what "*you* think, where *you* stand, what *you* have to say. Please don't turn yourself into a Board of Directors. Please don't tell me about Man, or about a view of Him that by some has been contended. Please don't speak with a megaphone. Please don't write a Theme. In the first few sets of papers of a term students have a tendency to sound the way they think they ought to sound, the way they think they have been taught to sound" (17).

Miller values Rachel's ability to test the limits of academic expectations and structures while she both fulfills institutional expectations and articulates the socially constructed identity that she values.

Like Straub, Miller provides a clear sense of what he values and practices in teaching writing. In both cases, the personal is mediated by the social, although more self-consciously so in Miller. Berlin's labels may not fully define the classroom work of these two compositionists, but they continue to provide a framework within which we can understand how practitioners define their aims.

Both Straub's and Miller's chapters focus more on individual student writers than do chapters where students actively promote social change. The complexities of the latter can be considerable, entailing collaborative and public writing, problem-posing and project-based learning, reshaped student/teacher relationships, and writing that extends well beyond an isolated paper or even the academic term. Such work splits compositionists' sense of responsibility between helping students improve as writers in a given social milieu and promoting social change in larger communities. However, even the chapters that seem most obviously grounded in social epistemicism—those most aimed at achieving social change—retain threads of cognitivist and expressivist rhetorics.

Steven Parks and Lori Shorr's "Reinventing Our Community" draws on the work of David Bartholomae, Anthony Petrosky, Paulo Freire, Ira Shor, Linda Flower, Lisa Delpit, and Anne Berthoff. Toward their aim of collective social action, Parks and Shorr discuss how and why Temple University restructured its lower-division writing curriculum as an opportunity to "establish a service-learning component in their entry level writing classes" (282):

> [W]here and when certain issues come to dominate the political, cultural, and social workings of a community (such as abandoned properties or welfare reform), the writing program should serve as a conduit for building alliances among different literacy/policy organizations involved in seeking solutions. Such alliances can provide students not only with an institutional bridge between university/community, which can help in their eventual postgraduation transition, but also provide them with a vision of writing connected to collective action, to collective agency. (279)

The social imperatives that Parks and Shorr articulate embody Berlin's ideological ideal. Students are "asked to study the debates around public education, the nature of literacy, and the history of their own education" (282). The program also includes academic reading and writing that explores "the social, economic, and political aspects of education," "literacy tutoring to middle school students through weekly visits to a public school," and professional development for schoolteachers to integrate writing into their curriculum. Furthermore, community and university tutors supplement literacy instruction. The first part of the new curriculum was "modeled after the work of Paulo Freire and Ira Shor," but Parks and Shorr acknowledge an eclectic praxis that includes expressivist and even current-traditionalist emphases as well. They note that students use "personal experience as a means to connect to larger systemic issues." And the student paper presented in the chapter is a critique of the popular film, *Stand and Deliver,* with its call to social action embodied in a common academic genre.

As Parks and Shorr state, "[a]ny individual paper occurs within the implicit and explicit expectations of a program," and such work cannot be separated from "the structures that support or inhibit it (278). Hence, programmatic structures—and not just epistemic aims—frequently determine teaching and rhetorical practices. When, as is the case at many research institutions, a few faculty members trained in composition and rhetoric direct programs staffed chiefly by part-time and non-tenure-track faculty, the opportunity to revise curricula on a regular basis can be rare. Few programs can provide the level of institutional support Temple has assigned to maintaining such a complex, community-based program. Hence, Berlin's social epistemic rhetoric operates within, but is also constrained by, the larger contexts of forces that influence specific classes. And the program-wide implementation of such a practice depends a great deal on both the institution's relationships with the community and its own resources, both human and capital.

This issue of programmatic reform is further complicated by pressures that push against institutional change, such as external norming pressures, funding allocations, and habitual teaching practices. The other two service-learning chapters in this volume reflect a social action that is teacher-initiated rather than program-determined. Both Libby Miles' "Writing with the Jonnycake Center" and Jane Carducci and Gary Eddy's "Discourse Community Service" describe courses designed for writing at the sophomore level or higher. In both, tenets of current-traditional and expressionist rhetorics inform obviously social-minded classroom teaching.

Miles explains how her pedagogy for this particular class is similar to all other writing courses that she teaches: "No matter what level writing course I teach . . . , five key assumptions about what writing *should* be drive my course design" (226). She names "writing as a social action," "writing as a collaborative enterprise," "writing as a form of inquiry," "writing as a technology," "writing as more than words on a page" (227). She explains further that her course is organized with "unlimited choices, and therefore unlimited opportunity for wrong turns" (227). Each of her students "grapples with understanding several different rhetorical situations, all of which call for different genre selections, different research paths, different stylistic and tone choices." The five assumptions she names are unique to her specific classes. The range of choices she makes available to students is rare across most institutions and nearly absent from less experienced classroom teachers. Yet, current-traditional rhetoric is recognizable in the terms "genre," "research," "style," and "tone." Though clearly social epistemicist in its approach, Miles' ambitious service learning class is grounded, like most chapters in this volume, in a set of common expectations of academic discourse.

Similarly, the overall focus of Carducci and Eddy's sophomore level writing-across-the-disciplines and service-learning class is grounded in Freirean problem posing. They explain how the final project of their course embodies "Paulo Freire's praxis of critical literacy: posing a problem, deriving the felt need, adopting a solution, acting, and reflecting on that action in pursuit of further problems and actions" (215). They describe a project in which a group of women's studies minors work to educate the community about Rohypnol, the date rape drug. Yet, as in the Miles chapter, the overarching goals for student work are squarely situated in current-traditional/cognitivist and expressivist practices. Carducci and Eddy explain that they supplemented

> the community service writing project with a variety of other types of writing: research essays on their chosen area of felt need, analytical and argumentative essays on public issues, defenses of controversial books, and essays that analyze the academic discourse of their major. (215)

The genre approach to writing that we describe in these three chapters accomplishes different purposes in each case, but it clearly characterizes patterns of teaching and learning across a range of the chapters we have collected. Indeed, many of them use elements of expressivism, and nearly all are concerned at some level with current-traditional issues such as genre, form, style, and correctness.

Thus the chapters of this book demonstrate that some of the best practices of social epistemic rhetoric retain threads of expressivist and cognitivist/current-traditionalist rhetorics. For instance, a current-traditionalist's "rule" may be cast by a social-epistemicist as a "convention" of the community that may alter meaning or mark outsider status if ignored; similarly, a cognitivist's heuristic may be cast in rhetorical terms by a social epistemicist who hopes to use audience or context as a means of invention and inquiry. Furthermore, as we see in Eddy and Carducci's chapter, personal experience (a "felt need") can motivate a cultural critique that fosters a reexamination of cultural assumptions or serves as an impetus to social action. In these ways, even though Berlin's labels no longer describe mutually exclusive rhetorical ideologies or their corresponding practices, his analysis still plays a useful role in describing the aims of compositionists. For a variety of purposes, compositionists continue to draw from the traditions of expressivist and cognitivist (as well as some current-traditional) rhetorics in achieving their ends. The collective praxis charted by contributors to *Teaching/Writing in the Late Age of Print* suggests, however, more so than any other, a primarily social epistemic aim—even though that aim may be complicated, mitigated, and even compromised by a host of administrative, intellectual, managerial, and financial concerns.

DISCURSIVE PATTERNS

To suggest that compositionists share a disciplinary discourse is to posit a set of common terms, assumptions, and oppositions that enables its community of participants to collaborate. Paul Diesing suggests that participants in such a "methodological community" "have common friends and acquaintances, intellectual ancestors, and opponents, and thus locate themselves at roughly the same point in sociometric space." He explains further that, "[a]lthough they do not all use exactly the same procedure in their work, there is a great deal of similarity, and the differences are accepted as variant realizations of the same values" (qtd. in North 2). Over the past decade and a half since North's *The Making of Knowledge in Composition*, it has become increasingly clear that composition is different from most scientific disciplinary formations. Unlike Diesing's social science model, which generally assumes a stable body of disciplinary knowledge, a unified field, and stable internal communities, composition is a "kind of piecemeal bricolage, cutting and splicing elements from the intellectual landscape" that makes composition "look more like a collage—a postmodern pastiche of juxtaposed parts . . ." (Trimbur 117). Yet, in all its diversity, composition has begun to coalesce around the very set of practices and discourses that North argued would pull it apart.[3]

---

[3]Stephen North argues that composition will either disarticulate as a cohesive field as it aligns with other disciplines such as anthropology, psychology, and cultural studies, or it will have to separate itself from departments of English.

The shared discourse of this community manifests itself in the works compositionists tend to cite; the conferences, listservs, and journals they populate; and the common threads that weave their teaching, scholarship, and research together. Perhaps even more tellingly, compositionists share sets of rhetorical tropes and discursive patterns that facilitate interaction between members of the community—if not, necessarily, outside it. Among the most common in these chapters are the consistent use of binary oppositions, scholarly references, and common metaphors—patterns that constitute the shared discourse of a disciplinary community.

Oppositions

More than half of the chapters in this volume use overtly dualistic terms such as "process and product" and "expressivist and social constructionist approaches" (Straub 17), often defining what is valued by what is not valued. Richard Miller, for instance, defines what he wants his students to accomplish by stating that he doesn't want students to produce writing that starts at some given place ("my thesis is X") and stays at that place ("and these are the examples that prove my thesis is X"). Instead, he wants "the students to produce writing that moves from here to there, writing that teaches as it goes." His job, he says, "is to show the students how to produce such writing" (76). As they appear throughout *TWLAP*, terms such as "empowerment," "literacy," "multiculturalism," "disability," "decenter," "problem posing," "risk taking," and "collaboration" derive their significance from relationships to their antonyms. Several chapters juxtapose oral or visual literacy with alphabetic, face-to-face discussion with computer-mediated-communication, correctness with content, lecture-based teaching with student-centered, consensus with dissensus, modern with postmodern, linear with multilinear, and univocality with multivocality. Whether compositionists agree that "post process" best characterizes the current state of composition, it is certainly not surprising that the term has become part of our shared discourse, given our tendency to articulate our values and practices in terms of what we juxtapose them against.

References

Our contributors' frequent references to key scholarly debates and definitive texts also suggest a set of shared assumptions across the intellectual community. Several of this book's chapters situate their work within the 1991 CCCC David Bartholomae-Peter Elbow debate. The

Works Cited for *TWLAP* reads like a bibliography for current disciplinary practices. Although references from literary theory (e.g. Mikhail Bakhtin), educational philosophy (e.g. John Dewey), and social science (e.g. Margaret Mead and Alfred North Whitehead) dot the list, they are tied to discussions of teaching writing at the college level. The most often-cited texts—specifically works by Bartholomae, Jay David Bolter, Deborah Brandt, Kenneth Bruffee, Lester Faigley, Paulo Freire, Andrea Lunsford, Cynthia Selfe, and Ira Shor—reflect the epistemic leaning of a large number of the contributors even as they suggest that their discourse is not governed by a single epistemological system. As Eric Hobson suggests, the search for a "pristine epistemological home" may be futile anyway: he argues that "we should instead negotiate the 'epistemological tightropes' and 'epistemological mix[es]' that are conditions of postmodernism" (73, 74). The contributors to this volume may not share a single epistemology, yet they are engaged in a common discourse that references a reasonably well defined set of debates and texts.

Metaphors

As Joseph Harris,[4] Jim Seitz,[5] and others have acknowledged, the metaphors that describe our work reveal our epistemological tendencies. As one would expect, they also reflect the practices that *TWLAP*'s contributors value, and they distinguish our discourse from others. *Growth*, a metaphor that has been consistently associated with expressivist pedagogies, is explicitly discussed by Straub and by Parks and Shorr but is implied in several chapters that deal directly with revision, such as Daniel Anderson's and Rebecca Rickly's. *Voice*, which is most often affiliated with personal writing and often used to represent authentic or stylized writing, finds its way into discussions of ethos and pathos and plays particularly important roles for Carrie Leverenz, Carducci and

---

[4]Joseph Harris describes in *A Teaching Subject: Composition Since* 1966 six key metaphors that have shaped composition historically: growth, voice, process, error, community, and contact/negotiation.

[5]Jim Seitz proposes in *Motives for Metaphor: Literacy, Curriculum Reform, and the Teaching of English* that a "reconception of the English studies curriculum might begin with a reconception of metaphor, both because of its overlapping position among the disciplinary domains within that curriculum (literature, composition, creative writing, and so on) and because of its unique way of negotiating 'difference'—a matter of considerable significance in recent attempts to reimagine the teaching of English" (194).

Eddy, and Betty Eidenier. The metaphor of *process* has played a significant role in the history of composition,[6] but it does not play a governing
role in any of the chapters. Nonetheless, process informs the pedagogies
of such diverse contributors as Christine Hult, Betty Eidenier, Mariolina
Salvatori, J Paul Johnson, and Jeremy Ball and Judith Hawkins. *Error*
has long served as shorthand for what is wrong with student writing.
The deficit model of teaching that the metaphor of error served in late
1960s and early 1970s pedagogies has survived today almost exclusively
outside of composition in populist notions of college writing and in the
instrumentalist pedagogies of nonspecialists. *Error* plays a minor role in
several chapters of this collection as a final stage of writing-process pedagogies, particularly those by Salvatori, Ball and Hawkins, and George
Otte. Nearly half of the chapters invoke the metaphor of *community*,
which reflects patterns of student and teacher interactions, usually within the context of socially constructed assumptions, ways of reading and
writing, and participation. Some compositionists claim that nearly all
writing is *argument*. Others use the metaphor to promote rhetorical
models or decontextualized heuristics, or, in some cases, to understand
their courses as studies in the art of argumentation. Even though teaching argument encompasses a wide range of practices, chapters by Joan
Latchaw, Rebecca Howard, Ball and Hawkins, and Susanmarie
Harrington all value argumentation as a form of academic discourse.
Metaphors of *conversation* and *contact* or *negotiation* are often juxtaposed. Latchaw, Rickly, and Anderson, for example, describe collaborative work as *conversation;* Wini Wood, Miller, and a host of others
address relations of power and cultural conflict in metaphors of *contact*
(as in contact zones), *negotiation,* and *authority.* One only has to think
of how "the idea of a writing center" has changed over the last 30 years
to witness the vigor of these metaphors first-hand: there, remedial
"labs" for error correction have given way to centers that foster *writing
communities* through *negotiation* and *conversation.*

Other metaphors are less recurrent, but equally revealing.
Reflection generally entails self-evaluation, examination of cultural
assumptions, and mediation of one's position through those of others.
Dialogism draws together metaphors of contact, negotiation,
power/authority, and discourse as a way for authorial discourse to be
challenged or unmasked. *Engagement* is almost always understood as a
matter of both students vesting themselves in their work and instructors
designing curricula that make this investment possible. *Difficulty* is gen-

---

[6]Harris discusses the metaphor of process in order to "get at what it might
have meant to teach writing 'as process not product'" and to assess how much
process teaching did or did not transform the actual teaching of writing (55).

erally associated with risk taking and is often juxtaposed against low-risk environments that are comfortably collaborative and rarely address issues of contact or negotiation. *Web* and *network* generally refer to work on the Internet but have increasingly been used to conceptualize the cultural, institutional, and ideological complications of writing in and beyond the classroom. For example, Johnson writes that his aim is to "support writing that is responsive to, and purposeful in, a rich network of textual interactions (oral/written, reading/writing, classroom/computer, teacher/student, student/student) via a complex web of contexts, opportunities, and responses for student writers" (314).

As in any disciplinary discourse, these key metaphors are specialized, often so much so that readers outside the community are less likely to grasp their significance. For example, the metaphors of *problem posing, contact zones, reflection,* or *dialogism* are unlikely to evoke the same systems of meaning outside of composition and some circles of English and sociology. Paul Heilker and Peter Vandenberg's recent collection of *Keywords in Composition Studies* demonstrates both the complexity of their accumulated meanings within composition and their apparent impenetrability beyond the field. This disjuncture is even more acute in the more common metaphors of *argument, voice, process,* and *error* that carry meaning outside of academic circles. When nonspecialists use these terms to discuss writing, they do not call upon the scholarly debates that have shaped their disciplinary uses. For example, compositionists can hardly discuss *error* without invoking disciplinary markers such as Mina Shaughnessy's *Errors and Expectations,* arguments over students' rights to their own languages, and the continuing stream of books, journal articles, and listserv exchanges on the topic. For those outside the community, however, *error* is less charged with meaning, simply an unwelcome phenomenon in student writing that compositionists have been unable to remedy. Just as the common use of binary oppositions and scholarly references frame the community's discourse, metaphors like *error* can both allude to a rich disciplinary dialogue for compositionists and represent the boundaries of their discussions.

PROBLEMS AND ISSUES

Stephen Toulmin extends Paul Diesing's notion of methodological communities and their attendant discursive patterns in his 1970s discussion of disciplinary evolution. In *Human Understanding,* Toulmin suggests that the "existence and unity of an intellectual discipline, regarded as a specific 'historical entity,' reflects the continuity imposed on its problems by the development of its intellectual ideals and ambitions" (155). Although it concerns scientific disciplines, Toulmin's definition is useful for considering composition's disciplinary discourse and identity. We can better understand composition as an "historical entity" by looking at how the intellectual ideals and ambitions of our contributors, which have developed over the past 30 years, impose continuity on the persistent problems that compositionists face. The problems articulated by *TWLAP* contributors range broadly but seem to include three types: rhetorical, pedagogical, and professional/institutional.

Rhetorical Problems

The rhetorical problems that students face—their writerly and readerly concerns—are perhaps best understood as a negotiation of expectations between teacher and students. These include writing that focuses too exclusively on structure and form (such as five-paragraph theme writing) and encourages students to organize "information mechanically, simplistically, without embracing the complexities of difficult subjects and without engaging difficult and contradictory viewpoints" (Heilker, qtd. in Johnson 319). They also include "balancing creativity with academic content" (Leverenz 123), paying attention to "real audiences" (Hawkins and Ball 333), and a host of other issues, from traditional notions of writing as a process or in a genre to writing for global audiences, writing and reading in and about new genres such as hypertext and electronic communication, and negotiating electronic technologies for writing. And a range of chapters confront students with the challenges of collaborative and project-based writing, peer evaluation, and writing-in-the-disciplines. Students often face several of these problems at once across multiple points along their reading and writing processes.

Reading-based problems are equally as broad-ranging. In contrast to the purely expressive writing classes of three decades ago, every class represented in this volume requires reading other than student texts. So the problem of writing is perceived also as a problem of reading. As Salvatori writes, "[t]he use of reading in composition courses, in fact teaching writing through reading, is something that I have argued for and written about since my first foray into the field of composition" (368). Several contributors, particularly Salvatori, Miller, Galin, Latchaw, and Kathleen Welsch, are concerned that students read critically, closely, and/or "against the grain"[7] rather than passively or simply

---

[7]David Bartholomae and Anthony Petrosky write in their introduction to *Ways of Reading* that "reading . . . requires a difficult mix of authority and

for information. The problems presented by reading new genres and transferring reading strategies beyond the classroom are taken up by contributors such as Leverenz, Hult, Katherine Fischer, and Libby Miles. Others concern themselves with how students read for research or validate sources on the World Wide Web.

The ways that instructors read student writing bridges the distinction between rhetorical and pedagogical problems. Although most chapters concern themselves with effective ways for teaching students to read and reflect critically on writing (their own and others'), few chapters explicitly explore this issue. Haviland notes the risks her students take when encouraged to write what they don't already know, to collaborate on papers with uncharted outcomes. She also notes the risks she poses for herself when she invites students to write papers that may not look like typical graduate student papers. Thus, an important emerging problem for compositionists is how they will read new texts—their own and their students'—for any kind of "different writing" demands different reading. The decisions that teachers make to address these issues are defined by problems of theory and pedagogy—problems of praxis.[8]

Pedagogical Problems

By far the most unifying and persistent problem is an issue of both scholarship and teaching: how do we teach writing and why? This problem undergirds the premise of this book and is central to the disciplinary discourse of composition. The question raises complex issues of governing principles, authority, technology, identity, and agency, and it foregrounds alternative modes of learning and knowledge making (collaboration, service learning, visual rhetorics, integration of new technologies, etc.). These issues have become increasingly critical in scholarly debates over the past fifteen years.

---

humility" (10). They explain further that most of the questions in their reader have students moving back and forth between "tak[ing] charge of a text" and giving "generous attention to someone else's (a writer's) key terms and methods," or "reading with and against the grain of a text, reproducing an author's methods, questioning his or her direction and authority" (10).

[8]Antonio Gramsci defines "praxis" as "the socio-practical activity, in which thought and action are reciprocally determined" (333). Raymond Williams defines praxis as "*practice* informed by *theory* and . . . less emphatically, *theory* informed by *practice*. In each case, praxis is understood as an integration of theory and practice as consciously theorized practice" (qtd. in Heilker and Vandenberg 188-89).

Some chapters are organized around a single governing problem, and others concern themselves with clusters of intersecting problems. For example, the governing problem for Salvatori is one of academic discourse. She works to determine how she might coax her class to engage poetry critically and reflectively. Her solution involves students writing "difficulty papers." She explains in her assignment: "My goal . . . is to move all of us from judging a difficulty as a reader's inability to understand a text to discerning in it a reader's incipient awareness of the particular 'demands' imposed by the language/structure/style/content of a text" (368). By encouraging students to identify difficulties as generative moments, she helps them discover that what might otherwise be perceived as a lack of ability or understanding on their parts might instead serve as an avenue to understanding.

Salvatori's articulation of this problem of academic discourse has its roots in resistance to the deficit models of writing that have so steadfastly maintained their grip on composition in the form of "bonehead" English of the 1960s and many representations of "remedial" writing present today. Salvatori suggests that, particularly in lower-division writing courses, some educational approaches circumvent difficulties by streamlining and providing answers for students, thus nurturing "continuous dependence on a hierarchy of experts most of whom are unwilling or unable to share with others the processes that enable them to acquire and amass their cultural capital" (376). She notes further that the students who are generally characterized as the least prepared or least sophisticated readers are often the ones who "demonstrate a remarkable awareness of textual bumps, irregularities, twists, deviations from or transgressions of rules—linguistic, conceptual, structural" and that the students who deem themselves most prepared or sophisticated readers often "glide right over those features, and turn them into prompts to display and give notice of a kind of knowledge that, in many cases, is formulaic, prepackaged, static" (376). Such insights have enabled Salvatori to develop a praxis that subverts typical student expectations of success and confronts them with the kinds of reading- and writing-based problems that we discussed earlier.

Although not all of the contributors see difficulty as a central element of their pedagogies, most, like Salvatori, direct our attention to the ways in which faculty construct students and students perceive their own work. These reflective moves for teaching and learning distinguish earlier discourses of teaching from those that have emerged over the past fifteen years. We have shifted our attention from assimilating distinct methodological practices from other disciplines to consolidating them into our own network of interrelated debates, methods, practices, claims, and problems. This realization is particularly important for new instructors and those whose teaching loads preclude research or reading in composition. These are the instructors who are least likely to see particular practices as rooted in disciplinary principles and are least likely to understand how effective teaching of writing must merge theory with pedagogy in informed praxis. They are also the instructors who are most likely to rely on textbooks to guide their teaching, which places a heavy burden on publishers to ensure that their books and teachers' manuals are carefully grounded in the scholarly/pedagogical problems of composition. However, when faculty depend chiefly on textbooks to shape their classes and writing projects, it is difficult for both faculty and students to make the kinds of reflective moves that Salvatori argues should be at the heart of teaching and learning.

Many chapters present a governing problem but identify clusters of additional ones that inform their classes. The following three classes demonstrate how balancing clusters of competing problems complicates teaching and learning. Like a host of other chapters, Karla Kitalong, Michael Moore, and Dickie Selfe structure their courses around the complications that new technologies are bringing to teaching. They suggest that "classroom experience is increasingly complex as we integrate communication technologies within the technologies of teaching and learning" (144). Based on a belief that technologies are neither transparent nor ideologically neutral, they argue that these attitudes, strategies, and approaches should likewise influence how future technological power relations are exercised in the social sphere of the classroom.

In addition, Kitalong, Moore, and Selfe address a series of problems that are not concerned with computer technologies. The question of how power is exercised within a classroom has been raised in Freirean problem-posing education, but also by Foucauldian notions of power, truth, and knowledge. The problems that social construction poses for students and teachers are apparent here: it is difficult for students to examine the ways their approaches to using technologies are shaped by those technologies and for teachers to shape their courses around the elements that students bring to the table. Such additional problems are characteristic of the chapters that take on the most complex forms of teaching—practices that include service learning, problem-posing, computer facilitation, collaboration, and project-based learning.

Christine Hult's project-based upper-division Rhetoric, Composition, and Computers class is constructed around the controlling scholarly/pedagogical problem of implementing a "postmodern writing pedagogy based on community and communal construction of knowledge." She uses a computer-facilitated project because she argues that "[w]e do a disservice when we ignore electronic writing and instead privilege print writing" (237). She rejects the romantic commonplace of the "solitary writer composing along in a garret" (237) and presents the collaborative nature of her class as a response to the student "listening to the teacher talk about writing (as is often the case in traditional writing classrooms)" (239). Furthermore, she argues that students must extend their understandings of reading and writing to include media production. She explains,

> [s]tudents in these twenty-first century classrooms are learning to read and write with media that were unheard of even a decade ago. It is incumbent upon writing teachers in the new millennium to help our students become intelligent users and producers of these media. (238)

Hult's orchestration of a project-based, service-learning, and computer-facilitated class is a class that only an experienced professional could have conceived and enacted successfully, and then only in a supportive context.

Professional/Institutional Problems

As if the complexities of Hult's course were not enough of a challenge, her chapter also addresses a managerial one that involves distance education—how to accommodate students with special needs. One of her students, confined to a wheelchair and unable to attend on a daily basis, had asked if he could attend virtually. His team's project focuses on the wheelchair sports organization to which he belonged. Meanwhile, Barbara Heifferon's chapter, "Disabling the Disability Label," argues that new technologies provide both unanticipated problems and opportunities for students traditionally defined as "disabled." Although many managerial problems occur at the programmatic level (including placement, staffing, training, and assessment), these two chapters suggest that teachers often find themselves addressing issues raised by their students' individual rights, needs, and concerns.

In addition to these kinds of managerial concerns, classroom practices are often tied to problems of professional status. Judith Hawkins and Jeremy Ball define their joint critical thinking and honors writing course as a response to institutional commonplaces that most faculty face. They write that students "don't seem to be using basic skills outside the immediate classroom context" (334). Nor are they "able to integrate the various basic skills they have accumulated into an organic whole and apply these skills in new ways in new situations" (334). Like Miles and Hult, they couple these rhetorical problems with larger institutional problems of professional status. "All too often," they explain, "composition instructors' and critical thinking instructors' competence is challenged by other faculty who seriously question how their upper-division students ever passed freshman composition and critical thinking classes" (334). This cluster of problems is certainly familiar, but it has inspired Ball and Hawkins to develop a mock trial, "project-based learning system" based on Freire's pedagogy of "'problem-posing education'" that enables students to work collaboratively in a computer-facilitated classroom as they "respond and answer to wider, more diverse audiences as they would in real-life writing situations" (336). When faculty in other disciplines question the subject matter of composition, their perceptions ignite debates over composition's ability to teach its subject matter as well as interrogate its members' professional stature.

Grounded in problems of textual difficulties, computer technologies, identity formation, and professional stature, these three chapters illuminate Toulmin's claim that the "existence and unity of an intellectual discipline, regarded as a specific 'historical entity,' reflects the continuity imposed on its problems by the development of its intellectual ideals and ambitions" (155). The problems of teaching writing in higher education have not changed over the past 30 years nearly as much as we might have expected, although responses to them have begun to shift substantially. For the most part, these problems concern how to teach and how to manage writing programs. Problems of professional status have always been part of the programmatic concern of composition, but they have affected the intellectual ideals and ambitions of writing faculty in more complex ways over the past two decades, particularly in the area of worsening material conditions and increasing reliance on part-time and nontenured teachers.

The exponential growth of PhD programs in composition and the increasing opportunities for recent graduates are leading to greater specialization of teaching practices. Since the 1970s, when new pedagogies in expressive writing introduced instructors to personal issues that they were unprepared to help students address, the degrees of complexity in teaching composition have dramatically increased. Even as some faculty lament that the teaching of writing has somehow gone astray as it has shifted its focus from the principles of stylistics, few seem to believe that composition should return to an exclusively stylistic focus. Yet, the competing and sometimes overlapping epistemologies, the dualistic tensions and metaphors, and the problems through which we define our work lead us to the kind of conflicted assertions about the disciplinary status of composition that Harris articulates at the outset of this chapter. Harris' separation of knowledge making from practical concerns represents one of the most significant obstacles for new or marginalized teachers of writing to address in their own teaching. At the same time, however, these problems—though they may remain much the same from one generation to the next—are now faced by a generation of teacher-scholars with training specific to composition and informed by decades of published scholarship. The fact that our contributors face common problems may remain one of the most convincing indications that they share not only common aims and discursive patterns, but also an emerging disciplinary identity.

DISCIPLINARY IDENTITY

Some scholars who have rejected composition's disciplinary status argue along with Stephen North and John Trimbur that composition is simply too diverse and too conflicted to represent a stable body of disciplinary knowledge. Others such as Kurt Spellmeyer have charged that composition has followed the wrong model of disciplinarity, and many have suggested that composition needs its marginal status to sustain a "postdisciplinary" identity "where multiple, heterogeneous, and polyvalent discourses, projects, and interests intersect" (Trimbur 136). Each of these positions is helpful as we use our discussion of these chapters to argue a clear disciplinary identity for composition. The identity we examine challenges traditional models and points to a more optimistic one than Spellmeyer projected at the 2001 Composition in the 21st Century conference, when he suggested that composition indeed had arrived at disciplinary status, albeit one of questionable value. He described the "achievement" as finally moving out of steerage to the main deck of a sinking ship, confidently offering graduate students deck chairs alongside the ones into which we have wriggled. As Spellmeyer's critique might suggest, the question of composition's disciplinary identity is one that has been, and continues to be, vehemently debated, with participants in the dialogue assuming varying, and conflicting, notions of disciplinarity.

John Trimbur opens "Composition Studies: Postmodern or Popular" by stating that although "Composition studies has emerged over the last two decades as an intellectual project to constitute the study and teaching of writing as a field of knowledge," he prefers the term "field" instead of "discipline" because he is concerned that disciplinary status means "staking out sharp boundaries" and engaging in "exclusionary practices." He amplifies: "the founding of composition studies as a mobile and heterogeneous set of interests has been influenced by dedisciplinary impulses in contemporary intellectual work" (117). However, even as he notes the importance of converging postmodern studies with emerging composition studies as a field, he fears that an uncritical embrace of postmodern theory can lead to the "decline of public discourse and utopian aspirations to create popular spheres of influence within civil society" (119).

Other scholars such as Stephen North, Louise Wetherbee Phelps, Joseph Harris, James Berlin, Edward Corbett, and Theresa Enos have described the disciplinary status of composition variably as a "fragmenting field of study," "a teaching subject," "three rhetorics of teaching writing," "a human science," an "enabling discipline," or a "maturing discipline." Although historically valuable, most of these narratives now can be seen best as descriptions of an emerging field, tracing responses and counterresponses to knowledge making, methods, institutional practices, and patterns of institutional growth.

Just as it is useful to situate the conversation historically, it is useful to interrogate the definitions within which we operate. The nineteenth-century model of disciplinarity generally assumes a stable body of knowledge that posits a unified field rather than the "kind of piecemeal bricolage, cutting and splicing elements from the intellectual landscape" that make composition "look more like a collage—a postmodern pastiche of juxtaposed parts . . ." (Trimbur 117). Indeed, it is precisely this turn-of-the-previous-century model of disciplinarity that compositionists have most resisted as they worked toward greater institutional recognition and disciplinary status.

When North applied Diesing's law to a discipline that supported no more than a dozen graduate programs, sponsored no more than a handful of scholarly journals, and drew on both a leadership and a work force trained primarily in literature, he arrived at the only conclusion he could: "Composition as a knowledge-making society" was "gradually pulling itself apart," fragmenting, gathering into communities or clusters of communities among which relations [were] becoming increasingly tenuous" (364). However, North applied Diesing's description of scientific disciplines without acknowledging that they could not, in all their diversity, form a single community, notwithstanding their common methods. Diesing looked at disciplinary formations such as physics and anthropology to describe the kinds of subcommunities within the larger fields of sciences and social sciences that "have common friends and acquaintances, intellectual ancestors, and opponents, and thus locate themselves at roughly the same point in sociometric space" (qtd. in North 2). Had rhetoric been designated the broader field, which would have been more equivalent to Diesing's *science*, composition might have been seen as an emergent community that was well on its way toward disciplinary identity, rather than a divergent collection of "practitioners, historians, philosophers, critics, experimentalists, clinicians, formalists, and ethnographers" (qtd. in North 4).

In contrast with North and Trimbur now, we posit with Diesing that "communication and co-operation occur primarily within the boundaries of a method [or set of epistemologies], not within a field" (qtd. in North 4). Thus, rather than hedging the status of composition as a field, we work to redefine composition as a postmodern disciplinary identity, one with important implications beyond the classroom walls.

An understanding of composition as a network of tensions between the decentralizing and centralizing forces that Mikhail Bakhtin describes in "Discourse in the Novel" provides us with a vision of a disciplinary identity that is markedly different from most nineteenth-century models.[9] It is a vision that shapes the ways we teach our classes and prepare our teaching assistants as well as the issues we address and the ways we theorize our work. We have argued thus far that these chapters demonstrate a substantial consolidation of theoretical aims, discursive patterns, and common problems that, taken together, suggest the centripetal forces of unification toward disciplinary identity. At the same time, however, composition has achieved its greatest period of consolidation within an era of great decentralizing forces. Susan Miller describes the current state of composition in the Foreword to this volume as having arisen "largely from the unexpected disruptions that impinged on theories and systematic practices of writing instruction" (xiv). Composition's embrace of postmodernism has enabled the emergence of a discipline that values complexity, diversity, collaboration,

---

[9]Mikhail Bakhtin writes that, "The centripetal forces tend toward a unitary language that is ideologically saturated, "language as a world view, even as a concrete opinion, insuring a maximum of mutual understanding in all spheres of ideological life" (270-71). At the same time, these unifying forces are situated within the heteroglossia of socio-ideological languages: languages of social groups, 'professional' and 'generic' languages, language of generations and so forth" (272). He continues, "Alongside the centripetal forces, the centrifugal forces of language carry on their uninterrupted work; alongside the verbal-ideological centralization and unification, the uninterrupted processes of decentralization and disunification go forward" (272).

engagement, dissensus, and reflection. This tension—between the centripetal forces that bring together composition as a knowledge-making discipline and the centrifugal forces of postmodernism—marks our work in this current historical conjuncture.

The problems of teaching writing that define our work in higher education represent these opposing forces. For instance, rhetorical problems within composition tend most often to move our teaching centripetally toward organized essays that satisfy institutional and societal expectations of good writing; yet our local issues, curricula, students, and budgets generate centrifugal forces. Likewise, our scholarship moves our teaching centrifugally toward increasingly complex and diverse settings and problems (such as writing in hypertext or in service-learning programs), even as our journals, organizations, conferences, and outcomes statements function centripetally, centralizing our aims and disciplinary identity. We can even look at our professionalization in light of these terms. The dramatic growth and institutionalization of PhD programs in composition over the past fifteen years competes with the centrifugal forces of our labor pool, which has dramatically increased as our PhD programs and undergraduate populations have expanded.

If we conceive the disciplinary status of composition as one governed by centrifugal and centripetal forces alike, nineteenth-century definitions of discipline do little to inform our analysis. The dissensus and bricolage that characterize our work need not suggest simple fragmentation; they need not prevent us from recognizing the institutional authority that composition has begun to acquire; nor need they lead us to ignore the shared theoretical aims and discursive patterns as defining features of our disciplinary work.

In "disciplinary identity" we include:

1. *Knowledge-making* of divergent and, at times, conflicting fundamental claims that nonetheless are recognized as belonging to composition and represented in increasing numbers of specialized academic journals, scholarly book series, textbooks, and specialized conferences;

2. *Institutional practices* that mark composition as a legitimate profession, including graduate programs with PhDs in composition, stand-alone programs for writing and rhetoric, secure and rewarding positions with appropriate tenure and promotion practices for composition specialists, and university programs and services that are directly or indirectly affiliated with composition, such as WAC/WID programs, writing centers, and computer-facilitated teaching facilities;

3. *Discursive patterns* that are unique to and definitive of a recognizable disciplinary identity, such as the dualisms, metaphors, and terms that mark our claims;
4. *Programmatic logistics* including the allocation of university, college, and departmental resources, numbers of students who take writing classes, educating of teaching assistants and writing center tutors, managing programs and other funded projects such as technology grants, National Writing Project sites, and service-learning/other community outreach projects;
5. *Day-to-day practices* that are generally acknowledged as composition-based work, such as course materials from first-year, advanced, honors, and graduate-level courses in composition, technical and professional communications, practices of and work produced in writing centers, community service projects, and other contexts; and
6. *Recurring, governing problems* that most directly determine daily practices, which range from the recurrent calls for accountability for editing skills and critical reading and writing to practices of epistemic rhetoric for academic and community service.

No one of these characteristics alone can present a sufficient case for composition's disciplinary status. Taken together, however, and situated within this rich context of theorized teaching, they paint a compelling picture of a disciplinary identity—not one in isolation, but one that is richly diverse and interdependent. We suggest that the tensions and conflicts we observe within our own community need not lead us to reject our disciplinary identity. Indeed, we often affirm other, less familiar disciplinary communities, missing or minimizing their gaps and fissures, even as we think our own gaps and fissures glaring simply because we know them so well. Rather, we see these disjunctures as necessary, useful, and even healthy indicators of vibrant intellectual activity. Thus we believe that these chapters imply a disciplinary community, albeit it one that, like most postmodern formations, is often questioning itself, a necessary condition that keeps itself engaged in the self-reflection essential to disciplinary growth and renewal.

IMPLICATIONS

Gone are the days when our biggest concerns centered on whether professional readings, including literature, should be included in composition courses. Our discipline faces now daunting responsibilities as post-modernism is pressed by globalism on both theoretical and material planes. This confluence of diversifying and unifying cultural forces confronts us on theoretical planes when aims and praxis collide. For example, we have begun to theorize alternative texts and invite our students to write them; yet we are faced with increasing pressures to prepare our students for the global corporate workplace. Indeed, any recognition of the interdependence globalism implies forces us to wrestle with the ways our expectations of students are mediated by corporate pressures. One response to this tension, colonialism, allows those with the most power to impose their practices as norms that others must adopt or be seen as deficient and excluded. Another more collaborative approach asks all participants to learn reading practices that account for difference. As both Susan Miller and Min Lu urge, faculty can teach themselves and their students to consider seriously the multiple ways texts can be composed and read, working to "illuminate rather than mask" the possibilities emerging from cultural and other differences. Rather than reify the "oppressive cultural forces inherent in institutional discourses" (qtd. in Hindman 89), such practices could lead Western readers to develop their rhetorical flexibilities as they look for both the argument and its nuances in more circular and implied language rather than reject any argument that isn't "efficient and straightforward." As Walter Truett Anderson notes, we begin to understand and accept other people's realities only as we find new ways to inhabit our own (267).

Many of our chapters point to the importance of training increasing numbers of instructors, for increasing numbers of students, in increasingly complex pedagogical agendas across a widely diverse set of institutional settings and expectations. These chapters describe projects designed to keep on writing beyond their classrooms, projects that may appear unfinished to both writers and readers, and projects that appeal to alternative readings. We have, however, only just begun to take the implications of new textual forms seriously—in our students' writing as well as our own. We are only beginning to see some of our colleagues working, for example, in contrastive rhetoric, resisting, in thoughtful and theoretically sound ways, corporate universities' moves to one-size-fits-all practices. Some of our journals have begun to risk printing differently formatted texts, and some of our conferences have shifted away from formal papers and toward open-ended roundtable or workshop sessions. However, editors still chide authors for ignoring "the readers' expectations," graduate students still feel encouraged to omit their student statuses in biographies in favor of their "real" work, and CCCC old-timers still grumble about having their proposals rejected and having to hear too many graduate students who "really don't have everything tied neatly together."

If we, as readers and teachers of readers, are serious about valuing a broader range of topics, methods, and presentations, we will have to reshape our own criteria for course papers, dissertations, journal articles, and conference presentations. We will have to struggle against the metacurriculum both inside and outside of the academy. If we do not reach beyond our own campuses, we tacitly support a bottom-line globalism that demands efficient, homogenous writing (read, organized, and presented according to white, corporate American norms), and we deceive our students by creating false expectations for workplace writing. If we are serious about the possibilities of transnationalism being informed by feminist practices and cultural studies in ways that engage rather than displace or erase diversity, we have to take both awareness and praxis beyond our usual borders and to convince administrators who fund our programs to share our vision.

Equally important are the material considerations. As we noted earlier, this collection represents differently situated compositionists, but with one significant exception: nearly all enjoy secure positions. Thus, even as these writers acknowledge the risks they choose to take in valuing alternative writing and teaching practices, most of them do so from relatively safe positions. Although faculty members generally, particularly those who teach in large public university systems, are being squeezed by business-model administrators to adopt top-down models and do more with less (or nothing), they still have greater autonomy and security than do adjunct faculty who teach term-to-term on multiple campuses. They still have more freedom than will new compositionists being expected to settle for the many new "rehabilitated" lectureships with diminished status and salary. Composition positions are plentiful, but good ones are not. Few other disciplines accept such a bifurcated faculty, yet composition appears to be leading the way for even greater division under the guise of "these are so much better than part-time positions." Of course they are, but they are not the kinds of positions that any discipline should be willing to commend as their legacies to their colleagues.

A responsibility to our discipline's material circumstances demands that current faculty reach outside their departments to show other faculty, administrators, and trustees what composition is and what kinds of faculty it requires. Rather than protect the sacred turf of past practices and privileges, our claims obligate us to press the boundaries of disciplinary and institutional norms.

Among the ways to initiate such changes, although perhaps the most obvious and potentially most difficult, is for those who manage and shape composition programs not to act as if their work is "merely" service to the university. When we cherish fixed syllabi or pedagogies that are not open to experimentation after our first years of teaching, when we "train" TAs in three-day workshops before they enter classrooms, when we rely upon adjunct faculty who have untenable work loads, next to no pedagogical support, and few opportunities or incentives to read professional journals and share their ideas with others, we do as much to contribute to composition's identity as a dry-cleaning like service as do administrators and faculty in other disciplines who ignore the tensions and complexities that shape our discipline. Rather, we need to embrace the centrifugal forces that foster change and growth in our work while we balance the needs of our students and institutions. We need to continue complicating our roles within our institutions. And our continual process of professionalization needs to accomplish much, much more than merely managing the number of students we move through our courses.

Our continual professionalization, then, entails developing philosophic and economic support for broadly based composition work. It means providing financial incentives for innovation and curricular reform. It means securing university support for centers for the teaching of writing that can house scholars-in-residence, more complex writing centers, WAC/WID programs, service-learning, and other project-based learning pedagogies. It means paying more careful attention to how we teach our TAs to teach and ensuring that they are mentored effectively. It means providing incentives and support for faculty, instructors, adjuncts, and TAs to pursue scholarship in the teaching of writing. It means sponsoring department- and university-wide forums on issues that we often debate internally but seldom engage in with others. It means seeking partners outside of the current funding circles within academic institutions by cultivating community benefactors. And it means a continued process of reflection, of gathering our best teaching practices and scholarship to assess what we value and where we are headed.

Our discipline continues to reach outward, beyond the confines of English departments and university service, toward the globalization that business, politics, and social practices have already embraced. As it does so, we will do well to remember Rich Straub's opening statement: "It is in the writing we have students practice and the values of writing we hope to instill—the ways we read, evaluate, respond to, and talk about the work of our students—that we most clearly define ourselves as teachers and characterize our courses in composition." The close study of these "practices" and "values" reflects not only "our courses" in composition, but our broader disciplinary identity as well, one defined by complex (but identifiable) theoretical aims, discursive patterns, and recurring problems. In the more intimate spaces of our classrooms, listservs, and conference sessions; in our programmatic and institutional decisions, policies, and actions; in our more public interactions with our constituencies and communities—in all of these ongoing interactions, we represent composition's disciplinary identity in the late age of print, where "teaching writing" has come to suggest a complex, dialogic, and ongoing intellectual and ideological activity.

WORKS CITED

Anderson, Walter Truett. *Reality Isn't What It Used to Be*. San Francisco: HarperCollins, 1990.

Bakhtin, Mikhail. "Discourse in the Novel." *The Dialogic Imagination*. Ed. Michael Holquist. Austin: U of Texas P, 1981.

Bartholomae, David. "Writing with Teachers: A Conversation with Peter Elbow," *College Composition and Communication* 46:1 (1995): 62-71.

Bartholomae, David and Anthony Petrosky. *Ways of Reading: An Anthology for Writers*. 5th ed. Boston: Bedford/St. Martin's, 1999.

Berlin, James A. *Rhetoric and Reality: Writing Instruction in American Colleges, 1900-1985*. Carbondale: Southern Illinois UP, 1987.

—. "Rhetoric and Ideology in the Writing Class." *The Writing Teacher's Sourcebook*. 4th ed. Eds. Edward P. J. Corbett, Nancy Myers, and Gary Tate. New York: Oxford UP, 2000. 9-25.

Coles, William. *The Plural I—And After*. 1978. Portsmouth, NH: Boynton/Cook Heinemann, 1988.

Corbett, Edward P. J. "Rhetoric, the Enabling Discipline." Corbett, Myers, and Tate 26-35.

Elbow, Peter. "Being a Writer vs. Being an Academic: A Conflict in Goals." *College Composition and Communication* 46:1 (1995): 72-83.

Gramsci, Antonio. *Selections from the Prison Notebooks*. Trans. and Ed. Quintin Hoare and Geoffrey Smith. New York: International Publishers, 1992.

Harris, Joseph. *A Teaching Subject: Composition Since 1966*. Upper Saddle River, NJ: Prentice Hall, 1997.

Heilker, Paul and Peter Vandenberg. *Keywords in Composition Studies*. Portsmouth, NH: Heinemann Boynton/Cook, 1996.

Hobson, Eric H. "Maintaining Our Balance: Walking the Tightrope of Competing Epistemologies." *The Writing Center Journal* 13 (1992): 65-75.

North, Stephen M. *The Making of Knowledge in Composition: Portrait of an Emerging Field.* Upper Montclair, NJ: Boynton/Cook, 1987.

Phelps, Louise Wetherbee. *Composition as a Human Science: Contributions to the Self-Understanding of a Discipline.* New York: Oxford UP, 1988.

Seitz, James E. *Motives for Metaphor: Literacy, Curriculum Reform, and the Teaching of English.* Pittsburgh: U of Pittsburgh P, 1999.

Shaughnessy, Mina. *Errors and Expectations.* New York: Oxford UP, 1979.

Toulmin, Stephen. *Human Understanding.* Princeton: Princeton UP, 1972.

Trimbur, John. "Composition Studies: Postmodern or Popular." *Into the Field: Sites of Composition Studies.* Ed. Anne Ruggles Gere. New York: MLA, 1993.

ABOUT THE CONTRIBUTORS

Daniel Anderson is assistant professor of English at the University of North Carolina at Chapel Hill and Director of the Studio for Instructional Technology and English Studies. He oversees computer-assisted writing classes and coordinates research into the impacts of information technologies on teaching and learning. His current interests include Web design, the development of online platforms for instruction, and the administration of programs and initiatives for integrating information technologies into the teaching and research missions of writing programs and institutions of learning.

Jonathan Anderson has returned to college composition after a two-year sojourn into high school language arts. He currently teaches Freshman Composition and Basic Writing at Crafton Hills College and is working to complete his Master's thesis.

Jeremy C. Ball earned his PhD in philosophy from Claremont Graduate University in January 2001. Currently, he is an associate professor of philosophy at the College of San Mateo. He is the co-author of a forthcoming series of critical thinking texts for Wadsworth Publishing Company, an International Thomson Publishing Company.

Jane Carducci, professor of English at Winona State University, earned her BA in English from Colorado College and then moved to Lake Tahoe, Nevada, and dealt blackjack for eleven years. Feeling that, for her, work in the casinos was a dead-end street, she completed the MA and PhD programs at the University of Nevada in Reno. Her publications on Shakespeare have appeared in such journals as *Literature and Psychology, Language and Literature,* and *Shakespeare Yearbook.* She has presented workshops on service learning for faculty development at WSU and NCTE.

Gary Eddy, professor of English at Winona State University, grew up in Niagra Falls, NY, and had a string of menial jobs before poetry led him through a string of degrees, including the MFA (University of Arizona) and PhD (SUNY Binghamton). His poetry appears in such journals as *The Georgia Review* and *Tamaqua.* He has presented workshops on service learning and writing in Minnesota and delivered papers on rhetorical theory at Penn State and CCCC.

Betty Eidenier is lead teacher in the Seminar Program at Orange High School in Hillsborough, North Carolina. A National Board Certified Teacher of English with over 20 years of experience teaching high school students and adults, she has published work in *English Journal, Icarus,* and *Cities and Roads* and has presented workshops in writing and literature at NCTE and Coalition of Essential Schools conferences.

Helen Rothschild Ewald is professor of English at Iowa State University, where she teaches graduate and undergraduate courses in rhetoric and professional communication. She has published three books, the most recent being *Mutuality in the Rhetoric and Composition Classroom,* co-authored with David Wallace. She has also published articles in such journals as *College Composition and Communication, Journal of Advanced Composition,* and *Journal of Business Communication.*

Katherine M. Fischer teaches writing at Clarke College in Dubuque, IA. Her poetry, articles, and essays appear in numerous journals, magazines, and anthologies as well as in the academic press. Currently she is writing a book about women's experience of the Mississippi River. When not in the classroom or writing studio, she can be found crick stomping the back sloughs of the Mississippi and singing to the catfish.

Jeffrey R. Galin is an assistant professor of English at Florida Atlantic University. He has co-edited *The Dialogic Classroom* with Joan Latchaw and published articles in *Computers and Composition* and *Kairos*. In addition to *Teaching/Writing in the Late Age of Print*, Galin is working on a book-length project tentatively entitled *Intellectual Property in the Academy: Who Owns Our Work and Why Should We Care?* His current research interests include the history of educational reform, literacy studies, intellectual property, and use and impact of computers on teaching and academic policies.

Susanmarie Harrington is Director of Writing and associate professor of English at Indiana University Purdue University Indianapolis. Her research focuses on writing assessment and literacy in a range of contexts, and her work has appeared in the *Journal of Basic Writing*, *WPA*, and various edited collections. With Linda Adler-Kassner, she has written *Basic Writing as a Political Act: Public Conversations about Writing and Literacies*.

Carol Peterson Haviland is an associate professor of English at California State University, San Bernardino, where she she directs the Writing Center and WAC programs, coordinates the upper division writing course, and teaches undergraduate and graduate composition courses. Her research interests include feminist theories, collaboration, intellectual property, writing centers, writing-across-the-curriculum, and writing program administration. She has presented sessions at regional and national conferences and written several articles and chapters on these topics; she is coeditor of *Weaving Knowledge Together: Writing Centers and Collaboration.*

Judith Hawkins currently teaches Composition and research writing at California State University, San Bernardino and University of California, Riverside. She is co-author of a forthcoming series of critical thinking texts for Wadsworth Publishing Company, an International Thomson Publishing Company.

Barbara Heifferon is an assistant professor of English at Clemson University, where she teaches in the Master of Arts in Professional Communication program. With Stuart Brown she edited a special edition on medical rhetoric for *Technical Communication Quarterly*. She has published in *CCC*, *Literature and Medicine*, *Feminist Working Papers*, *Alternative Rhetorics*, *Theorizing Composition*, *Critical Reviews in Biomedical Engineering*, and *Science and Engineering Ethics*, and other journals and books.

Rebecca Moore Howard chairs and directs the Writing Program at Syracuse University. She is author of *Standing in the Shadow of Giants: Plagiarists, Authors, Collaborators*; coauthor of *The Bedford Guide to Teaching Writing in the Disciplines*; coeditor of *Coming of Age: The Advanced Writing Curriculum*; and author of a variety of chapters and articles about plagiarism, pedagogy, and composition theory.

Christine Hult is professor of English and associate Department Head at Utah State University. Her research interests include computers in writing and program and teacher evaluation, as reflected in recent publications including the *New Century Handbook* (with Tom Huckin) and *Evaluating Teachers of Writing*. She has published books and articles on a range of composition and administrative topics in various composition journals, including *WPA, JAC, Rhetoric Review*, and *Computers and Composition*, along with a series of WAC textbooks and book chapters. She has recently assumed the position of Director for the Center for Online Education (COLE) at Utah State University.

James Inman is assistant professor of English at the University of South Florida. He serves as co-editor and co-publisher of *Kairos: A Journal for Teachers of Writing in Webbed Environments* and as co-coordinator of the Netoric Project. Inman's publications include *Taking Flight with OWLs: Examining Electronic Writing Center Work* (edited with Donna Sewell) and articles in *Computers and Composition* and *Writing Center Journal*.

J Paul Johnson is Writing Center Director and professor of English at Winona State University, where he teaches courses in writing, literature, and film. His publications in *Kairos, Thought and Action*, and *Practice in Context* focus on the politics and technologies of writing instruction, and he has presented papers, talks, and workshops at various local, regional, and national conferences, ranging on topics from the pragmatics of dialogue in fiction (MMLA) to turn-taking in synchronous computer chats (Penn State) to the rhetoric of hypertext theory (CCCC).

Karla Saari Kitalong is an assistant professor of technical communication at the University of Central Florida in Orlando. She also teaches in UCF's Honors College and digital media program. Her research interests include media representations of technology, usability and audience studies, visual communication, and generational differences in the acquisition of technological literacies.

Joan Latchaw is an associate professor at the University of Nebraska at Omaha specializing in rhetoric and composition. After two stints as Director of First Year Writing at Shepherd College and North Dakota State University, she is focusing on the scholarship of computer-mediated-communications. She co-edited *The Dialogic Classroom: Teachers Integrating Computer Technology, Pedagogy, and Research* with Jeffrey Galin. Latchaw and Galin have co-authored articles on intellectual property and have designed and taught joint graduate seminars, using MOOs and listservs and other technologies.

Carrie Shively Leverenz is associate professor of English and Director of Composition at Texas Christian University where she teaches courses in composition, cyberliteracy, and composition theory and pedagogy. She has published essays about collaboration, multicultural pedagogy, writing center theory and practice, and computers and writing, and is currently working on a book on ethical issues in institutionalized writing instruction.

Maureen A. Mathison is a faculty member in the Department of Communication and the University Writing Program at the University of Utah, where she teaches courses related to disciplinary rhetoric at the graduate and undergraduate levels. Her work has appeared in *Communication Theory, The Journal of Literacy Research, Written Communication*, and in numerous edited volumes.

Libby Miles is an assistant professor at the University of Rhode Island, where she directs the Writing Center and teaches undergraduate and graduate rhetoric courses. In both her teaching and research, she has focused on writing as a vehicle for change within bureaucracies and institutions; this interest led to the development of her service learning pedagogy. A recipient of the 2000 CCCC James Berlin Outstanding Dissertation Award and the 2001 CCCC Braddock Award, her recent scholarship appears in *College Composition and Communication, College English, Writing Program Administrator*, and edited collections such as *Coming of Age: The Advanced Writing Curriculum*.

Richard E. Miller is the Associate Director of the Writing Program and an associate professor in the English Department at Rutgers University. He is the author of *As If Learning Mattered: Reforming Higher Education*; his abiding research interest is in the relationship between institutional constraints and the desire to excel, transgress, and/or transcend.

Susan Miller is a professor of English and member of the faculty of the University Writing Program at the University of Utah. A contributor to Coles and Vopat's *What Makes Good Writing Good*, she teaches writing, cultural studies, and history and theory of writing. She has recently published articles on composition pedagogy, basic writing instruction, distance curricula in composition, a textbook on writing with computers written with an undergraduate collaborator (*New Ways of Writing: A Guide to Writing With Computers*) and a study of commonplace books in eighteenth- and nineteenth-century Virginia (*Assuming the Positions*). She is an advisor for the Salt Lake City Community Writing Center and has served as a University Public Service Professor. She coordinates the University of Utah's interdisciplinary PhD in rhetoric and composition and an undergraduate cross-curricular Literacy Minor.

Michael Moore is a graduate student and instructor in Rhetoric and Technical Communication at Michigan Technological University. His interests include composition studies, computer-mediated pedagogy, and intellectual property. His current research involves studying the enactment of public and performative rhetorics and citizen participation in online environments.

George Otte is a long-time writing program administrator at Baruch College (CUNY), member of the doctoral faculty in English at the CUNY Graduate Center, and co-editor of the *Journal of Basic Writing*. He was recently appointed Director of Instructional Technology for the City University of New York.

Steve Parks is an associate professor in the Department of English, Temple University where he is the Director of Literature, Literacy, and Culture as well as Director of Teachers for a Democratic Culture (www.tdc2000.org). He is author of *Class Politics: The Movement for a Students' Right To Their Own Language* and has published essays on language politics, writing across the curriculum, and the university.

Rebecca J. Rickly is an assistant professor at Texas Tech University where she serves as co-Director of Composition and teaches undergraduate and graduate courses in rhetoric and writing. Her work revolves around rhetoric, but includes such diverse applications as technology, feminisms, methods and methodologies, literacy study, contrastive rhetorics, and administration. She has served on the CCCC Committee on Computers and Composition, NCTE's Assembly on Computers in English, and she has chaired NCTE's Instructional Technology

Committee. Her publications include *The Online Writing Classroom* (with Susanmarie Harrington and Michael Day), and her work has appeared in several edited collections, as well as *Computers and Composition, CMC Magazine, The ACE Journal*, and *Kairos*.

Mariolina Rizzi Salvatori teaches and does research in the areas of hermeneutics, composition, literacy, and pedagogy. She is particularly interested in exploring the transactions of knowledge, and the relations between teachers, students, and texts that different theories of reading make possible. Her publications include: "Conversations with Texts: Reading in the Teaching of Composition," "The Personal as Recitation," "On Behalf of Pedagogy," "Pedagogy in the Academy: 'The divine skill of the born teacher's instincts'," *Pedagogy: Disturbing History 1819-1929*, and "porque no puedo decir mi cuento: Mexican Ex-Votos' Iconographic Literacy." In 1999 she was selected as Carnegie Scholar by the Carnegie Foundation for the Advancement of Teaching for her work on "pedagogy of difficulty." She is editor of *READER*, with Paul Kameen.

Richard (Dickie) Selfe is the Director of Computer-based Instruction in the Humanities department at Michigan Technological University and directs the Center for Computer-Assisted Language Instruction, a technical communication-oriented computer facility. He teaches a range of computer-intensive technical communication and graduate computer studies courses. His professional interests include technology-rich communication pedagogy as well as the social/institutional influences of electronic media on our work culture.

Lori Shorr is the Director of School and Community Partnerships at Temple University. She earned her PhD in Critical and Cultural Studies at the University of Pittsburgh. She is affiliated faculty in Women's Studies at Temple and has published essays on film, pedagogy and university politics.

Rick Straub was associate professor at Florida State University, where he taught courses in writing, rhetoric and composition, literature, and literary theory. He wrote three books on teacher response—*Twelve Readers Reading: Responding to College Student Writing, A Sourcebook for Responding to Student Writing*, and *The Practice of Response*—and a dozen articles on reading, evaluating, and responding to student writing. Just before his untimely death, he was editing a collection of noted statements on teacher commentary, *Key Works on Teacher Response to Student Writing*.

Lisa Toner is a post-doctoral scholar in writing program administration at the University of Kentucky. As an assistant professor at Wheeling Jesuit University, she taught courses in first-year and advanced composition and business and technical writing, implemented a computerized writing classroom, and chaired the Institutional Review Board. She received a PhD in rhetoric and composition from Purdue University in 1996 and is currently researching implications of a digitalized society for ethics and student-teacher power relations in writing instruction.

Kathleen A. Welsch is an assistant professor of English, Writing Center director, and Writing Across the Curriculum co-ordinator at Clarion University of Pennsylvania. She teaches a range of writing courses from First-Year Composition to Nonfiction Prose, provides year-long training for Writing Center peer tutors, and support to faculty in writing intensive courses. Her research interest is in nineteenth-century composition textbooks and student writing. After 20 years of teaching her favorite course to teach is still First-Year Composition.

Wini Wood began her career as a linguist, became an ESL teacher, and then a writing instructor. She has taught at Wellesley College for 16 years, where she also directs its first-year writing program. Her research interests include electronic discourse and WAC methodology; she is currently working on a dissertation (from UMass/Amherst) that is an ethnographic study of the ways students use electronic space to negotiate entry into the public sphere. She has less of an online life than she used to.

Charles Williams is an assistant professor of English at Chaffey College, where he teaches a range of composition courses and African-American literature. He has written articles on African-American literature and writing issues in multicultural spaces, and his current academic interests include exploring the relationship between critical theory and composition, the works of Ralph Ellison and Albert Murray, and visual literacy. He received an MA in English Composition from California State University, San Bernardino, where he worked as a writing tutor, taught as a TA, and directed a summer Bridge English program.

AUTHOR INDEX

SUBJECT INDEX

Printed in the United States
1252500001B/79-146